Hello, Norma Jeane

The MARILYN MONROE

You Didn't Know

ELISA JORDAN

APPLAUSE
THEATRE & CINEMA BOOKS
Essex, Connecticut

APPLAUSE
THEATRE & CINEMA BOOKS

An imprint of Globe Pequot, the trade division of
The Rowman & Littlefield Publishing Group, Inc.
4501 Forbes Blvd., Ste. 200
Lanham, MD 20706
www.rowman.com

Distributed by NATIONAL BOOK NETWORK

Library of Congress Cataloging-in-Publication Data

Names: Jordan, Elisa, author.
Title: Hello, Norma Jeane : the Marilyn Monroe you didn't know / Elisa Jordan.
Description: Essex, Connecticut : Applause, [2023]
Identifiers: LCCN 2023010691 (print) | LCCN 2023010692 (ebook) | ISBN
    9781493053957 (paperback) | ISBN 9781493053964 (ebook)
Subjects: LCSH: Monroe, Marilyn, 1926-1962. | Motion picture actors and
    actresses—United States—Biography.
Classification: LCC PN2287.M69 Z55 2023 (print) | LCC PN2287.M69 (ebook)
    | DDC 791.4302/8092 [B]—dc23/eng/20230809
LC record available at https://lccn.loc.gov/2023010691
LC ebook record available at https://lccn.loc.gov/2023010692

Contents

Part III: The Spotlight

Part IV: A Household Name

Part V: The End

Acknowledgements

Writing a book about Marilyn Monroe has been a lifelong dream for me. I am profoundly grateful for the opportunity and every single person mentioned here has been part of making this happen. This book wouldn't have been possible without the support of my amazing family, friends, colleagues, and fellow Old Hollywood fans.

I am forever indebted for their amazing research, community, and just plain being there for me: Rhonda Bell, Hazel Birdsall, Sandra Buigues, Elba Carrillo, April Clemmer, Ashlee Davis, Caren Roberts-Frenzel (one of the best Old Hollywood historians out there), Remi Gangarossa, Craig Harvey, Juliet Howlett, Bryan Johns, Joanna Linkchorst, Doug Mader, Benjamin Meissner, Scott Michaels (without you I couldn't have run my Marilyn tours), Eve Watson Minkler (who I consider a bit of a mentor), Michelle Morgan, Tiffany Nitsche, Jill Parresol, Fraser Penney, Trish Procetto, Gary Vitacco-Robles, Darrell Rooney, Laura Saxby, Greg Schreiner, Mikael Sharafyn (who shared his theory about Marilyn using Dietrich's nightclub act as a basis for her own), Mike Shear, Jacki Shepard, Tiffany Spellman, Stephanie Starr, Colleen Supan, Libby Supan, Martin Turnbull, Amy Wiedner, Eric Woodard (whose early Marilyn research was groundbreaking).

To my family, who have patiently endured a lifetime of Marilyn Monroe fandom with me. This book was written as much for them as for anyone. They deserve all the credit in the world. To Mom and Dad, who were fairly convinced they had an alien on their hands while I was growing up. My brother, Matt, and sister-in-law, Tami; Aunt Virginia; Aunt Carrie; cousins John, Margaret, and Elizabeth; and my nieces, Marissa and Madison, have all been helpful, loving, and supportive during this journey.

To my "Marilyn family," who were always available for me to fact check, brainstorm, exchange information with, and just be my buddy. Margaret

Barrett, who answered questions and shared her vast knowledge; Jackie Craig, who lets me pick her brain regularly; Lorraine Nicol, who can recall Marilyn facts off the top of her head and one of the funniest people I know; Lisa Sexton, who is a voice of reason and my biggest cheerleader; Marisa Van Der Pest, a passionate and dedicated fan and friend; April Vevea, who very graciously shared some of her research with me. And to Scott Fortner, my cohost on the All Things Marilyn podcast, who shared information from his collection.

Finally, to everyone at Rowman & Littlefield who believed in me and allowed me to write this book. I will never be able to thank you enough. A special shout out to the Norma Jeane Team: Chris, Laurel, Barbara, and Melissa. My editors Chris and Laurel were patient, kind, and understanding throughout the entire process. You are the best editors I could have asked for. Barbara worked with me on finding photos and getting clearances. Melissa in production kept things moving. None of it went unnoticed!

Introduction

$\mathscr{I}$ first fell in love with Marilyn Monroe when I was five. *Gentlemen Prefer Blondes* was on television and I just happened to catch her singing "Diamonds Are a Girl's Best Friend." It was love at first sight. As an adult, I've looked back at that moment and tried to figure out exactly what it was that captivated me. Was it because that musical number was everything little girls love? It was pink, sparkly, happy, had ballet dancers, and in the center of it all, a woman who looked like an angel. I'm still not sure if those were the reasons, but suddenly I wanted to know everything about this magnificent creature.

It might be hard to believe this now, but there weren't nearly as many books about Marilyn then as there are today. The few I could find, I gobbled up. When my mom took me to the library, I was disappointed to find the same books on the shelf that I already had at home. Then I figured out that this magical place called Hollywood was only a short freeway drive away! I begged my parents to take me on a visit to see her handprints at the Chinese Theatre and her star on the Walk of Fame. I also finally got a visit to her crypt and a day walking around the Hotel Del Coronado in San Diego where *Some Like It Hot* was filmed. When I was old enough to drive, I had the freedom to retrace many of her locations. When I traveled, I tried to work in Marilyn sites when I could.

No matter where I was in my life or how busy my schedule became, I tried to keep up with the latest Marilyn news, books, and documentaries. While there was once a lack of information about Marilyn, now there is an oversaturation and much of it is biased, sensational, gossipy, or outright absurd. As time went on, there was an increasing focus on her death, conspiracies, drug abuse, and her affairs. Each book was worse than the last; the more outlandish the stories the better the sales. It was disheartening. Dissatisfied with much of the material coming out, about fifteen years ago, I started sharing what I know about Marilyn. I answered questions online from people who wrote in and I also started a regular column on the internet. To my delight, I discovered a lot of people enjoyed learning about the real Marilyn. Encouraged, I began giving tours about Marilyn around Los Angeles. (All that hard work finding Marilyn sites in my youth paid off!)

This brings us to this book and what I set out to accomplish. With the hundreds (thousands?) of books out about Marilyn Monroe, why add another one? The reason, quite simply, is that I never felt like these books helped the reader know Marilyn as a person. Sure, biographies have facts and dates, but I'm often asked, "What was she really like?" It's impossible to boil anyone down to a few sentences, let alone someone with a life as complicated as hers. And, of course, I didn't know Marilyn personally. Still, the human element of her character is often missing.

This is not a typical biography. Apologies in advance if you are in the market for something more traditional—no hard feelings if you prefer another book. There are several great ones out there. I tried to group the chapters by topic instead of in chronological order, which means you'll see some crossover here and there. There might be a reference to the same subject more than once. You are not tied to reading the book in order if you don't want to—you can drop in wherever you want. Examining Marilyn's life by topic is my way of getting closer to the person she was in life. She wasn't all good and she wasn't all bad, just like any person. To present Marilyn in one light would be a disservice to her memory. She was many things—a hard worker who focused on goals, someone who loved generously, a witty conversationalist, a person who stood up for what she believed was right, and a gentle personality. She was also disorganized, difficult to work with, codependent, and at times inconsiderate of others by showing up late. I try to present all sides of her.

I should also point out another goal with this book. There are a lot of stories about Marilyn that simply are not true. Some are harmless and others have damaged her reputation. In keeping with the theme of presenting Marilyn as a real person, I make it a point to clear a lot of these up. There isn't enough time to hit every topic, but I tried to get many of them.

Finally, I have gone into some deep dives when it comes to areas of Marilyn's life that may not appear important at first glance. Fair warning if this isn't what you are interested in. My reasoning is that by understanding her environment, the people she admired, and those close to her, then putting everything and everyone into context, you get a better sense of Marilyn.

In 1961, Arthur Miller said: "Marilyn has become a sort of fiction for writers; each one sees her through his own set of pleasures and prejudices."

Marilyn was still alive when he said that and it's even more true now.

So here is how I see Marilyn and why I have continued to keep her as part of my life. At an early age, I realized that Marilyn Monroe started with nothing—no family, education, money, or stability. And yet she become the most famous woman in the world. If she could accomplish that, there was nothing I couldn't do. She lived a life of courage and conviction. In times of struggle and doubt, she kept going. For me, during challenging times, I would think of how Marilyn continued striving to improve herself, make her dreams come true, and keep going.

For all of these reasons, the book is called *Hello, Norma Jeane*. I hope you enjoy meeting her.

I

NORMA JEANE MORTENSEN

· 1 ·

Marilyn's Los Angeles

To better understand Marilyn is to put her in the context of her birth city and in particular the time frame in which she grew up. Marilyn was born in Los Angeles right as it was transitioning from a smaller, dusty Western town to a giant metropolis booming with oil, ports, aerospace, military, urban sprawl, freeway expansion, and, of course, the hub of the entertainment business.

In the 1880s, the railroad reached Los Angeles, making the city in the far West of the United States more accessible to the rest of the nation. Marilyn's grandfather Otis Monroe was part of that industry. Then oil was struck, which brought industry and laborers looking for work. Starting at the turn of the twentieth century, those who had visited Los Angeles raved about the warm climate and clean, dry air. Soon tourists were flocking to town and buying land for vacation homes. Much of the land was ripe with natural blossoming fruit trees. A couple of short movies were filmed in Los Angeles in 1911, but the movie industry remained rooted on the East Coast for the time being.

Two things happened in 1913 that forever changed Los Angeles from a quaint little town with Victorian houses and fruit tree groves to what it would become. One, the Los Angeles Aqueduct opened, bringing water to the area. Two, Cecil B. DeMille filmed the first full-length movie, *The Squaw Man*, in the area of the city known as "Hollywood."

Los Angeles proved to be the ideal center for moviemaking. The sunny, warm weather allowed for year-round production, especially in the early days when so much filming was done outside. Within just a couple of hours of driving, there was access to any kind of terrain needed, from mountains, snow, and beaches to forests and deserts. Land was cheap and studios swooped in to purchase large parcels of land where they could build backlots and sound stages, which were ideal once artificial lighting improved.

View of the Cahuenga Pass, Mount Hollywood, and San Fernando Valley from Hollywood in 1915. Within just a few years this area would be teeming with people, industry, and cars.
Pierce, C.C. (Charles C.), 1861-1946 / Wikimedia Commons

Meanwhile, the population of Los Angeles jumped from 102,479 in 1900 to 576,673 in 1920. It also marked the point that the population of Los Angeles surpassed San Francisco (although Los Angeles also has a significantly bigger square mileage). During the 1920s—the decade in which Norma Jeane was born—the population jumped again, this time to 1,238,048. California supplied 29 percent of the nation's oil and was the largest supplier of crude oil in the United States. In the 1920s, this expanded further when several additional large oil fields were discovered in Southern California.

It was also a time of change in the United States. During the 1910s, American homes felt the devastation of World War I and the 1918–1919 influenza epidemic. On January 17, 1920, the Eighteenth Amendment, better known as Prohibition, went into effect just as the nation wanted to party away the misery of the last decade. With alcohol consumption pushed underground, women were now free to enter spaces designated for drinking. Prior to Prohibition, bars and saloons had been previously regulated to men. That same year, the world further opened for women when the Nineteenth Amendment passed, granting females the right to vote. It was a time of liberation, and women flaunted their new freedoms by not just drinking and voting, but also shortening their skirts, cutting their hair, and wearing cosmetics. One of those ladies was none other than Marilyn Monroe's own mother, Gladys.

The year 1920 marked the first year that the population was higher in cities than in rural areas. The number of factory workers doubled from 4.7 million in 1900 to 9 million in 1920, with many of the positions being filled by a wave of recent immigrants. It was the decade vehicles changed the United States. In 1920, 8,131,522 cars were registered in the United States. The number was 23,120,897 by 1929. With average folks now better able to afford their own automobiles, the exotic land of Los Angeles that everyone seemed to love so much was more accessible than ever. And of course—after decades of lobbying, women received the right to vote in 1920 thanks to the Nineteenth Amendment.

In the 1920s and 1930s, the Hollywood Bowl was built, as were countless movie theatres and palaces. It was an early indication that Los Angeles would be a city by artists, for artists. In 1923, a large wooden sign reading HOLLYWOODLAND was erected on Mount Lee as a temporary advertisement for a real estate development. Instead the sign came to symbolize the region's growing entertainment industry.

It was an extraordinary time for architecture. World War I soldiers coming home from Europe were inspired by the buildings they saw overseas. Los Angeles, now attracting creative types, was especially lucky because many of these folks had the skills to build anything from homes to small retail businesses to grand high rises (tall for the time, anyway). Tudor, Normandy, Arts & Crafts, Craftsman, Spanish, Colonial, Storybook, Mexican, Art Deco, Streamline Moderne, Googie, Beaux-Arts, Moorish—all styles had a place and were appreciated. Many artistic types found Los Angeles inspiring so musicians, writers, photographers, painters, architects, and all-around dreamers and freethinkers found the city welcoming.

This was the Los Angeles Norma Jeane was born into on June 1, 1926. During the years of her childhood, she was in the middle of the city's transformation. In a way, she and Los Angeles grew up together and she was a product of her environment.

· 2 ·

Marilyn 101: The Basics

Born: June 1, 1926, at 9:30 a.m.
[1] Los Angeles General Hospital (now Los Angeles County USC Medical Center)
1200 North State, Los Angeles

Birth name: Norma Jeane Mortenson

Died: August 5, 1962
[2] 12305 Fifth Helena Drive
Brentwood, a neighborhood in Los Angeles

Burial: Westwood Memorial Park
[3] 1218 Glendon Avenue
Westwood, California

Mother: Gladys Pearl Monroe Baker Mortenson Eley (married three times)
Father: Charles Stanley Gifford (biological)
Edward Mortenson (listed on her birth certificate)

Half sisters: Berniece Baker Miracle, Doris Elizabeth Gifford
Half brothers: Robert Kermit "Jackie" Baker, Charles "Chuck" Stanley Gifford Jr.

Hair: Her hair was blonde and straight in childhood. As an adult, she was a brunette with curly hair. Starting with modeling days, her hair was dyed various shades of blonde. Marilyn's curly hair required straightening. The many years of bleaching and straightening damaged her hair, as can be seen later in life.

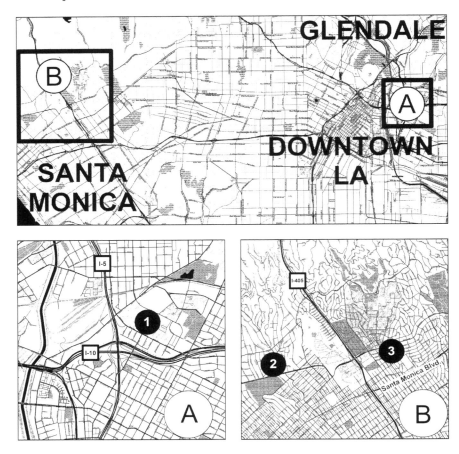

Eyes: Blue

Height: 5 feet, 5½ inches

Weight: Generally, between 115 and 120 pounds. During her marriage to Arthur Miller, she weighed about 135. After her divorce from Arthur and her gallbladder removal in 1961, she lost weight and weighed 117 pounds at the time of her death.

Dress size: Ten, twelve, sixteen (Depends on who you ask; and this doesn't account for custom-made clothing). However, clothing sizes were significantly different in Marilyn's era than they are now. By today's standards, Marilyn would likely have been a size two or four at her thinnest, and an eight or ten at her heaviest.

Shoe size: Seven, although many of her shoes were custom-made and had no sizes printed on them.

Dominant hand: Right

Marilyn in 1952. By New York Sunday News / Wikimedia Commons

· 3 ·

Marilyn's Family

*M*arilyn Monroe is commonly called an "orphan," and there is a kernel of truth in this because she spent most of her childhood in foster care and a couple of years in an orphanage. Marilyn did, however, have a family. To better understand Marilyn is to look at how her family shaped the woman she grew into.

TILFORD HOGAN

Marilyn's great-grandfather, Tilford Marion Hogan, was a humble farm laborer from rural Adams County, the westernmost county in Illinois. He was born on February 24, 1851, to George and Sarah Hogan, both of Kentucky stock. Little is known about his life, other than he married at least twice, moved to Missouri at some point, and outlived three of his four children.

Tilford Hogan's death predicts a sad reality for his descendants—mental illness, as his death certificate indicates suicide by hanging on May 27, 1933, in Missouri at the age of eighty-two.

One of the three children he outlived was his daughter, Della Hogan Monroe, who died in California about five years before her father. Della's lineage produced Marilyn's maternal line.

DELLA HOGAN MONROE

Della Mae Hogan, Marilyn's maternal grandmother, was born in Missouri on July 1, 1876, to Tilford and Charlotte Virginia Sellers, who was born in Carroll County, Missouri, on April 10, 1857. When Della was thirteen, Tilford and Charlotte made the unusual decision for the time to divorce, leaving her to bounce between her parents. During her youth, Della was known for her outgoing and mischievous personality, traits that no doubt attracted the attention of her future husband, Otis Monroe, whom she met in 1898.

OTIS MONROE

Born May 14, 1866, in Marion County, Indiana, to Jacob Monroe and Mary Stewart, Otis Elmer Monroe had big dreams of moving to Europe, studying the great painting masters, and becoming an artist. He was never able to realize his dreams, but he did succeed in winning the love of a young and vivacious Della Hogan, whom he married in 1899, one year after meeting her.

Instead of the European life of an artist, Otis and his bride traveled the country looking for work. The search took him to Mexico, where he accepted a job for the Mexican National Railway, not too far from the Texas border.

While living and working in Mexico, Della gave birth to the first of two children, a girl named Gladys Pearl Monroe, on May 27, 1902. The job in Mexico did not last long, and the Monroe family was once again on the move, returning to the United States in the spring of 1903.

Otis once again accepted work for a railroad, this time Pacific Electric Railway (sometimes called Red Cars) in Southern California, which was rapidly expanding and in need of transportation. The private transit system connected Los Angeles, San Bernardino, and Orange counties via streetcars and buses.

Otis, Della, and baby Gladys settled in Los Angeles, and soon the family expanded once again. A second child, a boy named Marion Otis Monroe, was born in Los Angeles on October 6, 1904.

Now a foursome, the young family may have decided on a life in Los Angeles, but they still moved several times every year. Otis was known to drink heavily, so when his memory began failing it probably went largely unnoticed—at least in the beginning.

Otis's health continued deteriorating at a rapid clip, soon developing into migraines, shakes, and violent rages, which frightened Della and the children. It was clear more was going on than just drinking.

As the symptoms of dementia overtook Otis, he was admitted to Patton State Hospital, a psychiatric hospital, in 1908. There he was diagnosed with syphilis, which one can contract through sexual contact, deep cuts in the skin, or mucous membranes. In the case of Otis, it is generally believed he contracted the disease from unsanitary living conditions in Mexico. By the following year, Otis was unable to recognize his own family and passed away at Patton in 1909, at the age of forty-three.

Although there was a medical diagnosis explaining the death of Otis Monroe, Della, and his children were convinced he had suffered from hereditary mental illness.

LIFE WITHOUT OTIS

In 1909, there were not many options for single mothers with young children. Della soon married one of Otis's coworkers from Pacific Electric Railway, but the marriage only lasted two years.

As for the children, Gladys and Marion had not experienced much stability in their formative years. They had moved frequently, making it difficult for them to make friends or develop a sense of security. Now without a father to provide for them, life continued to unravel.

Believing Marion needed a male influence, Della sent her son to live with relatives in San Diego. Gladys stayed with her mother, and by the time she was a young teen, mother and daughter moved into a modest boarding house within walking distance of the Pacific Ocean in Venice Beach.

Della had begun dating again and fell in love with a man who clashed bitterly with fourteen-year-old Gladys. The poor relationship between Gladys and her mother's suitor created problems at home, especially because Della was hoping to marry this man, or at least settle into a long-term relationship.

A TEEN BRIDE

A solution to Della's problem presented itself in a way she wasn't expecting but seemed to welcome nonetheless. Like her mother, Gladys was dating. Unlike her average-looking mother, however, Gladys had developed into an unusually beautiful young woman.

Gladys's suitor was Jasper Baker, an older man of twenty-nine (born on March 16, 1886) and a native Kentuckian. When Gladys discovered she was pregnant, Della eagerly married off her teenage daughter. Gladys married Jasper (listed as John Baker on the marriage certificate) on May 22, 1917, five days short of her fifteenth birthday. Her age was falsified on official paperwork to make her appear older than her actual age of fourteen. With Gladys out of the way, Della was now free to pursue her romantic relationship without interference.

Gladys delivered her son, Robert Jasper Baker, nicknamed Jackie, on January 16, 1918, in Venice Beach, California. A daughter, Berniece Inez Baker, also born in Venice Beach, followed on July 30, 1919.

The Baker marriage was a catastrophe. Gladys was a young girl from a dysfunctional family, and not at all prepared for motherhood. When Jackie was a toddler, he nearly lost an eye after Gladys placed broken glass in a trash can within his reach. Jasper blamed Gladys for the infraction.

Just as Gladys struggled, Jasper was hardly a model husband. He was known to verbally and physically abuse Gladys, including whipping her across the back with a horse bridle after speaking too long with one of his brothers.

During a physical fight between the couple in their car's front seat, Jackie accidentally opened the backseat door and fell from the moving vehicle into the street.

Unable to tolerate the abuse any longer, Gladys filed for divorce in 1921. It was granted in 1922, but it was not the end of Gladys's drama with her husband. On the contrary, Jasper kidnapped their two small children and fled to his native Flat Lick, Kentucky. A devastated Gladys traveled to Kentucky in pursuit of her children, even settling in town and working as a housekeeper for a family with young children, one of whom was a little girl named Norma Jean.

Jasper remarried, this time to a woman who was the exact opposite of his first wife. An older, matronly woman would serve as stepmother to Jackie and Berniece, a move on Jasper's part that effectively cut their biological mother out of their lives. Unable to regain custody, Gladys reluctantly traveled home to Los Angeles to start her life over—without her two children.

RETURN TO LOS ANGELES

Los Angeles in the 1920s was a rapidly growing metropolis. Gladys took a job as a film cutter in the burgeoning movie industry to support herself, but she seemed to go through a second adolescence—or perhaps the adolescence she never had in the first place.

By day she worked, but at night she lived the life of a flapper. She stayed out late to dance, drink, and date. Her best friend and adventure buddy was Grace McKee, a friend she met at work. Still only in her early twenties, Gladys continued to radiate beauty. Grace, on the other hand, was a few years older and plainer, but her outgoing personality made her the life of any party. Despite their opposite appearances, they had the same interests and became inseparable. Although no one knew it early on, Grace's friendship would make her a pivotal person in Gladys's life, someone loyal to her through thick and thin.

One person who did not see the value of Gladys's partying ways was her mother, Della. Gladys needed to settle down, Della argued, and become a respectable wife. Feeling pressured, Gladys gave in and married again, this time to a man roughly her same age with a good job working for the gas company. Gladys Monroe Baker married Martin Edward Mortensen on October 14, 1924, in Los Angeles.

The marriage sounded good in theory, but in reality Gladys was far from finished when it came to sowing her wild oats. Mortensen was a respectable young man, but Gladys was not ready for a quiet life dedicated to homemaking. She quickly grew bored living as Mrs. Mortensen, and the marriage crumbled accordingly. Gladys and her new husband soon separated, and she resumed the life she'd had with Grace before marriage.

A LITTLE GIRL COMES INTO THE WORLD

Gladys began dating her supervisor at work, Stan Gifford. Sometime around the holidays of 1925, Gladys discovered she was pregnant. When she informed Stan, he said it was a good thing she was already married because she could put her husband's name on the birth certificate.

Gladys delivered a baby girl in the charity ward of Los Angeles General Hospital on June 1, 1926. She took her ex-lover's suggestion and named her estranged husband, Martin Edward Mortensen, on the birth certificate as the father to avoid the stigma of illegitimacy.

The lie on the birth certificate took care of the illegitimacy issue, but it did not solve the fact that Stan Gifford refused responsibility for his child. Gladys was alone in an era with few resources for single mothers. Worried she could not raise a child on her own, Gladys placed her infant daughter in the care of Wayne and Ida Bolender on June 13. Soon after accepting Norma Jeane into their home, the Bolenders took in another infant, a boy named Lester who was born in August. The children were so close in age that Wayne and Ida sometimes referred to them as "the twins" and raised them as brother and sister.

The Bolenders lived across the street from Della in Hawthorne, a Los Angeles suburb, and were known for taking in foster children. Gladys visited occasionally and even took Norma Jeane out on day trips, but everyday responsibilities fell to Wayne and Ida.

With Norma Jeane at the Bolenders' house, Gladys resumed life as a single woman. She worked during the day, including a stint at the RKO studio in Hollywood, and partied at night, often with Grace. Della still lived across the street from the Bolenders, but it wasn't

Baby Norma Jeane was born to a single mother who was unable to properly care for a child and a father who denied responsibility. As an adult, the woman who became known to the world as Marilyn Monroe recounted feeling unwanted from the beginning of her life. By Dell Publications, Inc. New York / Wikimedia Commons

an ideal situation. She was now struggling with mental illness, and one day took it upon herself to cross the street and violently break the glass of the Bolenders' front door. They were unable to calm her down and called the police for assistance. Shortly after, Della died in Norwalk State Hospital on August 23, 1927. The official cause of death was myocarditis (heart disease) with "manic depressive psychosis" listed as a contributing factor.

Just a little over two years later, Gladys's brother Marion disappeared in November 1929. One day he left home, which included his wife Olive and three small children, and was never seen again. Olive finally had Marion legally declared dead in 1939 so she would be eligible for state financial aid. Although he never received a diagnosis, it is generally believed Marion may have had schizophrenia.

After Norma Jeane turned seven, life was about to take a turn when the Bolenders approached Gladys about formally adopting the little girl. They were adopting Lester and wanted to make the family they had created with both children permanent.

Gladys didn't just refuse the offer; she removed Norma Jeane from the Bolender home and took back custody of her daughter. It is unclear exactly why Gladys believed she could suddenly care for a child—or why she didn't just simply refuse the adoption request and continue allowing Norma Jeane to live with her foster family. Most likely, Gladys was afraid of losing yet another child after her first two had been taken from her. Whatever Gladys's reasoning was, mother and daughter were reunited.

Initially, Gladys rented an apartment in Hollywood near RKO, where she was employed, but soon set her mind on purchasing a house, probably to establish stability for her child. Grace advised against the purchase of a home. A new mortgage, raising a child she was trying to reestablish a bond with, working full time—it would all be too much, Grace warned. Gladys disregarded the good advice and bought a three-bedroom house near the Hollywood Bowl.

As it turns out, Grace had been correct all along. Life was becoming overwhelming for Gladys. For the first time she found herself in the role of single mother. She was working full time. She struggled to make her mortgage payments, so she was forced to rent part of the house to an English couple who worked as actors. Then in 1933, she received news of two deaths in the family. In May, her grandfather Tilford committed suicide by hanging himself. Not long after, she received word that her estranged fifteen-year-old son, Jackie, died in August of tuberculosis of the kidneys.

Gladys's emotional health deteriorated and, in retrospect, was already showing signs of the mental illness that would eventually overtake her. She exhibited severe depression and had difficulty expressing affection, including for her daughter.

In January 1935, all these factors came together in a perfect storm and climaxed when Gladys suffered a complete mental breakdown. The English couple who lived with Gladys initially tried to calm her but were ultimately forced to call an ambulance for assistance. Gladys was admitted into Norwalk State Hospital, the same psychiatric hospital where her mother had died a few years before. Doctors were finally able to diagnose Gladys and reached the conclusion she had paranoid schizophrenia with delusions of persecution.

Gladys was "adjudged insane" on January 15, 1935. Gladys and Norma Jeane's time together had been brief, and a maternal bond never had time to develop.

Just as Grace had been Gladys's best friend during the good times, she continued to be a friend when Gladys needed her most—and when Norma Jeane needed her. Grace filed legal paperwork to become Norma Jeane's permanent guardian. She also began the laborious task of cataloging Gladys's possessions so she could sell them off and pay any outstanding debts.

Once diagnosed, Gladys spent her life in and out of sanitariums and rest homes. The treatment of schizophrenia in the 1930s was in the early stages of development, and nowhere near what is possible today. For Gladys, life would be anything but peaceful. On January 20, 1937, Gladys escaped from a guard's custody in Atascadero, California, during a transfer from Norwalk State Hospital to Portland, Oregon. It was the first of several escape attempts to come over the years.

There is, however, a bright spot during this time frame. Gladys finally realized her wish to make contact with her oldest surviving child, Berniece, but her letters were so rambling and confusing the now-adult daughter initially wondered if her long-lost mother had brain damage.

Berniece came to visit her mother during the summer of 1946 while Gladys was attempting to live outside the confines of a sanitarium. The family lived in one of Ana Lower's duplexes.

During one of her extended stays on the outside, Gladys married for the final time in 1949. Her new husband, John Eley, was still technically married to his previous wife, but he and Gladys continued to live as a married couple until he died in 1952. When it came time to institutionalize Gladys again, Grace suggested to the now-successful movie star Marilyn Monroe the possibility of a private sanitarium instead of a state-run facility.

Through Grace's research, she found Rockhaven Sanitarium in 1953, a private facility located in the Crescenta Valley, not far outside of Hollywood. Rockhaven opened in 1923 and had a long-standing reputation for high-quality care. It accepted women only and, furthermore, hired female employees, which was intended as a means to keep vulnerable women safe from predatory male patients and employees.

Marilyn financed Gladys's stay at Rockhaven, but it is unknown if Marilyn visited. Given her commitment to a time-consuming career and, later, move to the East Coast, the likelihood seems low.

Grace's hunch that Rockhaven would make an ideal home for her longtime friend was correct. Gladys thrived at Rockhaven. The registered nurse who founded Rockhaven, Agnes Richards, had observed while working at asylums what helped patients and what increased their discomfort. Keeping their minds busy with projects could sometimes slow the progress of mental illness, so Gladys, along with other residents, participated in crafts, knitting, and gardening.

Schizophrenia presents itself differently in each person, but a common symptom is a preoccupation with a particular subject. For Gladys, it was religion, Christian Science in particular, and at Rockhaven she was permitted to study her Bible in peace.

Although it is unlikely Marilyn visited her mother during this era, paying for Gladys to live at Rockhaven was an act of love. She even took the step to set up a trust for Gladys's care in her will.

In November 1959, Marilyn consented for her business manager Inez Melson to become Gladys Eley's conservator. A few weeks later in December, Los Angeles Superior Court Judge Burdette Daniels granted Inez's request and named her as Gladys's legal guardian.

It's not clear when Gladys was informed of her youngest daughter's death on August 5, 1962. She knew within a few weeks, though, because a letter written to Inez was postmarked August 22. What's clear was Gladys knew Marilyn died and comprehended the loss. "I am very greatfull [*sic*] for your kind and gracious help toward Berniece and myself and to dear Norma Jeane," the letter read. "She is at peace and at rest now and may Our God bless her & help her always. I wish you to know that I gave her (Norma) Christian Science treatments for approximately one year."

Marilyn had provided for Gladys and her continued care in her will, but it would take time for everything to go through the probate process. There was also a process for paying Marilyn's outstanding debts before moving forward with the trust and paying Rockhaven for Gladys's stay. Inez and Berniece wanted to keep Gladys at Rockhaven, which was the best place for her, but the issue of payment was worrisome while Marilyn's will and estate worked out legalities.

Marilyn's will was signed and dated January 14, 1961, which was while she was in the process of divorcing Arthur Miller. Her estate was valued at one million dollars. Marilyn's will revealed she had left her mother a trust of $100,000 with $5,000 to be paid per year for Gladys's care.

The value of Marilyn's estate was due to television interest in her movies, but it took a few years to pay off the heavy taxes and creditors. Marilyn's on-set acting coach, Paula Strasberg, for example, was owed $22,200 and Joe DiMaggio was owed $5,000 for a loan that was used as a down payment for Marilyn's house in Los Angeles. Her agents filed the largest claim for $80,168.

These debts and taxes gobbled up Marilyn's estate for the first few years and left no funds to pay Gladys's bill, which in theory meant she could have been asked to leave. At some point, the Rockhaven staff decided to permit Gladys to stay for free until Marilyn's estate could repay the debt.

In the meantime, although Rockhaven was the best place equipped to handle Gladys, it wasn't always an easy stay. On July 4, 1963, Gladys knotted a bedsheet and dropped it out her window so she could climb out to freedom. It was a dramatic escape—but it was also a first-floor window. She could have easily walked out the front door of her bungalow.

Regardless, she disappeared off the property. Gladys was found about twenty-four hours later hiding in the boiler room of Lakeview Baptist Terrace Church, located ten miles away from Rockhaven. In her hands were a Bible and a Christian Science handbook.

One of the hallmarks of Rockhaven Sanitarium was the peaceful, home-like setting the ladies lived in while receiving treatment. Pictured is The Pines building, where Gladys lived at the time of Marilyn's death and later escaped. She was found the next day hiding in a church ten miles away. Courtesy Friends of Rockhaven

Authorities determined she must have walked there and had probably spent the night in the church. When the media learned of the story, photographers snapped Gladys's picture and printed photos of Marilyn Monroe's mentally ill mother in newspapers. J. Brian Reid, pastor of the church Gladys had been found hiding in, was considerably kinder than the media. When reporters asked him for a quote, he replied, "She was very calm and cool, the kind of person to whom your heart goes out."

It is not clear if Gladys tried to escape as a response to grief after her daughter's passing or if it was simply the continuation of a pattern, as she had tried to escape before. Rockhaven accepted her back and weathered the scandal even though Gladys's bill was overdue.

By July 1965, Marilyn's estate owed Rockhaven $4,133 in back payments for the $425 monthly bill. Inez Melson and Marilyn's attorneys, Aaron Frosch, who was executor of the estate, and Milton Rudin, continued working with Rockhaven through the mid-1960s. Around this time, Rockhaven received an envelope with a handwritten message reading, "Put this on Marilyn's mother's bill." Two one-dollar bills were enclosed. It was not much money, especially considering the amount of debt, but likely a show of goodwill or intent on the estate's behalf. The note was probably written by Inez Melson, who was still Gladys's guardian and had maintained her visitation schedule. It was also Inez who made a statement to a newspaper: "the sanitarium, which has been so nice, isn't going to set her out on the street."

Syndicated newspaper columnist Earl Wilson wrote on June 21, 1965, "Although Marilyn, in death, still earns about $150,000 a year in deferred salaries, and while her total earnings, including movie sales to TV, have come to over $800,000, virtually all is going for taxes. There have been no business expenses to deduct and Marilyn's continuing income is taxed at the highest bracket, 70 percent. There were also back federal income taxes of $118,000 to be paid for 1958 to 1962."

In 1965, Aaron Frosch made two payments against the outstanding bill totaling $2,547. Inez made another statement to the press to correct information about Rockhaven's treatment of her. "There have been reports in some foreign papers that she is being humiliated because she is in a public ward at the hospital, but these are untrue. Mrs. Eley is an ambulatory patient—she walks around. She has always shared a room with another patient. Even very wealthy patients live in rooms for two people. The institution officials have been kind and generous and she is as contented there as one who is ill can be."

It is doubtful Gladys knew anything about the trouble with her bill. Also, given the graciousness of how everyone handled her 1963 escape, it is clear Rockhaven and Marilyn's estate were trying to work together to keep Gladys safe. "Marilyn's mother and I go shopping at least once a month," Inez was quoted as saying. "Nobody seeing us having lunch would ever suspect that the little white-haired woman who once looked like Marilyn is actually Marilyn's mother. Her only concern, since she doesn't read the newspapers, is for her religious books."

Marilyn's estate continued to make good on the outstanding bill, but Gladys's mental health took a darker turn the following year. First in April and then again in May 1966, Gladys attempted suicide at Rockhaven by trying to stifle herself with bedsheets. "My soul has gone to God, my body might as well go also," she said.

The matter was larger than Rockhaven, and Gladys's case ended up in court, which concluded she was a danger to herself and others. A newspaper article from September 1966 indicated Gladys was required to move from Rockhaven to a California state mental institution for higher-risk patients. A state hospital is what Marilyn had been trying to avoid for her mother. Although Marilyn was no longer able to step in on Gladys's behalf, another daughter was—Berniece Baker Miracle.

The daughter who had been stolen from her so long ago now took responsibility. She did not have the financial resources of her younger half sister, Marilyn Monroe, but in November 1966 Berniece requested her mother be released to her care instead of a state-run institution. The request was granted and Gladys moved to Florida to live with her daughter's family. As she had done in the past, sometimes Gladys lived in facilities, and other times she lived in the outside world. At times she also lived in nursing homes. When Marilyn's estate had finally been probated and paid taxes, some money was available to care for her mother.

Gladys Pearl Monroe Baker Mortensen Eley passed away in Gainesville from heart failure on March 11, 1984. Her remains were cremated and there was a small memorial for family, close friends, and Christian Science associates. Her final resting place is unknown to the public, per her request. Her life was profoundly impacted by mental illness, both her own and members of her family. What defines her, however, was how badly she wanted to be a good mother to her children, two of whom she outlived. Although it was not the ending she had hoped for or expected, Gladys's desire to have bonds with her children came true. It was much later than she anticipated or hoped, but her daughters cared for her when she needed them most.

GRACE GODDARD: THE WOMAN BEHIND MARILYN

Without Grace Goddard, there wouldn't be a Marilyn Monroe.

Clara Grace Atchinson was one of five children born in Great Falls, Montana, to Wallace and Emma Atchinson. Not long after Grace's birth on January 1, 1894, the Atchinsons moved to California, as the 1900 census shows the family living in Bakersfield.

Her first marriage took place in Fresno on February 17, 1913, at the age of nineteen to twenty-eight-year-old Asher Ewing Service. The marriage didn't last long and in less than two years, Grace was not only remarried but living in Los Angeles. She married garageman Reginald Evans on February 2, 1915, and the couple settled in the Sawtelle area of Los Angeles. Although the marriage certificate notes she is divorced, she used her maiden name, Grace Atchinson, for the paperwork. The Evans marriage also didn't last, but this time it was due to death. Reginald Evans died at the age of twenty-four on January 21, 1919, in Los Angeles, from pneumonia brought on by acute influenza. (There was a worldwide flu pandemic in 1918–1919. The CDC estimated about five hundred million people, or one-third of the world's population, were infected with the H1N1 virus, which killed nearly fifty million worldwide. Of those, 675,000 were Americans.)

On June 12, 1920, she married again, this time to John Wallace McKee, a draftsman in the construction industry. The marriage certificate states Grace Evans is "widowed" and this is her "second" marriage—however, it was her third marriage. Her brother Bryan served as a witness. The marriage soon crumbled and the couple separated.

After three marriages in rapid succession, Grace entered the roaring 1920s ready for a fresh start and jumped into the life of a flapper. She supported herself by working at Consolidated Film Industries, where she met Gladys Baker. The two young women had a lot to bond over—failed marriages, heartbreak, and surviving trauma. They quickly became best buddies, a friendship initially dedicated to dancing, drinking, and parties. Over the years, however, they supported each other through life's most challenging moments. During the first years of their relationship, they shared an apartment at 1211 Hyperion in east Hollywood.

Grace was a force of nature, as Olin G. Stanley, a coworker at Consolidated Films, remembered, "[Grace] was freewheeling, hard-working and fast-living. Ambitious to succeed. A busybody. Whoever and whatever she wanted, she went and got. Partying and booze seemed the most important things in her life, and work was just a means to that end."

When Gladys gave birth to a little girl in 1926 and placed her with a foster family, Grace extended her friendship to the baby, Norma Jeane. Gladys tried to build a relationship with her daughter by visiting frequently and taking Norma Jeane out for day trips. Grace often accompanied Gladys and Norma Jeane on their adventures and she doted on her friend's girl. The trio went to lunch, the beauty parlor, and the movies—Grace and Gladys both loved the movies. It was a passion they passed along to Norma Jeane, who found refuge in watching movies, an activity encouraged by Grace, who loved telling her she was going to grow up to be a great woman like Jean Harlow.

Through these visits, Grace grew to know Norma Jeane well and developed a deep affection for her. She had no children of her own and channeled any maternal instincts she may have had into Norma Jeane.

Little did anyone know the relationship Grace had built with Norma Jeane would become so paramount to both their lives. The first indication came in 1935 when Grace assumed responsibility for her friend—Gladys had no family to handle her estate or daughter when she was institutionalized.

That year, Grace filed legal paperwork to become the legal guardian of "Norma Jean Baker."

Part of the process to become Norma Jeane's guardian required the little girl to stay at an orphanage, although Grace paid for her board and visited frequently. Despite Grace's efforts to still be part of Norma Jeane's life during this transition, the orphanage experience traumatized the impressionable and deeply sensitive young girl.

While Norma Jeane lived at the children's home, Grace married for a fourth and final time on August 10, 1935, in Las Vegas. Her new husband, Ervin "Doc" Goddard, was ten years younger. Like Grace, he was divorced but unlike Grace, he had three children. Grace didn't have biological children but was awarded legal guardianship of Norma Jeane on March 27, 1936. When the mandatory stay at the orphanage was fulfilled, Grace removed Norma Jeane from the orphanage on June 7, 1937.

Grace was a constant in Norma Jeane's life during her formative years, but even after assuming legal guardianship, Norma Jeane still bounced from foster home to foster home. She was never part of a government-run foster care system. Instead, Grace arranged placement through her network of friends and family.

Norma Jeane continued to live off and on with the Goddards, but other temporary homes included the family of Grace's brother, Bryan Atchinson, and her sister Enid's family, the Knebelkamps. Norma Jeane's favorite guardian was Ana Lower, Grace's paternal aunt. It was Aunt Ana who showed the troubled child an unconditional motherly love she had never before experienced. (There is a story that Norma Jeane was sent to live with Grace's other family members after Doc Goddard tried to molest Norma Jeane. There is no evidence to support this claim. The man who allegedly attempted to molest Norma Jeane was likely a boarder who lived with another foster family.)

In 1942, Doc Goddard accepted a work promotion that took the family to West Virginia. The Goddards determined they couldn't afford to take Norma Jeane along—they were taking Doc's three children with them, and another mouth to feed was cost-prohibitive. But what would happen to Norma Jeane?

Berniece Baker Miracle was Marilyn's half-sister through their mother Gladys. They enjoyed a warm, friendly relationship but had missed out on being raised together and met as adults. She is pictured here in 1962 while in Los Angeles for Marilyn's memorial service. Along with Joe DiMaggio and business manager Inez Melson, Berniece helped make the arrangements. Photofest

Grace arranged a marriage for Norma Jeane to a neighbor's son, Jim Dougherty. Norma Jeane turned sixteen on June 1 and she married Jim on June 19. Grace had already moved away and did not attend. Norma Jeane had no relatives at the wedding, only Ana Lower, who sewed a white wedding dress for her to wear.

In an instant, Norma Jeane went from a high school girl to a married woman. Grace leaving for West Virginia and marrying her ward off deepened Norma Jeane's fear of abandonment and feelings of being unwanted.

After Grace moved away and Norma Jeane was married, they kept in touch through letter writing. The Goddards moved back to California in 1946, the same year Gladys's first daughter, Berniece Miracle, came to visit. Gladys was living outside the hospital at this point so both now-adult daughters could try getting to know their mother. It wasn't easy, as Gladys was often remote, but Grace filled in many of the gaps by answering questions about their family history. Because she had known Gladys so well before her breakdown, Grace was the link to the past they needed when asking questions.

By this time Norma Jeane's schedule was full with modeling assignments, making the frequency of their contact increasingly sporadic. Sometimes she accepted Grace's invitations over for visits; often she did not. But Norma Jeane needed Grace for one more act of guardianship. Even though Norma Jeane had been married and was divorced in 1946, at twenty years old she was still considered a minor. To sign her first movie studio contract, she needed her legal guardian to cosign. Grace accompanied Norma Jeane to Twentieth Century-Fox and proudly signed a movie contract for the girl she had hoped would grow up to be a movie star like Jean Harlow. It was an accomplishment for both women.

Grace died in 1953, the result of a barbiturate overdose and years of alcoholism. Marilyn did not attend the funeral at Westwood Memorial Park, where Grace was laid to rest in a family plot along with Ana Lower.

Marilyn joined Grace at Westwood Memorial just nine years later—the result of a barbiturate overdose.

BELOVED AUNT ANA

The woman Marilyn Monroe called Aunt Ana was not her biological aunt, although one might never know from the loving way Marilyn spoke of her.

Ana Lower was an older, divorced woman with no children of her own, but with the nurturing disposition of a kindly mother or grandmother figure.

As an adult, Marilyn repeatedly spoke of how she felt loved for the first time when she moved into Aunt Ana's house. As a youngster, Marilyn lived with Aunt Ana off and on between 1937 and her marriage to Jim Dougherty in 1942, and then again in 1946. The only times she didn't stay with Aunt Ana during that time was when the elderly woman's health was suffering. She provided the young girl with the security she needed and the love she craved.

Edith Ana Atchinson was born on January 17, 1880, in Bakersfield, California. In her early twenties, she moved to Los Angeles, where she married William Lower in 1910. In the 1920s, she and her husband purchased some bungalows and cottages around the Los Angeles area to serve as rental properties and provide income. She and Will divorced in 1933 and Ana retained two of their properties, one of which was a duplex on Nebraska Avenue where Ana lived in one of the units. The rental properties provided a modest living but the Great Depression often left the landlady in need of tenants.

Counseling people in the Christian Science faith brought some extra pocket change but mostly she enjoyed sharing her faith free of charge. Her generosity took her to the Lincoln Heights jail, where she volunteered to read the Bible to inmates once a week. She was a devoted, but not fanatical, member of the church and attended services regularly.

When Grace placed young Norma Jeane with her aunt in 1937, Ana Lower was fifty-eight years old and not in the best of health. Still, she managed to shower the adolescent with love and stability. Norma Jeane blossomed in her care.

She began attending Christian Science services with Aunt Ana, who instilled many of the religion's values in the little girl. Anything is possible if you put your mind to it, Ana instructed, and further encouraged Norma Jeane's dream to become an actress. To help Norma Jeane overcome her shyness and stutter, Aunt Ana listened as she read aloud.

It was when Norma Jeane was living with Ana Lower that she came of age and entered puberty. It was also during this time frame that she began experiencing the severe pain of what would later be diagnosed as endometriosis. In adherence to Christian Science beliefs, Ana prayed with Norma Jeane for her pain to be cured. The condition, however, would continue to cause her physical pain and emotional distress for the remainder of her life.

When Norma Jeane traveled to meet her half sister, Ana sent her this letter, which was dated October 10, 1944.

My precious Girl

You are outward bound on a happy journey. May each moment of its joyous expectations be filled to the brim.

New places, faces and experiences await you. You will meet these all with your usual sweetness and loving courtesy.

When you see your sister, you will truly both receive a blessing. Give her my love and a kiss, also the dear little daughter. My love also to the fortunate father and husband.

My happiness is much that you are to have a needed rest and lovely visit with dear ones. Give Bibi [Bebe Goddard, Norma Jeane's foster sister] a kiss for me, too.

One joy of going away is the coming back, where all who love you (and who does not?) will be waiting with open arms to receive you.

My Prayer will be—Dear Father Keep thou my child on upward swing tonight, and always.

The following lines will help you know your protection at all times.

"I know
That where I am
Is God. Since this is so,
No place can safer be than where I go."

Good night dearest
With Love and Kisses
Aunt Ana

After Norma Jeane's separation from Jim Dougherty in 1946, she again turned to Ana Lower, who welcomed her home with unconditional love. Aunt Ana let her stay in the vacant downstairs apartment of her duplex, right below her residence.

Aunt Ana's weak heart finally failed her at the age of sixty-eight on March 14, 1948, just as Norma Jeane was evolving into Marilyn Monroe. After all those years of encouragement, Aunt Ana never got the opportunity to see her former charge's great success. Marilyn was devastated by her foster mother's death and spoke of her lovingly for the rest of her life.

Her affection for the kindly foster mother is probably what led Joe DiMaggio and Berniece and Inez Melson to lay Marilyn to rest in the same cemetery as Ana Lower.

CHARLES STANLEY GIFFORD

One of the key factors in Marilyn Monroe's life was the absence of a father. As an adult, she spoke of being an unwanted child and projecting her desire for a father onto Clark Gable, who she fantasized was her father.

Anecdotally, it appears she longed to fill the void by seeking out older men who could potentially give her the approval and love she never received during her childhood. Marilyn often gravitated to older, often intellectual, men. She typically called her romantic partners some form of "daddy" or "pa," but her search for a father figure stretched beyond romantic relationships. She also sought out older men who served as mentors, idealizing men who could provide the guidance and intellectual insight a nurturing father imparted to his children as they grew.

In her book *Fatherless Daughters: Turning the Pain of Loss into the Power of Forgiveness*, author Pamela Thomas writes that girls who grow up fatherless or lose their fathers while young are impacted in nearly every aspect of their lives. Whether death, divorce, or abandonment is responsible for the loss, these girls often grow into women who fear—and therefore have difficulty maintaining—close relationships. Fearing rejection and further loss, such women can end up isolating themselves from others. It can also profoundly affect a girl's (and then a woman's) self-esteem and sense of worth.

The issue of Marilyn Monroe's paternity has been debated for decades. Although declaring no one knows who Marilyn's father was made for a juicy story, which was the case in many books, documentaries, and magazine articles, Gladys never wavered when it came to identifying the man who fathered her youngest child—Charles Stanley ("Stan") Gifford. Marilyn herself never believed anyone but Stan Gifford to be her biological father, as well.

Had DNA existed in her lifetime, the question of who fathered the world's most famous blonde could have been answered long ago. In 2022, modern technology was finally able to put the question to rest. Thanks to a strand of Marilyn's hair and hair from Stan Gifford's granddaughter, DNA proved Stan Gifford and Marilyn Monroe were indeed father and daughter.

Stan Gifford was born in Newport, Rhode Island, on September 18, 1898, to Fred Gifford, a carpenter, and his wife Elizabeth, who were married in 1888. The Giffords moved to Los Angeles sometime before 1910 with their children, Ethel and Stan, all of whom appear in the Los Angeles census that year.

As a young man, Stan found work in a photography lab, and in July 1919, married a woman named Lillian, with whom he had two children. The oldest, Doris Elizabeth Gifford, was born September 22, 1920, in Los Angeles. Two years later, Charles Stanley Gifford Jr. was born in Santa Monica on September 21, 1922.

The marriage was an unhappy one, with Lillian filing for divorce in October 1923 when her children were still babies.

Citing "extreme cruelty," her legal filing read "that continuously during and throughout said period, as well as throughout the entire married life of plaintiff and defendant, the defendant has continuously pursued toward plaintiff a course of abuse, threats and intimidation calculated to harass, annoy, hurt and worry the plaintiff . . . has boasted of his conquests of other women, exhibiting to plaintiff marks on his body and declaring that same were caused by a hypodermic injection of narcotic drugs, and boasted that he was addicted to the use thereof, and wrongfully and untruthfully charging plaintiff with being the cause of the defendant having been addicted to the use thereof."

During his separation, but not yet legally divorced, Stan began dating one of his coworkers, Gladys Monroe Baker.

Both had marriages that had ended and had two small children, although Gladys's children were in Kentucky. Both had lived most of their lives in the Los Angeles area. Both were charming and good-looking. Needless to say, they found common ground and appealed to one another.

Stan didn't want any serious attachments because his divorce from his wife was not yet final, so Gladys did not receive a positive response when she informed him she was pregnant sometime around Christmas in 1925.

Gladys later recalled Stan made it clear he had no intention of helping or participating in the child's life. Stan disappeared from Gladys's life, leaving her pregnant and alone. Records indicate Stan Gifford was still living in Los Angeles through the 1940s. Norma Jeane grew up within just a few miles of the man Gladys insisted was her father.

While Norma Jeane dreamed of having a dashing father figure, her biological father remarried. This time, he married a teacher by the name of Mary Seiwell, and at some point, the couple headed out to Hemet, a desert community about ninety miles outside Los Angeles in the San Jacinto Valley.

Once in Hemet, the Giffords opened Red Rock Dairy, a farm, dairy, and cash-and-carry business. The dairy blossomed into a successful venture. According to an interview with his granddaughter Francine Gifford Deir in 2022, Stan took great pride in caring for his cows and bulls, even naming them after his grandchildren.

Norma Jeane, now a young woman whose mother has been institutionalized, still longed for a connection with her father. For help, she turned to Grace, who had been Gladys's best friend and confidant during the 1925 affair between Stan and Gladys.

In a letter dated September 14, 1942, newlywed Norma Jeane opens her letter with, "I want to thank you so much for writing Mom and explaining things about Stanley G. I'm sure she understands now." It is unclear what was meant by this, but after describing her new life as a young bride and housewife, Norma Jeane circles back around to the subject of Stan Gifford in the postscript. "How can I get in touch with Stanley Gifford? Through Consoladated [*sic*] films? Or something like that? Which dept?"

Marilyn's openness about who she believed her father was went beyond her inner circle of friends. Francine Gifford Deir, the daughter of Charles Stanley Gifford Jr., said in an interview she knew of the rumors that her grandfather was Marilyn Monroe's biological father as far back as the 1960s. "Marilyn talked about it with everyone," she said. "That's what Gladys, her mother, had told her. I had discovered it in the 1960s, on the cover of *Esquire* magazine. They had managed to get a picture of my grandfather. My father, who was in it, was furious."

In an interview with the *All Things Marilyn* podcast in 2023, Gifford Deir said Stan Gifford denied paternity of Norma Jeane because he feared losing visitation rights with the two children from his marriage. Although separated from his wife, he was still legally married and in the 1920s that would have put him at risk for losing his children. Gifford Deir's father, Chuck, was furious because he believed and defended his father. The rumors, he insisted, were not true. Stan had been a devoted and loving father to his kids, so it was difficult to comprehend that he would have denied a child of his.

At some point, Stan appeared to have had a change of heart, as he reached out to Marilyn by sending her a get-well card (addressed to "Marylyn"). It reads, "This cheery little get-well note / Comes specially to say / That lots of thoughts / and wishes, too, / Are with you every day." He underlined "Are with you every day" and wrote underneath it "a little prayer too." Because it is undated, it is unknown when the card was sent. There was no envelope when it was discovered in Marilyn's personal files, so it is also unknown if it was sent in the mail or if Stan had hand-delivered it.

In her book *My Sister Marilyn*, Berniece Baker Miracle says Marilyn told her that she had finally met her father. "'I feel . . . it was a very important event in my life,' Marilyn's voice quavers. 'I wouldn't say it was exactly . . . happiness . . . that I felt. As far as my feelings toward him . . . I don't think I can . . . express it. I guess . . . perhaps I'm not sure what the feeling was.

"'The first time I saw my father,' she continues, her voice gathering energy, and perhaps resentment, 'I was lying flat on my back in the hospital. I looked at him and I studied his face and features, and I saw that Mother had told me the truth, that he was my father.'

"'I said, "My ears are just like yours." You know how the tops of my ears are thin. They don't curl over; they just sort of stand up. I keep them covered most of the time.'

"'We talked . . . a long time,' Marilyn speaks haltingly again. 'I enjoyed talking . . . with him.'"

She didn't offer much more about the visit and it's not clear which hospital stay she was referring to; however, it's quite possible he gave her the get-well card in person.

The card was offered for auction in 2022.

Regardless of the relationship she had always wanted, at some point Marilyn finally gave up attempting to contact Stan Gifford and seemed disinterested in him. For her, it was too late, and no relationship developed between the two.

Marilyn may have given up, but Stan appears to have been weighed down with guilt after her death. As he was dying, he wrote a letter to Chuck disclosing he had been talking to a minister about something important. Stan encouraged his son to contact the minister to discuss something important. "What else could it be?" Gifford Deir said in the *All Things Marilyn* podcast.

The situation started because Stan Gifford was frightened, Gifford Deir said, and motivated by the love for his children. She also revealed that Doris died young from polio, so after Marilyn's death he had lost both daughters. It was apparently something he struggled with until the end. "It was sad in that respect," she said. "He got himself caught up in not telling the truth. Even when she became famous, I think he had lived the lie for so long."

Because so little was known about the relationship between Stan and Gladys, their romance has often been presented as a fling. As it turns out, it was a genuine love affair. Years later, Chuck learned from a relative that Stan and Gladys were seeing each other steadily and used to go away for the weekends together. Although it did not help Marilyn during her lifetime, time would reveal that she had, in fact, been born out of love. "He was a very good man that did a bad thing," Gifford Deir said. "A very sad thing."

· 4 ·

Marilyn Monroe: What's in a Name?

$\mathcal{I}$n *Romeo and Juliet*, William Shakespeare reflected, "What's in a name? that which we call a rose / By any other name would smell as sweet."

Shakespeare, a master of shining an insightful light into the human heart and spirit, eloquently argues that what matters is an individual's character, which remains constant despite his or her name.

Such is the case with Marilyn Monroe.

Few things in the life of Marilyn Monroe are simple and her name is no exception. There is much debate over nearly every aspect of Marilyn's original and, later, professional name.

It is interesting to note that her last name did not reflect her actual lineage until she chose the name Monroe for herself. Monroe was her mother's maiden name and represented her maternal bloodline.

NORMA JEANE IS BORN

On June 1, 1926, Gladys Monroe delivered a baby girl named Norma Jeane Mortenson, which is the name printed on the birth certificate. Gladys Monroe was indeed the mother's maiden name, and as such is printed on her baby's birth certificate. By this point in her life, however, Gladys had been married twice. The first time was to Jasper Baker and then to Martin Edward Mortensen in 1924.

Gladys Baker had given birth to two children while married to Jasper Baker. After their divorce, Jasper kidnapped the two youngsters and moved to his home state of Kentucky to raise the children.

Gladys accepted a proposal of marriage from Martin Edward Mortensen and the couple married on October 11, 1924. Gladys struggled to settle into a quieter life and within just a few months the marriage crumbled.

Gladys and her second husband filed for divorce in May 1925, although the resolution legally wasn't finalized until 1928. In the meantime, Gladys began dating again, including a handsome supervisor at her place of employment, Consolidated Films, in Hollywood.

Charles Stanley Gifford, who went by Stan, was a charismatic blue-eyed native of Rhode Island with light brown hair and a medium build.

They had not been dating very long when Gladys discovered around the holiday season of 1925 that she was expecting a baby.

Gladys informed her lover she was carrying his child. By all accounts, the conversation did not go well and ended with Stan tell-

Rare photo of Gladys Monroe with her younger brother Marion in childhood. Courtesy Scott Fortner Collection

ing her, "It's a good thing you're already married." The reference, of course, hinted at the fact that the child would not be considered illegitimate because she was still *technically* married. Because she was *technically* Mrs. Mortensen she could claim Mr. Mortensen as the father.

To avoid saddling her daughter with the undesirable "illegitimate" label, Gladys protected the baby girl by using "Mortenson" on the birth certificate. But there is a slight wrinkle when it comes to the spelling of the last name. For reasons unknown, *Mortensen* appears as *Mortenson* on the birth certificate. The most reasonable conclusions are a simple typo or absent-minded misspelling on Gladys's part. On the marriage certificate to Gladys, "Mortensen" is spelled with "sen" and on Norma Jeane's birth certificate Gladys spelled it "Mortenson" with "son."

The result meant Norma Jeane's name appears both as Mortensen and Mortenson on documents throughout her young life. Essentially, the spelling comes secondary to what it was meant to accomplish in the first place—avoiding the titles of "bastard" and "illegitimate," which in a legal sense was successful. (Mortensen's name would reappear later under "Father" on Norma Jeane's marriage certificates. He is listed as "E. Mortensen" on her certificate to Jim Dougherty in 1942 and again as "Edward Mortensen" on her marriage certificate to Joe DiMaggio in 1954.)

Mortensen (or Mortenson) was her legal name, but a third name was frequently used instead: Norma Jeane Baker—Gladys's first husband's last name. On the 1930 census for Los Angeles, mother and daughter are listed under the home of Wayne and Ida Bolender as "boarders," both with the last name Baker.

So why would Gladys revert to the name Baker, an abusive ex-husband who had kidnapped her children? And why would she give her new baby the last name of a man who was not the father?

The answer lies in Gladys's fantasy of regaining custody of her children, Jackie and Berniece, and bringing them back to California to live with her. When she reunited with her two children, she believed, all three children would have the last name Baker and live together as a unified family. Gladys called her youngest child Norma Jeane Baker in anticipation of a dream that would never come true. Stan Gifford, the man who denied paternity and rejected his daughter, never had his name associated with the child, which is clearly what he wanted all along.

As for the combination of her first names, it's typically reported Norma is in honor of silent movie queen Norma Talmadge and Jeane for Jean Harlow. Norma Talmadge was among the top-tier actresses of the 1920s and it is a reasonable stretch to assume the movie-obsessed Gladys Baker may very well have bestowed her daughter with the name of a movie star.

The story of Marilyn Monroe being named after movie stars is a popular one, as though her name predestined her for stardom. The story, however, is just that—a story. There is no evidence to suggest Norma Talmadge inspired the Norma half of her name, and Jean Harlow is an outright impossibility.

Jean Harlow didn't receive her first bit part until 1927, one year *after* Norma Jeane's birth, and didn't star in her breakout role in *Hell's Angels* until 1930. Although Norma Jeane would later idolize Harlow, she could not possibly have been named after her. Also, the spellings of Jean and Jeane are different. It's unknown why Gladys decided to add the extra "e" although it's interesting to note Berniece's name also has an extra "e," as opposed to the traditional Bernice spelling. To further complicate matters, although "Norma Jeane" is the legal name printed on her birth certificate, she used the names Norma Jeane, Norma Jean, and Norma while growing up.

The reality of Norma Jeane's name is much more mundane in origin. Gladys had traveled to Kentucky in pursuit of her kidnapped children, and during her brief stay lived with a family as a nanny and housekeeper. One of the girls was named Norma Jean—and Gladys simply liked the name.

When Norma Jeane married her first husband Jim Dougherty in 1942, the marriage certificate listed her name as "Norma Jeane Mortensen," which is not the spelling on her birth certificate—although it is the correct spelling of Martin Edward Mortensen's name—nor is it the last name she had used most of her life, Baker.

As of 1942, Norma Jeane settled into a quiet new life and for the next four years lived decisively as Norma Jeane Dougherty.

While Jim Dougherty dutifully served his country during World War II, Norma Jeane began fulfilling her childhood dreams of modeling, to then break into acting.

Like many young hopefuls in Hollywood, Norma Jeane Dougherty had a name the studios wanted to improve.

There is controversy over who helped the future superstar select her new name. Many people took credit, including actor Mickey Rooney, who claimed he told the young starlet she "looked like a Marilyn." At that moment, he later claimed, an agent named Monroe called. He informed the gentleman on the other end of the receiver he couldn't take the call right then because, "I'm talking to Marilyn, Monroe." And with that, a lightning bolt of inspiration struck and Mickey Rooney had the perfect stage name for Norma Jeane Dougherty.

The real story is much more typical of how stage names were selected during Hollywood's studio era. Twentieth Century-Fox, the first studio to sign Norma Jeane to a contract, holds the distinction of creating the moniker "Marilyn Monroe." The head of talent at Twentieth Century-Fox, Ben Lyon, helped Norma Jeane become Marilyn Monroe. The actor-turned-executive coincidentally had starred in *Hell's Angels*, the movie that propelled Norma Jeane's idol, Jean Harlow, to fame. (After meeting with the twenty-year-old starlet, he reportedly said, "It's Jean Harlow all over again!")

Several possibilities were discussed, considered, and rejected. One of the first real contenders was Carole Lind, but it didn't stick. Neither did Jean Norman, a play on Norma Jeane (or Jean). Norma Jeane proposed Monroe, her mother's maiden name, for her new last name. Yes, they decided. That would work. Now for the first name.

Norma Jeane wanted to keep the Jeane part, changing it to the more common Jean spelling, which would also honor Harlow. Jean Monroe? She liked it, but Lyon felt it wasn't quite right. It was a no-go.

Lyon selected the name Marilyn after actress Marilyn Miller, who had played his love interest in the movie *Her Majesty, Love* (1931) during his acting days. He still held an affectionate association with the name. (Remarkably, ten years later Marilyn's name would become Marilyn Miller when she married Arthur Miller.)

Marilyn, he decided, it would be and it fit perfectly with Monroe.

The newly named Marilyn Monroe began an acting career and her catchy name and pinup girl curves helped her gain considerable momentum.

Everyone she knew began addressing her as Marilyn. When she became a movie star as Marilyn Monroe, she signed this name on studio contracts, personal checks, and autographs. As was so often the case, though, the subject of her legal name remained a complicated matter. Although using the name Marilyn Monroe in every aspect of her life, she had never bothered filing paperwork with the court to make the name change official.

When she married Joe DiMaggio at the height of her fame in 1954, it was one of the few instances in which she still had to use her old—legal—name. Like a ghost from the past, she signed the marriage certificate "Norma Jeane Dougherty." She hadn't seen Jim Dougherty in about eight years at that point. (An interesting note about the marriage certificate: it reads "Norma Jean Mortenson" under MAIDEN NAME IF BRIDE IS PREVIOUSLY MARRIED. Jean is spelled without the "e" in Jeane and Mortenson matches the name on her birth certificate, but not the Mortensen on her first marriage certificate.)

After marrying Joe DiMaggio, the newlyweds embarked on a trip to Japan. It doubled as a work opportunity for Joe and as a honeymoon. While abroad, Marilyn accepted an invitation to entertain the American troops fighting in the Korean War. On her military identification card, which was government-issued, she is Norma Jeane DiMaggio.

It wasn't until 1956, two years after her divorce from Joe and the same year she married Arthur Miller, that she went to the trouble to legally change her name to Marilyn Monroe. She didn't say why she waited, although she later admitted, "I've never liked the name Marilyn. I've often wished that I had held out that day for Jean Monroe. But I guess it's too late to do anything about it now."

Perhaps she procrastinated because she didn't like the name. Or perhaps she just didn't get around to it. She was, after all, building a career of phenomenal proportions.

During her marriage to Arthur Miller, she sometimes signed her name as Marilyn Miller; her personal stationery had MMM monogrammed on it. However, this was never a legal name change.

Technically speaking, she wasn't named Marilyn Monroe for very long. She legally became Marilyn Monroe in 1956, but passed away just a few years later in 1962 so her death certificate, will, and crypt placard all read the correct name: Marilyn Monroe.

· 5 ·

The Influence of the Movies

$\mathcal{L}$ike a lot of people during the Great Depression, movies became an escape from the harsh realities of life during the 1930s. The movie industry's growing popularity was perfectly timed, albeit by accidental and unfortunate circumstances.

When the stock market crashed in 1929, movies were in the early stages of incorporating synchronized sound, increasing their appeal. In the days before television, the only real mass-entertainment competition movies needed to worry about was radio. Movies offered an affordable option for a desperate nation in need of relief from poverty and lack of work.

For Norma Jeane, movies were an especially big part of her childhood and helped shape her worldview. Her biological mother, Gladys, and primary foster mother, Grace, were obsessive moviegoers. Both Gladys and Grace took Norma Jeane to the movies, so from an early age they provided respite and became a coping mechanism.

Unlike for the average American, Hollywood as an industry and actual physical location were tangible realities for Norma Jeane. Growing up in the Los Angeles area, including time in Hollywood itself, for Norma Jeane movies were a part of everyday life. Studios dominated the cityscape, great movie palaces lined the streets, and celebrities placed their hands and feet in wet cement within walking distance. Even Norma Jeane's mother had worked in the film industry as a cutter.

When Norma Jeane lived in Hollywood with her mother, she frequently walked to Grauman's Chinese Theatre to watch movies by herself. Like millions of other people, she liked trying to fit her hands and feet into the prints of Hollywood's great stars.

She also liked walking a little farther down the street to the Chinese's sister theatre, Grauman's Egyptian.

Jean Harlow and Clark Gable were among the top box office draws in the 1930s, both as individual actors and when they were paired up. By Studio—eBay / Wikimedia Commons

Once inside, Norma Jeane found solace in the soft glow of the flickering pictures before her. She sat in the front row and often stayed all day. "I was supposed to come home when it got dark, but of course I didn't know when it was dark," she said.

With movies playing such an important part in her youth and providing a sense of comfort, it is little wonder Norma Jeane wanted to be an actress when she grew up. She loved many popular actors of the era, but two movie stars in particular caught Norma Jeane's attention: Jean Harlow and Clark Gable.

"I was fascinated by Jean Harlow. I had white hair—I was a real towhead—and she was the first grown-up lady I had ever seen who had white hair like mine," Marilyn told Associated Press reporter Victor Sebastian in an interview dated February 26, 1961. "I cut her picture out of a magazine, and on the back of it was the picture of a man. I pasted his picture in a scrapbook—just his picture. There was nothing else in the book. It was Clark Gable."

CLARK GABLE

Best remembered for his role as Rhett Butler in *Gone with the Wind* (1939), Clark Gable was given the nickname "The King of Hollywood" during his lifetime as a reflection of his fame and overall impact on the movie industry. The King ruled over his kingdom for nearly thirty years as a top box office draw.

Clark Gable would also, unknown to him, become one of the most important people in Norma Jeane Baker's young life. To Norma Jeane, the handsome, mustachioed actor resembled a photo she had seen of Charles Stanley Gifford, the man she believed to be her biological father. For a lonely, fatherless little girl, Norma Jeane channeled her energy into creating a fantasy around Clark Gable being her real dad. She even liked to daydream about him visiting her at the orphanage and bringing coloring books and crayons for her and the other children.

After Norma Jeane grew up to become Marilyn Monroe, she still looked up to Clark as a hero-like figure. In 1954, Clark Gable and his wife Kay were among the guests at a party thrown after the completion of *The Seven Year Itch* filming. Clark's attendance was an honor. He rarely went to Hollywood parties and public events, instead preferring to stay at home on his ranch in Encino, outside Los Angeles. Marilyn was delighted he attended and photos of them dancing that night show her face beaming up at him.

Marilyn recalled the moment to reporter Victor Sebastian, "I nearly collapsed. I'm sure I must have turned the color of my red chiffon dress. I don't remember what I said or if I said anything. But I remember thinking, wouldn't he be surprised to know how I really feel about him?"

Shortly after the party, when Marilyn was briefly hospitalized for a surgical procedure related to endometriosis, the Gables sent her flowers.

A few years later, Marilyn was beside herself with joy when Clark Gable was cast as her leading man in *The Misfits*.

Filming for *The Misfits* was done on location in Northern Nevada during the summer months, with temperatures regularly soaring between 100 to 110 degrees Fahrenheit in the afternoons. It was a difficult shoot for all involved, but Marilyn especially was in a tough place emotionally—her marriage to Arthur Miller was at its end; she had miscarried her babies; she struggled to work in the intense heat; and her dependence on prescription medication was increasing. Her chronic tardiness to the set worsened and her insecurities made it difficult for her to remember lines. As was her habit, Marilyn listened more to her acting coach, Paula Strasberg, than her director, which caused friction on the set.

In front of Clark Gable, however, Marilyn tried to stay on her best behavior. For as temperamental as Marilyn was on set, it was clear she wanted his approval. For his part, Clark recognized Marilyn was not well and treated her tenderly.

Ralph Roberts, the on-set masseur during *The Misfits* filming, recalled Clark's kindness to her. "Marilyn," he began, "I have to tell you that I had reservations about you from before the beginning of the picture. All the rumors of you and your temperament. I wanted to do this picture more than I can tell you, and even if it meant working with you, I was determined to do it. As far as I can see, you're about the least temperamental person involved."

Marilyn beamed. "Oh, Clark, thank you," she responded. "I'm so glad I've had you these years to hold onto in my dreams. I feel like Judy Garland and her song."

Clark became friends with Arthur Miller on the set, and the writer later recalled, "[Clark] behaved as though Marilyn was a woman in physical pain, despite his having to spend what might have been humiliating hours each day waiting for her to start working, no hint of affront ever showed on his face."

Marilyn later recalled he would bring her a chair between takes so she could rest.

"There are so many things I'll never forget about Clark Gable," she said. "Little things, incidents, moments. His unfailing politeness. He was one of the greatest gentlemen I have known. He had concern for everyone.

"I had gone direct to *The Misfits* from another picture. I was exhausted. I fought illness most of the time I was working on the picture. I had to go into the hospital for a couple of days. 'Rest yourself,' he'd say. 'Do like I do—take it easy.'"

While Marilyn struggled to show up for her call times, Clark typically showed up a half hour early. Huston tried to shoot around Marilyn when she was unavailable, but during the times when the crew was waiting on her, Clark took to amusing himself by performing many of his own stunts. At one point, the fifty-nine-year-old actor was dragged by a truck going thirty-five miles per hour to look like he was wrangling wild mustangs. The blazing heat and his heavy clothing added to the intensity and, even though his wardrobe took the scene's physicality into account, Clark ended up with bruising and cuts.

Despite the grueling filming experience, Clark was thrilled with his performance in *The Misfits*. It would turn out to be his last. Arthur recalled in *The Misfits*, a book about the movie's production, "I know Clark was very happy with this picture because just before he left the studio to go hunting— we did not know he was going to die three days later—he saw the rough cut and he told me, 'This is the best thing I did in my life.' I don't know if it was true, but he felt it was. He was pleased with this work and with the making of the film."

Shortly after completing *The Misfits*, Clark Gable died of a heart attack at the age of fifty-nine. He was entombed in a crypt next to his third wife, Carole Lombard, in Forest Lawn Glendale.

After his death, Marilyn gave an interview to the Associated Press as a tribute to her childhood hero. "He was everything I had expected him to be," she said. "They called him the 'King,' you know, and he was like that—he had a quality that commanded respect and admiration. I never saw anyone who had such an effect on everyone with whom he worked. The crew loved Clark. And he had that magnificent masculinity. But my biggest surprise was when we started our work together. That's when I realized what a real actor he was. That's when I became aware of his tremendous sensitivity. But, of course, that was what attracted me in the first place."

KAY GABLE

During the filming of *The Misfits*, Marilyn became friendly with Mrs. Gable, Clark's fifth and final wife. Kay Gable was pregnant with a baby then known to be Clark Gable's first and only child. (Decades later, it was revealed Clark had fathered a daughter with Loretta Young. As far as anyone knew at the time, however, Clark was childless until Kay became pregnant in 1960.)

"Kay Gable and I became very close," Marilyn said in 1961. "She used to come out to the set and call to me, 'Hey, how did Our Man do today?'

"I'd laugh, 'Our Man? I must say you are generous, Kay.' And it was a joke between us always. 'Our Man!'"

When Marilyn learned of Clark's death, she was heartbroken, but when she heard the rumor his widow blamed her for Clark's death, she was absolutely devasted. The story as Marilyn understood it was that Clark had been performing his own stunts in the intense heat while specifically waiting for her, which caused stress on his heart.

Marilyn was already in a fragile mental state, and the accusation she had caused the death of the King of Hollywood—and her childhood hero—was unbearable. Her depression deepened.

When Marilyn did not show up at Clark's memorial service in Los Angeles, the theory only gained traction. The gossip was that she must not have been invited. Or she wouldn't show up because her estranged husband Arthur Miller planned to attend.

In reality, neither story as to why Marilyn didn't go to Clark's funeral turned out to be true. Her friend Ralph Roberts wrote in his memoir that Marilyn was too emotional. "I can't face Sunday," she told him. "The funeral. I can't go out there. It would be wrong, and I just can't do it anyway. I can't do anything here to face the day. I called to leave my love and concern for Kay. I wrote. I sent flowers. Lee insists I come over for the day. Will you come with me?"

Instead of flying out to Los Angeles, Marilyn stayed in New York and was surrounded by her support network: the Strasbergs and Ralph Roberts.

Kay Gable delivered a healthy baby boy, John Clark Gable, on March 20, 1961. In June, Kay invited Marilyn to attend her son's christening. Marilyn was thrilled and relieved. It was proof Kay did not, after all, blame her for Clark's death. Marilyn arrived at St. Cyril's Roman Catholic Church dressed demurely in a black suit dress. Other guests included Jack Benny, Hedda Hopper, Edgar Bergen, Leo Carillo, Fred Astaire, Ray Milland, Robert Stack, Cesar Romero, and Rhonda Fleming.

JEAN HARLOW

Jean Harlow, born Harlean Harlow Carpenter in 1911, made a lasting impression on movies and popular culture.

As movies were becoming America's favorite form of entertainment in the 1910s and 1920s, they were still reflecting many of the ideologies of the

Victorian and Edwardian ages. After World War I, women began wearing makeup and shorter skirts, but many of the old tropes remained. This included "vamp" women who still reflected how they were portrayed in more conservative times—dark and mysterious, with erotic undertones. Theda Bara perfectly epitomizes these earliest versions of on-screen femme fatales.

Everything changed in the 1930s—talking pictures had replaced silent flickers and it was time for a new type of vamp.

Enter Jean Harlow.

When she appeared in MGM's star-studded *Dinner at Eight*, Jean Harlow's image represented a complete pivot in what movie audiences were used to. Instead of a silent, slinking woman with heavy eyeliner and downturned eyes, Jean Harlow had big, bright eyes, moved fluidly and with grace, and she *talked*. And not only did she speak on film, but she also was funny and exhibited a quick, sharp-tongued humor never before seen in movies.

Gone were the almost supernatural, spooky women with black hair and exotic clothing. Everything about Jean Harlow was light. She became famous for wearing form-fitting, glamorous white satin dresses and was placed in white sets. What made Jean Harlow a sensation, though, was that white blonde hair!

Women everywhere wanted their hair to look like Jean Harlow's and publicity men took note. While under contract to Howard Hughes, whose movie *Hell's Angels* provided Jean with her first break, he challenged his marketing team to come up with the perfect term to describe the hair color everyone was talking about. Their solution: *platinum blonde*.

When Jean moved to MGM, where she became a top-tier box office star, studio head Louis B. Mayer insisted on a new nickname for her. "Platinum blonde" was a Howard Hughes term, but she was now an MGM property and the old name would not suffice. MGM brass came up with the "blonde bombshell."

Both terms were invented specifically for Jean Harlow and were so powerful in their descriptiveness that they are still in use today.

Jean Harlow died in 1937 at the age of twenty-six, so Marilyn would never meet her like she later had the opportunity to meet Clark Gable. It is clear, however, Jean Harlow's powerful imagery influenced Marilyn Monroe, and Marilyn herself always gave credit to her platinum lineage.

Platinum Blonde Sisters: The Harlow-Monroe Parallels

Although Marilyn never met Jean Harlow in person, she felt a strong connection with her. The parallels between the lives and careers of these two blondes are stunning. Here's a brief overview:

Complex Relationships with Their Mothers: Harlow's mother was domineering and manipulated her daughter and her career.

Monroe's mentally ill mother was often absent from her daughter's life.

Acted under Their Mothers' Maiden Names: Harlow, born Harlean Carpenter, signed her Central Casting paperwork with her mother's maiden name—Jean Harlow—on a whim.

Monroe, born Norma Jeane Mortenson, was renamed when she signed her first contract with Twentieth Century-Fox. An executive, Ben Lyon, selected the name Marilyn; she selected her mother's maiden name, Monroe.

Were "Discovered" by Ben Lyon (Kind Of): Harlow was working as an extra on a movie when Ben Lyon, who was in the middle of filming *Hell's Angels*, walked to a neighboring set while on a break. There he spotted a sexy extra with white-blonde hair. *Hell's Angels* had been filming when sound technology became available, so studio head Howard Hughes scrapped the original silent version and started filming again from scratch. This meant leading lady Greta Nilsson and her thick Norwegian accent were no longer suitable for the part of femme fatale Helen. Lyon, according to his own story, whisked unknown Jean Harlow over to Howard Hughes to show him the new "Helen."

Monroe's first movie contract was with Twentieth Century-Fox, which would eventually become her home studio. When she was presented to a Fox executive for consideration, it was none other than Ben Lyon, who was now retired from acting and working behind the scenes. It was Lyon, he later said, who came up with the name "Marilyn."

Eschewed Underwear: Harlow literally jiggled on the screen.

Monroe was bustier and wore bras but went without panties when she could.

Sought out Father Figures: Harlow's spitfire mother divorced her mild-mannered father when she was still a young woman. Although Jean loved her father, she was rarely permitted to see him after her parents' divorce. As a result, Jean tended to seek out men who were older and more worldly.

Monroe was told by her mother that her biological father was a man named C. Stanley Gifford. Gifford, however, always denied paternity and she grew up without knowing a father. As a result, Marilyn tended to seek out men who were older and more worldly.

Exposure to Christian Science Faith: Harlow's mother dabbled in Christian Science. Monroe's foster mother, "Aunt" Ana Lower was a devoted Christian Scientist, as was Monroe's biological mother.

Worked Hard to Improve Acting Skills: Harlow knew she wasn't a great actress at the beginning of her career and sought to improve by working with directors on her skills. As a result, her performances got significantly better.

Monroe enrolled at the Actors Studio and also studied privately with its director, Lee Strasberg.

Experienced Anguish over Their Sex Symbol Images: Harlow referred to her characters as "sex vultures."

Monroe hated playing "dumb blondes."

Both Women Went on Strike at the Height of Their Careers for Better Parts and More Money: Harlow went on strike in 1934 in a bid for a better salary and parts stretching beyond her "sex vulture" image.

Monroe went on strike in 1955 in a bid for a better salary and parts stretching beyond her "dumb blonde" image.

Both Married Three Times, with the First Marriage Taking Place at Age Sixteen: Harlow fell in love with and married a dashing young millionaire named Chuck McGrew. She loved Chuck, but the marriage also got her out from under her mother's thumb (for a while).

Monroe's guardian, Grace Goddard, moved East and couldn't take her charge so she arranged for the teenager to marry a neighbor's son, Jim Dougherty. She cared for Jim, but the marriage kept her from returning to an orphanage.

Were Avid Readers: Harlow read several books per week.

Monroe opened one of her first charge accounts at a bookstore; she also took a literature course at UCLA.

Loved Animals: Harlow had several pets, including dogs.

Monroe had several pets, including dogs.

Directed by George Cukor: Harlow: *Dinner at Eight* (1933)

Monroe: *Let's Make Love* (1960) and *Something's Got to Give* (1962, incomplete)

Lived on Palm Drive in Beverly Hills: Harlow's last home was on Palm Drive; here she languished with kidney failure until moving to Good Samaritan Hospital in her final hours.

Monroe lived on Palm Drive twice—once in 1950 with Johnny Hyde and again, down the street, with Joe DiMaggio during their short marriage in 1954. The house with Joe was just two doors down from the Harlow house.

Their Last Movie Costarred Clark Gable: Harlow: *Saratoga* (1937)

Monroe: *The Misfits* (1961)

Both Died While in the Middle of Filming a Movie: Harlow: *Saratoga* (1937, Jean had finished enough of her role that a double was used to complete the movie)

Monroe: *Something's Got to Give* (1962, the movie was shelved because there was not enough usable footage)

Died Young and Under Mysterious Circumstances: Harlow: Rumors swirled about the cause of Harlow's early demise, including a story that the products used to bleach her signature platinum blonde hair were responsible for her death. The most commonly repeated story, though, is that Jean's Christian Scientist mother refused to allow doctors to treat her. In reality, Jean Harlow received around-the-clock medical attention but there was no cure for kidney failure in 1937.

Monroe: A cottage industry has built up around the subject of Marilyn Monroe's death. Officially, her passing has been ruled a "probable suicide." Since then, however, many have expressed doubts over the verdict. Some theories are more believable than others, but they include everything from an accidental overdose to various murder scenarios.

The heydays of Harlow and Monroe were twenty years apart; Harlow was the queen of the box office in the 1930s and Monroe claimed that title twenty years later in the 1950s. Jean Harlow didn't live long enough to form an opinion of Marilyn Monroe, but Marilyn Monroe was keenly aware of Hollywood's original platinum blonde and her influence.

Whether or not all the similarities were coincidences remains a mystery and even Marilyn herself wasn't sure. She once told her business partner Milton Greene, "I kept thinking of her, rolling over the facts of her life in my mind. It was kind of spooky and sometimes I thought, 'Am I making this happen?' I don't think so. We just seemed to have the same spirit or something. I don't know. I just kept wondering if I would die young like her, too."

There were, however, some important differences between the two women. While Marilyn was raised in poverty in Los Angeles and dreamed of becoming a movie star, Harlow, in contrast, was born to a financially comfortable family in Kansas City, Missouri.

It wasn't until newlywed Harlean Carpenter McGrew moved to Los Angeles with her husband that a movie career presented itself. Friends of the teenage bride dared her to audition for movie roles. She took the dare for fun and registered with Central Casting. Unlike Marilyn, Jean Harlow had no innate desire to be a movie star. It was her overbearing mother who lived out her dreams of stardom through her daughter.

Both women also didn't give themselves enough credit as natural comediennes. Their real-life wit crept into their pictures and the ability to be funny is not easily learned. Audiences responded well to them because, quite simply, they are fun to watch.

Perhaps it is not just their screen legacies that continue to fascinate film buffs. Years before the Women's Movement, they risked their careers to demand fairness in a male-dominated industry. Struggles in their personal lives, the desire to continually better themselves, and their tenacity make more than untouchable celluloid images; they are human and relatable.

Marilyn Monroe was likely born with these qualities, but her admiration of Jean Harlow was also well placed. In Jean Harlow, Marilyn found a strong, sexy, and intelligent role model.

In a 1958 photo shoot with Richard Avedon, she dressed as screen enchantresses who had come before her. With childlike glee, Marilyn dressed up as Marlene Dietrich, Lillian Russell, Theda Bara, Clara Bow—and Jean Harlow. In her lifetime, Marilyn dreamed of making a movie about Jean Harlow. There are even stories about Marilyn meeting with Jean Harlow's mother to get her blessing, but this story can't possibly be true, as the date given for the meeting takes place *after* Jean's mother died.

That movie was never made, of course, but Marilyn's prediction she would die young was, sadly, correct. And here her last parallel with Jean Harlow surfaces: After Jean Harlow's June 1937 death, her boyfriend, actor William Powell (who starred in *How to Marry a Millionaire* with Marilyn in 1953), regularly sent flowers to the final resting place of his beloved. In death, Marilyn's devoted ex-husband, baseball legend Joe DiMaggio, sent flowers to her grave three times a week for twenty years.

• 6 •

Like a Rolling Stone

Marilyn at Home

$\mathcal{D}$uring her youth, Marilyn did not have much choice in where she lived. After divorcing her first husband, Jim Dougherty, at the age of twenty, she was truly on her own for the first time. Her lack of finances, however, limited her choices when it came to living situations during her early twenties. Modeling and bit parts in movies provided some income, but work was irregular for her first few years in the industry.

After signing a seven-year contract with Twentieth Century-Fox in 1951, a guaranteed weekly income afforded her more freedom when it came to selecting places to live. Even as she made more money later in her career, her adult patterns for how she lived had already been established.

A PARADOX WRAPPED IN A FUR

Outwardly, she projected the image of an ideal movie star. Having an innate sense of image and presentation, Marilyn never disappointed fans with an appearance worthy of a movie star when she attended a public event. She delighted in wearing glamorous, if not risqué (for the era), gowns, wrapped herself in furs, and saw to it that her hair and makeup, usually tended to by professionals, were perfect. As was popular at the time, Marilyn often wore large rhinestone bracelets or long dangly earrings, all costume jewelry.

In contrast, at home Marilyn was casual. She walked around in slouchy sweaters, casual trousers, or a white terrycloth robe. She rarely wore jewelry, except for wedding bands during the periods when she was married.

Her homes reflected a similar paradox in how she lived. Marilyn's tastes were not typically ostentatious, but she enjoyed shopping and decorating. When not sharing a home with a romantic partner or surrogate family, she generally lived in smaller accommodations, such as modest apartments or hotel rooms. At the same time, Marilyn usually pushed her budget to its limit, if not outright living beyond her means. She may have been staying in apartments or hotel rooms, but they were often in Beverly Hills or expensive areas of Manhattan. Marilyn had difficulty managing finances throughout her lifetime, and her spending habits are reflected in her accommodations.

ON THE MOVE

A hallmark of Marilyn's life is how often she moved. Throughout her thirty-six years, she lived in more than fifty places. Marilyn had a fairly stable life with the Bolender family for her first seven years, although after leaving their house she didn't stay in one place very long. She moved around frequently while in foster homes, and it was a pattern she continued in adulthood.

After Norma Jeane grew up and became Marilyn Monroe, her pattern of living with "foster families" continued. In addition to her husbands' families, who all welcomed her, Marilyn created surrogate families for herself just as she had become accustomed to in childhood. In some cases, this trait went so far as to move in with families.

The connecting thread for these relationships and surrogate families is the intensity Marilyn put into them. When not studying for her roles or reading to better herself, she spent much of her time with the families to whom she had grown attached, including dinners, holidays, vacations, and special occasions.

BOOKS

Throughout Marilyn's adult life, one of the constants was her book collection. Wherever she moved, so, too, did her books. They were one of the most important components of all her homes.

Dropping out of school after tenth grade weighed heavily on Marilyn. That, combined with her natural desire to learn, ambition, and a mean-spirited comment by her boyfriend Fred Karger about her "embryonic" brain, led Marilyn to pursue self-betterment throughout her life. The desire to improve herself dictated much of her free time, whether it was lessons for dancing, modeling, singing, or acting.

It didn't stop there. Marilyn's interests stretched beyond her professional aspirations, and she bought books to further educate herself. When she began making a modest living as a model, one of the first things she did was open a charge account at a local bookshop in Hollywood. Interests ranged from art to psychology to religion to philosophy. She also collected novels, poetry, drama, and biographies of historic figures. She even had cookbooks, which she wrote in along the margins. In total, Marilyn owned more than 430 books at the time of her death.

How many of them she read is unknown. Arthur Miller once said Marilyn had a knack for skimming books but retaining the most important details. Ultimately, she absorbed enough to become knowledgeable about a variety of topics and was a delightful conversationalist on numerous subjects.

Having an extensive library was one thing, but Marilyn was keen for others to know she had one. From the earliest days of her acting career, she was photographed holding books and in front of her bookshelves on multiple occasions. She was also known to walk around carrying books, often with the title facing out.

LOCATION, LOCATION, LOCATION

The following is a listing of the places Marilyn called home.

5454 Wilshire Boulevard, Los Angeles | June 1926

Gladys brought Norma Jeane home from the hospital to her apartment, but the newborn didn't stay long. When Norma Jeane was just thirteen days old, Gladys entrusted her baby to Wayne and Ida Bolender. The Bolenders were known for taking in foster children. Gladys's mother—Norma Jeane's grandmother Della—lived across the street at 206 E. Rhode Island Street, which is how the Monroe family was acquainted with the Bolender family.

[1] 459 E. Rhode Island Street, Hawthorne | 1926–1933

Norma Jeane lived here with her first foster parents, Wayne and Ida Bolender. Norma Jeane spent her first seven years here, making it the longest she lived in one home.

The Bolenders provided a strict, but stable, environment for Norma Jeane's most formative years. She even had a foster brother, Lester, who was just two months younger and raised as her "twin" because of their proximity in age. The Bolenders functioned as a nuclear family.

It's not much of a stretch to surmise that much of Marilyn's self-discipline exhibited later in life likely came from the stability she received while living with the Bolenders. Here

Norma Jeane spent the first few years of her life in the home of Wayne and Ida Bolender, a strict but caring couple who wanted to adopt her. Photofest

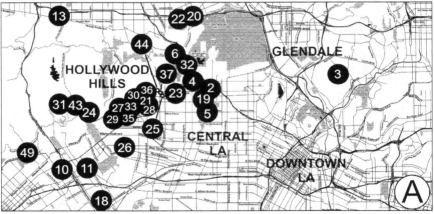

she had regular meals and bedtimes, and learned basic chores. Beyond this, however, the Bolenders were a devoutly religious couple who lived in a framework to achieve a pious life. Whether or not she consciously realized it, little Norma Jeane was immersed in a world in which guidelines were set to achieve a specific outcome.

[2] 6012 Afton Place, Los Angeles (former location) | 1933

When Gladys regained custody of Norma Jeane, mother and daughter lived briefly in an apartment. It was in stark contrast to the quiet suburb of Hawthorn with the Bolenders. This home was in a bustling Hollywood neighborhood close to movie studios, including RKO, where Gladys worked, Paramount, and Columbia. The block was demolished in the 1960s.

[3] 6812 Arbol Drive, Los Angeles (former location) | 1933–1935

To create a sense of stability, Gladys purchased a modest but comfortable house near the Hollywood Bowl, just off Highland Avenue, in 1933 for $5,000. Norma Jeane took lessons on a piano, a piece of property she would track down and repurchase in adulthood. Gladys struggled to afford the mortgage on her film cutter's salary and was forced to lease out part of the house to Mr. and Mrs. George Atkinson, English actors working in the movie industry. The house was within walking distance of the Chinese and Egyptian theatres, where Norma Jeane liked to lose herself in movies for the day. It was while living in this house that Gladys suffered her life-changing breakdown. The Atkinsons briefly cared for Norma Jeane until a suitable foster family could be found and the house sold. This house was razed in the 1960s for the Hollywood Bowl's expansion.

[4] 2062 Highland Avenue, Los Angeles | Spring and Summer 1935

After Gladys's hospitalization, her best friend Grace stepped in to arrange care for Norma Jeane while beginning the process of settling Gladys's estate. In 1935, Grace placed Norma Jeane with the Giffens, neighbors near the Arbol house. Like the house Norma Jeane shared with her mother, the Giffens' house was within walking distance of the Hollywood Bowl and the Chinese and Egyptian theatres. Harvey, a sound engineer for RCA, and his wife, Elsie, had three children, including a daughter Norma Jeane's age. Most likely, Norma Jeane had attended Selma Elementary School with the Giffen kids. She lived here in the spring, possibly to finish out her school year. Grace surmised Harvey and Elsie had a full house and wouldn't want to keep an extra child for very long. It was rare that Grace guessed incorrectly, but in this case her instincts proved wrong. The Giffens were native to the New Orleans area and wanted to return. They offered to adopt Norma Jeane, which would have given her three siblings and a comfortable middle-class life, and include her in their move to Louisiana. When Gladys was contacted at Norwalk State Hospital with the family's request, she declined permission, just as she had done with the Bolenders. The Giffen family moved back to New Orleans without Norma Jeane.

[5] Los Angeles Orphans Home (Now Hollygrove/Uplift Child Services)
815 N. El Centro Avenue | September 13, 1935–October 1936

When Grace applied to become Norma Jeane's legal guardian, part of the process was placing Norma Jeane at this orphanage for a mandatory waiting period. Under the points of Grace's petition, it reads, "7. That said Norma Jean [*sic*] Baker is now in the care of the Los Angeles Orphans' Home Society at 815 North El Centro, Los Angeles, California; 8. That said Norma Jean Baker has no guardian legally appointed by will or otherwise, and she is incapable of taking care of herself or any estate that she may acquire, and that it is necessary that a guardian of her person and estate be appointed. WHEREFORE, your petitioner prays that she be appointed the guardian of the person and estate of Norma Jean Baker and that notice of this petition and hearing thereon be given as required by law."

When Grace pulled up to the orphanage with Norma Jeane, the little girl began to shake and cry. She pleaded not to be left at the orphanage, and repeatedly said she had a mother—she wasn't an orphan. Grace visited regularly and took Norma Jeane for outings, but was forced to complete

Norma Jeane stayed at the Los Angeles Orphans Home for a mandatory waiting period in the mid-1930s while guardian Grace Goddard obtained custody. Now called Hollygrove/ Uplift Child Services, the structure has been rebuilt since Norma Jeane's time. Elisa Jordan

the waiting period before removing the child from the orphanage permanently.

An entry from Norma Jeane's file while living here reads, "Sometimes she seems anxious and dull . . . and then she begins to stutter. Norma Jean is also prone to coughing fits and frequent colds. . . . If she's not treated with much patience and constantly reassured, she is prey to panic attacks. I would recommend for her a strong and good family."

[6] 3107 Barbara Court, Los Angeles

When not at the orphanage, Norma Jeane visited Grace and her new husband, Erwin "Doc" Goddard in this home near the Cahuenga Pass. Doc had three children from his previous marriage, and Norma Jeane became one of

The RKO water tower was visible from the girls' dormitory at the orphanage. Norma Jeane used to gaze upon it at night and dream of becoming a movie star when she grew up. Elisa Jordan

the bunch. At the time, Grace was breeding Cocker Spaniels, who became playmates for the kids.

[7] 6707 Odessa Avenue, Van Nuys | October 1936–November 1937

Norma Jeane lived here with Grace and Doc.

[8] 12000 block of Oxnard Street, North Hollywood | Late 1937

For a while Norma Jeane moved in with Olive Monroe, her aunt by marriage to Marion (Gladys's brother), and her three children—Norma Jeane's cousins—along with Olive's mother Ida Martin. Gladys's estate paid Olive $30 per month for Norma Jeane's care. Olive was parenting her three children alone, as Marion Monroe, Norma Jeane's uncle, had disappeared, never to be seen again.

[9] 1826 E. Palmer Street, Compton | Spring 1938
Grace placed Norma Jeane with her brother, Bryan Atchinson, his wife Lottie, and their daughter Geraldine, for a brief period in this Los Angeles suburb.

[10] 11348 Nebraska Avenue, Los Angeles | Summer 1938–Summer 1939
On August 29, 1938, Norma Jeane moved to the home of Grace's aunt, Ana Lower, the sister of Grace's father. Aunt Ana was a kindly older woman with a nurturing personality but had health problems and a bad heart. When her health permitted, however, Norma Jeane liked staying here.

[11] 2246 Glendon Avenue, Los Angeles | Summer 1939–February 1940
During the summer of 1939, Norma Jeane moved in with Grace's sister, Enid Knebelkamp, her husband, Sam, and their daughter, Diane. Norma Jeane babysat Diane and the twin daughters of their neighbors, the Howells, who lived down the street at 2310 Glendon. This was a charming street on the west side of Los Angeles.

[12] 14743 Archwood Street, Van Nuys | February 1940–February 1942
Norma Jeane moved back in with the Goddards starting in February 1940 for what would be an extended period. Norma Jeane and Doc's daughter, Bebe, slept on a screened-in porch. Things changed when Doc accepted a job in West Virginia, and the family moved without Norma Jeane. Grace arranged a marriage to neighbor Jim Dougherty for Norma Jeane.

[10] 11348 Nebraska Avenue, Los Angeles | February 1942–June 1942
Norma Jeane moved back in temporarily with Aunt Ana while awaiting marriage to Jim Dougherty.

[13] 4524 Vista Del Monte Avenue, Sherman Oaks | June 1942–January 1943
In preparation for their wedding on June 19, Jim and Norma Jeane signed a lease for a studio apartment behind their landlord's house on June 8, 1942. They paid $40 per month. Sherman Oaks is the city next to Van Nuys, where Jim and Norma Jeane had been living when they were neighbors.

[12] 14747 Archwood Street, Van Nuys | January 1943–Spring 1943
Newlyweds Jim and Norma Jeane didn't stay in their little studio for long. In January 1943, they returned to Van Nuys and moved into his parents' house.

[14] 14223 Bessemer Street, Van Nuys | Summer 1943

The Dougherty family moved out of the Archwood Street house around summertime when their lease was up. The elder Doughertys moved to North Hollywood, and Jim and Norma Jeane moved into this house. While living here, Norma Jeane began to make some friends, adopted a dog she named Muggsy, and sometimes visited the beach. She also began experimenting with her look. She liked playing with hair and makeup and was developing a stringent grooming routine, including obsessively washing her face. It is here where Norma Jeane reportedly tried to rescue a neighbor's cow from the rain by attempting to bring it inside.

[15] 323 Metropole Avenue, Avalon, Santa Catalina Island

To serve his country during the war, Jim enlisted in the Merchant Marine and was stationed on Santa Catalina Island for training. During the war, Catalina was closed to tourists and turned into a military training facility.

Norma Jeane and Muggsy were permitted to join Jim. Men significantly outnumbered women on the island, but Norma Jeane made friends with other military wives. She also continued to experiment with her look and style of dress. She noticed, for instance, that she attracted the attention of men. Her interest was not in actually seducing men, but rather in figuring out how she impacted the opposite sex. Form-fitting clothing that accentuated her figure,

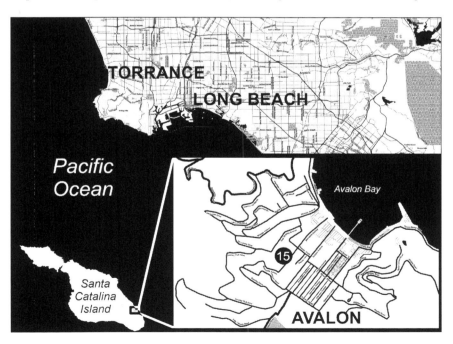

bathing suits, and bright hair ribbons made an impact. Walking Muggsy provided a perfect excuse to parade around Catalina's city of Avalon. One man in particular noticed—Jim Dougherty—who was none too pleased his young wife was dressing provocatively.

It was also during her time around military personnel that she learned the importance of physical fitness. A military trainer taught her the basics of exercise and weight training, skills she would utilize for the rest of her life.

[16] 5254 Hermitage Street, North Hollywood | Spring 1944
Now ready to ship out to war, Jim moved Norma Jeane into his parents' new house in North Hollywood. Ethel Dougherty worked at Radioplane Company, and she helped her teenage daughter-in-law also get a job there. It was also while living here that Norma Jeane began modeling, much to the disapproval of her mother-in-law.

[10] 11348 Nebraska Avenue, Los Angeles | Spring 1945–Spring 1946
After her burgeoning modeling career was met with disapproval from her in-laws, Norma Jeane moved back in with Aunt Ana, the one person she had always counted on to show love and support.

[17] 604 S. 3rd Street, Las Vegas | Spring 1946
In May 1946, Norma Jeane lived here with Grace's aunt, Minnie Willettes, to establish her six-week residency to obtain a divorce from Jim Dougherty. Mostly, Norma Jeane needed an address for her mail to go. In reality, most of her time was spent in Los Angeles so she could continue accepting modeling jobs. The divorce took a little longer than the expected six weeks because Jim had been reluctant to sign divorce papers.

[10] 11348 Nebraska Avenue, Los Angeles | Summer 1946
After a joyous arrival home from Las Vegas, Norma Jeane moved back in with Aunt Ana for the summer of 1946. It was an exciting time. Norma Jeane was in the process of becoming Marilyn Monroe, having signed a contract with Twentieth Century-Fox and changing her name. It was also the closest she came to experiencing life with her family. Gladys had returned home and, for a while at least, was living outside the confines of a sanitarium. Norma Jeane's half-sister Berniece came to visit with her daughter, Mona Rae. Norma Jeane was thrilled. She had long been encouraging Berniece and her husband to try living in California.

Everyone stayed in Ana's duplex, with Berniece and Mona Rae sharing the bottom unit, with Gladys and Norma Jeane upstairs with Aunt Ana. The Goddard family had returned from West Virginia, so it was the only time

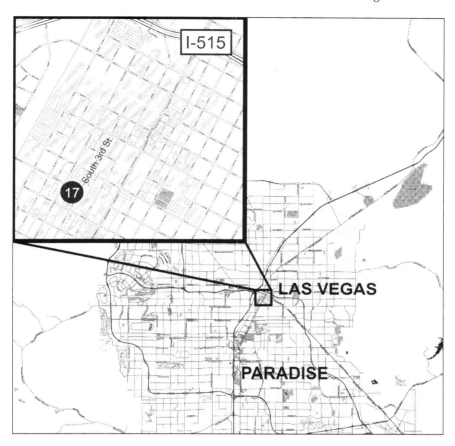

everyone was together. Norma Jeane was able to spend time with her mother and get to better know her half sister and niece. The two sisters had met once before, but the extended visit enabled them to build their relationship. Berniece, who had grown up without her biological mother, was finally able to establish a connection with Gladys, which wasn't always easy. Gladys's mental illness meant she was often emotionally distant.

Although Gladys was able to fill in some gaps, it was Grace and Ana who better communicated the family's history to Berniece. It was, Berniece later said, a time when she finally obtained the answers about her family she had always longed for. She heard the story of how Gladys met Berniece's father, Jasper, and how he had kidnapped their children. It was the first time Berniece was able to hear the story from her mother's perspective. Berniece enjoyed her summer in Los Angeles so much she started to take seriously the notion of relocating to California. Ana and Norma Jeane were delighted at the idea and encouraged Berniece to speak with her husband, Paris, about the move. Paris, however, did not want to move so far away from his family in the south.

[18] 3539 Kelton Avenue, Los Angeles
After Berniece left Los Angeles and Gladys decided to move to Oregon, Marilyn rented a place of her own. This was the first time she lived alone.

[19] 1215 N. Lodi Place, Los Angeles
Hollywood Studio Club | Fall 1946–Early 1947
Now a starlet, Marilyn moved into the Hollywood Studio Club on September 13, 1946. The Hollywood Studio Club was a chaperoned dormitory for women in the entertainment industry. In addition to actresses, the Studio Club also welcomed writers, designers, singers, dancers, script girls, and film cutters. Rules included a curfew and no men in dorm rooms. Amenities included two meals per day, sewing machines, hair dryers, laundry facilities, typewriters, practice rooms, and a sundeck. Marilyn shared room number 307 with another actress named Clarice Evans.

In the early days of Hollywood, both as an industry and a city, actors often found it difficult to find accommodations, as landlords were often unwilling to rent to "show people." Studios needed to house their employees, so many of them financed apartment buildings around town.

In the case of the Hollywood Studio Club, funding came from multiple studios, including Famous Players-Lasky (later renamed Paramount), Metro Goldwyn (later to merge and become Metro-Goldwyn-Mayer), Carl Laemmle, Warner Bros., and Christie Comedies. The Hollywood Studio Club's Mediterranean-style building was designed by pioneering female architect Julia Morgan, who later designed Hearst Castle. Mary Pickford attended the grand opening in May 1926.

Other famous residents over the years included Barbara Eden, Dorothy Malone, Maureen O'Sullivan, Kim Novak, Ayn Rand, Virginia Sale, Sharon Tate, Marie Windsor, and Joanne Worley.

Times changed, and the club closed in 1975. The building still stands, but is now an adult education center.

[20] 131 South Avon Street, Burbank | Summer 1947
Marilyn housesat here for part of the summer in 1947.

[21] 8491-8499 Fountain Avenue, West Hollywood | August 1947

Marilyn moved to the El Palacio Apartments and lived in a unit belonging to actor John Carroll and his wife, movie executive Lucille Ryman, who were assisting Marilyn financially. The couple were grateful for their success in the entertainment industry and liked paying their good fortune forward by sponsoring young actors. Often this included a financial allowance and use of their properties when someone had no place to live. During this time in 1947, Marilyn became one of those people who required assistance. Her first contract with Twentieth Century-Fox was not renewed, and she needed financial help.

[22] 4215 Rowland Street, Burbank (now renamed 4215 Warner Boulevard) December 1947 through early 1948

This small house is within walking distance of the 110-acre lot belonging to Warner Bros., one of the largest and most powerful movie studios of the era. Little is known about Marilyn's brief time here, but the address appears on a contract Marilyn signed with actor John Carroll. There is a picture of her standing on the front porch.

It is at this location that Marilyn reported an off-duty police officer named Charles Rosenberger who attempted to break into her home. A *Valley Times* newspaper article dated December 12, 1947, described the incident and arrest. Interestingly, Marilyn's age is given as nineteen, when in reality she was twenty-one.

"Miss Monroe, starlet at Twentieth Century-Fox studio, said she was awakened late last night at her home, 4215 Rowland ave., [*sic*] by someone attempting to force the front door. Unsuccessful, the intruder went around to the back door and finally came to her bedroom window and started tugging at the screen, the actress related to the police.

"When she called out, 'What are you doing—leave or I'll call the police,' the would-be burglar replied, 'Go ahead.'

"Miss Monroe ran outside and to a next-door neighbor's home and called the police. At that time the intruder disappeared.

As a struggling starlet, Marilyn lived in this small house in Burbank. She had to call the police for help when a drunk man tried to forcibly enter. Elisa Jordan

"Shortly thereafter Burbank Officers Jon Johnson and Harold Brennan were questioning the actress at her home when Rosenberger appeared at the front door. Miss Monroe positively identified him as her molester, the officers reported."

Rosenberger, who was twenty-five years old at the time, was arrested and charged with drunkenness and suspicion of burglary. The burglary charge was dropped, Rosenberger was fined $50 and he was given a thirty-day suspended jail sentence. He was also placed on probation for a year with the stipulation that he quit drinking.

The newspaper further reported, "He said he had been to the actress' home earlier in the evening but that she was absent so he had gone to a nightclub and had 'seven or eight drinks,' the arresting officer reported.

"He had just left the café and was driving home, Rosenberger assertedly related, when he heard the police broadcast on his auto's 'two-way radio' of the attempted burglary and went to the actress' aid."

[23] 1171 N. Stanley, Los Angeles | March and April 1948
Marilyn received a couple of letters from Twentieth Century-Fox executives at this address.

[24] 141 South Carolwood Drive, Beverly Hills | April 1948–June 1948
Although the address is technically Carolwood Drive, this estate borders busy Sunset Boulevard. During Marilyn's stay, the home belonged to former Twentieth Century-Fox head Joseph Schenk, who was a close friend. Marilyn lived in the guesthouse.

This home, now called Owlwood Estate, is one of the most famous and celebrated houses in Los Angeles still standing. It was designed by architect Robert D. Farquhar in 1937 for businessman Charles H. Quinn. At the time it was completed, the 12,600 square-foot-house was the largest in Los Angeles. The second owner was Joseph Drown, who founded the Hotel Bel Air, another of Marilyn's residences. Schenk was the third owner, and after his residency, owners have included several notable names. Schenk sold the estate to William Keck of Superior Oil in 1956. Tony Curtis, Marilyn's *Some Like It Hot* costar, bought the home in the 1960s and later sold it to Sonny and Cher. The estate was sold again in 1976 after Sonny and Cher's divorce. In 2002, the owners of Owlwood absorbed the property next door, 10100 Sunset—the former home of fellow blonde bombshell Jayne Mansfield, who had painted her mansion pink. Mansfield's former property, called the Pink Palace, was razed to increase the land surrounding the Owlwood estate.

[19] 1215 N. Lodi Place, Los Angeles
Hollywood Studio Club | June 1948–March 1949

Marilyn returned to the Studio Club, this time without a roommate. Her unit, number 334, was paid for by Lucille Ryman. During her second stay, Marilyn was under contract to Columbia Pictures, which was within walking distance of the Studio Club.

[25] 1312 North Harper Avenue, Los Angeles (now West Hollywood) | Summer 1948

New boyfriend Fred Karger brought Marilyn "home to mother," literally, to live with him, his mother Ann, and sister, Mary.

In her book *My Meril*, Fred's daughter Terry described the house the Kargers shared. "It was a large house, with a rolling front lawn, a big backyard, and a long driveway leading to the garage in the back."

Marilyn took up residence in the guest room and tried her best to fit in. She helped out around the house, performed chores, and wanted to be a good example for Terry.

Marilyn lived here only three weeks, but became extremely close to Ann and Mary and remained friends with them for the rest of her life.

[25] 1306½ North Harper Avenue, Los Angeles (now West Hollywood) | Fall 1948

Natasha Lytess lived next door to the Kargers and Marilyn frequently stayed here, too. Marilyn wasn't always a permanent fixture, as she lived here on and off.

[26] 9400 West Olympic Boulevard, Beverly Hills
Beverly Carlton Hotel (now the Avalon) | March 1949

After (officially) leaving the Studio Club, Marilyn moved to the Beverly Carlton Hotel and kept a room with a kitchenette. She leased it to keep up the appearance of living alone and received her mail here. In reality, she lived with agent and lover Johnny Hyde. Marilyn was photographed extensively here by the swimming pool in 1950.

[27] 718 North Palm Drive, Beverly Hills | Spring 1949–1950

Marilyn moved into this large Beverly Hills home with Johnny Hyde after he left his wife for his much younger lover. There is a story that Johnny went so far as to install a dance floor and restaurant booth to resemble Romanoff's, her favorite restaurant. Although Marilyn "officially" lived by herself at the Beverly Carlton, Earl Leaf extensively photographed her in this house—playing with her Chihuahua Josefa, watering flowers, in the kitchen, on the stairs, and—of course—with her bookcase.

While living with Johnny Hyde, Marilyn used the Beverly Carlton Hotel (now called the Avalon) for her mailing address to keep up appearances. Fun fact: This exterior was used as the hotel in I Love Lucy *during the show's Hollywood episodes.* Elisa Jordan

Marilyn and Johnny Hyde lived in his Beverly Hills mansion during their relationship. As a top talent agent in Hollywood, he spent the last two years of his life promoting his protégé. Elisa Jordan

After Johnny died on December 18, 1950, his family evicted Marilyn from the Beverly Hills house she shared with him.

[25] 1301 North Harper Avenue, West Hollywood
Marilyn moved back in with Natasha after Johnny Hyde's death, but exact dates are difficult to pin down because she stayed here on and off.

[28] 8573 Holloway Drive, West Hollywood | 1951
This apartment is located within walking distance of Barney's Beanery, an affordable roadhouse diner on Route 66 (now Santa Monica Boulevard), popular with Hollywood locals. According to actress Shelley Winters, the two young starlets were roommates for about a year in this apartment building. Marilyn's residence at this address is somewhat controversial because there is no solid proof she lived here, such as mail, contracts, documents, signed checks, or her talking about this location. Marilyn typically lived by herself, with romantic partners, or with surrogate families—not friends.

Although there is no proof other than Shelley's word that Marilyn was her roommate at one time, they were at the very least acquainted. A few photos of the two actresses pictured together exist.

[29] 611 North Crescent Drive, Beverly Hills | September 1951–January 1952
Marilyn stayed here with acting coach Natasha Lytess for a couple of months. Marilyn was back at Twentieth Century-Fox and the two worked on her role in the upcoming *Don't Bother to Knock* while living here.

[30] 1211 Hilldale Avenue, West Hollywood | January 1952–Spring 1952
Friend David March helped Marilyn find this apartment, which was steps off the famous Sunset Strip. Marilyn was living here when she met Joe DiMaggio for their first date up the street at Villa Nova.

[26] 9400 West Olympic Boulevard, Beverly Hills
Beverly Carlton Hotel (now the Avalon) | Spring 1952
Marilyn returned to the Beverly Carlton, this time staying in the annex across the street from the main hotel in room 233. She was photographed extensively here by Phillipe Halsman for *Life Magazine*, which included a cover shot. In addition to the photo that landed Marilyn her first *Life* cover, pictures from this session depict Marilyn in her room reading, listening to music, and exercising. The tiny room contained just enough room for a bed, record player, and, of course, her books.

[31] 701 Stone Canyon Road, Los Angeles | May–Summer 1952

In May 1952, Marilyn moved into the exclusive Hotel Bel-Air while recovering from her appendectomy. Located above Beverly Hills and nestled deep in Stone Canyon, the secluded hotel offered Marilyn the tranquility she lacked at her previous location, where fans had started ringing her doorbell. Her monthly rent was $750 per month, a substantial sum for 1952—and also for an actress still in the starlet phase of her career. Andre de Dienes photographed Marilyn at the Hotel Bel-Air, including pictures of her by a fireplace, dancing outside her bungalow and exercising by the swimming pool. While living here, Marilyn received an exciting birthday present on June 1 in the form of great news about her career: Twentieth Century-Fox had awarded her the role of Lorelei Lee in *Gentlemen Prefer Blondes*.

[32] 2393 Castilian Drive, Los Angeles | September 1952–March 1953

On September 15, 1952, Marilyn signed a deposit check for $450 on a six-month lease. A note on the back of the check reads, "1st and last months rent on 2393 Castilian Drive, LA." Marilyn's relationship with Joe DiMaggio was getting serious, and a house nestled in the hills offered a level of privacy they had trouble finding elsewhere. Unlike the smaller accommodations Marilyn preferred when she lived alone, the Castilian Drive house was a grand mansion with sweeping canyon vistas. The couple's time here did not last long. In October, Joe stormed out of the house after a fight and returned to his hometown of San Francisco. A check dated January 23, 1953, for $237.82 has a handwritten note on the back reading, "This check releases Miss Monroe of all obligations on lease of 2393 Castilian Dr. L.A. It does <u>NOT</u> cover the telephone bill."

[33] 882 Doheny Drive, West Hollywood | March 1953–January 1954

After leaving the large house in the hills, Marilyn moved back into a small apartment. Positioned on the border of Beverly Hills and then-unincorporated Los Angeles (now West Hollywood), Marilyn moved into this five-apartment building on March 18, 1953, and stayed until she married Joe in January 1954. Her rent was $200 and the location was ideal. It was an easy drive to Twentieth Century-Fox, the Sunset Strip was a few blocks away for evenings out, and she was close to favorite locations, such as Romanoff's and Chasen's for dining, and Jax, where she frequently shopped for clothes.

It was during this year her life changed as her career flourished into genuine stardom. *Niagara* had recently been released, and *Gentlemen Prefer Blondes* was soon to follow. While living here, Marilyn filmed *How to Marry a Millionaire*, which was released in November.

Marilyn lived at 882 Doheny twice. The first time was in 1953 when her career was ascending, and the second time was after her return from the East Coast. Elisa Jordan

[34] 2150 Beach Street, San Francisco | 1954

Joe DiMaggio was born and raised in the San Francisco Bay area. When he moved to New York to play baseball for the Yankees, the majority of his family remained in California. Having come from a large, tight-knit Italian family, Joe continued to maintain a foothold in San Francisco. During his career with the Yankees, he purchased this home in 1939 for his family. Retiring in 1951 enabled him to spend more time at the family home.

When Marilyn and Joe got married, it was in his hometown at the San Francisco City Hall on January 14, 1954, about three miles away from the DiMaggio house. Soon after their marriage, the newlyweds honeymooned in Japan, a trip that doubled as a work trip for Joe. On her passport,

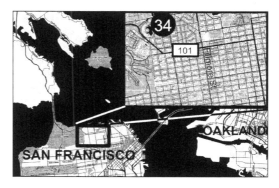

Marilyn listed the Beach Street address in San Francisco as her own. On the same passport, Marilyn listed Mr. Joseph Paul DiMaggio as her emergency contact and also gave the Beach Street house as his address.

[35] 508 North Palm Drive, Beverly Hills | Spring 1954–October 1954

After returning home from Japan, Mr. and Mrs. DiMaggio rented a large home in the heart of Beverly Hills.

It marked the second time Marilyn lived on North Palm and was just two doors down from Jean Harlow's final home. The couple paid $750 per month and, like the Doheny apartment, made for an easy commute to Fox.

The house on North Palm Drive was not a happy home.

On October 6, 1954, the press gathered on the lawn of the DiMaggio house for a press conference. Joe got into his car without making a statement and drove away. Later that day, a tearful Marilyn emerged and stood on the front step with her attorney, Jerry Giesler. With Marilyn by his side, Giesler announced the couple's divorce due to "a conflict of careers."

Marilyn crying in front of her marital home is one of the few times she lost her composure in public. Over the years, some critics have gone so far as to say Marilyn's tears were her finest performance as an actress. More

The DiMaggios lived on North Palm Drive during their brief marriage in 1954. Marilyn would later stand on the front porch with her attorney Jerry Giesler to announce her separation from the baseball great. Elisa Jordan

realistically, it is not unreasonable for someone to cry and show emotion while in the fresh stages of a separation.

As Marilyn prepared to move out for good, Joe returned to the house one last time and asked her to reconsider her divorce petition. He also wrote her a letter, postmarked October 9, and sent to the Palm Drive address, which opens with "Dear Baby." In the handwritten letter, he continues, "Marilyn, I keep reading reports about you being sick and naturally I'm concerned. I love you and want to be with you. There is nothing I would like better than to restore your confidence in me so that I can help you regain your healthy self.

"My heart split even wider seeing you cry in front of all these people and looking as though you were ready to collapse at any second. . . . I can tell you, I love you sincerely—way deep in my heart, irregardless [*sic*] of anything. Will you call me tonight if you should receive this letter by then? It will be happily received."

Marilyn was resolute in her decision—she would not reconcile.

[36] 8338 DeLongpre Avenue, Los Angeles (now West Hollywood) | November 1954

After her separation from Joe DiMaggio, Marilyn moved into the Brandon Hall Apartments. As was typical of her accommodations when she was single, Marilyn chose a smaller place to live, although the building itself was upscale. She brought her books, a definitive characteristic of her home. From an outsider's perspective, it looked like she was here to stay for the foreseeable future. Instead, she was secretly planning her escape from Hollywood. Ultimately, Marilyn stayed at this apartment for only a matter of weeks.

[37] 1428 Crescent Heights Boulevard, Los Angeles (now West Hollywood) December 1954

Eager to escape the tyranny of Twentieth Century-Fox, Marilyn secretly planned on fleeing to New York. While plotting her move, she quietly moved in with Ann Karger, who now lived in this building.

[38] Fanton Hill Road, Weston, Connecticut | December 1954

Marilyn slipped out of Los Angeles and secretly arrived on the East Coast, where she stayed with business partner Milton Greene and his family, wife Amy and young son Joshua. Marilyn arrived in time for the holidays, which she spent with the Greenes. As with the Kargers, she had become an extended family member. Marilyn stayed with the Greenes on and off when she wasn't living in a hotel in the city. A couple of months after her arrival, Marilyn emerged from hiding when she, Milton, and Amy appeared on *Person to Person* with Edward R. Murrow. The interview was filmed in this home in April.

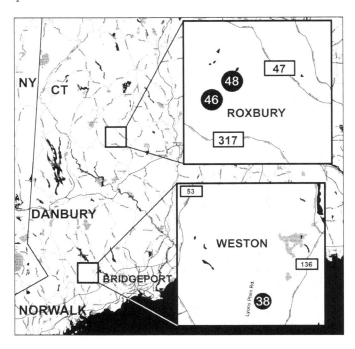

[39] Gladstone Hotel, 114 East 52nd Street | January–March 1955
As Marilyn got acquainted with her newly adopted hometown, friend and photographer Sam Shaw helped her get a room at the Gladstone Hotel, where he knew the owner. Estranged husband Joe DiMaggio helped her move in. Marilyn was in a transitional phase of her life—moving to a new city, studying at the Actors Studio, negotiating for a better contract with Twentieth Century-Fox, divorcing her husband, cutting Natasha out of her

Marilyn thrived after she moved to New York in 1955. To capture her new life away from Los Angeles, photographer Ed Feingersh followed her around the city and even captured her at the Gladstone Hotel, where she was living at the time.
By Ed Feingersh / Wikimedia Commons

life, and setting up a production company with Milton Greene. To help get Marilyn on her feet, Milton paid her expenses during this time.

To document Marilyn in New York, photojournalist Ed Feingersh followed her around town for *Redbook*, which included capturing her at the Gladstone. In one session, Feingersh took a series of pictures of Marilyn getting ready for a night on the town, including one of her applying Chanel No. 5 perfume, which has since become an iconic photo.

[40] Hotel Ambassador, 345 Park Avenue, New York City (former location)
March–April 1955
In late March, Marilyn moved into the Hotel Ambassador. Marilyn, Milton Greene, and Edward R. Murrow had a meeting at the hotel regarding the upcoming appearance on his television show, *Person to Person*. She stayed at the Ambassador for only sixteen days and Milton Greene paid her $1,035.36 bill. She moved out on April 8, 1955.

[41] Waldorf Astoria Hotel, 301 Park Avenue, Suite 2728, New York City
April–Autumn 1955
Since its opening in 1931, the Waldorf Astoria Hotel has symbolized luxury accommodations and elegance in Manhattan. With Marilyn and Milton Greene's partnership in Marilyn Monroe Productions in place, he sublet a suite on Marilyn's behalf from actress Leonora Corbett. The twenty-seventh-floor apartment cost the new production company $1,000 per week. Marilyn moved in on April 12, 1955, and lived here through the fall. During her stay, Marilyn immersed herself in classes at the Actors Studio and attended plays. It was while she was living here that *The Seven Year Itch* was released and became a blockbuster.

Marilyn's time at the Waldorf ended when it became too expensive for Marilyn Monroe Productions to continue paying the exorbitant rent. Milton moved Marilyn into his apartment in the city.

With the Waldorf being a cultural center, however, Marilyn returned for a couple of special events. In December 1956, Marilyn made an appearance on CBS radio from the Waldorf. She and Arthur were also guests at the April in Paris Ball in 1957.

[42] 2 Sutton Place S, Apartment E8, New York City | Fall 1955–1956
Marilyn moved into Milton Greene's apartment to save money. His main residence was in Connecticut with his family, but as a busy fashion photographer, he kept an apartment in Manhattan for when work required long hours.

With his apartment now unavailable to him and his family, when the Greenes needed overnight accommodations in the city, they instead stayed at his studio on Lexington Avenue.

The move was hardly a downgrade for Marilyn. Milton's apartment was located in a small, high-end neighborhood overlooking the East River. The Upper East Side location was defined by stately, prewar buildings, and leafy trees. It was an area known for low foot traffic, which provided Marilyn with something she had come to crave—privacy.

During her time at the Sutton Place apartment, Marilyn continued her affair with Arthur Miller, whose relationship with Marilyn finally gave him the push he needed to leave his unhappy marriage.

When the press learned of her engagement to Arthur, reporters cornered Marilyn in the carport of 2 Sutton. Wearing a spaghetti-strapped black dress and a black sweater draped over her shoulders, Marilyn answered questions with her usual quick wit. When asked if they were planning on children, she quipped, "I'm not married yet, dear!" Everyone, Marilyn included, burst out laughing.

[43] 595 North Beverly Glen Boulevard, Los Angeles | February–June 1956

On February 25, 1956, Marilyn arrived in Los Angeles after a year in New York. There was much reason to celebrate with the new contract Twentieth Century-Fox awarded her. The press greeted Marilyn at the Los Angeles airport, where she sat down to answer questions in front of news cameras. Marilyn spoke with reporters about her new contract, director approval, and her triumphant return to Hollywood. Not every newsperson chose to focus on Marilyn's accomplishments.

Marilyn had the opportunity to show off her sense of humor when a reporter said, "You're wearing a high-necked dress now. The last time I saw you, you weren't. Is this a new Marilyn?" To which Marilyn quipped, "No, I'm the same person. It's just a different suit." Remarkably, the person who asked that question was a woman. The same female reporter asked Marilyn if her measurements had changed or if she had gained weight. Marilyn's polite reply: "I think I'm about the same."

Now back in Los Angeles, Marilyn and the Greene family rented a large house near Beverly Hills for $995 per month. Marilyn Monroe Productions paid the rent.

Marilyn and the Greenes threw a grand cocktail party in the home for Marilyn Monroe Productions. She spent the weekdays here while working and slipped off to the Chateau Marmont for weekends with Arthur Miller, who flew in from Reno, Nevada.

[44] Chateau Marmont, 8221 Sunset Boulevard, Los Angeles | February–June 1956

While maintaining a room at the Beverly Glen house with the Greenes during the week, weekends were a different story. Marilyn spent weekends at Chateau Marmont in Los Angeles with Arthur Miller, who was supposed to be in Reno, Nevada, establishing residency so he could divorce his wife. Unable to stay apart, Arthur would sneak back to Los Angeles to see Marilyn.

The Chateau, as locals call it, is a contradiction. The commanding, castle-like exterior serves as a dramatic, if unofficial, entrance to the Sunset Strip. In contrast, the Chateau's interior has always been one of the most private locations in Los Angeles. The Chateau Marmont opened in 1929 as an apartment complex so the rooms are self-sufficient with their own kitchens, making it ideal for long-term stays or negating the need to dine out. Soon after opening, the stock market crashed and plunged the United States into

While filming Bus Stop, *Marilyn and Arthur Miller spent the weekends at Chateau Marmont. This landmark hotel is famous for tight security and discrete employees.* Elisa Jordan

the Great Depression. The Chateau switched from an apartment building to a hotel and quickly became a favorite place for the very wealthy and Hollywood elite. Its location is ideal for those who want to indulge in the Sunset Strip or retreat into privacy, as the hotel forbids paparazzi and employees are famously tight-lipped. Columbia Studios head Harry Cohn once told his actors, "If you must get into trouble, do it at the Chateau." Marilyn and Arthur's romance was a safely held secret at the Chateau.

[45] 444 East 57th Street, Apartment 13E, New York City | Spring 1957–1962

In the spring of 1957, Marilyn and Arthur moved from Milton Greene's apartment to their own—but they did not go far. The 2 Sutton Place apartment was located on the corner of Sutton Place and East 57th Street, and the new apartment (444 E. 57th) was next door, but the entrance faced East 57th Street.

Like the Sutton Place apartment, the new location was close to the East River and offered privacy. Marilyn gave the home a white color palette, probably inspired by Jean Harlow's bedroom set in *Dinner at Eight*.

The prewar, three-bedroom apartment had windows on three sides and a partial view of the river. The couple took the master bedroom, a second bedroom was outfitted with two twin beds for Arthur's children's visits, and the third bedroom was turned into a writing studio. Most importantly, the piano Marilyn had played in her mother's house as a little girl was moved to this location.

With Arthur, she began splitting her time between the city and the country. When staying in town, the Millers were quite social, attending plays, dinner parties, and visiting friends. They also welcomed a new family member, a hound named Hugo, who was frequently seen out on walks with the famed playwright and actress.

When the Millers separated in 1961, Marilyn retained the New York City apartment and Arthur kept the Connecticut house—and Hugo.

When Marilyn moved back to Los Angeles in 1961, she still maintained her New York home. In fact, she considered herself a New Yorker until she died. It is probably what she would have considered the most "home" of all the places she lived as an adult. It was here that Marilyn recovered after her stay at Columbia Presbyterian Hospital for mental exhaustion and from her gallbladder removal surgery. During her convalescence after the operation, her half-sister Berniece arrived for a couple of weeks to care for her. It was one of the few times the sisters spent extended time together and the last time they saw each other. It was also when former husband Joe DiMaggio reentered her life.

With Marilyn bicoastal in the last year and a half of her life, she considered Los Angeles her base. New York, however, was now where she lived. She visited her New York home shortly before her passing in May 1962 while in town to appear at a Democratic party fundraiser and sing "Happy Birthday" to President John F. Kennedy at Madison Square Garden. She was photographed after rehearsal in front of her apartment wearing a headscarf and a green Pucci blouse.

[46] 153 Tophet Road, Roxbury, Connecticut | 1956

Arthur Miller originally purchased this property in 1947 when he was married to his first wife, Mary Slattery. He still owned it after his divorce had been finalized. It is here that Marilyn and Arthur met with the press before their wedding on June 29, 1956.

The press was in a frenzy over the couple that day and trying to get photos. As Arthur and Marilyn drove home after lunch at Arthur's cousin's house nearby, reporters gave chase. A paparazzi car missed a sharp turn and ran head-on into a tree. Hearing the crash, Arthur turned his car around to see if anyone needed help. Arthur ran to the twisted car and found the passengers, including *Paris-Match* reporter Mara Scherbatoff, who had been thrown through the windshield and was gravely injured. Arthur would not let Marilyn view the scene. The nearest phone was a short drive to their home, so the couple sped off to call for help. They alerted authorities, but Scherbatoff died at a hospital later that day from her injuries. The press conference with Marilyn and Arthur commenced that afternoon as originally planned in front of their house. While standing under a tree on the property, Arthur and Marilyn spoke about their plans to marry but did not offer a date. No mention of the accident was made, but privately Marilyn was devasted and viewed it as a bad omen.

Arthur and Marilyn met with the press in front of their home on June 29, 1956, to announce their wedding, although they did not divulge any details. They married in a civil wedding later that evening at the Westchester County Courthouse. Earlier that day, a reporter died while in pursuit of the couple's car. Marilyn was devastated and considered the tragic event a bad omen.
United Artists / Photofest © United Artists

Later that night, Marilyn and Arthur drove to Westchester County Courthouse where they were married in a four-minute ceremony. The newlyweds returned home without anyone from the press knowing about their wedding.

Two days later, on Sunday, July 1, they married again in a Jewish ceremony at the home of Kay Brown, Arthur's agent. The next day, July 2, Arthur put the house up for sale. The money from the sale went toward another house on the same street—a house where the Millers could start a new life in a house without a past.

[47] Parkside House on Wick Lane, Englefield Green, Egham, England | July–November 1956

The Millers lived here while Marilyn was filming *The Prince and the Showgirl* from July 1956 through November. The five-bedroom mansion dated back to the eighteenth century, sat on four acres, and had a rose garden. Arthur and Marilyn rented the estate from Lord Charles Garrett Moore, managing director of the *Financial Times*, and his wife, concert pianist Joan Carr.

It is in Parkside House that Marilyn reportedly saw an entry in Arthur Miller's diary indicating he was disappointed in her behavior.

It is clear from Marilyn's own notes, written on Parkside House Stationery, that she was unhappy during this period.

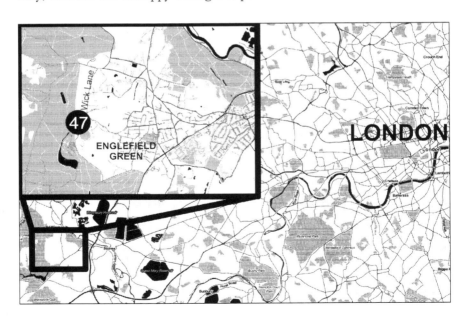

I guess I have always been
deeply terrified to really be someone's
wife
since I know from life
one cannot love another,
ever, really

My Week with Marilyn, which is a fictional story of Marilyn's time in England, returned to Parkside House when filming in 2010 to shoot scenes. The house looked much the same as it did when the Millers were there in 1956.

[48] 232 Tophet Road, Roxbury, Connecticut | October 1957–1960

After selling Arthur's other house on Tophet Road, the couple moved into this nearby farmhouse originally built by Captain David Leavenworth, a Revolutionary War veteran. Best of all, the house was surrounded by 325 acres of land, which included maples and fruit trees. When not in the city, the Millers enjoyed complete privacy.

After moving in, Marilyn contacted architect Frank Lloyd Wright about possibly replacing the circa 1780s house with a new one. Marilyn met with Wright at the Plaza Hotel in Manhattan and instructed him on their requirements: a screening room, swimming pool, large office for Arthur, and a dressing room. Arthur told Wright that he wanted to live simply. The famed architect drew up plans for the proposed house, which centered around a grand circular living room overlooking a swimming pool in the yard. Two wings shot off either side of the house. The house was both too grand and cost prohibitive, so the Millers declined and kept their original house. Marilyn set about updating the property and redecorating. The house had been remodeled over the years, and Marilyn enjoyed restoring many of the elements that had been removed. They also built a garage and separate writing studio on the property so Arthur could have a quiet place to work.

After their divorce, Arthur kept the Roxbury house and turned it into his primary residence. With Arthur and Marilyn dividing up their belongings and homes, she had to make a couple of trips back to Connecticut to retrieve some of her things. During one trip, she asked Ralph Roberts to drive up with her. "I loved this place," she told him. "It was such heaven buying it, repairing it, changing it back to what it was at the beginning of time. Planting. Dreaming. Hoping. Praying."

On the final trip to Roxbury, Marilyn's half-sister Berniece and Ralph accompanied her. There Hugo ran and played with Marilyn's new dog, Maf.

Berniece wrote, "Arthur wears an old sweater with elbow patches as he greets his guests, the familiar pipe between his teeth. He gives a tour of the large house, discussing its features, and pointing out the new additions he and Marilyn made, such as the dark wood beams crossing the ceilings. Arthur brews tea, and they chat in a sunroom decorated by Marilyn with black and white photographs of Arthur. Here and in the hall are posters, advertisements for *Death of a Salesman*, framed newspaper reviews, and full-length photos of Arthur blown up to almost life size."

In February 1962, he married for the third and final time, to Inge Morath, a photographer who had been on the set of *The Misfits*. The couple lived in the farmhouse for the entirety of their forty-year marriage.

Arthur passed away on February 10, 2005, in the farmhouse where he had lived for so long. It was fifty-six years to the day that *Death of a Salesman* debuted on Broadway.

[33] 882 North Doheny Drive, West Hollywood | April 1961–March 1962

With Marilyn contractually obligated to Twentieth Century-Fox, she decided to split her time between New York and Los Angeles. She still considered New York her permanent home and continued filing her taxes there. When she first arrived back in her hometown, she moved to an apartment that was familiar to her—the one on Doheny, where she lived in 1953. Marilyn was comfortable here, although her return was not without issues. During her second residency at Doheny, Marilyn struggled with depression. At the encouragement of her psychiatrist, Dr. Ralph Greenson, Marilyn began searching for a house to purchase instead of her pattern of renting. His reasoning was that Marilyn should create a feeling of security and put down roots.

[49] 12305 Fifth Helena Drive, Los Angeles | March 1962–August 1962

It wasn't until 1962 that Marilyn finally purchased a house, and when she made the commitment, it was in the upscale neighborhood of Brentwood in Los Angeles. Dr. Ralph Greenson was the inspiration to buy a house, but Marilyn wanted one similar to his, which was built in Spanish or Mexican-style architecture.

The Greenson family home was beautiful, which Marilyn found aesthetically pleasing, but she felt safe there and wanted to replicate that sense of security in her own house. There was also a familiarity with Spanish-style architecture, which had been one of the hallmark styles of Los Angeles while Marilyn was growing up in the 1920s and 1930s.

Marilyn purchased the house for $77,500 from William and Doris Pagen. She made a down payment of $45,000, which Joe DiMaggio helped pay. She qualified for a fifteen-year or twenty-year loan (depending on the source) and began monthly payments of $320 on March 1, 1962. The little hacienda was cheerful and perfectly sized for a single woman. Famously, the

Latin inscription *Cursum Perficio*, roughly translating to "I'm Completing My Journey," is inscribed in tiles at the front door; it came with the house. In terms of feeling safe, a sturdy block wall surrounded the property, obscuring the house from public view and helping to ensure privacy.

Marilyn relished the opportunity to decorate her new house. In addition to adding her own touch to the place, the house had been built in 1929 and needed updating. It had also been remodeled at some point, a process that removed some of the Spanish influence. Marilyn was delighted with the prospect of adding these details back into the décor. She promptly restored the kitchen and bathrooms with brightly colored tiles reminiscent of Spanish architecture. (Her kitchen bore a striking resemblance to the Greenson kitchen.) During this process, she also updated the plumbing in the thirty-year-old house.

The roof was overhauled, a cost that had been factored into the final sale of the home. Because there was no attic or crawl space to serve as a buffer between the roof and ceiling, a sturdy roof was imperative.

With major renovations to the roof, kitchen, and bathrooms completed, Marilyn began the process of decorating. Marilyn went so far as to travel to Mexico and purchase authentic furnishings to complement the architecture. Many of the furnishings were custom, which required time for manufacturing to her specifications. The delay caused some of Marilyn's furniture to arrive after her death. Several other items, however, were in place and the interior was coming together.

The exterior also underwent a renovation when it came to landscaping. Marilyn wanted plants authentic to Mexico and lots of colors. Through this process, she discovered she enjoyed gardening. The property, being at the end of a cul-de-sac, was large and featured a kidney-shaped swimming pool. She was proud of the pool but likely didn't use it much during what turned out to be a short residence.

Marilyn's house purchase comes at a pivotal point in her life, making it an important element in her final months. The house was meant to bring her stability at a time she needed it, and many believe she was on an upswing, with her house symbolizing a renewed energy and mental outlook.

During the summer of 1962, Marilyn was happy when discussing her new home. "Now that I've turned thirty-six, this is a dream come true for me—my having my own home, my own house," she told photographer George Barris. "I have an apartment in New York City on Sutton Place, and I'm officially a legal resident of New York, but since pictures are still made in Hollywood, that's where I have to be for work. I decided it was time for me to buy a house, instead of leasing one all the time. . . . It's a cute little Mexican-style house with eight rooms, and at least I can say it's mine—but not alone.

I have a partner—the bank! I have a mortgage to pay off. The address is cute, too: 12305 Fifth Helena Drive, Brentwood. And get this, I'm in a cul-de-sac or, as we call it, a dead-end street. It's small, but I find it rather cozy that way. It's quiet and peaceful—just what I need right now."

Marilyn gave an interview to *Life Magazine* in her home. It would be her last interview and reporter Richard Merryman recalled that day: "As she led me through the rooms, bare and makeshift as though someone lived there only temporarily, she described with loving excitement each couch and table and dresser, where it would go and what was special about it. The few small Mexican things—a tin candelabra, folding stools, ingeniously carved from single pieces of wood, a leather-covered coffee table, tiles on the kitchen walls—revealed her impetuous, charming taste."

Unfortunately, she never got the opportunity to finish her project. Marilyn passed away in the home and was found on August 5, 1962.

Since Marilyn's short tenure at Fifth Helena Drive house, ownership has changed hands several times and undergone multiple remodels.

The 2,300-square-foot, three-bedroom house was enlarged when the main and guest houses were connected. The wood paneling in the living room, kitchen tile, and bathroom tile have all been removed since Marilyn's time. A few touches, however, remain, including the tile around the living room fireplace, a pointed arched doorway in the living room, the swimming pool, and the *Cursum Perficio* tile work at the front door, which for many has come to symbolize Marilyn's stay here.

· 7 ·

School Days

One of the most prominent aspects of Marilyn's character was her love of learning. Even when it wasn't a formal learning situation, Marilyn was always educating herself.

[1] Ballona Street School | 306 E El Segundo Boulevard, Hawthorn
Norma Jeane and her foster brother, Lester, began kindergarten here in September 1931. She also attended first grade in 1933.

[2] Selma Avenue Elementary School | 6611 Selma Avenue, Los Angeles
After moving to Hollywood with her mother, Norma Jeane attended second and third grade at Selma from 1933 to 1935. Actress and comedienne Carol Burnette is also an alumnus of Selma Elementary.

[3] Vine Street Elementary School | 955 Vine Street, Los Angeles
While living at the Los Angeles Orphans Home, Norma Jeane and the other children walked here to school every day. She attended fourth and fifth grade at Vine Elementary, from 1935 to 1937.

[4] Lankershim School | 5250 Bakman Avenue, North Hollywood
Presently living with her aunt Olive (Marion Monroe's wife) and her three cousins, Norma Jeane started school at Lankershim Elementary School in November 1937 for sixth grade.

[5] Sawtelle Elementary School (now Nora Sterry Elementary School) | 1730 Corinth Avenue, Los Angeles
Norma Jeane moved in with Ana Lower and attended seventh grade for the 1938–1939 school year. She served on the safety committee. The school was renamed in 1941 after the school's principal, who was also a Red Cross volunteer and community activist.

[6] Emerson Junior High | 1650 Selby Avenue, Los Angeles
Still living with Aunt Ana, Norma Jeane enrolled in Emerson Junior High in the fall of 1939. She attended Emerson for eighth and ninth grade, graduating in June 1941. Her activities at school included the glee club and working on *The Emersonian*, the school newspaper. Her smiling face can be found in a large class photo in front of the school.

[7] Van Nuys High School | 6535 Cedros Street, Van Nuys
Once again living with Grace Goddard's family, Norma Jeane moved to Van Nuys in the San Fernando Valley and began tenth grade at Van Nuys High School.

[8] University High School | 11800 Texas Avenue, Los Angeles
Norma Jeane transferred mid-school year to University High School after the Goddards relocated to West Virginia. She moved to Aunt Ana's while awaiting her wedding to Jim Dougherty. Her marriage marked the end of her high school education, which bothered her deeply for the rest of her life.

[9] Actors Lab | 1455 N. Laurel Avenue, West Hollywood (former location)
In 1947, Marilyn took classes at the Actors Lab on Laurel Avenue, around the corner from Schwab's Drug Store.

[10] University of California, Los Angeles | 405 Hilgard Avenue, Los Angeles
Determined to further her education despite not having a high school diploma, Marilyn enrolled in UCLA's adult extension program. The class she took was called Backgrounds in Literature. She posed for a series of photos at the university. Marilyn later commented, "When I started out in movies, I used to go to night school. The headmistress didn't know who I was and couldn't understand why boys from other classes sometimes popped their heads through the door during a class to look at me and whisper. One day, she decided to ask my classmates, who told her I acted in movies. She said, 'And I took her for a young girl straight out of a convent!' That's one of the biggest compliments I've ever been paid."

Norma Jeane Baker finished her formal education after completing the tenth grade at University High School. Almost immediately after, she married neighbor Jim Dougherty.
Elisa Jordan

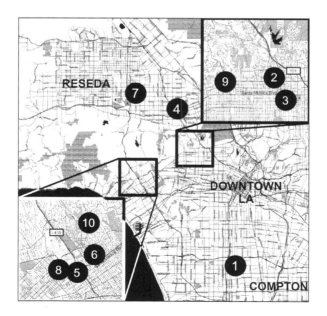

[11] Actors Studio | 1955–1960

Founded in Manhattan in 1947 by Elia Kazan, Cheryl Crawford, and Robert Lewis, the Actors Studio has come to be recognized as a leading school for professional actors. It is best known for teaching the Method, inspired by the "system" developed by Konstantin Stanislavski in Russia.

Lee Strasberg took over the school in 1951 and remained in charge until he died in 1982. In 1955, Marilyn began both group classes and private lessons and remained a student until her death.

Rosie the Riveter

During World War II, women began filling jobs traditionally held by men. These included everything from manufacturing, freight, heavy machinery, shipyards, welding, construction, steel mills, and more. Recruitment campaigns were launched to encourage women into entering such "masculine" lines of work.

In 1942, Redd Evans and John Jacob Loeb wrote a song that first used the name "Rosie the Riveter," giving an identity to an idealized fictitious woman working to support the war effort. Artwork gave a face to "Rosie." In 1943, a Norman Rockwell painting of a female defense worker appeared on the cover of *The Saturday Evening Post*. Perhaps the most lasting image

The iconic Rosie poster produced by the US War Production Board. National Archives / NAID 535413.

was artwork created by J. Howard Miller, who produced a series of posters, one of which was a woman showing off her bicep with the slogan "We Can Do It!"

Over the years, Rosie the Riveter inspired a social movement that outlasted the war. For many women, images of Rosie have come to symbolize female independence and empowerment. When Norma Jeane Dougherty was a teenager during World War II, she was one such woman who went to work in the defense industry and became a "Rosie the Riveter."

· 9 ·

Radioplane Company

Originally founded by British actor, World War I veteran, and aviation enthusiast Reginald Denny, Radioplane Company was located in Van Nuys, a suburb of Los Angeles in the San Fernando Valley. The company specialized in manufacturing drones for gunnery practice. During World War II, Radioplane made approximately 9,400 OQ-3 models, small propeller-powered monoplanes. When shot down during practice, a small parachute opened and floated the drone down for a landing. The company also produced radio control and self-guided missiles.

Norma Jeane Dougherty went to work at Radioplane Company in 1944 after her husband Jim shipped out to war. His mother, Ethel Dougherty, was a nurse at the factory and it was she who found her daughter-in-law a position at the company. Norma Jeane was paid $20 for working sixty hours per week. Over the next two years, she coated fabric aircraft fuselages with varnish and inspected the parachutes. She earned a certificate of excellence for her work.

Years later in an interview, she recalled her duties:

> I first had a job inspecting parachutes—not the kind of parachutes a life depends on, the little parachutes they use to float down the targets after the gunners are through with them. That was before I worked in the "dope" room, the hardest work I've ever done. The fuselage and various parts of the ship were made of cloth at that time—they use metal now— and we used to paint the cloth with a stiffening preparation. It wasn't sprayed on; it was worked in with brushes, and it was very tiring and difficult. We used a quick-drying preparation—a type of lacquer, I guess, but heavier—the smell was overpowering, very hard to take for eight hours a day. It was actually a twelve-hour day for other workers, but I only did eight because I was underage. After the cloth dried, we sanded it down to glossy smoothness.

To cheer up the brave boys fighting overseas, photographer David Conover took pictures of pretty girls doing their part for the war effort by working at Radioplane. Teenage Norma Jeane Dougherty was among the employees selected to participate. She was a natural in front of the camera, and Conover encouraged her to model professionally. By U.S. Army photographer David Conover / Wikimedia Commons

The hard work paid off in ways she would have never imagined. It was because of her job at Radioplane that the future Marilyn Monroe first posed for a professional photographer. At the suggestion of actor Ronald Reagan, then the commander of the Army's 1st Motion Picture Unit, David Conover was dispatched to Radioplane to photograph pretty girls who were doing their part to support the war effort and boost the morale of the brave boys fighting for their country.

The teenage Mrs. Dougherty was a natural choice when it came to finding pretty girls who photographed well at the factory. Conover took pictures of Norma Jeane working on the line and was so impressed with the results that he also photographed her outside Radioplane, and suggested she look into modeling professionally.

In a letter dated June 4, 1945, Norma Jeane wrote to Grace Goddard recounting the experience:

> The first thing I knew, the leadlady and leadman had me out there having the Army taking pictures of me. . . . They all asked where in the H—l I had been hiding. . . . They took a lot of moving pictures of me, and some of them asked for dates, etc. (Naturally, I refused.).
> . . . After they finished with some of the pictures, an army corporal by the name of David Conover told me he would be interested in getting some color still shots of me. He used to have a studio on the Strip on Sunset. He said he would make arrangements with the plant superintendent if I would agree, so I said okay. He told me what to wear and what shade of lipstick, etc., so the next couple of weeks I posed for him at different times. . . . He said all the pictures came out perfect. Also, he said that I should by all means go into the modeling profession . . . that I photographed very well and that he wants to take a lot more. Also he said he had a lot of contacts he wanted me to look into.
>
> I told him I would rather not work when Jimmie was here, so he said he would wait, so I'm expecting to hear from him most any time again.
>
> He is awfully nice and is married and is strictly business, which is the way I like it. Jimmie seems to like the idea of me modeling, so I'm glad about that.

David Conover was true to his word, and photographed Norma Jeane a few more times. By August 1945, she had gained enough confidence to contact Blue Book Modeling Agency, which not only booked jobs for models but also offered training in the form of classes.

Ethel Dougherty expressed her disapproval of Norma Jeane modeling to the point that the young woman no longer felt welcome in the Dougherty home. Norma Jeane moved out of her mother-in-law's house and returned to Aunt Ana's duplex on Nebraska Avenue. Norma Jeane had always dreamed of a career in front of the camera, and she recognized this was the opportunity she had always longed for.

II

THE MAKING OF AN ICON

· 10 ·

Emmeline Snively, Blue Book Models, and a Bridge to Show Business

> She was a clean-cut, American, wholesome girl—too plump, but beautiful in a way. We tried to teach her how to pose, how to handle her body. She always tried to lower her smile because she smiled too high, and it made her nose look a little long. At first she knew nothing about carriage, posture, walking, sitting, or posing. She started out with less than any girl I ever knew, but worked the hardest. She wanted to learn, wanted to be somebody, more than anybody I ever saw before in my life.
>
> —Emmeline Snively

Without the guidance of Emmeline Snively and her Blue Book Modeling Agency, it's very likely Marilyn Monroe would not have been as effective as she was in front of the camera. It's also because of Emmeline and her agency that Marilyn got the exposure and camera experience she needed to proceed with her dream of acting.

Emmeline Snively, the woman who mentored a teenage Norma Jeane Dougherty on how to work in front of a camera, was born in Ohio on May 2, 1909. She was the only child born to Frank and Myrtle Snively.

After Frank passed away in the 1930s, Myrtle and Emmeline moved to Los Angeles at the height of the Great Depression. Myrtle managed a boarding house and Emmeline attended classes at Holmby College before transferring to UCLA. Upon graduating in 1934, she began teaching art classes, but within a few years, turned her attention to opening the Village School, a modeling school in Westwood Village, near the UCLA campus.

In addition to teaching modeling to young women, Emmeline taught them how to pose in front of the camera and even acted as their agent for professional photo shoots. The school also offered classes for nonprofessionals who wanted to learn poise, charm, and personal development.

Her business took off to the point that an Associated Press article about Emmeline Snively and her modeling agency appeared in print by 1943. One of her quotes all but predicts what will happen to her future pupil, Norma Jeane. "Don't consider modeling as a career. Make it a stepping-stone to something really worth while. You may reach a high-salaried place in motion pictures, the stage, radio, advertising or merchandising. Some of our girls start modeling as young as 14 or 15, and by 18, if they show any promise, they are snatched up by the movies. Hollywood models seldom get to be the sophisticated mannequins of the east and their fees are much lower. However, they usually go on to something better than their eastern sisters."

Emmeline also details the steps needed to be a successful model.

1. A good disposition, for she will have to work with temperamental people under difficult conditions.
2. Good health, because it will be reflected in clear skin, sparkling eyes, and hair that looks alive.
3. A structurally good face. Perfect teeth and large eyes are priceless assets.
4. A reasonably good figure, preferably between 5 feet, 2 inches, and 5 feet, 7 inches.
5. Adequate training in makeup, hair styling, posing, and taking camera direction.

Eventually, Emmeline moved her business to Sunset Boulevard before finally moving again in 1944 to a space at the Ambassador Hotel, which was centrally located in Los Angeles. The Ambassador was more than just the literal center of Los Angeles and more than just a hotel. The Ambassador Hotel was also the figurative center of Los Angeles in terms of culture, politics, business, leisure, and entertainment. Political figures, royalty, and other high-profile visitors in need of high levels of security found safety when staying there. For culture, the Ambassador's world-famous Cocoanut Grove hosted the most important singers and bandleaders, in addition to the Oscars and Golden Globe Awards.

The Ambassador was like a mini city; it had restaurants, a post office, barbershop, I. Magnin department store, furrier, small businesses, and long-term rental options for those choosing to live on the property, including bungalows that opened up directly to the spacious grounds. Emmeline's leasing office space at the Ambassador Hotel was hardly an accident. It was a step in raising the profile of her business.

The school and agency, now called Blue Book Models, was located on the casino floor in suite 37 of the Ambassador. It became a family business when Emmeline's mother Myrtle joined the staff.

A nineteen-year-old Norma Jeane Dougherty was introduced to Blue Book on August 2, 1945, by photographer Potter Hueth. Emmeline wrote down Norma Jeane's measurements, clothing size, height, and hair color. Her hair color, Emmeline noted, was, "California blonde," meaning it was darker in the winter and lighter in the summer when the sun naturally lightened it.

Emmeline Snively agreed to take the young woman on as a student and client. One of the ways Emmeline liked to build interest in her models was by entering them into beauty pageants, but because Norma Jeane was married, she did not qualify. She also didn't have the money to pay for classes at Blue Book, but seeing the eagerness in Norma Jeane, Emmeline arranged for her to pay for classes out of the money she was sure to earn as a model.

Blue Book's curriculum covered posing for photographs and how to conduct oneself in interviews, but it also went further. The classes at Blue Book included everything from grooming and presentation to "making the most of your background" and "sell[ing] yourself to the public as a starlet." No detail went overlooked. Emmeline noticed that when Norma Jeane smiled, a little bit of gum showed on top. She instructed Norma Jeane to lower her smile as a way to hide her gums. It was a habit she kept for the rest of her life and the reason Marilyn Monroe would later be known for her signature lip movements.

Norma Jeane was at a disadvantage from the beginning because she was married and struggled with tuition money. Still, Emmeline was able to find work for the pretty girl. Norma Jeane's first modeling job was at the Pan Pacific Auditorium for Holga Steel Company. She spent Labor Day weekend of 1945 smiling and standing next to metal filing cabinets. She earned $90, which she promptly handed over in full to Emmeline for her classes.

Norma Jeane excelled in her studies when it came to learning makeup, posture, and hand poses, but she was too busty to become a fashion model. Instead, Norma Jeane was labeled as a wholesome, all-American girl. Rather than modeling clothing and working for catalogs, Norma Jeane did more photographic work, such as modeling for pinups, magazine covers, and advertisements. From there, Norma Jeane began booking more jobs, including modeling for Hollywood Star Suit, which had a storefront on Hollywood Boulevard, and Douglas Aircraft.

Emmeline had another suggestion for Norma Jeane when it came to improving her appearance—bleaching and straightening her brown, very curly hair. Norma Jeane, who would one day become the world's most famous blonde, was reticent about changing her hair. She didn't want anything that wasn't natural and initially declined Emmeline's suggestion.

Emmeline continued pressing Norma Jeane to change her hair, finally convincing the young model she would work more if she went blonde. Ambitious and in need of work, Norma Jeane finally agreed and walked into the Frank and Joseph Salon right across the street from the Ambassador. As it turns out, Emmeline Snively's instincts were correct and Norma Jeane's bookings steadily increased.

As Norma Jeane's popularity grew on the modeling circuit, her husband Jim Dougherty's time in the Merchant Marine was coming to an end. He would be coming home soon, he informed her, and when he

Norma Jeane Dougherty's first modeling job was standing next to metal filing cabinets for Holga Steel Company at a trade show in 1945. For her work over the three days of Labor Day Weekend, she earned $90, which she used to pay for her modeling classes. Edward Roth / Alamy Stock Photo

arrived it was time to quit modeling and settle into life as a housewife. But it was too late. Norma Jeane was certain she wanted to pursue acting. She confided her wishes to Emmeline, who took Norma Jeane to meet with an agent named Helen Ainsworth.

Norma Jeane continued modeling on and off for the next few years, even after she signed her first contract with Twentieth Century-Fox. Modeling began to drop off, however, when Marilyn's career resulted in some small, but breakout, performances in such movies as *All about Eve* and *The Asphalt Jungle*. These roles paved the way for a seven-year contract with Twentieth Century-Fox. There was no formal resignation or good-bye with Emmeline Snively and Blue Book Modeling Agency, but the guaranteed income from her Fox contract made the need for modeling obsolete.

As Marilyn's career began to take off, Emmeline instinctively saw a good opportunity to publicize her modeling school and agency. She began offering to write magazine articles about how she taught Marilyn Monroe everything she knew about being in front of the camera.

In 1954, Emmeline called Twentieth Century-Fox to arrange for some photos with her former pupil, who was in the middle of filming *There's No Business Like Show Business*. While in costume for the "Heat Wave" dance number, Marilyn posed for photos with Emmeline measuring her former model's now-famous bust and hips—the same bust and hips that once prevented her from becoming a fashion model.

After the reunion, Emmeline and Marilyn sporadically kept in touch, although soon Marilyn would move to New York in 1955 and remain on the East Coast until 1960. Emmeline's business continued successfully, and she even wrote a play about her experiences in the modeling world and asked Marilyn to read the script. They were in contact during the summer of 1962 when Marilyn was living once again in Los Angeles. It's possible the two women met in person, but there is little information to conclude whether they did or not.

After Marilyn's death, Emmeline continued trying to get her script produced as a play or a movie, without success. She even tried to publish a book about the early years of her star pupil's career, but no publishers were interested.

As the 1960s turned into the 1970s, Emmeline Snively's health began to fail and she retired from the modeling industry. She moved to an assisted living facility in Huntington Beach, a community about thirty-five miles south of Los Angeles. She passed away on September 17, 1975, at the age of sixty-six from a stroke. No one attended her memorial service.

Although Emmeline Snively's name isn't recognizable today, the detailed notes in her Blue Book files have provided valuable information on Norma Jeane's early life in show business and the training that later helped her achieve star quality.

• 11 •

Creating Marilyn

*M*arilyn Monroe's image is one of the most recognizable and identifiable of all time. Wavy blonde hair and red lipstick are so iconic it is almost cliché. Throw in the beauty mark and the "Marilyn look" is unmistakable.

Marilyn's priority was to look sensational as an entire presentation and not have a single element stand out. One of her hairdressers, George Masters, once said if someone had told her, "Your hair looks great," he would have never seen her again. He also once said something similar about her approach to makeup. "Marilyn Monroe always turned her back to the mirror, then looked around. Whatever she saw first—eyes or lips—she would tone down."

Marilyn had specific ideas about beauty and took the concept of mind and body complementing each other and working in tandem to heart. "Try to be beautiful, but don't underestimate your frame of mind," she said in 1953. "You must feel attractive and desirable to make others feel it. You can't be mentally fighting a battle of the sexes. This sometimes happens unknowingly—a carry over from your childhood when you wished you were a boy because they had more freedom. The basis of being attractive to men is your enjoyment of being a woman."

SKINCARE

Even before she was famous, Marilyn took an interest in makeup and skincare. Her first husband, Jim Dougherty, remembers perfectionism led to her washing her face multiple times per day to prevent breakouts.

During an era when a healthy tan was considered fashionable and healthy, Marilyn was ahead of her time by staying out of the sun. Some of her motivation was so her fair skin would match her platinum blonde hair

Classic Marilyn Monroe: She was an expert in her own right when it came to her image, but she also had the best in the business when it came to assisting with hair, makeup, and clothes. Frank Powolny / Wikimedia Commons

(she liked to "feel blonde all over"), but it helped preserve her skin from premature aging.

Her diligence when it came to taking care of herself paid off as she built a career in modeling and movies. She continued to keep up a regular skincare routine and invest in high-quality products and professional facials.

In Los Angeles, Marilyn regularly booked sessions with Madame Renna, who was considered the facialist of the stars. Her salon was located at [1] 8663 Sunset Boulevard, right on the Sunset Strip in the center of exclusive restaurants, expensive clothing boutiques, and nightclubs. Madame Renna and her husband, Dr. G. W. Campbell, created a line of skincare products, often tailoring them to a client's specific needs.

It was Madame Renna who was the "face" of the business, but her husband was just as important to the quality of the salon's services. As a former dentist, Dr. Campbell had a deep knowledge of the face's bone structure and

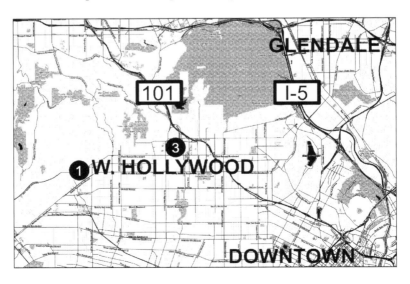

musculature. He developed massage techniques to help stimulate blood flow to facial muscles. One of his hobbies was reading philosophy, and Marilyn enjoyed discussing his favorite books.

Because Marilyn typically ran late for everything, she booked two adjacent appointments to give herself a buffer in case she couldn't show up on time.

In New York, Marilyn visited the salons of Elizabeth Arden and Erno Laszlo, both of whom went on to create popular skincare products and, in the case of Elizabeth Arden, makeup.

Hungarian-born Erno Laszlo treated such beauties as Greta Garbo, Katharine Hepburn, and Audrey Hepburn. (In the 1960s, Sharon Tate also used Erno Laszlo products.) The salon Marilyn visited originally opened in 1939 and was located at [2] 677 Fifth Avenue in Manhattan. In 1959, Erno Laszlo created a regimen for Marilyn's specific needs, which included skin that tended to be a little on the dry side.

Dated March 17, 1959, and addressed to Mrs. Marilyn Monroe Miller, the instructions take her through the day.

Morning: Wash face and neck in warm water with ACTIVE pHELITYL SOAP in the following manner: fill basin with warm water, wet face and neck, and rub on soap making a lather. Make a separate lather in hands and rub well into skin. Rinse thoroughly in the same soapy water and dry with towel. Apply well-shaken NORMALIZER SHAKE-IT on entire face, - except around eyes, - with a large piece of cotton saturated to the dripping point. Blot off with tissues immediately. Apply pHELITONE under eyes only in tiny dots, spreading it gently over the surface. Blot off with tissues. Dab DUO-pHASE FACE POWDER amply on entire face

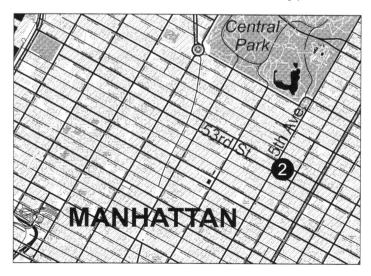

and neck; after one minute brush off superfluous powder with a large piece of cotton.

Evening before dressing: Follow Instructions for "Morning".

On formal occasions: After blotting off NORMALIZER SHAKE-IT, apply pHELITONE on top of it on entire face, also under eyes, and neck and decollete. Blot off with tissues. Apply DUO-

Evening before retiring: Apply ACTIVE pHELITYL OIL on entire face, lips and neck with a large piece of cotton saturated to the dripping point. Wash immediately oily face and neck according to Instructions for "Morning". After drying, apply ACTIVE pHELITYL CREAM on entire face, lips, neck and decollete. Wash off cream immediately with a large piece of cotton saturated to the dripping point with well-shaken CONTROLLING LOTION, - except around eyes and on lips where you shall blot cream off with tissues. Dry face and neck with towel. Reapply on nose and chin with another thoroughly saturated large piece of cotton, covering thickly and let dry on overnight.

Do not eat: Any kind of nuts, chocolate, olives, oysters and clams.

In addition to the routine for Marilyn's face, the Erno Laszlo company states the doctor created Phormula 3-8 (now Phormula 3-9) especially for her to help heal a scar on her stomach, likely from her gallbladder surgery in 1961.

Of all the products Marilyn used, Erno Laszlo's are arguably the most closely associated with her. She had several jars in her possession at the time of her death, including a container found by her bedside on the morning she died. The brand's distinctive black-and-white jar is pictured on Marilyn's floor, alongside a drinking glass and pill bottles.

MAKEUP

Marilyn's love for makeup and beauty began in childhood. While on outings with her mother, little Norma Jeane was often treated to appointments at beauty salons. When she lived at the Los Angeles Home for Orphans, the director let Norma Jeane play with her makeup.

Taking care of her appearance became an outlet, and she put the effort into every aspect. She was naturally gifted at doing her makeup, but when she met makeup artist Allan "Whitey" Snyder while filming her first screen test, she found her soulmate when it came to makeup. Over the years, Marilyn and Whitey worked together to craft her makeup and finally hit on the signature Marilyn Monroe look.

Whereas Marilyn worked with several hairdressers over the years, Whitey remained her primary makeup artist for her entire career.

"I can sit here and do the whole thing in my sleep," Whitey said years later of Marilyn's makeup routine. "Put the base all over, lightly. The formula we used that perfectly matched her natural flesh tone was to mix a quart of Max Factor's 'sun tan base,' a half cup of 'ivory' coloring, and an eyedropper of 'clown white.' Then, highlight under her eyes. Pull the highlight out over and across the cheekbones to widen. Highlight her chin. Eyeshadow was toned, and that also ran out to her hairline. Then the pencil on top. I'd outline her eyes very clearly with pencil, but I'd make a peak right up—say almost three-sixteenths of an inch—above the pupil of her eye, and then swing it out there. And from there on out was where we put eyelashes. Also, the bottom line was shaded in with a pencil to make her eyes stand out fully and good. Her eyebrows came to a point as far as I could get them to widen her forehead. So I'd bring them to a peak just outside the center of her eyes and then sweep down to a good-looking eyebrow. You couldn't go out much farther than that or it would look phony. Shading broke the bones underneath her cheekbone. I just brought a little line down there, a little darker shadow, so that it helped her stand out. Lipstick, we used various colors. As the industry changed, we got down to normal colors. At first, we had a hell of a time with [Technicolor]—no red photographed anything but auburn. We had to go light pink."

Marilyn often used as many as three shades of lipstick to give her lips a more contoured appearance. In an era where gloss wasn't yet manufactured, she liked to dab Vaseline on her lips for a sexy moist pout. She also lightly dabbed Vaseline on her browbone and cheekbones for dewy highlights.

Her signature beauty mark was in actuality a tiny colorless mole on her left cheek, which she could darken or cover depending on the desired effect she wanted.

If makeup and her appearance were an outlet for her, they were also an excuse. Marilyn's debilitating anxiety delayed her appearance on the set. She used her makeup as a reason to refrain from showing up by focusing on self-perceived "flaws" in her cosmetics and insisted on redoing her face.

The entire process for Marilyn's makeup took anywhere from an hour and a half at a minimum and went up from there. "She looked fantastic, of course, but it was all an illusion," Whitey said. "In person, out of makeup, she was very pretty but in a plain way, and she knew it."

Indeed, Marilyn's ability to change her appearance was almost like a superpower. George Winslow, the little boy who played Henry Spofford III in *Gentlemen Prefer Blondes*, recalled that every night after work a nice woman would say goodnight to him as they left. As an adult, he realized the woman was Marilyn Monroe without makeup.

As Marilyn settled into her fame and began studying acting in New York, her makeup evolved and toned down. Another aspect is likely the changing times. The 1950s were a bridge (albeit a glamorous one) between the dramatic look of the 1940s and the lighter lipstick shades and changing eyeshadow trends of the 1960s.

The Makeup Kit

> Elizabeth Arden cream eyeshadows in shades Autumn Smoke and Pearly Blue
> Elizabeth Arden highlighter
> Elizabeth Arden eyelashes
> Elizabeth Arden eye pencil in dark brown
> Elizabeth Arden Eye Stopper eyeliner in brown and black
> Elizabeth Arden liquid eyeshadow in Pearly Blue
> Three lipsticks by Max Factor labeled L.S./7-22/N.I. (these were prototype colors)
> Max Factor highlighting tube "Highlight by Lilly Dache/White"
> Winter White lipstick by Michel Cosmetics
> Leichner of London Light Green cream eyeshadow
> Leichner of London Gray cream eyeshadow
> Leichner of London Light Blue cream eyeshadow
> Glorene of Hollywood eyeliner and eyelashes
> Hollywood Wings
> Shisheido "Quintess" line perfumed lotion
> Anita d'Foged "Day Dew" cream makeup and coverup
> Dorin Inc. Rouge Brunette No. 1249
> Helena Rubinstein black mascara
> Martha Lorraine eyelashes
> Erno Laszlo face powder, face cream, brush cream, "fair" cream, skin paste, "rosy" cream, scar cream
> Erno Laszlo pHelityl
> Erno Laszlo Normalizer Shake-it
> La Maire cosmetics jar
> Vaseline
> Flents Ear Stopples Ear Plugs
> Comfort Eye Mask

FINGERNAILS

Except for certain roles or specific photo sessions, Marilyn's nails were generally free from polish, relatively short, and rounded. She did have some nail polishes found in her belongings, however, including Cherries a la Mode and Hot Coral by Revlon.

FASHION AND JEWELRY

When it came to clothing, Marilyn typically eschewed the full skirts that were popular in the 1950s. She preferred more form-fitting dresses and clean lines. She was on to something. Years later, her style would seem less dated and have a more timeless appeal than many of her contemporaries.

She had very clear ideas about clothing and what worked for her. In "I Dress for Men," Marilyn states, "To begin with, I believe your body should make your clothes look good—instead of using clothes to make the body conform to what is considered fashionable at the moment, distorted or not. That's why I don't care for 'unorganic' clothes that have no relation to the body, not to be something distinct from it."

While performing her movie roles, the costumes served the characters, although many of Marilyn's personal preferences, such as the slimmer fitting skirts, sometimes made their way into the designs. Marilyn was often such a fan of the clothing she wore on film that she borrowed the outfits and wore them for personal appearances.

Another habit was to buy something in multiples. She was fond of black-and-white checked slacks and had several pairs over the years. She loved slim-fitting, peddle pusher-style pants and owned several black cocktail dresses with spaghetti straps that were practically identical. She also went so far as to buy the same pants, blouses, and dresses in different colors. When she found something that worked for her, she stuck to it.

For public appearances requiring glamour, such as movie premieres, award ceremonies, or high-profile parties, Marilyn delighted in showing up as the beautiful movie star fans and media expected. Early in her career, Marilyn set herself apart from other starlets by wearing risqué dresses, which drew ire from others. As she notes in the "I Dress for Men" article, "The only people who have criticized my clothes so far are other women."

Once when asked what she wore to bed, Marilyn coyly replied "Chanel No. 5." Photographer Ed Feingersh captured Marilyn applying a dab before a night on the town in 1955.
By Ed Feingersh / Wikimedia Commons

Once Marilyn became a star, she settled into a more classic and elegant style. She loved wearing black, gray, white, or red—red, especially because "red gets a response!" She also believed, "Busy prints or busy lines in a dress get tiring."

For a little girl who grew up in poverty during the Great Depression, dressing for events appeared to have been fun for Marilyn. "My love for dressy clothes might have a psychological implication," she writes. "When I went to school, I had exactly two navy skirts and two white blouses. I washed one and wore the other. But because they looked so much alike, my school mates made fun of me because I had only one outfit."

At home and out of the range of a spotlight or professional camera, Marilyn was distinctly more casual. She tended to prefer fuzzy white terry-cloth robes (a favorite), slouchy sweaters, and flat shoes.

Although forever associated with diamonds and a love of jewelry thanks to her portrayal of Lorelei Lee in *Gentlemen Prefer Blondes*, as a general rule Marilyn didn't wear much jewelry, especially at home. If she was married, her wedding band was usually about all she wore. For public appearances, she would sometimes wear such jewelry as the wide, decadent rhinestone bracelets or long dangly earrings that were popular with movie stars at the time. When she wore necklaces, they were usually fairly simple by the era's standards.

"Flashy earrings, necklaces and bracelets detract from a lady's looks," she said. "And even if I have to wear that stuff, I don't have to own it. The studio lends it to me whenever they want to show me off."

THE GLAM SQUAD

It took a village to create "Marilyn Monroe" when she was stepping in front of a camera or crowd. Here is a sampling of some of Marilyn's very talented team.

Hair: The Stylists Who Tended to the World's Most Famous Blonde

Sylvia Barnhart: It was Sylvia who turned the brunette Norma Jeane into a blonde Marilyn Monroe. With the help of hairdresser Sylvia Barnhart, Marilyn's hair got lighter and straighter over time. When Sylvia moved from Frank and Joseph's near the Ambassador Hotel to a second location at [3] 6513½ Hollywood Boulevard, Marilyn followed and began getting her hair bleached and cut right in the heart of Hollywood. Sylvia continued doing Marilyn's hair on and off for the next couple of years (at times Marilyn was so broke she bleached her own hair) until she found herself under contract with studios, which took over much of Marilyn's hair care during times when she was filming.

Kenneth Battelle: Mr. Kenneth, as he was known professionally, had a "Hairdresser of the Stars" reputation and began styling Marilyn in New York, probably sometime in the late 1950s. He styled her hair for the "Happy Birthday, Mr. President" performance in May 1962.

Gordon Bond: When Marilyn traveled to England in 1956 to film *The Prince and the Showgirl*, Gordon Bond was her hairdresser for the movie. Marilyn and Gordon got along well, and he appeared to have a genuine connection with her. Before Marilyn was presented to Queen Elizabeth II, Bond styled her hair for the event.

Agnes Flanagan: Of all the stylists to work with Marilyn, Agnes had the longest relationship with her. They began working together on the Twentieth Century-Fox film *The Fireball* in 1950 and continued on and off for the rest of Marilyn's life. She did Marilyn's hair for *Some Like It Hot* and (along with Sydney Guilaroff) *The Misfits*, which was a wig. In addition to movie work, Marilyn often hired Agnes to do her hair for public appearances, special occasions, and photo shoots, sometimes working on location or out of Marilyn's home for such events. Like many hairdressers and clients, over the years Marilyn and Agnes developed a close friendship, with Agnes becoming a treasured confidant. Agnes's last job as hairdresser for Marilyn was styling the wig for Marilyn's funeral, as her real hair had been damaged during the autopsy process.

Sydney Guilaroff: As MGM's primary hairstylist during the Golden Era, Sydney Guilaroff's clientele list is a who's who of Old Hollywood. When Marilyn made *The Asphalt Jungle* for MGM in 1950, it was Guilaroff who convinced her to trade her long Rita Hayworth hair for a shorter style better

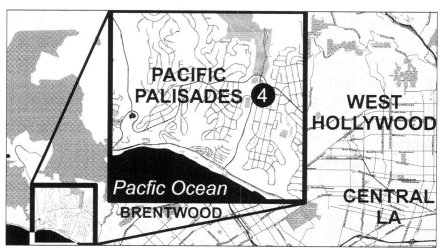

suited to her face. This was the beginning of Marilyn finding her own look. Although Marilyn's hairstyles changed frequently over the years, often coinciding with movie roles, her hair typically stayed above her shoulders after this point unless a part called for her to wear a long wig. Sydney worked with her on *Right Cross*, a movie she appears in only briefly. Along with Agnes Flanagan, he worked as a hairstylist on Marilyn's last film, *The Misfits*. In his 1996 memoir, *Crowning Glory*, Guilaroff claims to have bedded many of Old Hollywood's most famous actresses, Marilyn included. There does not appear to be any evidence to support an affair with Marilyn except his account.

Helen Hunt: In 1948, Marilyn was signed to a six-month contract at Columbia Pictures, the home of Rita Hayworth. During her time at Columbia, Marilyn's hair was styled by none other than Helen Hunt, the woman who created Rita's signature flowing locks. Helen styled Marilyn's hair in a similar fashion to Rita's for the movie *Ladies of the Chorus*, and the results were sensational. It was ultimately Rita's look, though, and Marilyn would go on to find her own style.

Peter Leonardi: When Marilyn moved to New York for a new life in 1955, Leonardi served as her hairdresser.

Rita Hayworth, the undisputed queen of the Columbia lot, was one of the most famous movie stars of the 1940s and a popular pinup with American soldiers during World War II. By Crowell-Collier Publishing Company, photograph by George Hurrell / Wikimedia Commons

He also helped out Marilyn Monroe Productions by acting as an assistant and a driver. When Marilyn traveled to Bement, Illinois, for an appearance at an Abraham Lincoln event, Leonardi accompanied her. Their relationship ended after he threatened to sue Marilyn and Milton Greene for falsely promising to help him open his own salon. His claim is doubted by several

Marilyn biographers, but either way, Marilyn and Milton no longer employed him after the accusations. Decades later, Leonardi told James Haspiel he once drove Marilyn to the Bowery, where she gave money to homeless people.

George Masters: Masters worked with Marilyn later in her career and accompanied her to Mexico in 1962. On this trip to buy furnishings for her new home, she appeared at a press conference and made a couple of public appearances, for which Masters styled her hair. In 2011, George Masters's nephew, Jeff Platts, claimed to have deathbed confession tapes of Masters talking about Marilyn boarding Frank Sinatra's private airplane to have a secret rendezvous with mobster Sam Giancana on the last full night of her life (August 3); the FBI murdered her via a barbiturate-filled enema; and an ambulance picked up Marilyn alive but turned around and brought her home, where she died. These stories are easily disproven and were debunked long ago. Soon after Jeff Platts's claims were published, the story lost merit and disappeared. George Masters died in 1998, broke and drug addicted.

Jimie Morrissey: Marilyn spent Thanksgiving 1961 (her last) at the home of Gloria Lovell, Frank Sinatra's secretary. At the time, Gloria lived in the same building as Marilyn on Doheny Drive. The others present were Danny Thomas's secretary, Janet; Inez Melson, Marilyn's business manager; a woman named Jo; and Jimie Morrissey, Gloria's hairdresser. Later, Jimie styled Marilyn's hair a couple of times in 1962.

Pearl Porterfield: Pearl Porterfield had done the hair of Jean Harlow, the first-ever platinum blonde and, of course, Marilyn's favorite actress. Marilyn invited Pearl to bleach her hair before starting *Something's Got to Give* in 1962.

Gladys Rasmussen: Gladys was an employee of Twentieth Century-Fox and worked with Marilyn regularly, including on several key films, such as *How to Marry a Millionaire*, *River of No Return*, *The Seven Year Itch*, and *Bus Stop*. She also styled Marilyn for special occasions and public appearances, including the *How to Marry a Millionaire* premiere, the *Jack Benny Show*, and a Christmas party for the *Herald Examiner* newspaper at the Shrine Auditorium. Later, Gladys worked on the television show *Little House on the Prairie* along with Marilyn's longtime makeup artist, Allan "Whitey" Snyder.

Gladys said of her, "There are several problems with doing Marilyn's hair. Her hair is very fine and therefore hard to manage. It gets oily if it isn't shampooed every day. And her hair is so curly naturally that to build a coiffure for her I have to first give her a straight permanent. . . . The way we got her shade of platinum blonde is with my own secret blend of sparkling silver bleach plus twenty volume peroxide and a secret formula of silver platinum to take the yellow out."

Marilyn Monroe Hair Care Facts

- She parted her hair on the left. During her lifetime, there were only a couple of exceptions to how Marilyn parted her hair.
  - There is a modeling photo of Marilyn in her starlet era in which her hair is parted in the middle.
  - Marilyn's hair was parted on the right for the premiere of *Baby Doll* in 1956 and a photo shoot in 1962 with Bert Stern in which she's holding a Nikon camera.
- As a natural brunette who maintained a platinum color, Marilyn had to get her hair bleached once a week to avoid roots showing.
- Some of the hair products Marilyn used included Arrive Beautiful hairspray and Erno Laszlo Kolestral hair conditioning cream.
- According to actress Simone Signoret, Marilyn disliked her widow's peak. "It was a very pretty widow's peak, which divided her forehead neatly in half. But she detested it, despised it; it was her personal enemy. She hated it because, curiously, the roots of that hair, fluffy as the hair of a small child, didn't take the platinum dye as well as the rest of the hair on her blond head."

Makeup

Allan Brooks ("Whitey") Snyder was born on August 7, 1914, in Morgan, New Jersey, to Myron Brooks Snyder and Dorothy Parker Snyder. In 1940, his draft card reveals he was living at [4] 860 Radcliffe in Pacific Palisades, a beach community in Los Angeles County; his father lived nearby at 1803 Euclid in Santa Monica. It was also during this time he was working in the makeup department at RKO, but at some point he moved over to Twentieth Century-Fox. At the time he met Marilyn, he was married to a woman named Beverly Bray and had two children, Ron and Sherrill.

Whitey was Marilyn's makeup artist on her very first screen test in 1946. As the story goes, Marilyn did her makeup for the test, only for the director to humiliate her in front of the entire crew when he called Whitey over to fix it. She must have appreciated what he did for her because as soon as she had any clout, she wanted to work with Whitey for all her major parts.

The first movie he worked on with Marilyn was *Monkey Business* and he continued with her on all her movies after that, whether or not he received official credit. Whitey also did Marilyn's makeup for important photo shoots and appearances, but most importantly, he became one of her closest friends and confidants. Photos of the two on movie sets show them holding hands, embracing, and comforting one another.

Marilyn was known to telephone those in her inner circle when she needed support, sometimes at odd hours. Whitey was one such person and he tried to encourage her the best he could. "She used to call me. She'd be lonely. She was a lonely girl all the way through. Not so much in the mornings but many, many times at night, and she'd call me in the middle of the night. She'd just want to talk to you, talk to me, say, or anybody."

Whitey saw firsthand how anxiety prevented her from appearing on the set at an appointed time. "She was just frightened—inferiority complex," he recalled in an interview from the 1980s. "She'd be there in time and play around, and the worst thing was when she had to sing a song or something later, which she could do nicely. She wasn't a great voice, but a nice voice. She would just pick up anything—the eyebrows were wrong or something—to redo it. Anything not to just appear out there."

Marilyn used to joke with Whitey that if she died first, she wanted him to do her makeup for her memorial service. To underscore the joke/request, she gave him a gold Tiffany money clip with the engraving:

Whitey Dear:
While I'm still warm
Marilyn

As it turns out, Marilyn did die first and Whitey found himself in the unenviable position of having to fulfill a request that broke his heart. Marilyn passed away on August 5, 1962, and her memorial service was just three days later on August 8. Whitey was born on August 7, which means he may very well have had to fulfill his promise to Marilyn on his birthday. Thanks to liquid courage in the form of gin, Whitey kept his promise to Marilyn and made her look beautiful one last time.

Whitey continued in his successful makeup career. He was notably associated with *Rosemary's Baby* (1968), *The Poseidon Adventure* (1972), and the television series *Little House on the Prairie*. In her book *Confessions of a Prairie Bitch*, Alison Arngrim, who portrayed Nellie Oleson on the show, recalls Whitey still carrying the money clip Marilyn had gifted him years earlier.

Hairstylist Gladys Rasmussen also worked on *Little House*.

"Whitey always carried a gold money clip. One day when Gladys was telling me about how fabulous Marilyn had been to work with and how much they all loved her (this really kind of blew the lid off the whole 'diva' mythology—those who worked with her described her as a sweet, vulnerable, almost delicate creature), she showed me the gold pendant necklace Marilyn gave her and told Whitey to show me what Marilyn had given him. He took a wad of bills out of his pocket; he didn't just keep the money clip, he actually used it for its intended purpose on a daily basis. It was engraved with the words 'While I'm Still Warm—Marilyn.'

"I thought the inscription was very weird and started to open my mouth to ask what on earth that meant, when he put it away hurriedly, and Gladys gave me a 'don't you dare' look and shook her head. After Whitey left the room, she explained that he was very sensitive about the whole thing. What the engraving referred to was this: Marilyn used to laugh and tell Whitey, 'Oh, Whitey, your makeup is so wonderful; when I die, I want you to make me up while I'm still warm!' One day, she gave him the engraved clip. The gift would have remained a cute, funny story, except that when she died, tragically and horribly at thirty-six, he in fact went to the funeral home and applied makeup to the face of his now dead friend.

"According to Gladys, this task was extremely traumatic for him and required large amounts of alcohol to complete. She said he never fully recovered emotionally and told me that I should always be careful when discussing Marilyn in his presence and, if I had any sense, to never say anything else about the money clip. I heard and obeyed."

After *Little House on the Prairie*, Whitey moved on to *Highway to Heaven* from 1984 to 1987. He retired to Washington state, where he passed away on April 16, 1994. He had remarried in 1970 to a woman named Marjorie Plecher, who had worked as a wardrobe director on several of Marilyn's films. Whitey was still married to Marjorie at the time of his passing.

The fourteen-karat gold money clip Marilyn had gifted to Whitey resurfaced in 2012 when the Snyder family sold many of his possessions at auction in 2012. Julien's Auctions sold the clip for $21,250.

The Main Designers

Several designers worked with Marilyn during her career, with a few of them helping to shape her lasting image and legacy. Here's a quick look at three of them.

Dorothy Jeakins: Dorothy Jeakins helped shape Marilyn's lasting image when she designed the wardrobe for *Niagara*, Marilyn's breakout role.

A San Diego native, Dorothy relocated two hours north to attend school at the prestigious Otis Art Institute in Los Angeles. From there, she moved on to work as a sketch artist at Disney. She eventually made her way to the I. Magnin department store on Wilshire Boulevard, where she started designing clothes for customers. While employed at I. Magnin, director Victor Fleming discovered her talents, and recruited her to help create costumes for *Joan of Arc* (1948) starring Ingrid Bergman.

Remarkably, Dorothy won an Oscar for *Joan of Arc* (shared with Barbara Karinska), her very first picture and the first year the Academy handed out the Best Costume Design award. She won a second Oscar for *Samson and Delilah* in 1949 (shared with Edith Head) starring Hedy Lamarr.

Unlike many of her colleagues, Dorothy primarily worked as a freelancer and wasn't tied to one particular studio. She was hired by Twentieth Century-Fox to design outfits for *Niagara*, a noir-style film set against the backdrop of Niagara Falls starring a new leading lady the studio wanted to promote—Marilyn Monroe. Dorothy had only been working in the movie industry for a few years, but she had already won two Oscars.

Dorothy Jeakins designed this magenta dress for Marilyn in her breakout role as Rose Loomis in Niagara. *In addition to making a big impact on-screen, Marilyn liked it so much she wore it during personal appearances, as well.* By Studio publicity still. Twentieth Century-Fox / Wikimedia Commons

For *Niagara*, Dorothy created one of Marilyn's most famous costumes and one that would go on find its way to her personal wardrobe—the sexy magenta dress Marilyn wears while singing "Kiss." With a bow knotted at the bust and a peek-a-boo midriff, the dress emphasizes the character Rose as a femme fatale. Elsewhere in the movie, Dorothy balances Rose's seductive character with tailored suits—they're formfitting enough to accentuate her sex appeal but not overtly vulgar. It's while wearing one of these suits that Marilyn walks away from the camera and establishes the "Marilyn walk."

Marilyn and Dorothy paired up once again in 1960 for *Let's Make Love*, a romantic comedy in which Marilyn plays an actress starring in an off-Broadway musical. This collaboration was less successful than the first one in *Niagara*. Marilyn was unhappy with several of the pieces Dorothy created. In the final scenes, Marilyn wears a dress from her personal wardrobe, a two-piece black suit designed by John Moore, instead of what Dorothy had prepared.

Dorothy Jeakins was scheduled to design Marilyn's costumes for *The Misfits*, but it was clear Marilyn was still deeply dissatisfied with her *Let's*

Make Love clothing. In a letter dated March 3, 1960, Dorothy wrote to Marilyn, "I am sorry if I have displeased you." And if Marilyn does not like the costume sketches for *The Misfits*, "someone else can take over."

Jean Louis went on to design Marilyn's *Misfits* wardrobe, but Dorothy Jeakins continued to have a successful career. She won another Oscar for *Night of the Iguana* (1964) and received nominations for *The Children's Hour* (1961), *The Music Man* (1962), *The Sound of Music* (1965), *Hawaii* (1966), *The Way We Were* (1973), and *The Dead* (1987). Some of her other credits include *The Ten Commandments* (1956), *South Pacific* (1958), *Little Big Man* (1970), *Young Frankenstein* (1974), and *On Golden Pond* (1981).

Travilla

> She had a delightful quality, being so beautiful, of wanting to show herself. Some people were offended by it—and of course she did it on purpose. She was so childlike she could do anything, and you would forgive her as you would forgive a seven year old. She was both a woman and a baby, and both men and women adored her. She was not well educated, but an extremely bright woman, and she had the whims of a child.
>
> —Travilla

Of all the designers Marilyn Monroe worked with, William "Billy" Travilla (known professionally as just Travilla) had the most prolific partnership with her. It was Travilla who created the white halter dress she wore to stand over a subway grate in *The Seven Year Itch* and the pink gown for the "Diamonds Are a Girl's Best Friend" dance number in *Gentlemen Prefer Blondes*. Not to mention the pleated gold lamé dress with a plunging V-neckline that was ruled too risqué for *Gentlemen Prefer Blondes*, so she wore it for photo shoots and public appearances instead.

The clothing Travilla designed for Marilyn had a dramatic—and lasting—impact on her overall image. Whether it was flamboyant showgirl costumes for musical numbers, tailored skirts and dresses for more conservative scenes, or glamorous movie star-style gowns, Travilla did it all.

Like Marilyn, Travilla was a Los Angeles native. From an early age, he showed an aptitude for art and attended Chouinard Art Institute while still in adolescence. In his teens, he began selling costume sketches to burlesque dancers who performed in downtown Los Angeles theatres. The experience later made his skills ideal when designing showgirl costumes for elaborate Hollywood musicals. He studied fashion design at Woodbury University in Burbank and graduated in 1941 at the age of twenty-one.

After graduation, he got a job sketching designs at Western Costume Co. in Hollywood, another invaluable experience that helped develop his skills. From Western, he moved to Hal Roach and then on to gigs at Columbia Pictures, Warner Bros., and finally Twentieth Century-Fox. In 1950, he shared an Oscar win with Leah Rhodes and Marjorie Best for *The Adventures of Don Juan* (1948). When he met Marilyn in the early 1950s, he was not only an Oscar winner but had dozens of film credits to his name.

Travilla proved to be the perfect partner in helping Marilyn craft her style. When dressing her, he created ensembles that suited the character and enhanced her body. He was also responsive to Marilyn's requests and incorporated her preferences for straight skirts as often as possible.

For a few years, Marilyn very much became Travilla's muse. He was responsible for the majority of her most memorable costumes, including the movies *Monkey Business, Gentlemen Prefer Blondes, How to Marry a Millionaire, River of No Return, There's No Business Like Show Business, The Seven Year Itch*, and *Bus Stop*.

For "Diamonds Are a Girl's Best Friend," Travilla's original design drew from his experience creating costumes for burlesque dancers. The costume was initially a body stocking with strategically placed jewels and fishnet tights. However, Marilyn had just survived a scandal involving a nude calendar she posed for in 1949. Executives at Fox were in no mood for a half-naked Marilyn dancing around on the screen. They instructed Travilla to cover Marilyn up—now!

His new design was nothing like the first. Instead of a revealing burlesque-style costume, Travilla came up with a strapless pink gown, cinched at the waist with a belt and accented with an oversized bow in the back. Opera-length gloves completed the look. To keep the dress from exposing Marilyn as she danced, Travilla used a stiff silk fabric called *Peau d'Ange* (which translates to "angel's skin" in English) and reinforced the bodice with boning. Marilyn's gown appears glamorous and feminine.

For the subway dress in *The Seven Year Itch*, Travilla relied on his skills with pleating. Although Marilyn didn't typically like fuller skirts, the scene called for something with enough volume to billow up around her legs. With Travilla's design, Marilyn's pleated skirt was relatively slim as she walked normally, but the pleating allowed the skirt to open and fan out. As Marilyn tried holding down her skirt for the photo shoot, the rest of it created a voluminous unfurled effect around her.

Travilla received Oscar nominations for his work on *How to Marry a Millionaire* (shared with Charles LeMaire, the head of Twentieth Century-Fox's wardrobe department and Travilla's boss) and *There's No Business Like Show Business* (shared with Charles LeMaire and Miles White).

After *Bus Stop*, Marilyn traveled to England to film *The Prince and the Showgirl* for Warner Bros., and the two collaborators drifted apart, but

Travilla's career remained successful. In 1963, he received another Oscar nomination for *The Stripper*. He went on to design for *Valley of the Dolls* (1967) and Diahann Carroll's breakthrough character in *Julia* (1968–1971), the first television show with a nonstereotypical African American woman in the lead. Some of his other notable credits include *The Thorn Birds*, *Knots Landing*, and *Dallas*, receiving a total of seven Emmy nominations for his work in television.

Jean Louis: Marilyn's first collaboration with designer Jean Louis was in 1948 during her brief employment at Columbia Pictures—although collaboration might be too strong of a word. When Marilyn starred in *Ladies of the Chorus*, she did indeed wear designs by Jean Louis, who was the studio's head designer at the time. The costumes she wore, however, were not made specifically for her. They were pulled from Columbia's warehouse of stock costumes.

At the time of Marilyn's tenure, Jean Louis was best known for dressing Columbia's brightest star, Rita Hayworth. His designs for her vehicle, *Gilda*, furthered Jean Louis's reputation as not just a designer, but as a master craftsman.

When Rita Hayworth filmed *Gilda*, she was getting back into shape after the birth of her first child. The dance numbers in *Gilda* required maximum movement without Rita Hayworth falling out of her costumes. The interiors of the dresses, particularly the strapless black gown for the "Put the Blame on Mame" dance number, were a marvel of structure and form. They cinched and accentuated Rita in all the right places while keeping her body parts exactly where they needed to stay.

Jean Louis's career only continued to gain momentum. From 1950 to 1967, he was nominated fourteen times for an Academy Award, winning in 1956 for *The Solid Gold Cadillac*. He also began taking freelance assignments, including for Marlene Dietrich's cabaret shows. It was his partnership with Marlene that would inspire Marilyn's "Happy Birthday, Mr. President" dress.

The sexy black gown Rita Hayworth wears in Gilda *is considered a masterpiece of construction and design. Jean Louis established a reputation as a master craftsman while working at Columbia Pictures before opening his own atelier.*
By Edward Cronenweth (1903–1990)—ebay / Wikimedia Commons

WORKING WITH MARILYN

Jean Louis was hired to design Marilyn's wardrobe on *The Misfits* after Dorothy Jeakins was let go. For the character Roslyn, a recent divorcee who finds herself in the Nevada desert with cowboys, Jean Louis created two distinct looks. One was more feminine, with dresses and heels. The black suit she wears in the opening scenes of the movie transforms when she removes her jacket to reveal a cocktail dress. Her most famous costume from *The Misfits* is the white "cherry dress" with a deep V-neckline and ties at the shoulders. The other costumes are more casual, such as jeans, and more suitable for a life in the remote desert with cowboys.

Marilyn liked his work so much that she invited him back for her next movie, *Something's Got to Give*. Marilyn was slimmer when she reported to work for *Something's Got to Give*, making it easy for Jean Louis to create a wardrobe of slimming dresses and elegant suits. He designed a beige wool suit trimmed in mink with a matching hat, which she quickly incorporated into her own wardrobe. She wore it to throw out the first pitch at Dodger Stadium on June 1, 1962. It was her thirty-sixth birthday and turned out to be her last public appearance.

THE WORLD'S MOST EXPENSIVE DRESS

Now considered one of the most famous dresses in American history, Marilyn's flesh-colored, body-hugging gown by Jean Louis first made headlines in 1962 when she wore it to sing "Happy Birthday" to President John F. Kennedy. Marilyn wanted something show-stopping, and told Jean Louis to make her a dress "only Marilyn Monroe could wear."

Marilyn's dress drew inspiration from Marlene Dietrich's cabaret show, but Jean Louis reworked it to suit Marilyn. Marlene's dress had a similar "nude" illusion, but she wore it with a high neck and sleeves. Marilyn's dress featured thin straps and a low scoop neck. A nineteen-year-old aspiring designer named Bob Mackie sketched the dress. The concept was to make Marilyn appear as though she were shimmering in the nude, so the dress would have to look like a second skin.

Jean Louis employed Western Costume Co. to manufacture the dress and dye a pair of shoes to match.

To begin, Jean Louis ordered a silk souffle gauze fabric from France in a shade to exactly match Marilyn's skin tone. Souffle is delicate and no longer made because of its high flammability. Even in 1962, the fabric was rare and expensive. Silk souffle fabric is created with finer-than-average threads and woven on miniature looms. It looked and felt similar to soft skin.

After the fabric arrived in Los Angeles, Jean Louis and his staff got to work creating the dress. Because it was supposed to give the illusion of flesh, the team worked to mold the fabric perfectly to Marilyn's body. During this process, Marilyn stood on a stool in the nude as the fabric was fitted to her body.

Jean Louis was long known for his craftsmanship and ingenuity when it came to creating garments, as this dress demonstrates. For example, the dress forgoes traditional side seams in favor of making the fabric look as though it was cut, sewn, and tucked precisely to Marilyn—because it was.

There has been much discussion as to whether or not the dress was lined. The answer is . . . yes and no. Because Marilyn did not plan to wear undergarments, the dress had to have structure and maintain its shape without the aid of underwear or shapers. It also had to give the illusion of nudity without actually exposing Marilyn for real.

Jean Louis's solution was to layer the fabric. Various sized panels of the fabric were sewn into the interior of the dress to create shape and structure. In total, the inside of the dress utilized about two hundred fabric panels on the inside, including twenty in the bust, which kept her breasts lifted and in place.

The dress is not lined in the traditional sense, but the silk souffle fabric was layered and positioned in such a way that it created a lining and shaped the dress's interior. Because the form-fitting skirt was tight, in the back there was a kickout that allowed Marilyn to walk.

Once the dress was sewn, more than 2,500 crystals and several thousand beads were individually attached to the gown, a process that took more than a month. They were positioned strategically over the body and cascaded down the skirt, with the beads increasing in size and number toward the bottom.

Although there have been numerous stories about Marilyn being "literally sewn" into the dress, there was a zipper in the back. It began at the small of Marilyn's back and extended over her bottom. The zipper was clear plastic; hook-and-eye closures, which had to be closed by hand over the zipper, further ensured everything stayed safe and secure.

STAGE FRIGHT

Marilyn was known for her anxiety before a performance.

When preparing for her big night in front of a capacity crowd at Madison Square Garden, which included thousands of fans, other celebrities, and the president of the United States, Marilyn confided to Joan Greenson, her psychiatrist's daughter, that she was terrified about singing live on stage. To help give her confidence, Joan gave Marilyn her childhood copy of *The Little Engine That Could*. It was found in Marilyn's possessions when she passed away and sold at the Christie's auction in 1999.

To help further boost her confidence, a friend recommended she carry a chess piece with her as a reminder that she was not alone. It would symbolize the support network around her. In some pictures from that evening, Marilyn's hand is visibly cupping something—it's the chess piece.

THE INSPIRATION FOR MARILYN'S PERFORMANCE

Marilyn's performance at the Democratic Fundraiser in 1962 has become American history, in large part because of the (false) rumors she was having an affair with President Kennedy. Since that time, a lot of stories have surrounded Marilyn's performance that night—it was too sexy, she was drunk, she had to be sewn into the dress, she was late to the performance . . . anything that makes a good story.

The truth is much more mundane. The inspiration for Marilyn's performance was likely Marlene Dietrich's cabaret act. In the 1950s and 1960s, Marlene Dietrich transitioned from movies to a highly successful nightclub act. Performances often opened with complete darkness and when she stepped on stage, a single spotlight followed her to the microphone. One of her favorite gowns to wear was her "illusion" dress by Jean Louis; she accentuated the look by wrapping herself in a white fur coat. She stood in front of a single microphone and with her signature deep, husky voice sang songs from her movies.

Marilyn's performance was possibly an exaggerated imitation of Marlene's nightclub act. She specifically requested a similar dress from Jean Louis and her movements closely mirrored Marlene's—a dark stage to start, a spotlight that found Marilyn when she appeared and followed her to a microphone. She was

Marilyn told Jean Louis she wanted a gown that "only Marilyn Monroe could wear." The "illusion dress" was designed to give the impression that Marilyn was sparkling and shimmering in the nude. Cecil Stoughton. White House Photographs. John F. Kennedy Presidential Library and Museum, Boston

wrapped in a white fur coat, which she removed to reveal her Jean Louis "illusion" gown, and then launched into a rendition of "Happy Birthday" in a deep, husky voice that was not Marilyn's regular singing voice. Even Marilyn's hair was an exaggerated interpretation of Marlene's bouffant.

In all likelihood, Marilyn was lightheartedly spoofing Marlene's act, a comedic rendition of the great Dietrich's breathy, sexy singing style to sing something as innocent as "Happy Birthday." The Marlene Dietrich cabaret show was so popular during that era, the audience would have understood the reference and the irony—and it does appear they are in on the joke. The audience can be heard laughing as Marilyn dramatically pauses between lines.

It wouldn't be the first time Marilyn imitated Marlene Dietrich. As part of the photo series Fabled Enchantresses she did with Richard Avedon, Marilyn posed as five sexy movie sirens from Old Hollywood's past—Lillian Russell, Theda Bara, Clara Bow, Jean Harlow, and Marlene Dietrich. Marilyn and Marlene had met in person and liked one another; both were known for their sense of humor in real life.

Photos of Marilyn rehearsing the day before on the Madison Square Garden stage reveal she is practicing precisely the same movements as her actual performance the following night. In other words, she wasn't drunk. Nor was she late. The running gag for the evening was Peter Lawford introducing Marilyn throughout the night only for Marilyn to "not show up." It was a joke about her running late in real life and a good indication that Marilyn's appearance at the show was meant to be comedic.

SINCE 1962

Many of Marilyn's personal effects were sold by Christie's in 1999, including the dress she wore to sing "Happy Birthday" to President Kennedy. The sale price was $1,267,500, a significant increase from the $2,428.83 Marilyn originally paid for it. The dress was purchased by a private collector, who kept it as a showpiece in his climate-controlled penthouse, along with four matching collarless suits once belonging to The Beatles.

After his death, the collector's heirs put the dress up for sale through Julien's Auctions in 2016. This time, the dress sold to Ripley's Believe It or Not for $4,800,000, setting a record for the most expensive dress ever sold.

MET GALA CONTROVERSY

In May 2022, the history of the dress got another footnote when reality television star Kim Kardashian showed up wearing Marilyn's dress to the Met Gala. The annual fundraiser raises money for the Metropolitan Museum of

Art's Costume Institute in New York with the intention of garment preservation. It is considered one of fashion's most important events of the year and attracts not only important names in the industry but celebrities as well.

When Kim Kardashian stepped onto the red carpet at the Met Gala on May 2, 2022, she caused a sensation when she appeared in the very same gown Marilyn Monroe had worn in 1962 to sing "Happy Birthday" to President Kennedy. But it wasn't the good kind of sensation.

Kim, with a white fur coat draped over her backside, walked the red carpet and ascended the staircase; when she reached the landing, she changed into a replica dress.

In the weeks following the event, the dress went back on display at the Los Angeles location of Ripley's. While it was on display, observers noticed damage to Marilyn's dress, including a torn right shoulder strap, missing crystals, stretched-out fabric, and a kickout pleat that looked like it had been walked on.

Neither Kim nor Ripley's accepted responsibility for the damage; both parties claimed the dress had been treated with the utmost respect and caution. In the aftermath, however, a video surfaced of Kim trying the dress on and showed fitters yanking the delicate dress over Kim's hips. Crystals can be heard hitting the floor.

Even though Kim went on a crash diet to lose sixteen pounds in just three weeks, the dress still did not fit properly. The gown never did fit over Kim's buttocks, so the zipper was nowhere near being able to close. This explains the white fur coat covering her backside—the dress did not close. Kim is also at least three inches shorter than Marilyn, so she had to wear platform heels, which likely caused the damage seen on the kickout pleat.

Photos and footage of Kim Kardashian wearing Marilyn Monroe's dress made international news. Costuming experts and clothing preservationists criticized the incident. Justine DeYoung, PhD, of the Fashion Institute of Technology, called the incident "irresponsible and unnecessary." She went on to say, "She can—and did—commission a replica which would be indistinguishable from the original. Such an iconic piece of American history should not be put at risk of damage just for an ego-boost and photo-op."

The intensity of the controversy inspired the International Council of Museums to form a group that would update a code of conduct for historic garments. The problem is the new code of conduct applies to museums and Ripley's Believe It or Not does not qualify as a museum, so Marilyn's dress is still not protected.

Kim Kardashian and Ripley's Believe It or Not have continued to deny damaging Marilyn's dress, but photographic evidence proves otherwise.

· 12 ·

Cooking

Some people seem to find cooking quite tedious.

—Marilyn to *Cosmopolitan* magazine in 1960

*M*arilyn cooked with varying degrees of success but overall was never known for her talent in the kitchen. First husband Jim Dougherty reported Norma Jeane's skills in the kitchen were limited. His lunches consisted of egg sandwiches, which she dutifully packed for him every day. She also liked to make a combination of peas and carrots because of the appealing color combination. The teen bride tried, but her skills frequently fell short.

She salted Jim's coffee because she heard it brought out the flavor—instead it was just bitter. While entertaining, Jim asked her to make highballs but she served straight whiskey, which got their guests drunk after just one drink. Once, Jim brought home some fish he had caught and asked Norma Jeane to prepare and cook them. Inspired by Southern California's large Japanese population, she attempted to serve sashimi. Instead of a Japanese delicacy, however, he received a skinned, boned dead fish on his plate. She didn't understand there was more to the dish than just raw fish. This offense caused an argument, with Jim booming, "When the hell are you gonna learn how to took?" Norma Jeane called him a brute and threw a garbage pail at his head. Jim retaliated by placing her under cold shower water.

Her skills seemed to improve over time, mostly as an attempt to build goodwill with her husbands. While staying with the DiMaggio family, Marilyn learned the basics of Italian cooking from the DiMaggio women. At home with Joe, she made pasta dishes, complete with homemade noodles.

When Mr. and Mrs. DiMaggio separated after just nine months of marriage, a reporter tracked down a now-remarried Jim Dougherty, who joked Joe probably didn't like her cooking.

112

During her marriage to Arthur Miller, Marilyn again tried to expand her cooking skills to satisfy her new husband's culinary tastes. As she had done with Joe and his Italian roots, Marilyn wanted to fix meals catering to Arthur's Jewish heritage. It was during this time Marilyn developed a taste for Jewish cuisine and comfort foods.

While filming *Let's Make Love*, Marilyn and Arthur stayed at the Beverly Hills Hotel right across from costar Yves Montand and his wife Simone Signoret. Marilyn cooked a spaghetti meal for the two couples, drawing on the skills she honed during her marriage to Joe.

As time went on, friend Norman Rosten reports in his book that Marilyn experimented with cooking during the mid- to late 1950s, a time frame coinciding with her marriage to Arthur. Marilyn would invite Norman and his wife Hedda over to try out her dishes, which included such menu items as roast beef, stew, and bouillabaisse. "She was practicing cooking," he wrote in his book. "Cookbook stuff mostly. Stews. Wild omelets. Roast beef. I remember a stunning bouillabaisse. Salads of strange ingredients: sometimes lettuce with oil and no vinegar, while I swear once it was all vinegar with shreds of lettuce. Or sauce with meat instead of meat with sauce. However, she was very good at desserts, and her color schemes (peas and carrots), if not striking, were at least consistent."

During the 1960 *Cosmopolitan* interview, she spoke of cooking and how much trouble she went through to cook a meal. "For homemade noodles, I roll the dough out very thin, then I slice into narrow strips . . . then the book says, 'Wait till they dry.' We were expecting guests for dinner. I waited and waited. The noodles didn't dry. The guests arrived; I gave them a drink; I said, 'You have to wait for dinner until the noodles dry. Then we'll eat.' I had to give them another drink. In desperation, I went and got my little portable hair dryer and turned it on. It blew the noodles off the counter, and I had to gather them all up and try again. This time I put my hand over the strips, with my fingers outspread, and aimed the dryer through them. Well . . . the noodles finally dried. So they do leave out a few instructions. I've wanted to write in and ask, 'Please, let people know how long it takes to dry noodles.' But I never did."

Marilyn never did master the art of cooking, but it is fair to say she managed to create meals that worked for her, especially when she was single. When she wasn't cooking for a husband or dinner guests, she had an easier time coming up with food ideas. One of the important factors to remember about Marilyn in the kitchen—aside from her penchant for serving peas and carrots—was she never gave up trying even though she admittedly did not enjoy the process.

· 13 ·

Diet and Exercise

*M*arilyn was famous for her body shape and sexy figure. For the July 1952 issue of *Movieland Magazine*, Marilyn authored an article called "I Dress for Men." In it, she says, "I don't want to be bone thin, and I make it a point to stay the way I want to be."

So how did Marilyn keep that famous hourglass figure in shape? Was it natural? Did she work at it? What did she eat?

The answer isn't so simple.

Marilyn's diet and exercise routines were all over the place. What she ate largely depended on her finances, to whom she was married at the time, and whether she was preparing for a film. She did not enjoy cooking, so she usually kept things simple.

Like anyone, many of Marilyn's eating habits developed during her childhood. She grew up in the Great Depression and came of age during World War II, two eras in which food and money were often scarce. Also, Marilyn grew up in a series of foster homes and spent time in an orphanage, so she didn't have the opportunity to learn about cooking, health, or proper nutrition from a mother as most children would. There was little to no consistency.

When Marilyn was struggling financially in the 1940s, her diet reflected her poverty. She could not afford to eat a nutritionally balanced diet. Also, because she was modeling during this time, she needed to stay thin. She often survived on as little as $1 per day (1940s money) by eating things like raw hamburger, peanut butter, hot dogs, chili, crackers, oatmeal, and orange juice.

During the 1950s, she was continually on and off diets. When watching her figure, Marilyn ate a diet similar to the high-protein/low-carb diets popular today. She ate a lot of steak (sometimes for breakfast), eggs, liver, juice, grapefruit, and some greens.

In "I Dress for Men," she writes, "A breakfast of hot milk with two raw eggs means energy without fat. I like rare steaks and green salads and vegetables, too. Rather than wonder, should I eat dessert? I just go on an ice cream binge once a week (chocolate, please!)."

She supplemented her healthy eating habits by stretching, jogging, and lifting small weights. There are numerous photos of her from the late 1940s through the mid-1950s exercising to stay fit. In this respect, she was very much ahead of her time.

In the mid-1950s, Marilyn developed a taste for Italian food, thanks to her marriage to Joe DiMaggio and his mother's cooking. To please Joe, she experimented in the kitchen and began cooking simple pasta dishes. The marriage didn't last long, but the taste for Italian food did. She ate pasta for the rest of her life.

During her time in New York and her marriage to Arthur Miller, Marilyn was on and off diets. She was photographed by Sam Shaw in 1957 eating a hotdog (without the bun) and seemed to settle into married life. She was also trying to conceive a child, and this effort became the primary focus of her life at this point. She gained some weight during this time (although was never plus size) due to either marital bliss or her miscarriages.

When she wasn't watching her diet, she ate things like hot dogs, caviar, Mexican food, and, again, steak (her favorite). While filming *Let's Make Love* in 1960, she ate a lot of spaghetti and lamb stew.

Because of trouble with her gallbladder, Marilyn had occasional digestive issues that disrupted her appetite. After her gallbladder surgery in 1961 solved this problem, she lost about twenty pounds and returned to the same weight—between 115 and 120—that she had been in the early to mid-1950s.

A typical breakfast during 1961–1962 might consist of egg whites poached in safflower oil, toast, hard-boiled eggs, or a grapefruit. A typical lunch might be a broiled steak.

For taking care of her body, Marilyn learned the importance of exercise in her teens. While living on Catalina Island with Jim Dougherty, she struck up a friendship with former Olympian Howard Corrington, who was on the island training soldiers. Howard taught her the basics of weightlifting and proper technique, skills she utilized for the rest of her life. Jim recalled noticing a change in her strength right away after following Howard's advice. She even had her own weight set, which Philippe Halsman photographed her using in the early 1950s. (Her weights sold at auction at Christie's in 1999 for $59,700.)

In addition to lifting weights, Marilyn tried yoga and jogged regularly during her modeling and starlet years. Later in life she experimented with meditation, which wasn't yet popular at the time.

On the advice of Johnny Hyde, Marilyn took the idea of mind and body unification seriously. Like dancers and athletes, Johnny told her great actors thought of their bodies as instruments. To help her develop these techniques, she read books such as *The Thinking Body*.

· 14 ·

Body of Evidence

Some people have been unkind. If I say I want to grow as an actress, they look at my figure. If I say I want to develop, to learn my craft, they laugh. Somehow they don't expect me to be serious about my work.

—Marilyn Monroe

I'm more sexy than Pamela [Anderson] Lee or whoever else they've got out there these days. Marilyn Monroe was a size 16. That says it all.

—Roseanne Barr, 1996

I've always thought Marilyn Monroe looked fabulous, but I'd kill myself if I was that fat. I went to see her clothes in the exhibition and I wanted to take a tape measure and measure what her hips were. [laughter] She was very big.

—Elizabeth Hurley, 2000

*M*uch has been said about Marilyn Monroe's voluptuous, hourglass figure. As Hollywood's most glamorous movie star, maybe that's inevitable. It seems a little unfair to reduce a woman to mere numbers, but how big or small the proportions of her body were have become almost an obsession for many. In some ways it says more about our society and what we think about beauty and weight than it does about Marilyn and her attractiveness, which are not in dispute.

Both Roseanne Barr and Elizabeth Hurley are right—but at the same time they're both wrong. Marilyn's figure appeared more voluptuous than many beauty standards today because of her hourglass figure, but that hardly makes her "fat" or "very big," to use Elizabeth Hurley's words. Marilyn was quite thin, although she still had curves in the "right" places, making her appear curvy. Similarly, Marilyn did wear a size sixteen dress like Roseanne Barr said, but dress sizes from the 1950s have been renumbered and changed significantly over the years.

Dress sizing as we now know it with numerical labeling didn't exist until after World War II. Since then, the sizing has been modified more than once so the dress "sizes" of women in the 1950s and 1960s are meaningless by today's standards.

Marilyn, as a woman in the 1950s, did indeed have clothing ranging from ten to sixteen (depending on her current weight, the specific garment, and who you ask). However, those dresses would be anywhere from current sizes two to ten today, generally speaking.

Keep in mind, too, when using the term "dress size" it can mean something very different with blouse or trouser sizes. When a woman has an hourglass shape, as Marilyn did, it can sometimes be difficult to find a dress that fits all body parts. A woman may have to go up a size to accommodate her largest part, such as her bust or hips, but then the dress is too large in the waist, which is smaller. Mass-produced clothing is a business of averages, not specifics, for individual bodies.

Marilyn's costumes are a different story because once she became a leading actress, her wardrobe was custom-made to perfectly fit her body, making the size issue moot.

This leads to Marilyn's actual measurements, which vary on the year and who is giving the information. When she started modeling in 1945, the Blue Book Modeling Agency listed her measurements as 36-24-34 and her weight as 120 pounds. She was a "size 12" according to her modeling paperwork. (Her modeling stats also give her height as 5 feet, 6 inches and note "teeth perfect.")

In 1951, *Collier's* magazine claimed she was 37-23-34. The studio's claims about her measurements vary. Twentieth Century-Fox said at different times 36½-23-34, 38-23-36, and 37-23-36. One dressmaker's claim was 35-22-35, although other dressmakers' measurements have appeared, too.

In 1954, Marilyn traveled to Korea to entertain troops fighting in the Korean War, a mission that required a Department of Defense identification card. Her real legal name at the time—Norma Jeane DiMaggio—appears on the card along with her weight, 118 pounds.

Like most women, Marilyn's weight fluctuated depending on numerous factors, including her health, age, pregnancies (she was confirmed pregnant twice), diet, exercise, water weight, and so on. To pinpoint one dress size or one set of measurements as the "only one" is futile and would be inaccurate.

Marilyn stood 5 feet, 5½ inches tall (according to her autopsy report) and generally weighed between 115 and 120 pounds. During her marriage to Arthur Miller she gained twenty pounds or so, bringing her to an estimated 135–140 pounds at her heaviest. Scott Fortner, who owns several pieces of Marilyn's personal clothing, has measured the items in his collection to get a clearer picture of her size. A belt she wore in 1951 measures twenty-seven inches in the waist, but was worn *over* her clothing. Fortner also has a black cocktail dress custom-made for Marilyn in 1959 when she was at her heaviest and the waist measures 28⅓ inches. Because the dress was custom-made specifically for Marilyn, we know this measurement is accurate to her size that year.

After Marilyn's divorce from Arthur, which was finalized in early 1961, she had her gallbladder removed and started a stricter diet and exercise routine, resulting in weight loss and a more toned body. Some people over the years have even commented Marilyn was too thin after shedding pounds. In reality, she had merely returned to her weight from just a few years prior. Although her face was slightly thinner at this point, she was also now in her mid-thirties, an age when many people's faces begin thinning out due to collagen loss.

In May 1962, Marilyn sang "Happy Birthday" to President John F. Kennedy in front of an audience at Madison Square Garden in New York. She had a skin-tight evening gown designed for the event, and her measurements for this dress were 35½-23½-33¼. The fit of this dress is exacting to Marilyn's figure and comes straight from the designer.

At her rehearsal for the "Happy Birthday" performance, Marilyn wore a lime green Pucci blouse. The blouse is now in Scott Fortner's collection and the label inside indicates it is a size fourteen—however, this is a 1960s size fourteen and also an Italian brand.

The guessing game of what size she was may have either amused or horrified Marilyn herself. It's difficult to say. What she did *not* appreciate—as she said herself—was how she felt her desire to study and grow as a respected actress was belittled because of her looks. She was correct to believe her efforts were not taken seriously.

No matter what her size was, no one ever doubted the sexiness of Marilyn Monroe. A lesson to be learned for everyone maybe—she was much more than a dress size.

· 15 ·

Studios

$\mathcal{T}$hroughout her career, Marilyn worked with several studios, but she was only under contract to two: Columbia Pictures and Twentieth Century-Fox. Both had a profound impact on her professional trajectory.

COLUMBIA PICTURES: SIX MONTHS
THAT CHANGED EVERYTHING

An often overlooked, but pivotal, point in Marilyn's career came when she found herself under contract at Columbia Pictures in 1948. Her time there was brief, but her six months at Columbia Pictures left an impression on her both personally and professionally.

Marilyn arrived at Columbia after an uneventful time at Twentieth Century-Fox. After Fox released her, Marilyn struggled with unemployment and the poverty that accompanies it.

Upon the recommendation of Fox executive Joseph Schenck, Columbia agreed to sign the young blonde to a six-month contract. After not working, the guaranteed income brought relief to the money-strapped starlet. She signed on March 9, 1948, for a salary of $125 per week.

Liberated from hardship by her steady paycheck, Marilyn spent her money lavishly instead of saving. She purchased a professional hairdryer, cosmetics, and clothing. She also bought a Ford car; although in fairness, a vehicle to get around the sprawling, public transit-deprived Los Angeles was more a necessity than a luxury.

Marilyn may have gotten a break in terms of her finances, but within days of securing her new job, the worst happened: Aunt Ana Lower, who represented the closest thing Marilyn had to a real parent, passed away on March 14.

By all accounts, losing Aunt Ana devasted Marilyn, who channeled her grief into her work. Columbia provided a place for Marilyn to focus on improving her acting, dancing, and singing.

The month after signing her contract, Marilyn was assigned to work with Columbia's drama coach, Natasha Lytess, who spotted potential in the young contract player but observed that her acting was "cramped."

Marilyn's newfound coach/mentor/friend/protector/sometime room-mate was not the only person at Columbia she met who ended up changing her life. Fred Karger, her vocal coach, would turn into her first great love.

Finally, *Ladies of the Chorus* represented Marilyn's first starring role.

Ultimately, Marilyn's time at Columbia didn't last long. Harry Cohn, one of the most hated and feared men in Hollywood, invited Marilyn out for a day on his yacht. She happily accepted and said she was looking forward to spending time with him *and his wife*. Cohn did not renew her contract and she was once again unemployed.

TWENTIETH CENTURY-FOX

While still a teenager, Norma Jeane was an in-demand model for magazines, pinups, advertisements, and glamour portraits. But modeling was a means to an end. She always knew she wanted to transition to movies.

The opportunity arose in 1946 when twenty-year-old Norma Jeane Dougherty found herself across a desk from executive Ben Lyon, who arranged for a screen test and made the unusual request that it be filmed in color.

She filmed her first screen test on July 23, 1946. With Whitey Snyder's help, she went before the camera with a professionally made-up face and was impressive enough to land her first studio contract.

Fox offered her a fairly standard contract for a newcomer: six months at $75 per week with an option to renew for another six months.

Newly contracted and renamed, Marilyn Monroe went to the lot every day even though she had yet to receive a movie part. Under the studio system, actors typically worked five days a week regardless of if they were currently filming. There were plenty of other tasks to do—pose for still photos, classes in acting, singing, dancing, diction, and posture. Whatever a performer needed, studios had resources. Ever the perfectionist, Marilyn threw herself into everything available to her. She even went so far as to ask about makeup, costuming, lighting, and movie cameras. Ben Lyon noticed the newcomer was putting in long hours and was impressed when she told him if an oppor-tunity presented itself, she wanted to be prepared.

Marilyn didn't receive any roles until 1948 when she was given bit parts in *Scudda Hoo! Scudda Hay!* and *Dangerous Years*. They did nothing to enhance her career and Fox finally decided to drop her contract instead of renewing it. She spent six months at Columbia, then found herself unemployed. She relied on modeling jobs when they presented themselves, but she went through lean times.

Marilyn's fortunes changed when she met Johnny Hyde, who secured her two small parts in big movies, *The Asphalt Jungle* for MGM and *All about Eve* for Twentieth Century-Fox. From there, he was able to negotiate a new contract with Twentieth Century-Fox that set her up with an income for the foreseeable future. Johnny Hyde died in December 1950, but Marilyn signed a new, long-term contract on May 11, 1951.

Marilyn's contract was for seven years with a one-year option, meaning she would be paid $500 per week for the first year. The studio could renew her contract every year with a raise: $750 per week for the second year, $1,250 for the third year, $1,500 for the fourth, $2,000 for the fifth, $2,500 for the sixth, and $3,500 for the seventh.

Marilyn was a full-time employee of Twentieth Century-Fox. Unless approved by Fox, she was not permitted to work for another studio, nor was she allowed to seek employment anywhere or appear in any other medium.

Marilyn's immediate future was secure in terms of work and finances. She was now officially on the radar of Fox's highest-level executives—Darryl Zanuck, the head of production, and Spyros Skouras, the president. As far as Fox was concerned, they had now invested in Marilyn for seven years and the company went about creating a persona for her. During the Golden Age of Hollywood, studios were about making movie stars. No matter how versatile or talented an actor or actress may have been, the audience should never forget who they were watching on the screen. In Marilyn's case, her beauty funneled her into the sex symbol category and from there she was further narrowed down to a dim-witted one.

As she was still in her starlet phase, she had little to no say in which movies she was cast or the kind of roles she played. Marilyn had some smaller roles, often sexy secretaries. She was given a huge opportunity with the drama *Don't Bother to Knock* (1952), in which she plays an unstable babysitter opposite Richard Widmark. It's considered by many to be one of her finest performances, but Fox had other plans.

A STAR IS BORN

The same year *Don't Bother to Knock* came out, Fox finally gave Marilyn a starring vehicle in the form of *Niagara*, a modern film noir in vibrant Technicolor set against Niagara Falls. Marilyn played Rose, a femme fatale whose attempt to murder her husband backfires. After *Niagara* wrapped, Marilyn was given two star-making roles in the back-to-back movies *Gentlemen Prefer Blondes* and *How to Marry a Millionaire*. All three movies were released in 1953. What followed was an avalanche of publicity for Marilyn: magazine covers, billboards, awards for best newcomer and comedic performances, appearances at parties and premieres, guest starring on *The Jack Benny Show*, and the ultimate prize—placing her hands and feet in wet cement at Grauman's Chinese Theatre in Hollywood. Marilyn Monroe had finally achieved everything she had dreamed of as a little girl. And yet, something wasn't quite right.

To Marilyn's horror, she discovered her acting wasn't taken seriously. In *Gentlemen Prefer Blondes* and *How to Marry a Millionaire* she essentially played the same character—a sexy dumb blonde obsessed with finding a rich husband. Worse, fans believed the persona manufactured by the studio was who she was in real life. As soon as Marilyn was finding professional success, she realized her career was headed in a direction she disliked.

Marilyn was next placed in *River of No Return*, which she referred to as a "Z-grade Western." Then came *The Girl in Pink Tights*, an update of a 1943 Betty Grable vehicle called *Coney Island*. She didn't want to star as another one-dimensional blonde, but she was especially suspicious when she wasn't permitted to see a copy of the script. One thing she did know: Her costar, Frank Sinatra, was going to make $5,000 per week when she was now a big star and locked into her $1,500 per week. With *Pink Tights*, Marilyn showed the first signs of the rebellion that was yet to come.

On the first day of filming, Marilyn was a no-show. The studio threatened her with suspension and dangled Sheree North's name as a threat to replace her. She responded by traveling to San Francisco with Joe DiMaggio for the holidays. While she was away, a copy of the script was sent to her and, as it turned out, Marilyn had been right all along. It was a terrible part in a bland movie. The characters she played in *Gentlemen Prefer Blondes* and *How to Marry a Millionaire* may have been dumb blondes but at least the scripts were funny—and both movies had the rare distinction of being carried by female leads. Twentieth Century-Fox may have created a new superstar but they struggled when it came to finding a place for her. Meanwhile, Marilyn married Joe DiMaggio and left for Japan as the female half of a newly minted power couple.

Finally, Twentieth Century-Fox had no choice but to acquiesce and drop *The Girl in Pink Tights*. The company regrouped and offered Marilyn a package deal of two movies, *There's No Business Like Show Business* and *The Seven Year Itch*. She would also receive a bonus of $100,000 for *Itch*, which was to be directed by Billy Wilder. Marilyn had no interest in *There's No Business Like Show Business*, a lackluster tribute to Irving Berlin, but *The Seven Year Itch* had great potential. The female lead was another sexy blonde, but the movie was based on a sensationally successful Broadway play by George Axelrod, and Billy Wilder was one of the best directors working in Hollywood.

When Marilyn returned, she kept her word and performed in both movies, first filming *There's No Business Like Show Business* and then *The Seven Year Itch*. The latter went on to become not just what we would now call a blockbuster but created a cultural touchstone with the images of Marilyn holding down her skirt while standing on a subway grate.

Knowing they had a huge success coming with the release of *The Seven Year Itch*, Twentieth Century-Fox figuratively rolled out the red carpet for Marilyn when they threw her a lavish party to anoint her as the Queen of Hollywood. It took place in November 1954 shortly after the movie wrapped at her favorite restaurant, Romanoff's. Clark Gable, her childhood hero, attended and asked her to dance.

ON STRIKE!

And then she disappeared. Just before the holiday season of 1954, Marilyn slipped out of town and went into hiding on the East Coast with friend and new business partner Milton Greene at his family's home.

In an interview with *The Saturday Evening Post* dated May 19, 1956, Marilyn reflected on escaping Hollywood. "I disappeared because if people won't listen to you, there's no point in talking to people," Marilyn told journalist Pete Martin. "You're just banging your head against a wall. If you can't do what they want you to do, the thing is to leave. I never got a chance to learn anything in Hollywood. They worked me too fast. They rushed me from one picture into another.

"I know who started all of those stories which were sent out about me after I left Hollywood the last time," she continued. "One paper had an editorial about me. It said: 'Marilyn Monroe is a very stupid girl to give up all the wonderful things the movie industry has done for her and go to New York to learn how to act.' Those weren't the exact words, but that was the idea. That editorial was supposed to scare me, but it didn't, and when I read it and I realized that it wasn't frightening me, I felt strong. That's why I know I'm stronger than I was."

Milton Greene's attorneys and Marilyn's new agency, MCA, went to work on negotiating with Twentieth Century-Fox on a new contract, demanding more money, more control over scripts and director approval, and the right to produce with her own company. Fox retaliated by not paying Marilyn the $100,000 bonus they had promised her for *The Seven Year Itch*.

The first half of 1955 was spent with both sides going back and forth, each with valid points. Fox charged that Marilyn still owed the company four more years on her original contract. Marilyn's representatives pointed out she had not received her bonus.

The deciding factor came in the form of *The Seven Year Itch* becoming a juggernaut at the box office upon its release in the summer of 1955. The public had voted with their wallets and they wanted Marilyn. Twentieth Century-Fox relented, and Marilyn signed her new contract on December 31, 1955. The new terms included:

- Four movies over seven years
- $100,000 per movie, plus a percentage of the profits
- Script approval
- Director approval
- Cinematographer approval
- $500 allowance per week while filming
- Nonexclusivity for Fox—she was permitted to star in one independent film per year
- Annual retainer of $100,000
- Milton Greene was to receive an annual salary of $75,000

It was about as much control as a star could hope for under the studio system at the time. The nonexclusivity was important not just because she could work for other companies, but with her new company, Marilyn Monroe Productions, she could also produce. Marilyn was not the first female movie star to launch her own production company, but it was still an impressive step, as was the right to approve scripts, directors, and cinematographers.

In 1956, Marilyn jumped enthusiastically into *Bus Stop*, a drama based on the play by William Inge. Emboldened by her new contract, the Actors Studio training she had received while in New York, and a relationship with playwright Arthur Miller, Marilyn turned in one of her finest performances. But she did not come back to Fox again until four years later in 1960.

A ROCKY LAST FEW YEARS

Marilyn's absence was due to a couple of reasons. In addition to starring in films for other companies, at home she was struggling with fertility issues, which resulted in the loss of at least two babies. The emotional roller coaster of finally getting pregnant and then losing her children was physically and mentally exhausting for her.

It was also a time of great fear when it came to the House Un-American Activities Committee (HUAC), which was questioning—and often blacklisting—artists, writers, and entertainers with frequently unfounded accusations of Communism. Arthur Miller was now under the intense scrutiny of

HUAC, probably because his romance with Marilyn Monroe placed him in a brighter national spotlight. His left-leaning opinions made him a prime target to be called for testifying in front of the committee. Marilyn would have been guilty by association. Even after the HUAC drama, Marilyn did not return to Fox until *Let's Make Love.*

Marilyn returned to Fox again in 1962 for *Something's Got to Give* after a devastating 1960 and 1961. Marilyn looked as beautiful as ever but was difficult to work with when she returned.

Unable to cope with her any longer, the studio that had been Marilyn's home fired her on June 8, 1962. They pulled the plug on *Something's Got to Give*, then almost immediately regretted it.

Marilyn's representatives and the studio soon entered negotiations to resume filming. As it turned out, Marilyn passed away before a new contract was signed so it is unclear if her side would have tried to negotiate for better terms.

· 16 ·

The Calendar That Almost
Stopped Time

$\mathcal{I}$n the late 1940s, Marilyn's career was at the lowest it had ever been and would ever go. Both Twentieth Century-Fox and Columbia Pictures had dropped her. Modeling work was irregular.

She needed money, which is why on a day in 1948 she was so eager to arrive on time for a casting call. While driving on the stretch of Sunset Boulevard known as "the Strip," Marilyn was involved in a minor fender bender. No one was hurt, but she was now at risk of losing out on a job. A Good Samaritan by the name of Tom Kelley stopped his car when he saw a young woman at the side of the road in distress. When she explained why she was so upset, Kelley, a photographer, understood her despair. He handed her a few dollars, which was enough to catch a taxi, and he agreed to stay behind with the car. As Marilyn prepared to leave for her job interview, he also gave her a business card. If she ever wanted to pose for him, he said, give him a call.

That moment presented itself when Marilyn's car was impounded and she didn't have the $50 needed to get it back. Marilyn phoned Kelley and agreed to pose nude for him provided his wife was also present for the shoot. Kelley agreed and arranged for Marilyn's sitting on May 27. Kelley and his wife Natalie prepared a backdrop of red velvet, which Marilyn posed against for approximately two hours. To help Marilyn feel comfortable, Kelley played Artie Shaw music while he snapped pictures.

When the photo session ended, Marilyn signed the model release with the name "Mona Monroe" and received the $50 needed for her car. Then she went to Barney's Beanery for a bowl of chili.

In total, Tom Kelley took twenty-four photos of her although only two would go on to find publication. One of the photos was sold to a calendar called Golden Dreams, which was circulated to businesses catering to men—for example, mechanic shops, plumbers, and electricians. The model appearing on the 1952 calendar was not identified but somehow, someone figured out the identity of the nude woman partially covering her face was rising starlet Marilyn Monroe.

There are different stories as to how the story broke, but that didn't matter to Twentieth Century-Fox, which had recently invested millions on their budding movie star. They were at risk of losing her to scandal. No movie star had been proven to have posed nude at this point, although decades later photos of other stars would surface. Marilyn was the first, and the studio didn't know what to do. Initially, studio bosses were inclined to deny the woman in the photo was Marilyn Monroe. It's generally believed it was Marilyn who prevailed on executives that honesty was the best policy.

Marilyn turned to her friend and trusted ally, Sidney Skolsky, who also happened to be a powerful gossip columnist and brilliant at spinning stories. Together, Marilyn and Sidney came up with ways to address tough questions and speak with the press so the moviegoing public would listen to her story with sympathy instead of judgment. In their version, the story about getting her car back was changed to needing rent money. The reason was not everyone understood that cars were the only mode of transportation in Los Angeles. Most large cities have public transportation and unless someone lived in L.A., the car story didn't make sense—but everyone knows what it's like to come up with rent money.

The article ran on March 13, 1952.

Beautiful Marilyn Monroe Is That Blonde On The Calendar.
By Aline Mosby.
HOLLYWOOD
A photograph of a beautiful nude blonde on a 1952 calendar is hanging in garages and barbershops all over the nation today.

Marilyn Monroe admitted today that the beauty is she.

She posed, stretched out on crumpled red velvet, for the artistic photo three years ago because "I was broke and needed the money."

"Oh, the calendar's hanging in garages all over town," said Marilyn. "Why deny it? You can get one any place.

"Besides, I'm not ashamed of it. I've done nothing wrong."

The beautiful blonde now gets a fat paycheck every week from an excited Twentieth Century-Fox Studio. She's rated the most sensational sweater girl since Lana Turner . . . she lives in an expensive hotel room . . . she dines at Romanoff's.

But in 1949 she was just another scared young blonde, struggling to find fame in the magic city, and all alone. As a child she lived in a Hollywood orphanage.

She was pushed around among 12 sets of foster parents before she turned an insecure 16.

After an unsuccessful marriage, she moved into Hollywood's famed Studio Club, home of hopeful actresses.

"I was a week behind on my rent," she explained. "I had to have the money. A photographer, Tom Kelley, had asked me before to pose but I'd never do it. This time I called him and said I would as soon as possible, to get it over with.

"His wife was there. They're both very nice. We did two poses, one standing up with my head turned profile, and another lying on some red velvet."

Marilyn speaks in a breathless, soft voice, and she's always very serious about every word she says.

"Tom didn't think anyone would recognize me," she said.

"But when the picture came out, everybody knew me. I'd never have done it if I'd known things would happen in Hollywood so fast for me."

Marilyn's bosses at plushy Fox Studio reached for the ulcer tablets when the calendar blossomed out in January.

"I was told I should deny I posed . . . but I'd rather be honest about it.

"I've gotten a lot of fan letters on it. The men like the picture and want copies. The women, well . . .

"One gossip columnist said I'd autographed the pictures and handed them out and said 'Art for art's sake.' I never said that.

"Why, I only gave two away," said Marilyn, and blinked those big, blue eyes.

In the weeks following the initial article, Marilyn answered other questions presented to her by journalists. As was becoming typical of her interviews, she displayed a natural wit that disarmed even the harshest writers. During a now-famous exchange, when a reporter asked if it was true she had nothing on while posing, she replied, "Oh no, I had the radio on."

Marilyn's tactic worked, and soon the public—most of whom had not seen the photo—were decidedly seeing things through her eyes. Why yes, that poor orphan girl just needed rent money! And the female body is beautiful. She did nothing wrong!

Marilyn survived her first Hollywood scandal, but the publicity created a demand to see the photograph itself. The nude photos were officially considered obscenity so getting a copy of the calendar or photo proved difficult. In June 1952, Jerry Karpman and Morrie Kaplen were brought up on charges of conducting a mail-order business to distribute the photos. (Marilyn had to testify because they used the name "Marilyn Monroe" for their business.)

In 1953, Phil Max, who owned a camera store on Wilshire Boulevard in Los Angeles was arrested and fined for displaying a photo in his display window. Still, most Americans had yet to see Marilyn Monroe in the nude.

That changed when a former *Esquire* magazine copyeditor named Hugh Hefner published the first issue of *Playboy* in December 1953. He had taken out a loan and raised $8,000 from investors to buy the $500 publishing rights to the Kelley photo and for printing costs. The cover featured a photo of Marilyn smiling and waving, captured in a moment from her appearance as Grand Marshall at the Miss America pageant on September 2, 1952.

Now more readily available for the first time, Marilyn's nude photo from 1949 was on the newsstands—and the first edition of a brand-new magazine sold an astounding fifty thousand copies.

Hugh Hefner never met Marilyn Monroe, nor did he ever thank her for helping launch his empire. She had signed a model release, and therefore did not receive a portion of *Playboy*'s profits from that December 1953 issue, nor did she receive profits from the massive number of calendar reprints that went into production during the 1950s. Legally, the publishers of the photos didn't have to pay Monroe.

Despite the initial worry in 1952, in the end, Marilyn's career went on and she experienced great success. Although there was an elephant in the room—no one mentioned the fact that Hugh Hefner was willing to risk Marilyn's career for the sake of his magazine launch. If Marilyn's career hadn't survived, what would have happened to her? Would he have helped her?

If Marilyn held any resentment against him, she moved past it. In 1962, she was in talks to possibly do an article with *Playboy*. A memo from Pat Newcomb to Marilyn dated July 11 reads "The Playboy story awaits our decision."

After Marilyn's death, Hefner always spoke highly of her. In the January 2000 issue of *Playboy*, Marilyn was voted No. 1 in the feature "Centerfolds of the Century." The ultimate tribute he paid to her was purchasing the crypt next to hers for $75,000 in 1992.

It should be noted that Marilyn's calendar appearance was not the only time she appeared nude. In the late 1940s, Marilyn modeled for pinup artist Earl Moran numerous times and appears seminude in a couple of the photos. These photos were used as references for his artwork and were not released to the public until after Moran's death. Marilyn was always comfortable with her body and sexuality. She appeared seminude in photos by Bert Stern and on the set of *Something's Got to Give* in 1962.

III

THE SPOTLIGHT

· 17 ·

A Life Devoted to Movies

$\mathcal{S}$ome of Marilyn's earliest memories involved going to see movies.

When Norma Jeane was a little girl in Hollywood and lived within walking distance of theatres, it was not unusual for her to sit in a movie theatre all day. "I remember when I was a kid sitting in the front row at the movies on Saturday afternoon—and I would never come out of the movie. They would have to come and get me. I would sit in the front row and think how wonderful it would be to be an actress."

Dangerous Years
Twentieth Century-Fox
Release date: December 7, 1947
Plot: A teacher who tries to end local teen delinquency by opening a boys club discovers a group of kids stealing from a local warehouse. While confronting the thieves, one of the boys, Danny, shoots and kills the teacher, with whom he has already a bad relationship. The boys flee to a local hangout, the Gopher Hole, to make it look like they've been there the entire time. The District Attorney charges Danny with first-degree murder. During the trial, an elderly woman who used to run the orphanage where Danny grew up comes forward and reveals to him that he is the District Attorney's biological son from a marriage that was annulled. The old woman had substituted a young girl in Danny's place when she told the District Attorney he had a child with the wife, who disappeared because she believed the girl needed a secure home more than Danny. Not wanting to disrupt the home life this girl now has with her "father," Danny begs the old woman not to say anything. She dies before she can testify, taking the secret with her to the grave. Danny is convicted of the murder but does not receive the death penalty.

Behind the scenes: *Dangerous Years* was the first of Marilyn's movies to be released, although it was not the first movie she worked on. Her bit part was as a tough cookie waitress named Eve. *Dangerous Years* was made during Marilyn's original contract at Twentieth Century-Fox. The film received poor reviews and today is remembered primarily because of Marilyn's appearance.

Scudda Hoo! Scudda Hay!
Twentieth Century-Fox
Release date: April 14, 1948
Plot: Two stepbrothers in a rural midwestern community live with their mother on a farm. One brother hires on at another nearby farm and falls in love with the owner's daughter, who encourages both brothers to compete for her attention.
Behind the scenes: *Scudda Hoo! Scudda Hay!* was the first movie Marilyn reported to work on, although it was released after *Dangerous Years*. Most of Marilyn's "performance," which was brief, ended up on the cutting room floor and she is glimpsed only for an instant. She was uncredited at the time but is now closely associated with the movie because it is her first role. *Scudda Hoo! Scudda Hay!* served as a vehicle for one of the Twentieth Century-Fox's top leading ladies at the time, June Haver. A very young Natalie Wood, who would later successfully transition to adult roles, is also featured. Like *Dangerous Years*, this movie was made while Marilyn was under her first contract with Twentieth Century-Fox.

Ladies of the Chorus
Columbia Pictures
Release date: February 10, 1949
Plot: Mother Mae (Adele Jergens) and daughter Peggy (Marilyn Monroe) both work as burlesque chorus girls. A young man named Randy (Rand Brooks) from a rich family becomes smitten with Peggy after seeing her performance but soon learns her mother does not permit her to date. To win Peggy over, he begins anonymously sending her orchids every day. Peggy goes to the florist to learn her secret admirer's identity, and he coincidentally shows up to order the next orchid. They go out on a date, and he proposes. Mae has grave concerns, as her marriage to Peggy's father was also to a man from a wealthy family, and their social classes drove them apart. Randy invites Mae and Peggy to meet his mother, who is delighted her son is in love. Her old friend is a Burlesque comic, who has been quietly in love with Mae for years. Randy's mother tells her high society friends she used to be a dancer as

well, so they accept Randy and Peggy as a couple. Mae and Peggy later learn Randy's mother was never a dancer but made the story up to help the young couple find acceptance among her wealthy peers. Mae and Peggy then decide to both get married in a double wedding.

Behind the scenes: Actress Adele Jergens plays Marilyn's mother in the film, despite the fact she was just nine years older than her costar. Marilyn worked at Columbia for just six months, but it turned out to be a pivotal time. She met her first acting coach Natasha Lytess, fell in love with vocal coach Fred Karger and received her first starring role, albeit in a B film. (B-movies were lower-budget pictures that typically served as the second film of a double feature. The term has a broader definition today.) Even with the B status, it was a huge step for Marilyn's career. *Ladies of the Chorus* was a national, commercial release and she was one of two main stars. She gets to sing, dance, and have her first on-screen romance opposite Rand Brooks, who played Charles Hamilton, Scarlett O'Hara's first husband in *Gone with the Wind*.

Love Happy
United Artists
Release date: October 12, 1949
Plot: Based on a story by Harpo Marx, the original movie concept was intended as a solo vehicle for him. Harpo plays a thief and Grouch Marx plays Detective Grunion, who is searching for valuable diamonds belonging to the Romanoffs. The caper leads Detective Grunion to a troupe of performers putting on a revue called "Love Happy."
Behind the scenes: Marilyn's walk-on part was brief but memorable. As a "client," she seeks out Detective Grunion's help because "some men are following me." Groucho delivers his line, "Really? I can't understand why!" with trademark sarcasm. To promote the film, the studio sent her on a publicity tour, which raised her profile as a result. *Love Happy* also provided Marilyn with the opportunity to appear on screen with the Marx Brothers, who were still a box office draw more than two decades into their careers.

A Ticket to Tomahawk
Twentieth Century-Fox
Release date: May 19, 1950
Plot: Set in 1870s Colorado, *A Ticket to Tomahawk* is a musical Western about railroads expanding into the Rockies. Stagecoach operators, however, plan on sabotaging the operation.
Behind the scenes: Marilyn plays an uncredited chorus girl and won the role after Johnny Hyde encouraged her to audition.

The Asphalt Jungle
MGM
Release date: May 12, 1950

Plot: Based on a novel by the same name, *The Asphalt Jungle* follows professional criminal Doc Riedenschneider, who is released from prison only to begin setting up his next heist. Doc hires a safecracker, a getaway driver, and a petty criminal to help rob a jewelry store, but things go wrong when the safe explosion knocks out the power grid.

Behind the scenes: Marilyn secured her role as a mob mistress with the help of Johnny Hyde, who recognized appearing in a film directed by John Huston would benefit her career. Huston would later become one of the names on Marilyn's list of approved directors she would work with after her successful strike against Twentieth Century-Fox in the mid-1950s. An interesting side note is that the cinematographer was Hal Rosson, who had once been married to Marilyn's childhood idol, Jean Harlow.

Director John Huston instructs Marilyn on the set of The Asphalt Jungle *in 1950. The man standing behind her is cinematographer Hal Rosson, whose credits include such great movies as* The Wizard of Oz *and* Singin' in the Rain. *Coincidentally, he was once married to Marilyn's childhood idol, Jean Harlow.*
MGM / Photofest © MGM

The Fireball
Twentieth Century-Fox
Release date: August 16, 1950
Plot: Tired of being picked on for his short stature and lack of athletic skills, Johnny (Mickey Rooney) runs away from a home for boys and becomes a roller skating champion. His success leads him to become arrogant and intolerable until he is humbled by a bout of polio.
Behind the scenes: Marilyn played a small role as a roller derby fan in this mostly forgettable film. Mickey Rooney was one of Hollywood's greatest stars during the Golden Era, but his stories of Marilyn Monroe are often called into question for their accuracy. For instance, he claimed to have given her the name "Marilyn Monroe," introduced her to Johnny Hyde, personally awarded her the part in *The Fireball*, and even hinted there may have been a romance. There is no evidence to support any of his claims.

All about Eve
Twentieth Century-Fox
Release date: October 27, 1950
Plot: Considered one of the best movies in cinema history, *All about Eve* follows the great—but aging—Broadway actress Margo Channing (Bette Davis), who is pursued by sycophant fan and aspiring actress Eve Harrington (Anne Baxter). Soon Eve begins to manipulate her way into Margo's life and uses the accomplished star to further her own career goals. By the end of the movie, Eve is a star in her own right and a young woman named Phoebe (Barbara Bates) similarly begins to insert herself into Eve's life, implying the cycle will continue.
Behind the scenes: Marilyn won the part of Miss Casswell, a beautiful young starlet, with the help of Johnny Hyde. She was intimidated by working with Bette Davis and required multiple takes as a result. Another problem for Marilyn was the jealousy of Zsa Zsa Gabor, whose husband George Sanders was a costar in the film. Marilyn and George had lunch in the studio commissary one day while filming because only one table was open. Word got back to Zsa Zsa that her husband was seen dining with the beautiful blonde starlet. After that day, George began keeping his distance from Marilyn between takes to avoid conflict at home.

Right Cross
MGM
Release date: November 15, 1950
Plot: Mexican American boxer Johnny Monterez (Ricardo Montalban) has become ashamed of his heritage after suffering discrimination. Hiding an

injured right hand and in love with his trainer's daughter (June Allyson), Johnny decides to risk everything on getting a big payout to help her and the wheelchair-bound trainer. During an argument with his friend Rick (Dick Powell), Johnny throws a powerful right punch and permanently damages his hand. Johnny ultimately wins the girl and makes up with his best friend. **Behind the scenes:** Once again uncredited and appearing only briefly, Marilyn is a sexy dame who chats with Dick Powell's character while sitting at a table in a restaurant.

Home Town Story
MGM
Release date: May 18, 1951
Plot: Former politician Blake Washburn (Jeffrey Lynn) becomes editor of a small-town newspaper to regain traction in his political career. He plans to expose the evils of big business, but after his little sister is trapped in a mine during a school outing, his feelings change after large corporations help rescue her.
Behind the scenes: In a small role, Marilyn plays a secretary for the first time. Other sexy secretary roles during her starlet years awaited her. Marilyn Monroe wasn't the only future star in *Home Town Story*. Alan Hale Jr., who would later go on to fame as the Skipper on *Gilligan's Island*, was also in the movie.

As Young as You Feel
Twentieth Century-Fox
Release date: June 13, 1951
Plot: After printer John R. Hodges (Monty Woolley) is forced to retire, he disguises himself as a man named Harold Cleveland to tout the virtues of older and more experienced workers. His ruse causes company president Louis McKinley (Albert Dekker) to change his retirement policy and hire back some of the employees recently pushed out. When the real Harold Cleveland discovers someone is using his name, it creates a problem. After realizing Hodges meant no harm by using the Cleveland name, the real Harold Cleveland is impressed with John Hodges and offers him a job. However, McKinley offers to give Hodges his original job back. Marilyn stars in a bit part as a secretary named Harriet, whom company boss Louis McKinley shows an interest in, despite being married.
Behind the scenes: Marilyn struggled on the set, as Johnny Hyde had recently passed away. She was often in tears and had puffy eyes when called to the set. While making this film, Marilyn began dating director Elia Kazan. He visited her on the set, and during one of these visits brought a close friend, Arthur Miller. Marilyn and Arthur's romance was still a few years off, but as

they got to know each other over the next couple of days, the seeds of interest were planted on both sides.

Love Nest
Twentieth Century-Fox
Release date: October 10, 1951
Plot: Wife Connie (June Haver) purchases a New York City apartment building with the belief that being a landlord will give her husband Jim (William Lundigan) time to write his novel. Unfortunately, the building requires a lot of time and money to maintain. The building is also filled with colorful tenants, including Eadie (Leatrice Joy), a widow without much money, and a neighbor, Charley (Frank Fay) who swindles lonely wealthy widows for money. Charley falls for Eadie even though she doesn't have much money. Meanwhile, Jim rents an apartment to an old "Army buddy," Bobbie, who Connie thinks is a man. In reality, Bobbie is Roberta, a beautiful blonde (Marilyn Monroe) and Connie becomes jealous. Charley goes to jail for his past crimes, reforms while incarcerated, and reunites with his love Eadie after release. Jim writes about Charley in a book, which becomes a bestseller. Jim and Connie use the royalties to fix up the apartment and live happily ever after.
Behind the scenes: *Love Nest* was based on the novel *The Reluctant Landlord* by Scott Corbett. Now one of Twentieth Century-Fox's contract players, Marilyn found herself in another sexy blonde role.

Let's Make It Legal
Twentieth Century-Fox
Release date: November 6, 1951
Plot: Hugh (MacDonald Carey) and Miriam Halsworth (Claudette Colbert) are a married couple who separate due to his gambling. Miriam moves in with her daughter (Barbara Bates) and son-in-law (Robert Wagner) while Hugh lives at the hotel where he works. Millionaire Victor (Zachary Scott) reenters the scene after losing Miriam's heart to Hugh twenty years earlier. Intent on winning Miriam back, Victor tells her the two men gambled for her in a game of craps, with Hugh winning. Infuriated, Miriam confronts her estranged husband, who admits the story is true—but he cheated with loaded dice. Miriam is pleased with the explanation and they reconcile. Marilyn's character Joyce is vying for the attention of Victor, who only has eyes for his old love, Miriam.
Behind the scenes: Director Richard Sale became infuriated with Marilyn for her tardiness to the set. He dressed her down in front of the cast and crew and demanded that she apologize to everyone. Embarrassed, Marilyn stormed

off the set, only to return later. There are also shades of the real Marilyn in this role. She was squeezed into the picture as a way to get her some screen time and her name on a movie poster, so writers weaved inferences about her personal life into the brief role, and they weren't flattering. Her character, Joyce, is a gold-digging model posing for cheesecake photos. Joyce pursues a wealthy man on a golf course (Marilyn had met John Carroll on a golf course). Later, Joyce is seen at a poker party attended by several influential men (a reference to Joseph Schenck and his poker parties).

Clash by Night
RKO
Release date: June 16, 1952

Plot: *Clash by Night* follows Mae (Barbara Stanwyck), who returns to her bleak seaside hometown and her brother Joe (Keith Andes), with whom she does not get along. She marries Jerry (Paul Douglas), a nice man and fisherman who owns his own boat. Mae begins an affair with Jerry's friend Earl (Robert Ryan), another restless resident of the dreary town. When Jerry learns the truth, he confronts the couple and nearly strangles Earl to death. Mae changes her mind about wanting to leave Jerry for Earl and returns to her husband, who forgives her.

Behind the scenes: Based on a play by Clifford Odets, the original setting was Staten Island. Director Fritz Lang changed the location to Monterey, a fishing town on California's central coast, known for John Steinbeck's *Cannery Row*. Marilyn plays Peggy (her second time playing a character named Peggy), Joe's girlfriend who is more gracious to the returning Mae.

Marilyn made this picture for RKO while on loan from Twentieth Century-Fox and her friend, journalist Sidney Skolsky, is often credited with helping Marilyn get the part. It was Skolsky who arranged for Marilyn to lunch with producer Jerry Wald, who became convinced she was the right actress for the part. *Clash by Night* was a production she was already familiar with, as she had studied the Odets play during classes at the Actors Lab. Odets was also a friend and colleague of Elia Kazan, Marilyn's one-time lover.

The movie was filmed primarily on location in Monterey, and many of Marilyn's negative traits on set were starting to emerge during the shoot. She was already struggling to show up on time, but her anxiety and perfectionism caused her to break out in red blotches on her skin, get physically sick and ask for multiple takes, even when everyone else was satisfied with the scene. It was also the first movie where acting coach Natasha Lytess was asserting herself more prominently on set and caused conflict with the director. That wasn't the end of her troubles during production. Around this time, the scandal of her nude calendar began to break.

"She was awkward," Barbara Stanwyck later said. "She couldn't get out of her own way. She wasn't disciplined, and she was often late, and she drove Bob Ryan, Paul Douglas and myself out of our minds . . . but she didn't do it viciously, and there was a sort of magic about her, which we all recognized at once. Her phobias, or whatever they were, came later; she seemed just like a carefree kid."

We're Not Married
Twentieth Century-Fox
Release date: July 11, 1952
Plot: Five couples learn they are not legally married because a justice of the peace (Victor Moore) married them before his appointment went into effect. The plot follows each couple's response upon learning the news. Marilyn and David Wayne play Jeff and Annabel Norris. Jeff is fed up with Annabel's focus on her pageant career, as he is left caring for their baby while she competes. After discovering they are not married, he makes sure she loses her Mrs. Mississippi title. They reconcile and become re-engaged, and he cheers her on as she wins the Miss Mississippi pageant.
Behind the scenes: Twentieth Century-Fox created the role of Annabel specifically so Marilyn could wear bathing suits on screen. The movie was written by Nunnally Johnson, who would go on write other Marilyn projects, *O. Henry's Full House*, *How to Marry a Millionaire*, and *Something's Got to Give*. Marilyn reconnected with David Wayne in *How to Marry a Millionaire*, where they played a married couple for the second time. Wayne was also in *As Young as You Feel* and *O. Henry's Full House*, making him Marilyn's most frequent costar.

Don't Bother to Knock
Twentieth Century-Fox
Release date: July 18, 1952
Plot: Hotel employee Eddie (Elisha Cook Jr.) recommends his niece Nell (Marilyn Monroe) as a babysitter for guests. Once in the hotel room where she is sitting a little girl, Nell flirts with a handsome pilot (Richard Widmark) through a window. As the evening progresses, Nell starts to unravel and it becomes clear she is unstable.
Behind the scenes: Director Roy Ward Baker utilized Marilyn's real anxiety to the advantage of the film by often using first takes for the final cut. *Don't Bother to Knock* is considered by many

Marilyn and Richard Widmark in a promotional image for Don't Bother to Knock *(1952). By Historical Media—Ebay/Wikimedia Commons*

to be one of Marilyn's best performances. During production, the news Marilyn had posed nude a few years prior became a huge scandal.

Monkey Business
Twentieth Century-Fox
Release date: September 5, 1952
Plot: Dr. Barnaby Fulton (Cary Grant), a chemist working on a youth elixir, is unaware that one of his research chimpanzees has gotten loose in the laboratory, mixed a beaker, and dumped the contents into the office water cooler. Dr. Fulton drinks from the water cooler and finds himself acting like a younger man. Invigorated, he spends the day roller skating and swimming with his much-younger secretary, Lois (Marilyn Monroe).

Mrs. Fulton (Ginger Rogers) drinks the concoction and begins acting like a young schoolgirl. Other employees at the office begin drinking from the water cooler and they all begin acting like children. By the end, the couple mentally returns to their real ages but are emotionally renewed by the experience.

Behind the scenes: Although playing yet another sexy secretary, it was becoming clear Marilyn's star was on the rise. Audiences were starting to respond warmly to her, and the studio noticed potential. Furthermore, her private life was attracting attention. When new boyfriend Joe DiMaggio visited Marilyn on the set, photographers jumped to snap pictures of the couple—it was all about Marilyn Monroe, Hollywood's newest blonde, and American hero Joe DiMaggio.

O. Henry's Full House
Twentieth Century-Fox
Release date: October 16, 1952
Plot: The movie *O. Henry's Full House* was an anthology of five shorter films. Marilyn appeared in the installment titled "The Cop and the Anthem," which starred Charles Laughton and David Wayne. Soapy (Laughton) is a down-on-his-luck hobo-type who plans to commit a petty crime so he can spend the cold winter in jail where it's warm and he has shelter. He lets Horace (Wayne), a fellow ne'er-do-well, in on his plan.

One of Soapy's schemes involves harassing a woman on the street in the hopes her frightened screams will attract the attention of the police. The plan backfires when the woman he approaches (Marilyn Monroe) turns out to be a streetwalker, who is not only unafraid of his advances but asks him to buy her a drink. Realizing his mistake, Soapy apologizes and explains, "I haven't got a dime to my name." To apologize for the error, he gifts her his only possession, an umbrella. "My compliments to a charming, delightful young lady." As she watches Soapy bumble off, the nameless woman raises a handkerchief to her eye and says wistfully, "He called me a lady!"

After his encounter with the streetwalker, Soapy meets up with Horace in a church. He realizes he doesn't need to spend his winter in jail to stay warm. He can get a job and find a real home. Police then spot Soapy and Horace. Horace has clean shoes to show the officer but Soapy is arrested for vagrancy.

Behind the scenes: Marilyn is prominently featured in the trailer and on the poster, but she appears in *O. Henry's Full House* only briefly. The higher profile is an indication that Twentieth Century-Fox was beginning to invest in her potential.

When asked about her costar Charles Laughton years later by W. J. Weatherby, Marilyn said, "He played a gentleman bum, and I was a lady streetwalker. I was overawed at first, but he was very nice to me. He accepted me as an equal. I enjoyed working with him. He was like a character out of Charles Dickens."

The movie was narrated by author John Steinbeck. In 2016, a letter written by Steinbeck to Marilyn requesting an autograph for his teenage nephew-in-law surfaced. Dated April 28, 1955, the letter is filled with good-natured humor.

Dear Marilyn,

In my whole experience I have never known anyone to ask for an auto-graph for himself. It is always for a child or an ancient aunt, which gets very tiresome, as you know better than I. It is therefore, with a certain nau-sea that I tell you that I have a nephew-in-law who lives in Austin, Texas, whose name is Jon Atkinson. He has his foot in the door of puberty, but that is only one of his problems. You are the other.

I know that you are not made of celestial ether, but he doesn't. A sug-gestion that you have normal functions would shock him deeply and I'm not going to be the one to tell him.

On a recent trip to Texas, my wife made the fatal error of telling Jon that I had met you. He doesn't really believe it, but his respect for me has gone up even for lying about it.

Now, I get asked for all kinds of silly favors, so I have no hesitation in asking one of you. Would you send him, in my care, a picture of yourself, perhaps in pensive, girlish mood, inscribed to him by name and indicating that you are aware of his existence. He is already your slave. This would make him mine.

If you will do this, I will send you a guest key to the ladies' entrance of Fort Knox and, furthermore, I will like you very much.

Yours sincerely,

John Steinbeck

Initials typed at the bottom of the letter indicate it was dictated. The signature is also likely secretarial, as it does not match other examples of Steinbeck's handwriting.

The letter was part of Marilyn estate, indicating she had saved it. After the letter was discovered and put up for auction, the nephew-in-law in question, Jon Atkinson, was asked by a reporter if he had ever received an autographed photo of Marilyn Monroe. Now a retired minister, Atkinson expressed fond but vague memories of the era in which John Steinbeck requested an autograph on his behalf—but he does not recall ever receiving the autographed photo.

Niagara
Twentieth Century-Fox
Release date: January 21, 1953
Plot: Set against the backdrop of Niagara Falls, this noir-style movie centers around an unfaithful wife, Rose Loomis (Marilyn Monroe) who schemes with her lover to murder her deranged husband, George (Joseph Cotten). Ray and Polly Cutler (Max Showalter and Jean Peters) befriend the troubled couple at the cabins where they are all staying and are witness to their unusual behavior. George kills both Rose and her lover, before dying while saving Mrs. Cutler from going over the Falls.
Behind the scenes: *Niagara* was conceived when producer Charles Brackett wanted to set a movie against the backdrop of Niagara Falls. Instead of focusing on a honeymoon storyline, which is what was synonymous with the location, he turned the movie into a thriller. The "honeymoon" aspect is still somewhat represented by the Cutlers, who are celebrating a delayed honeymoon and have already been married for some time. *Niagara* was filmed during the summer of 1952 and released in January 1953, the first of Marilyn's movies to be released during her breakout year. (*Gentlemen Prefer Blondes* and *How to Marry a Millionaire* were the other two.) Marilyn fans will take note of two things: One, Marilyn's walk away from the camera is the longest in movie history and also establishes the sexy walk for which she is now known. And two, *Niagara* is the first movie in which the Marilyn Monroe persona appears fully formed.

Gentlemen Prefer Blondes
Twentieth Century-Fox
Release date: July 1, 1953
Plot: Lorelei Lee (Marilyn Monroe) and Dorothy Shaw (Jane Russell) are best friends and showgirls. They board an ocean liner to cross the Atlantic en route to France, where money- and diamond-obsessed Lorelei plans to marry

Augustus "Gus" Esmond (Tommy Noonan), a nerdy heir who is hopelessly smitten with Lorelei. During the trip, Lorelei looks for prospective suitors for Dorothy, who flirts with the Olympic team that is also aboard the ship.

Lorelei charms a wealthy old man, Piggy (Charles Coburn), who gifts her a tiara belonging to his wife, who in turn believes Lorelei stole it. Dorothy falls in love with Ernie Malone (Elliott Reid), an undercover private detective hired by Gus's father to follow Lorelei. Upon arriving in France, Lorelei and Dorothy find Gus's father has cut off their line of credit thanks to Malone's reports from the ship. In need of money, the women find work as showgirls in Paris.

Marilyn's rendition of "Diamonds Are a Girl's Best Friend" in Gentlemen Prefer Blondes *became a sensation and is still influential on fashion and dance numbers today.*
Twentieth Century-Fox / Photofest / © Twentieth Century-Fox

Gus arrives in Paris and is in the audience for Lorelei's performance of "Diamonds Are a Girl's Best Friend." Meanwhile, in a French court, Dorothy pretends to be Lorelei by wearing a blonde wig and resolves the tiara issue. Malone redeems himself by revealing Piggy now has the tiara and it was never stolen, which exonerates Lorelei. Back in the theatre, Lorelei impresses Gus's father by telling him a man being rich is like a girl being pretty—you might not marry someone because of wealth or beauty, but it helps.

Lorelei and Dorothy wear matching dresses to marry their respective sweethearts in a double wedding. Diamond-obsessed Lorelei's engagement ring is significantly larger than Dorothy's ring.

Behind the scenes: *Gentlemen Prefer Blondes* was based on a comedic 1925 novel by Anita Loos. The book is written in diary form (complete with grammatical and spelling errors) by Lorelei Lee, a blonde flapper. Although the movie version of *Gentlemen Prefer Blondes* does not indicate which era it is set in, it's generally assumed to be the 1950s. A few elements of the 1920s remain intact, however. For instance, Dorothy becomes enamored by the Olympic team as they sail to Paris, which hosted the 1924 Olympics.

Marilyn learned she had won the role of Lorelei Lee on June 1, 1952—her twenty-sixth birthday. She had not been the most obvious choice at first. Carol Channing had played Lorelei on Broadway to rave reviews and would have been an obvious selection. The most likely Lorelei, however, would have been Betty Grable, Twentieth Century-Fox's reigning top blonde. Two things made Marilyn the more desirable choice over Betty for studio head Darryl Zanuck. First, he liked Marilyn's sexy rendition of "Do It Again" and saw potential in her musical abilities. Second, Betty made more money than Marilyn, so the company would save money.

Marilyn studied hard for her role as Lorelei. Filming started in late 1952 and in February 1953, Hedda Hopper reported that Marilyn had gone to a burlesque show to watch the showgirls.

> When Marilyn Monroe sings "Diamonds Are a Girl's Best Friend," she'll be against a background of red velvet and on a red floor. She does the old burlesque bumps and grinds in "Gentlemen Prefer Blondes." Marilyn visited a burlesque show and when she came out, she said. "Just imagine. Some of those girls didn't have a stitch on!"

Gentlemen Prefer Blondes has become one of Marilyn's most beloved and best-remembered movies, in large part because of "Diamonds Are a Girl's Best Friend," which has been often imitated over the years.

It was during the filming of *Gentlemen Prefer Blondes* that Marilyn finally received the dressing room she had been asking for. Fox had repeatedly denied Marilyn's request with the reminder, "You're not a star." Fed up, Marilyn replied maybe she wasn't a star, but the movie was *Gentlemen Prefer Blondes* and she was *the blonde*. Fox finally granted her request.

Part of the movie's lasting appeal is the friendship between Dorothy Shaw and Lorelei Lee. No matter what happens during the story, the women stick together and look out for each other. That warmth and mutual respect, it turns out, were genuine. Marilyn's costar Jane Russell was a perfect complement to her both on and off screen. When Jane realized Marilyn's anxiety made it difficult for her to leave her dressing room, Jane began making friendly stops by Marilyn's door and offered to walk with her to the set. It helped Marilyn tremendously.

"Jane and I had an immediate rapport," Marilyn told Ralph Roberts. "I sure learned a lot from her. I also learned through her the importance of having friendly people around."

How to Marry a Millionaire
Twentieth Century-Fox
Release date: November 5, 1953
Plot: Three top fashion models, Schatze (Lauren Bacall), Loco (Betty Grable), and Pola (Marilyn Monroe) hatch a plan to rent a penthouse in the posh Manhattan neighborhood of Sutton Place to attract rich suitors. The penthouse has been rented out while its owner Freddie (David Wayne) is living in Europe to hide from the IRS.

For months the plan is unsuccessful until Loco comes home from the grocery store assisted by Tom Brookman (Cameron Mitchell), who promptly develops a crush on the brash Schatze, only for her to rebuff him. The models begin dating wealthy men, but none of their relationships work out. Loco's man turns out to be married and grumpy. While on a trip to the mountains with him, she falls in love with a local park ranger (Rory Calhoun).

Pola, who doesn't like wearing her glasses, gets on an airplane to meet her wealthy new beau's family only to have her seatmate tell her she's on the wrong flight. He turns out to be Freddie, the man who owns the penthouse

Betty Grable, Marilyn Monroe, and Lauren Bacall in a scene from How to Marry a Millionaire, *one of the first movies filmed in CinemaScope. The plot follows three fashion models looking for rich husbands and is often noted for the leading ladies' glamorous costumes, which were designed by Travilla.*
Elisa Jordan Collection

where the models have been living. When he encourages Pola to put her glasses on and then compliments her on how beautiful she looks in them, she falls hopelessly in love.

Schatze pursues a wealthy older man J.D. (William Powell), even though she does not love him. Tom Brookman continues to pursue her, and believing he is a "gas pump jockey," she tries to avoid his advances. Against her will, she falls in love with him anyway. A guilty conscience leads her to call off her wedding to J.D. at the alter, and she marries Tom instead. It is only after they are married that Schatze discovers her new husband is a millionaire.

Behind the scenes: *How to Marry a Millionaire* has the rare distinction of starring three women in the lead roles. Men came secondary to the ladies and their comedic caper.

Twentieth Century-Fox was known for its stable of beautiful blondes, and *How to Marry a Millionaire* in many ways represents the passing of the baton from Betty Grable to Marilyn Monroe. Many entertainment journalists eagerly awaited news from the set of a bitter blonde feud. Much to their disappointment, Betty and Marilyn got along just fine.

Betty's reign at Fox had been impressive. For thirteen years running she had been a top ten box office star. Now it was clear the studio was grooming Marilyn to take over as top blonde. First, Marilyn had been cast as Lorelei Lee in *Gentlemen Prefer Blondes*, even though Betty made it known she wanted the part. Now the two women were on relatively equal footing in *Millionaire* despite Marilyn being a newcomer. Betty's name appeared above Marilyn's on the screen credits, but in advertisements, Marilyn's name came before Betty's.

Lesser actresses might have taken out their frustrations on the newcomer. Betty realized, however, the issue was not with Marilyn but the studio itself and never appeared to resent the younger actress. On the contrary, the two women posed for photos together while attending Walter Winchell's birthday party at Ciro's on the Sunset Strip in 1953. Betty even noted the day when she had to leave the set early to pick up one of her daughters after a playground injury at school. Marilyn, she said, was the only person who called to make sure the child was okay. Betty also spoke up in Marilyn's defense when she was criticized for wearing a revealing dress to an awards ceremony.

There is a popular story in which Betty told Marilyn, "I've had mine, honey. Go get yours." According to Hollywood historian April Vevea, there is no evidence to support she said this.

In addition to being successful at the box office and solidifying Marilyn's status as a bankable leading lady, the movie was also a technological achievement. *How to Marry a Millionaire* and *The Robe* were the first movies to utilize CinemaScope, Fox's widescreen format. The two movies went into production around the same time but Twentieth Century-Fox released *The Robe* first, believing the biblical epic was more family-friendly and would find a larger audience.

In her first official appearance on television, Marilyn appeared on *The Jack Benny Show* to promote the movie and CinemaScope.

In her 1978 autobiography, *Lauren Bacall by Myself*, Lauren recalled her time on the set. "I returned home to prepare for my role of Schatze in *How to Marry a Millionaire*. Marilyn Monroe and Betty Grable were to be in it as well—it was about three girls looking for millionaire husbands, and it was funny, witty and even touching. I hadn't really known either of my co-stars before and hoped the association would be a good one.

"As CinemaScope was a new experiment for everyone, it was difficult. One had to keep actors moving and not too close together, as the screen was long and narrow. You shot longer scenes in CinemaScope, five or six pages without a stop, and I liked that—it felt closer to the stage and better for me. Betty Grable was a funny, outgoing woman, totally professional and easy. Marilyn was frightened, insecure—trusted only her coach and was always late. During our scenes she'd look at my forehead instead of my eyes; and at the end of the take, look to her coach, standing behind Jean Negulesco, for approval. If the headshake was no, she'd insist on another take. A scene often went to fifteen or more takes, which meant I'd have to be good in all of them as no one knew which one would be used. Not easy—often irritating. And yet I couldn't dislike Marilyn. She had no meanness in her—no bitchery. She just had to concentrate on herself and the people who were there only for her. I had met her a few times before, and liked her. Grable and I decided we'd try and make it easier for her, make her feel she could trust us. I think she finally did."

As it turns out, Lauren Bacall was correct in her assessment. "Betty was adorable. So funny and so witty. She kept us all in stitches," Marilyn told Ralph Roberts in 1960. "Bacall showed a professionalism I found remarkable. She was always prepared, knew her lines and her character, but she wasn't so rigid that she couldn't improvise when something unexpected came up."

River of No Return
Twentieth Century-Fox
Release date: April 30, 1954
Plot: Westerns had long been a popular genre, so it should come as no surprise that Marilyn would eventually make one. *River of No Return* is set in 1875. Marilyn plays saloon singer Kay; her fiancé is gambler Harry (Rory Calhoun). Matt (Robert Mitchum) has recently been released from prison for killing a man while defending another. As a widower, he reclaims his son Mark (Tommy Rettig), and the two set out to build a homestead.

River of No Return was filmed against the backdrop of majestic Banff, Alberta, Canada, but making the movie was not a positive experience for Marilyn. She was injured on the set, clashed with the director, and hated the finished picture, which she called a "Z-grade western."
By Bert Parry—Page 39 / Wikimedia Commons

Matt and Mark rescue Kay and Harry, who are poorly navigating a raft on the way to file a gold claim Harry won in a poker game. Harry offers to purchase Matt's rifle and horse. When Matt declines, Harry knocks Matt unconscious and proceeds to steal the rifle and horse anyway.

Kay stays behind with Matt and Mark, and the three continue down the rapids while encountering a series of dangerous scenarios. Although still engaged to Harry, Kay starts to admire Matt's bravery. Kay discovers Harry did not win the gold claim as he told her; he stole it. Mark, meanwhile, is heartbroken to learn his father had been in prison for murder and has trouble comprehending the idea of killing someone, even for defense.

Kay, Matt, and Mark finally arrive in Council City, where they are reunited with Harry. Matt and Harry get into a confrontation and when Harry tries to shoot Matt, Mark shoots Harry in the back to protect his father.

After Harry's death, Kay gets work singing in a saloon. Matt finds her sitting on a piano singing the song "River of No Return," strides across the floor, and throws her over his shoulder to take her home with him and Mark.

Behind the scenes: *River of No Return* was filmed on location in Banff, Alberta, Canada, in 1953. It was not an easy shoot for Marilyn. Director Otto Preminger was gruff and tyrannical under the best of circumstances but bullied Marilyn about her ability to learn lines and forced her to perform stunts she was not comfortable doing. Like other directors before him, Preminger struggled with the presence of Marilyn's acting coach Natasha Lytess, who was once again undermining a director's instructions on the set. The director and acting coach clashed, and Marilyn retaliated by showing up late and holding up production.

Marilyn's experience on the set went from bad to worse when she nearly drowned while rehearsing a raft scene. To protect her costume, Marilyn wore chest-high waders. She slipped and fell into the water. The waders filled with water, weighed her down, and held her under. Robert Mitchum and others on the set realized Marilyn was unable to come up for air and pulled her out of the water to safety. She badly sprained her ankle during the accident and ended up with a cast and on crutches, which Mitchum jovially referred to as her "supporting cast."

The sprained ankle was legitimate but many came to believe Marilyn milked the injury in an effort for Preminger to lighten up with her. At one point, Marilyn was so miserable during filming, boyfriend Joe DiMaggio flew to Canada and made a rare appearance on one of her sets to cheer her up.

Marilyn's sour feelings about the movie remained and a few years later called it "a grade-Z cowboy movie in which the acting finished second to the scenery and the CinemaScope process."

Otto Preminger similarly harbored negative feelings about *River of No Return* and vowed to never work with Marilyn Monroe again.

There's No Business Like Show Business
Twentieth Century-Fox
Release date: December 16, 1954

Plot: Conceived as a tribute to Irving Berlin, *There's No Business Like Show Business* showcases many of the master songwriter's beloved classics. The plotline follows husband and wife vaudevillians Terence and Molly Donahue (Dan Dailey and Ethel Merman). The Donahues' three children join their act, making them the Five Donahues. Eventually, the children begin pursuing other paths in life. The movie featured lavish costumes and production numbers but was considered a box office failure.

Behind the scenes: Marilyn did not want the part in *There's No Business Like Show Business* but had already refused to work on a movie called *The Girl with Pink Tights*. For her rebellion, she was suspended, making it more difficult to refuse another movie. To entice her, Twentieth Century-Fox promised Marilyn the lead role in *The Seven Year Itch* if she made *Business* first. *Itch*, a massive hit on the Broadway stage, was a plumb part and Marilyn knew it. She accepted the deal.

Marilyn later told her friend and masseuse Ralph Roberts, "Ethel Merman ridiculed my singing. Mitzi Gaynor klutzed over my dancing. It was an agonizing time. I felt it wrong, and unnecessary, for a real singer to make fun of a would-be singer, and an established dancer to likewise a non-real dancer."

Ralph noted, "She wasn't bitter about it, just observing how veterans sometimes act about newcomers." It should also be noted that Marilyn never complained publicly about her experience. Instead, her comments to Ralph were between friends.

Two important things happened on the *Business* set. One, Marilyn met Paula Strasberg, wife of acting coach Lee Strasberg, and their daughter, actress Susan Strasberg. Even though Marilyn was still working exclusively with Natasha Lytess for acting lessons, Susan later recalled Marilyn whispering to her how she intended to move to New York to study under her father, Lee.

Second, new husband Joe DiMaggio visited the set on exactly the wrong day—Marilyn was scantily clad for her musical number "Heat Wave." Joe was livid watching his wife gyrate around while singing suggestive lyrics.

The Seven Year Itch
Twentieth Century-Fox
Release date: June 3, 1955
Plot: Richard Sherman (Tom Ewell) finds himself alone with his overactive imagination after his wife and young son leave Manhattan for the summer. He discovers his upstairs neighbors are also away for the summer and have rented their apartment to a pretty aspiring actress (Marilyn Monroe) and soon he finds himself fantasizing about her. He invites her over for a drink but finds he is too tempted by her presence and asks her to leave.

Tormented by his lusty thoughts for his new neighbor, Richard convinces himself his wife is having an affair. For revenge, he takes his neighbor to the movies. As they walk home, he watches as she cools herself from the summer heat by standing over a subway grate. Back at the apartment building, he invites her in. She tells him she is appearing on television the next day and begs to spend the night in his air-conditioned apartment. She takes the bed and he sleeps on the couch. The next morning, Richard tells his neighbor she's welcome to stay in his air-conditioned apartment and he runs off to join his wife.

Behind the scenes: *The Seven Year Itch* was based on a successful Broadway play of the same name. Twentieth Century-Fox purchased the rights to the play by George Axelrod, who helped cowrite the screenplay with director Billy Wilder. Both writers expressed frustration that the Hays Office, which dictated Hollywood's morality codes in film, continually forced changes to the script, making the movie less funny than the original play. Axelrod and Wilder removed the single most significant plot point, which was an affair between Richard Sherman and "The Girl." For the movie, their relationship is reduced to two kisses.

The scene that literally stopped traffic: Marilyn standing on a New York City subway grate became a zeitgeist moment in the twentieth century.
Published by Corpus Christi Caller-Times—photo from Associated Press / Wikimedia Commons

The Seven Year Itch contains the now-famous scene in which Marilyn's white skirt billows up around her legs. The scene was filmed twice, once on the streets of New York in front of a crowd of onlookers, who shouted and hooted so loudly that the footage was unusable. Wilder filmed Marilyn again under the more controlled setting of a sound stage back in Los Angeles. In the film, Marilyn's skirt does not go as high as it did during the first shoot on the New York streets.

The scene created a stir for film fans and popular culture in general, but it was nothing compared to what happened in Marilyn's private life. Joe DiMaggio was one of the onlookers at the New York street shoot, and the sight of his wife showing off her body, especially in front of whistling men, was too much for him. He stormed off and their marriage ended shortly thereafter.

After what had been a very public breakup, reporters, photographers, and fans were shocked to see Marilyn arrive on Joe's arm for the movie's premiere on June 1, 1955—Marilyn's twenty-ninth birthday. Their appearance sparked gossip that the baseball legend and glamorous movie star would reunite and claim their place as a favorite celebrity couple. For outsiders, it seemed likely given the high-profile nature of the event and Joe's willingness to attend. In the past, he had typically eschewed making public appearances with her, especially larger-scale events. As it turned out, they did not reconcile and she went on to begin a relationship with Arthur Miller.

Today, Marilyn standing on a subway grate while holding her skirt down in *The Seven Year Itch* has become among the most iconic images in Hollywood history. In an odd twist of fate, the very scene responsible for ending Marilyn's marriage also catapulted her into immortality.

Bus Stop
Twentieth Century-Fox
Release date: August 31, 1956
Plot: Beau (Don Murray), a young and naïve cowboy from Montana, has traveled to Phoenix for a rodeo. He is chaperoned by a father figure named Virgil (Arthur O'Connell). While in Phoenix, Beau falls for Cherie (Marilyn Monroe), a saloon singer with ambitions of moving to Hollywood. After forcing a kiss on her, he comes to believe they are engaged even though Cherie insists she has no intention of marrying him.

Not taking no for an answer, the next day Beau applies for a marriage license. He finds Cherie sleeping in her apartment, and lets her know they can get married at the rodeo. He rousts her out of bed and drags her to the rodeo and its accompanying parade, but while he competes in an event,

Cherie runs away. Beau finds her at the saloon, kidnaps her, and forces her on the bus headed for Montana. The bus becomes stuck at a coffee shop due to snow. The bus driver, coffee shop owner, and waitress become aware Cherie is being held against her will. Virgil and the bus driver beat up Beau to make him apologize and leave Cherie alone. Humiliated, he is unable to apologize.

The next morning, the snow has melted and the bus is ready to move on to Montana. Beau finally humbles himself and offers Cherie a sincere apology. Cherie tells him she is not the woman he thinks she is—she has had many boyfriends. Beau confesses he is inexperienced when it comes to girls and still wishes she would come home with him. Moved by his vulnerability

Bus Stop was a huge leap in Marilyn's career, with many critics pinpointing the movie as one of her best performances. She plays saloon singer Cherie to Don Murray's Beau, a rodeo star who is inexperienced with women. Wax Publications publisher of Film Bulletin—Page 23 / Wikimedia Commons

and newfound respect, Cherie decides to accompany him back to Montana.

Behind the scenes: *Bus Stop* was a movie of firsts for Marilyn. It was the first movie Marilyn made after renegotiating a new contract with Twentieth Century-Fox. It was the first movie Marilyn made under the acting instruction of Lee and Paula Strasberg. It was also the first movie where friend and business partner Milton Greene was present on the set.

Marilyn was deeply involved with playwright Arthur Miller at this point, but because his divorce was not yet final, they kept their relationship secret. Filming took production to Arizona and Idaho, but while in Los Angeles, the couple worked out ways to rendezvous. During the week, Marilyn lived in a rented house in Beverly Hills with the Greene family. Simultaneously, Arthur was staying in Reno, Nevada, to establish six weeks of residency to get a quick divorce. On the weekends, Marilyn and Arthur secretly met at the Chateau Marmont, a hotel at the foot of the Sunset Strip. The Chateau has always been famous for its discretion and for keeping the secrets of its guests.

The Prince and the Showgirl
Warner Bros.
Release date: June 13, 1957 (United States), July 3, 1957 (United Kingdom)
Plot: Set in 1911 London just before the coronation of George V, an American showgirl, Elsie Marina (Marilyn Monroe), finds herself invited by a widowed Prince Regent (Laurence Olivier) to the Carpathian embassy for dinner. Expecting to attend a large party, Elsie is surprised to discover an intimate meal planned for just her and the Prince Regent. Although she drinks to excess during the evening, the Prince Regent tries but fails to seduce the showgirl.

While at the palace, Elsie overhears a treasonous plot by the Prince Regent's son to overthrow his father. Unwilling to wait until he comes of age, the young prince plans to take power early, which means unseating his father. She does not tell the Prince Regent but does inform his mother-in-law, who invites her to George V's coronation in place of her lady-in-waiting, who is ill.

Elsie's temporary lady-in-waiting status helps her resolve the conflict between father and son. The Carpathian royals ready themselves to return home, and the Prince Regent, now in love with Elsie, hopes she will accompany him. In eighteen months, his regency will be over and the obligations to his son completed. Elsie's commitment to her show in London is also eighteen months. Ultimately, they decide not to become a couple.

Behind the scenes: Marilyn Monroe Productions, which was co-owned by photographer Milton Greene, purchased the rights to the play *The Sleeping Prince*, which was adapted into a movie script. Both Marilyn and Milton were producers of the film, although Milton took on the day-to-day operations concerning legalities, finances, and supervision. Marilyn focused primarily on her responsibilities in front of the camera as a leading lady. Her director and costar for the movie, now titled *The Prince and the Showgirl*, was renowned British actor Laurence Olivier, who had played the part in the theatre version. His costar on the stage had been his real-life wife, Vivien Leigh. He did not say explicitly, but it is quite possible he resented the fact his wife would not be his costar in the movie adaptation.

In early photos of Marilyn Monroe and Laurence Olivier, the two appeared friendly toward one another. Once filming began, however, the Monroe-Olivier partnership soon fell apart. The two stars did *not* get along or agree on anything. Filming was contentious. Both Marilyn and Laurence Olivier were difficult in their respective ways. Marilyn was chronically late to the set and used Method Acting techniques, which infuriated Olivier. For his part, Olivier was dismissive of Marilyn's acting style and openly rude to her in front of the entire cast and crew. At one point, when Olivier directed Marilyn to just "be sexy," she walked off the set.

Marilyn Monroe Productions purchased the rights to the play The Sleeping Prince, *which starred husband and wife Lawrence Olivier and Vivien Leigh on the stage. Olivier retained his starring role and directed the film version. Marilyn played the role of the showgirl, Elsie Marina. Filming took place at Pinewood Studios in England, about 18 miles outside of London.* By Milton H. Greene / Wikimedia Commons

In later years, Olivier spoke negatively of his experiences with Marilyn, expressing frustration with her chronic tardiness on the set. He also dismissed her acting abilities. "Inside, somewhere or another, she doesn't want to act," he said. "She wants to show herself. That's another thing. She is a model. By accident or by a villainy of nature, forced to be an actress. That's the answer to her."

Olivier made some valid points about Marilyn's behavior, such as showing up late. At the same time, he had shown her considerable disrespect on the set. In the years following the release of *The Prince and the Showgirl*, many critics have praised Marilyn's performance above Olivier's. While critiquing a performance is a matter of conjecture, Olivier also had a long-standing and well-earned reputation for jealousy. His comments could be tainted by the criticism of his performance and her ever-increasing popularity.

In his autobiography, Arthur Miller remembers, "There was a genuine conflict, it seemed to me, between two different styles not merely of acting but of life. The comedy of the script came from the timeworn dilemma of the powerful representative of society, the prince, reduced to helplessness in the hands of the innocent prole ignorant of all but sex and ending with all the power. Marilyn knew more than most about such circumstances. But her want of training, as she saw it, in high comedy, not to mention her unrelenting uncertainty, pressed her to try to delve too deeply into a character that was essentially a series of lines crafted to address a situation, an outside with no inside. Olivier, who had mastered most of the great roles, knew how little there was in this one, but to say outright that all she needed for it was herself would be demeaning. And for Paula [Strasberg] this admission would mean that the Method had no application here. So the heart of the matter was that nobody could tell the truth, and Marilyn was finally in no position to hear it if it was told. I did not know how to help her, not least because in the rushes she seemed so perfectly delectable, despite all her anxiety, even lending the film a depth of pathos it did not really have."

The Prince and the Showgirl received renewed interest with the release of *My Week with Marilyn* (2011), a movie based on two books by Colin Clark. The story depicts his perspective as an assistant during the film's production but is generally considered fiction by historians.

Some Like It Hot
United Artists
Release date: March 29, 1959

Plot: Two male musicians and best buddies, Joe (Tony Curtis) and Jerry (Jack Lemmon), accidentally witness the St. Valentine's Day Massacre in 1929. To avoid mafia retaliation for witnessing the crime, they leave Chicago disguised as women and join an all-girl band for a musical engagement in Florida.

Problems soon develop when Joe falls in love with the band's beautiful blonde singer, Sugar (Marilyn Monroe), and when Jerry (while dressed as

Now considered the greatest comedy of all time by the American Film Institute, Some Like it Hot *became one of Marilyn's signature films.*
TCM Mediaroom / Wikimedia Commons

a woman) finds an eccentric millionaire, Osgood (Joe E. Brown), who has become infatuated with Jerry's female alter ego.

Their trouble increases when a large mafia convention arrives at the hotel where the band lives and performs every night. The mafiosos soon discover the true identities of Joe and Jerry, putting their lives in danger. Joe, Jerry, and Sugar escape via Osgood's boat and the movie ends with one of the most famous and funny lines in movie history.

Behind the scenes: *Some Like It Hot* was the second collaboration between writer-director Billy Wilder and Marilyn, who created magic together during *The Seven Year Itch* just a couple of years before. Unlike her recent experience with Laurence Olivier, who had no patience for Method acting and took his frustrations out on Marilyn for using such techniques, Billy Wilder didn't care how actors produced their performances. He cared only about the results.

Marilyn shines in her role as Sugar, although she did not initially want the part. By this point in her career, she had fought hard to get roles beyond "dumb blondes," and Sugar most certainly fell into the dumb blonde category. Two things changed her mind. One was the opinion of her husband Arthur Miller, who read the script and assured Marilyn the movie was a first-rate comedy. The second was simple necessity: The Millers needed money after Marilyn bought out Milton Greene, her business partner in Marilyn Monroe Productions, and for Arthur's legal bills after testifying before HUAC.

Before production began, one major casting change took place. Billy Wilder originally wanted Frank Sinatra to play Joe, but when the singer failed to show up at a meeting the part went to Tony Curtis instead. To kick off the movie's production, the cast—Tony Curtis included—and crew gathered for a press party at the Beverly Hills Hotel on July 8, 1958. The next big change was switching from filming in Technicolor to black and white. Marilyn had a Technicolor clause written into her contract and was disappointed when she arrived on the set to discover the change. Makeup tests during preproduction revealed that the thick makeup required to make Tony Curtis and Jack Lemmon look like women produced an unnatural, sickly tint to their faces. Black-and-white film hid the problem and ended up feeling accurate for a movie taking place in 1929.

Marilyn's performance is a bright spot in an already brilliant comedy, but her on-set behavior was taxing for the entire cast and crew. As was common with Marilyn, she was chronically late to the set and had difficulty remembering lines. Cue cards were hidden all over the set to assist her in reciting lines. Insecurity and perfectionism caused her to insist on an excessive number of retakes, which exhausted the other actors and crew and led to filming delays. It became clear her on-set difficulties had worsened since *The Seven Year Itch*.

Billy Wilder later said, "She was constantly late, and she demanded take after take after take—the Strasbergs, after all, had taught her to do things again and again and again until she felt she got them right. Well, now she had us doing things again and again, our nice sane budget was going up like a rocket, our cast relations were a shambles, and I was on the verge of a breakdown. To tell you the truth, she was impossible—not just difficult. Yes, the final product was worth it—but at the time we were never convinced there would *be* a final product."

This behavior was also seen by Jack Lemmon, who was typically gracious in how he spoke about the troubled star.

"I liked her very much and I got along great with her," he recalled. "She had a lot of problems, she was basically an unhappy girl. She drove Billy and Tony crazy, she drove me a little crazy too but I didn't let on and it didn't bother me as much as it bothered them, and it was almost always because of the same thing: the lateness. She had a problem, God knows what it was. She just could not come out of her dressing room, fully made-up and dressed and everything, the little portable dressing room on the set, until she was ready to face the camera psychologically. Until then you could knock on her door and she'd say 'fuck off,' literally. She just could not or would not come out."

To complicate matters, Marilyn was pregnant after trouble conceiving and a previous miscarriage. (She miscarried this baby, too, after production wrapped.) Arthur Miller approached Billy Wilder and asked if Marilyn could just work mornings due to her condition. Billy balked at the suggestion— Marilyn couldn't even get to the set until afternoon. Any resemblance to a civil relationship between the director and the playwright crumbled at that moment.

Marilyn did not get along with costar Tony Curtis, with whom she shared many of her scenes. After watching the daily rushes of his kissing scene with Marilyn, he stood up when the lights came on and proclaimed it was "like kissing Hitler." (Curtis was Jewish.) In the years following the movie, Curtis denied making the remark but everyone in the room had heard him. Jack Lemmon, who was there when it happened, diplomatically said he didn't blame him for denying it. Curtis later changed his story and claimed the Hitler remark was a joke. And contrary to popular belief, he claimed, he and Marilyn not only got along but had an affair during production—in fact, the baby she was carrying was his, not Arthur Miller's. Most historians do not believe Curtis's story.

After production wrapped, Billy Wilder vented his frustration with Marilyn publicly. Immediately after *Some Like It Hot* wrapped, his response to being asked if he would ever work with Marilyn again was, "I have discussed this with my doctor and my psychiatrist, and they tell me I'm too old and too rich to go through this again."

Infuriated, on February 11, 1959, Arthur Miller fired off an angry telegram to the director.

> Dear Billie [*sic*] I cannot let your vicious attack on Marilyn go unchallenged. You were officially informed by Marilyn's physician that due to her pregnancy she was not able to work a full day. You choose [*sic*] to ignore this fact during the making of the picture and worse yet, assiduously avoided mentioning it in your attack on her. Fact is, she went on with the picture out of a sense of responsibility not only to herself but to you and the cast and producer. 12 hours after the last shooting day her miscarriage began. Now that the hit for which she is so largely responsible is in your hands and its income to you assured, this attack upon her is contemptible. I will add only that she began this picture with a throat infection so serious that a specialist forbade her to work at all until it was cured. She went on nevertheless. Your jokes, Billie, are not quote hilarious enough to conceal the fact. You are an unjust man and a cruel one. My only solace is that despite you her beauty and her humanity shine through as they always have.
> Arthur Miller

In December 1958, the first sneak preview was arranged to disastrous results. The audience had been expecting to watch *Suddenly, Last Summer*, but instead were met with *Some Like It Hot*. Not once did the audience laugh and offended parents marched their children out of the theatre after just a few minutes.

Critics and audiences were considerably kinder to the movie once it was released to the public. The film was applauded for its comedic timing, snappy dialogue, and sophisticated performances. As time went on, Billy Wilder's assessment of Marilyn softened, and he said he *would* work with her again—the results on camera were worth the trouble. "She was an absolute genius as a comedic actress, with an extraordinary sense for comedic dialogue. It was a God-given gift. Believe me, in the last fifteen years there were ten projects that came to me, and I'd start working on them and I'd think, 'It's not going to work. It needs Marilyn Monroe.' Nobody else is in that orbit; everyone else is earthbound by comparison."

The exterior scenes of the "Florida" hotel were filmed at Hotel del Coronado, a historic Victorian-era resort on Coronado Beach near San Diego. Movie interiors were filmed at the lot in Hollywood. *Some Like It Hot* continues to garner praise since its release. Marilyn won a Golden Globe award for Best Actress in a Comedy or Musical. She was pictured proudly clutching her award on the night she won it. Billy Wilder was nominated for an Academy Award in the Best Director category. Other nominations included Best Actor

(Jack Lemmon), Best Screenplay (Billy Wilder and I. A. L. Diamond), Best Cinematography—black and white (Charles Lang), Best Art Direction—black and white (Ted Haworth and Edward G. Boyle). Orry-Kelly won Best Costume Design. The American Film Institute named *Some Like It Hot* the best comedy of all time.

Let's Make Love
Twentieth Century-Fox
Release date: August 24, 1960
Plot: French billionaire Jean-Marc Clement (Yves Montand) learns an off-Broadway show is satirizing his life. Clement visits the theatre and watches actress Amanda Dell (Marilyn Monroe) singing "My Heart Belongs to Daddy," a song by Cole Porter.

After the dance number, a director mistakes Clement for an actor and offers him the part of Jean-Marc Clement. Clement does not correct the director and accepts the offer to play himself. To keep up with his scam, he claims his name is Alexander Dumas. (Attentive viewers will recognize this name as the author of *The Three Musketeers*.) During rehearsals, Clement finds himself getting jealous of the friendship between Amanda and costar Alexander Kaufman (Tony Randall). To improve his performance, Clement hires Gene Kelly, Milton Berle, and Bing Crosby (all playing themselves) to coach him.

When production is threatened, Clement secretly funds the show. After Clement and Amanda fall in love, he confesses his true identity to her. At

Marilyn knew Let's Make Love *wasn't a good script, but she was contractually obligated to make another movie for Twentieth Century-Fox. Marilyn and leading man Yves Montand began an affair in real life, but their off-camera chemistry did not translate to the screen.* Film trailer screenshot (Twentieth Century-Fox) / Wikimedia Commons

first, Amanda doesn't believe him, but when she realizes he is indeed Jean-Marc Clement, she is furious with his deception. After a confrontation, Amanda runs to an elevator to escape, only for Clement to stop the elevator and let himself in. They continue arguing; Clement breaks out into song and wins Amanda's love.

Behind the scenes: When Marilyn signed her new contract with Twentieth Century-Fox in 1955, she agreed to make four movies for the studio. By 1960, she had completed only one: *Bus Stop. The Prince and the Showgirl* (1957) and *Some Like It Hot* (1959) were for Warner Bros. and United Artists, respectively. When Marilyn was presented with *Let's Make Love*, she was not in a place to turn it down, despite the lackluster script. Aside from problems with the script, several elements were put in place that made the movie look better on paper, including a star-studded cast, George Cukor directing, and Jack Cole, who guided Marilyn to excellence for "Diamonds Are a Girl's Best Friend," choreographing the dance numbers.

After nearly every leading man in Hollywood turned down the role of Jean-Marc Clement, Yves Montand was cast in the part, even though he did not speak English well and had to learn his lines phonetically. Additionally, Marilyn was unhappy with many of her costumes. Designer Dorothy Jeakins, who had dressed Marilyn beautifully in *Niagara*, had created some unflattering outfits for *Let's Make Love*, which ultimately cost her the job of designing for Marilyn on *The Misfits*.

The biggest production wrinkle, however, was the off-screen affair between Marilyn and Yves Montand.

Arthur Miller, already at work on *The Misfits*, required time away from Los Angeles to collaborate with John Huston at his home in Ireland. His absence allowed Marilyn and Montand to strike up a romance, which was a poorly kept secret around the studio. (Oddly, their off-screen chemistry did not translate to the finished movie, and the love story between Amanda and Clement lacked the spark needed for the screen.) Gossip columnist Hedda Hopper eventually broke the story to the public, causing great embarrassment to all involved.

Another issue arose when Arthur agreed to work on the troubled *Let's Make Love* script after a Writers' Guild strike removed the possibility of a contract writer taking on the responsibility. He took the job as a gesture of goodwill to his wife, who ended up resenting him for crossing the picket line during a strike.

Ultimately, when the movie finally premiered it was a moderate success in terms of box office sales, but in comparison to Marilyn's other movies, it was considered a failure by many—a first for Marilyn.

There were several difficulties during production, which in retrospect foreshadowed the turmoil in Marilyn's next film. The troubled Miller marriage, the need for a new costume designer, and the disappointing box office were all factors that showed no signs of going away.

The Misfits
United Artists
Release date: February 1, 1961

Plot: After establishing a six-week residency for a quick divorce in Reno, Nevada, Roslyn Tabor arrives at court, where her divorce is granted. Afterward, she and her landlady Isabelle (Thelma Ritter) head to a casino for drinks, where they run into Guido (Eli Wallach), a tow-truck driver who had earlier inspected Roslyn's car, and his friend Gay Langland (Clark Gable). Guido and Gay are cowboys who take odd jobs to avoid "wages," their word for jobs, and mainstream life.

Later that day, the foursome drives out to Guido's partially constructed house in an isolated section of desert, where they continue drinking. Gay and Roslyn develop a romantic relationship and move into the house, although it becomes clear parts of their personalities are at odds. For instance, Gay is a skilled hunter and Roslyn is an animal lover.

Marilyn idolized Clark Gable when she was growing up and even pretended he was her father. She was beside herself with joy when she had the opportunity to appear with him in The Misfits. By Macfadden Publications New York / Wikimedia Commons

When Guido and Gay decide to go "mustanging," they head to the Dayton, Nevada, rodeo to find another cowboy to help in the endeavor. At the rodeo, they find Gay's friend Perce (Montgomery Clift), who is too broke to pay the rodeo entrance fee. Gay offers to pay the fee in exchange for Perce's help with mustanging. When Perce is thrown from a bull and sustains a head injury, Roslyn becomes distraught and cries.

When Gay, Guido, and Perce venture out into the desert for mustanging, Roslyn tags along. She is soon horrified to learn "mustanging" means rounding up wild mustangs that will be slaughtered for pet food. Roslyn tells Gay she's disappointed in him because she thought he was kind. Gay responds that he is the same person he always was and "kind people" can kill. He hunts so he can stay free from stifling jobs.

Privately, Guido approaches Roslyn and offers to stop the hunt if she leaves Gay and goes home with him. Roslyn is furious and accuses Guido of having "to get something to be human!"

As the day progresses, Roslyn becomes increasingly upset, screaming at the cowboys and offering to pay $200 for the horses' release. Gay is insulted by her offer. Perce offers to set the mustangs free and when Roslyn declines because she is afraid the gesture will start a fight, he releases the horses—a stallion, a mare, and her foal—anyway.

In response, Gay chases and recaptures the stallion, only to set him free again—he wants to be in charge of the decision. Gay offers to drive Roslyn home. Moved by his kindness, Roslyn gets in his truck and offers to leave their house the following day. As they drive, Roslyn and Gay see the mare and her foal running free. Gay puts his arm around Roslyn and they drive off together.

Behind the scenes: The origin for *The Misfits* dates back to Arthur Miller's stay in Reno, Nevada, while establishing six weeks of residency to obtain a divorce in 1956. While in Reno, he encountered cowboys who avoided regular employment by hunting horses. Inspired by their lives, Arthur wrote *The Misfits* as a short story but later turned to the genre he knew best—drama—and began developing the story into a screenplay with the intention of writing a dynamic part for Marilyn. The process required fleshing out the female character, an element largely missing from the original short story.

Marilyn was given a sizable role with the opportunity to stretch in a different direction than her previous movies. In addition to challenging her acting skills, Marilyn wanted to push the boundaries of movie censorship by becoming the first woman to appear topless in a mainstream film. In the "morning after" scene in which she sits up in bed and kisses Clark Gable, she holds a sheet over her chest but her bare back is exposed to the camera. In one take, Marilyn dropped the sheet, revealing her breasts. John Huston refused to print the footage.

The Misfits was a turbulent shoot from beginning to end. By the time filming began, Marilyn and Arthur's marriage was disintegrating quickly and in its final stages. The tension between them affected the entire set. As filming progressed, the couple moved into separate hotel rooms.

Marilyn was in a dark place. Her miscarriages, the breakdown of her marriage, and her prescription drug use were all taking a huge toll. Additionally, production was held in the Nevada desert during the summer months and temperatures frequently soared above one hundred degrees Fahrenheit. The extreme heat was taxing physically and emotionally for the entire cast and crew, Marilyn especially.

To further complicate matters, Marilyn reportedly felt betrayed that some things she confided to Arthur turned up in the script. Roslyn, for instance, never finished high school, talks about her absent parents, and becomes overwhelmed when she suddenly misses her mother. There are also notable comparisons between Marilyn and Roslyn, such as both names ending in "lyn."

In his autobiography, *Timebends*, Miller draws comparisons between Marilyn and Roslyn. "I knew by this time that I had initially expected what she satirized as 'the happy girl that all men loved' and had discovered someone diametrically opposite, a troubled woman whose desperation was deepening no matter where she turned for a way out. By the start of *The Misfits* it was no longer possible to deny to myself that if there was a key to Marilyn's despair I did not possess it. . . . As *The Misfits* went into production, I clung to an expectation of change, not knowing quite why. Maybe it was that the role of Roslyn, her first serious one, had the womanly dignity that part of her longed for. And Roslyn's dilemma was hers, but in the story it was resolved. I hoped by living through this role she too might arrive at some threshold of faith and confidence, even as I had to wonder if I could hold on to it myself after we'd both been let down from expectations such as few people allow themselves in a marriage."

In another scene, authentic photos of Marilyn's early glam pinups are seen hanging up inside a closet door. After Guido ogles them, Roslyn closes the door and says Gay hung them up as "a joke." While the dialogue about her mother does seem like something Marilyn might have said in real life, it is less clear if Arthur literally or figuratively meant to call Marilyn a joke. Regardless, it is a moment in the film that has not aged well, especially considering he later wrote *After the Fall*, loosely based on his life with Marilyn. The flip side of that argument is that all three main male characters, Gay (Clark Gable), Guido (Eli Wallach), and Perce (Montgomery Clift) are competing for Roslyn's love, an indication, perhaps, of Arthur Miller's attachment to her. Years later crew members recalled Arthur referring to Marilyn's close-up on the set one day. They were confused, as Marilyn hadn't filmed a close-up. When they watched the footage back, the other actors were in the scene with her. It occurred to them that Arthur believed it had been a close-up because he quite literally could see *only* Marilyn.

As the movie closes, the characters Roslyn and Gay drive off under the stars—a more modern interpretation of riding off into the sunset. Arthur struggled with how to finish the movie, repeatedly changing the end. "Aware of the hopefulness with which I had conceived the story and my uncertainty about my future now, I still could not concede that the ending had to be what I considered nihilistic, people simply walking away from one another. . . . One afternoon Marilyn, with no evident emotion, almost as though it were just another script, said, 'What they really should do is break up at the end.' I instantly disagreed, so quickly, in fact, that I knew I was afraid she was right. But the irony was too sharp: the work I had created to reassure her that a woman like herself could find a home in the world had apparently proven the opposite."

Ultimately, production of the movie he wrote for her would not save their marriage.

Script issues aside, Marilyn's pattern of on-set behavior was once again a factor—arriving late, listening to her coach over the director, forgetting lines. At one point, director John Huston shut production down so Marilyn could enter a hospital in California for rest.

Production soon began running over budget and falling behind schedule. In the years following Marilyn's death, Huston placed much of the blame for production delays and cost overages on her shoulders. There is truth to Marilyn causing delays, but Huston conveniently neglected to mention the troubles he also caused, which included heavy drinking, gambling all night at craps tables, and losing large sums of money. His all-nighters in the casino caused him to fall asleep in his director's chair during the day and lose track of which scene was filming.

In the book *The Misfits* about the making of the movie, Arthur Miller recalled, "He loved to gamble. One night, he lost twenty-five thousand dollars, which he didn't have, as soon as he got it. The gangsters who ran the place told him politely he was never going to leave town unless he paid that bill. So, one evening, I left him around nine o'clock after dinner at this table. [Miller points to one photo.] I believe it was this table . . . I came down the next morning around six, and there he was. He had made his money back! Plus about five hundred or a thousand dollars! He stayed up at it the whole night. Then he goes on location and falls asleep. When he woke up, he said, 'Okay! We deal with scene number nine!' or whatever. And the script girl answered, 'But we did that one yesterday!' It was totally crazy. I'll never forget that one."

(Huston did something similar in his next movie, *Freud*, with Montgomery Clift. After Clift's death, Huston accused the lead actor, a known alcoholic, of causing trouble on the set, when Huston himself was also partially to blame. With Marilyn Monroe and Montgomery Clift dead, Huston could easily shift attention away from himself when it came to on-set drama. In the book *The Misfits*, Arthur said, "He [Huston] hated him [Clift], for reasons I never knew. But I did not see that on *The Misfits*. Huston was kind and considerate. But perhaps he was different on different films.")

With all the behind-the-scenes drama happening on the set, Marilyn confided to Ralph Roberts that she missed Johnny Hyde. He would have known how to handle everything, she said.

The worst was yet to come. Clark Gable, who was fifty-nine, had taken to performing some of his stunts, including being dragged by mustangs. Gable died of a heart attack shortly after production wrapped, an event that left an unexpected pall hanging over the troubled movie. An already fragile Marilyn was devastated to learn gossip pinpointed her as the cause of his heart attack. According to the stories, tired and bored while waiting for Marilyn to show up on set, Gable occupied himself with tasks beyond what he could realistically handle physically. Between the extreme heat and his age, Gable's on-set activity stressed his heart to the point of no return. Furthermore, the gossip asserted, Gable's pregnant widow Kay blamed Marilyn for her husband's death. (For his part, John Huston insisted he did not allow Gable to perform stunts he believed were beyond Gable's capabilities, effectively sidestepping the blame Marilyn received.)

The truth of Clark Gable and his health while filming *The Misfits* is considerably more nuanced than simply blaming Marilyn for showing up late, although she was indeed often late to the set. Clark Gable's health before production of *The Misfits* began filming was already in question. After years of heavy smoking, drinking, and fluctuating weight, he failed the physical examination required to obtain insurance for him on the production. He was dieting to lose weight before the start of the movie, and his doctor gave him strict instructions to rest, cut out smoking and drinking, and take medication for hypertension. John Huston even pushed the start date of the movie back to accommodate him. Gable passed the second physical and was cleared to begin filming. According to *Clark Gable: A Biography* by Warren G. Harris, he celebrated the good news with a cigar and brandy.

The start date had been delayed to ensure he could pass his physical, but now the entire company was forced to work during the hottest months of the year. The Nevada heat was difficult for all, but Arthur Miller remembers Gable's costumes were not well suited for the summer desert weather. "He was exhausted," Arthur said in *The Misfits* book. "The heat was so unbearable, and Clark had to wear heavy clothes to protect his skin when he was being dragged by the horses."

Furthermore, he performed at least some stunts when Marilyn was present, which disputes the stories of Gable combatting his boredom by performing dangerous stunts while waiting for her. As Ralph Roberts recalls, "The scene with Gable, with him bouncing over the radiator of the car in front of the saloon in 115-ish degree temperature, was completed with much success and with a burst of applause from the crew and spectators. Marilyn told him how wonderful she thought it went and then had Rudy [the driver] drive her to Reno and then to the airport."

The reason for Marilyn's trip to Los Angeles has been reported as the result of a breakdown and addiction to pills. Marilyn was not in good health either, but as with Gable, there was more to the story. According to Ralph Roberts, "The reason for going to L.A. was not for a dress or premiere. She wanted to see Engelberg and Greenson [her doctors]. She was suffering from complete exhaustion, having fights with Arthur. And she wanted one last meeting with [Yves] Montand." When Marilyn arrived at the hospital, "it had been determined that she suffered from heat exhaustion, complicated by her usual monthly agony." The "usual monthly agony" was her ongoing battle with endometriosis.

The Misfits *filmed on location in Nevada, including Dayton, where the rodeo and paddle ball scenes took place.* Elisa Jordan

The last scenes were finished in the more hospitable environment of a Paramount Pictures soundstage in Los Angeles.

A few months after Gable's death in November 1960, *The Misfits* was released in February 1961. Had he lived, Clark Gable would have turned sixty that month. It was also just a month after the Monroe-Miller divorce was finalized. Arthur Miller did not attend the premiere; Marilyn attended with Montgomery Clift. After all the work that had gone into finishing the film, at the time of its release *The Misfits* was considered a box office failure.

Time has been considerably kinder to *The Misfits*. In the years since its release, *The Misfits* has made its money back through home video sales, a technology not yet foreseen in the early 1960s. Modern critics have also praised the performances of the lead actors.

Something's Got to Give
Twentieth Century-Fox
Incomplete: 1962
Plot: *Something's Got to Give* was a reworked version of the 1940 movie *My Favorite Wife* starring Cary Grant and Irene Dunn. In the updated version, Marilyn would play Ellen Arden, a wife and mother who was legally declared dead after a shipwreck. Her widower Nick (Dean Martin) remarries, and he is on his honeymoon when Ellen—alive after surviving on a desert island—returns home unexpectedly. When she enters her backyard, her loyal Cocker Spaniel greets her enthusiastically. Her two children, however, were too young when she disappeared to recognize her. As the children swim in the family's pool, she approaches them without revealing her identity. Ellen dons a disguise as a Swedish woman named Ingrid. Now married to two

Marilyn created a stir when she stripped off her flesh-colored bikini while filming the skinny dip scene in Something's Got to Give. *The stunt momentarily knocked Elizabeth Taylor off the front of the newspapers.*
Twentieth Century-Fox / Photofest / © Twentieth Century-Fox

women, Nick tries to keep his new wife Bianca and Ellen separate until he can figure out what to do. Nick becomes jealous when he learns Ellen was stranded on the island with another man, prompting Ellen to try coaxing a meek shoe salesman into posing as the man with whom she was stranded on a desert island.

Behind the scenes: In 1962, Marilyn was still contractually obligated to Twentieth Century-Fox.

It was a critical time for both Marilyn and Fox. Marilyn's last two films were box office disappointments, and she needed another hit. As for Twentieth Century-Fox, the company was in dire financial straits, to the point that only two movies were in production during 1962: *Something's Got to Give* and *Cleopatra* starring Elizabeth Taylor. Fox was banking on Hollywood's favorite blonde and favorite brunette pulling the studio out of its financial slump. *Cleopatra* was costing the studio a fortune; the plan was to film *Something's Got to Give* quickly and cheaply for a Christmas release. Marilyn's star power would hopefully produce enough revenue to reinvest back into *Cleopatra*. Both movies and actresses, however, would prove challenging.

In the months leading up to the April 1962 start date for *Something's Got to Give*, a replica of director George Cukor's house was constructed on a Fox soundstage. He was using his own home as inspiration for the "Arden house" set. The actors did their wardrobe, hair, and makeup tests on the interior set. Marilyn reported to Fox for her tests much slimmer than she had been in years after losing twenty-five pounds from gallbladder surgery the previous year. The weight loss brought her back down to the same size as her modeling and starlet days.

For one of her costume tests, Marilyn wore a long blonde wig and appeared in a denim top and jeans for when her character Ellen was stranded on a desert island. For her more glamorous look, she wore a black-and-white spaghetti-strap dress with a pencil skirt.

Marilyn's hair for the movie was updated from 1950s waves to a more contemporary bouffant. Her hair was also bleached lighter than it had ever been, a shade she called "pillowcase white."

The costumes Marilyn ended up wearing in the film were designed by Jean Louis, who was returning after a successful partnership with Marilyn in *The Misfits*. The dresses he created for Marilyn were in the style of the early 1960s and favored the slimmer-fitting skirts she had always preferred.

Before filming, Marilyn asked for—and received—permission to attend a Democratic fundraiser at Madison Square Garden in New York on May 19. As part of the evening, which would feature performances by several celebrities, Marilyn was asked to sing "Happy Birthday" to President John F. Kennedy, as the event was close to his birthday.

Before filming even began, there was an indication of problems to come. Producer Henry Weinstein claimed to have gone to Marilyn's house and found her unconscious from barbiturates. He reported the incident to Twentieth Century-Fox and recommended delaying the film, only to have his suggestion rejected. When production began on April 23, Marilyn called the studio and informed Fox brass she was suffering from sinusitis and could not film.

Fox dispatched Dr. Lee Siegel to Marilyn's home and he indeed diagnosed her with sinusitis. He called for one month of rest. Instead of closing down production, director George Cukor rearranged the schedule to film around Marilyn's absence. Scenes with the children,

Marilyn as Ellen Arden in Something's Got to Give, *a remake of* My Favorite Wife *(1940) starring Cary Grant and Irene Dunn.* \By Eureka Humboldt Standard, August 7, 1962 / Wikimedia Commons

Cyd Charisse and Dean Martin were filmed while Marilyn recovered at home. Cukor filmed as much as he could without Marilyn, but she was the star of the movie and could only get so far.

Marilyn finally showed up for her first day of work on April 30.

"I would call three doctors every day," said Weinstein in a documentary about the making of the movie. "One was her nose man and eye man because she had sinusitis. She was afraid of all that. Then she had an internist and then, of course, her analyst. I mean, she had enormous problems that came with the territory. And the studio was naïve to think that this wouldn't happen. I mean, if the picture was budgeted for an eight-week shoot, they should have budgeted for a sixteen-week shoot because they wanted a film with Marilyn Monroe. But there are certain people you create films and don't manufacture films. You're not putting Elvis Presley in front of the camera and shooting it in six weeks. You have a very, very different persona. And I think that was the miscalculation and I think it became aggravated because of what was happening with *Cleopatra*. I'm convinced of it."

Dean Martin, known for his easygoing personality, shrugged off the delays and putted golf balls during the downtime.

As of May 10, Marilyn had missed sixteen of seventeen filming days. On Monday, May 14, Marilyn showed up and worked the entire day—just as she did Tuesday and Wednesday. On Thursday, May 17, Marilyn left work early to leave for the Democratic fundraiser at Madison Square Garden. Studio executives were furious and forbade her to go; George Cukor also did his best to dissuade her. They tried to use the reasoning that Marilyn had not been granted permission to attend or at the very least had rescinded permission. Marilyn was undeterred—she was going.

"Cukor was angry. The studio was angry," said Gene Allen, associate producer on the movie. "There was a feeling of resentment, you know, that everybody had been patient enough and trying as hard as they could for Marilyn and then to do this."

"I just remember being with Cukor at the time and we were both astonished that she had gone—and angry. Cukor particularly was angry. He was starting to feel, I think, a kind of helplessness in the situation that regardless of what he did, regardless of what the studio said or something, she was gonna get her way," said Walter Bernstein, the screenwriter for *Something's Got to Give*.

Thirty years later, Henry Weinstein had become more diplomatic about the incident. "They were very upset and so was I, and that was stupid," he said. "And had I been more experienced I would have said, 'Marilyn, I'll go with you. We'll get more publicity for the picture.' Which would be the natural thing to do. I should walk with a sign saying *Something's Got to Give* instead of worrying about whether she's gone or what the studio thinks. Immediately, the studio should have been alerted. We should have had our own cameramen there with her and the President. . . . That's what you would do instead of, 'How could she go?'"

Marilyn returned to Twentieth Century-Fox on Monday, May 20 but was exhausted from her trip and couldn't film close-ups. Instead, she filmed retakes with the young actors playing her children.

A highlight of the filming experience was when Ellen skinny dips in the family swimming pool as a way to push Nick into telling his new wife she has returned home. Marilyn wore a flesh-colored bikini for the shoot but when a cameraman noted he could see it, she stripped off the swimsuit. Her makeup man Whitey Snyder stood by the camera and alerted her if any parts that shouldn't be showing turned up on film. If Whitey indicated "yes," she wouldn't allow it to print. Still, she consented to distribute seminude photographs to the press—which bumped Elizabeth Taylor off the front pages of newspapers and magazines, at least temporarily. Had the movie been finished, it would have technically been the first "nude" scene with a major movie star in a mainstream film, even if she didn't show much.

Marilyn showed up to the set on Friday, June 1, her thirty-sixth birthday, but upon learning the crew planned to throw Marilyn a party, George Cukor insisted on a full day of work before the cake was brought out. It was Marilyn's stand-in Evelyn Moriarty—not the studio—who bought a cake for her.

On Monday, June 4, Marilyn did not show up to work. She called in sick again on Tuesday, June 5, and this time even the ever-patient and cool Dean Martin had been pushed too far. Frustrated, he walked off the set. Marilyn called in again on Wednesday and Thursday. Dr. Seigel confirmed Marilyn's sinuses were flaring and that her temperature was 102. Back on the set, the crew and studio bosses were dubious.

The production was sixteen days behind schedule and one million dollars over budget, which was nothing compared to *Cleopatra*, but still a drain on the studio's precarious resources. Marilyn's analyst, Dr. Greenson, was called home from a vacation in Switzerland and he promised to have her on the set by Monday, June 11. But Fox was in no mood to wait. When she didn't show up on Friday, June 8, the studio fired her. That same day, Fox filed a $500,000 breach of contract lawsuit against her. On June 9, the studio announced Lee Remick was taking Marilyn's place.

Twentieth Century-Fox almost immediately regretted firing Marilyn. In the haste to fire her, they overlooked a couple of pivotal factors. First, Dean Martin had a clause in his contract allowing him to approve his costar—and he very quickly informed Fox he would *only* work with Marilyn Monroe. Second, sixteen days behind schedule and one million dollars over budget were still better than no movie at all, and Twentieth Century-Fox was desperate to release a movie and recoup some of the money *Cleopatra* was spending. *Something's Got to Give* had been the only other Fox movie in production, so finishing it with Marilyn was the only realistic option.

· 18 ·

The Updated Fox Contract

The circumstances around Marilyn's dismissal can get complicated. It was more than just Marilyn calling in sick a lot, leaving for a few days to sing "Happy Birthday" to President Kennedy, and filming getting behind schedule, all of which did happen. The undercurrent involved years of back and forth between her and the studio; on-set behavior; a very public strike and rebellion; the production of *Cleopatra*; and the financial duress of Twentieth Century-Fox.

After Marilyn had been fired from *Something's Got to Give*, she began a media campaign to restore her career and get her version of events out to the public. She sat for an in-depth interview with Richard Merryman from *Life* magazine and posed for several photographers during the summer of 1962. Her message was clear—she was still able to work but believed she had been treated unfairly by her studio, Twentieth Century-Fox. She had been sick with a serious case of sinusitis and had a doctor's diagnosis as proof. She had also been granted permission to attend President Kennedy's fundraiser and birthday party in New York, and it wasn't her fault the company tried to renege on the agreement. Ultimately, both sides had valid points.

With *Something's Got to Give* closed down, there were now no movies filming on the Los Angeles lot—a point Fox manipulated to sound like Marilyn's carelessness had caused crew members to lose their jobs. Marilyn was devastated at the claim and quickly fired off telegrams to colleagues begging them to believe she would never be so thoughtless as to not consider them.

Twentieth Century-Fox was disingenuous; the plan was never to cancel *Something's Got to Give* permanently but to halt production while a replacement actress could be found. The studio quickly announced Lee Remick was Marilyn's replacement. This, too, came to a halt when Dean Martin rejected Lee Remick.

Given Dean Martin's ultimatum, the money Fox had already spent on *Something's Got to Give*, Marilyn's star power, and the crippling financial losses of *Cleopatra*, Fox soon realized hiring Marilyn Monroe back was the best option.

In theory, it would seem Marilyn would have been thrilled. What she had wanted all along was to save her career and restore her reputation. It was only in the years following Marilyn's death that it was revealed Fox was in the process of hiring her back, which led to the belief that Marilyn should have had much to look forward to. She was returning to work and restoring her newly purchased home—she seemingly had reasons to continue living.

The contract Fox sent her, however, left much to be desired. In fact, it was downright insulting. The updated contract Fox offered Marilyn stripped her of everything she had worked for over the years. If Marilyn did not sign, Twentieth Century-Fox would sue her in court. It was more of a legal threat than an invitation back to work.

The contract terms were drawn up and possibly intended for Marilyn's attorney, Milton "Mickey" Rudin. It was a draft and therefore does not have proper punctuation in some places.

By our letter of June 11 we notified you of our election to terminate, effective June 8, all of our obligations re said photoplay

Since it is your desire and Monroe's desire that we resume production of the Photoplay on July 23, 1962 or within a reasonable amount of time thereafter

You agree to the following:
1. Neither you nor Miss Monroe shall have any right of consultation or approval in the selection of a director. Co-stars, feature players, bits, extras stand-ins or any other players. Our decision will be final.
2. No say in director
3. Miss Monroe will perform her services whether the Photoplay is based on the script which is presently in existence or as it may be modified, neither you nor Miss Monroe will have any rights to approval or consultation.
4. No rights of approval or consultation with regard to cameramen, makeup-man, wardrobe woman, hairdresser or hair stylist.
5. Miss Monroe will be prompt in observing our work calls and will take her lunch break only when we specify and will be available all day as we specify. When she appears, she will be fully prepared in connection with the scene and she shall have memorized her dialogue.
6. Neither you nor Monroe will have any right of consultation as to the number of "takes" to be made on each scene or printed. She will have no right to attend the dailies or any other exhibition prior to its final cut.

7. No employees of yours or hers will be allowed in the studio without the express consent of our studio.

8. No rights with regard to portrait photographs or still photographs.

9. Miss Monroe will be paid $100,000 and there will be additional compensation and there will be no additional compensation [*sic*] payable to you for the use of Monroe's services beyond the 14 week period.

10. Once this is signed, we will dismiss the suit we filed in the Superior Court of the County of Los Angeles.

Under any circumstances, a contract with so little control would be offensive to an actor of any notable stature, but especially one of Marilyn Monroe's caliber. This would have been especially devastating after risking her career by going on strike and fighting for better terms. She had not only lost everything she won during her strike, but she now had even less say in her career than she ever had before.

Marilyn's behavior over the years had been, at times, unprofessional. She had been late to the set regularly, asked for repeated takes, and listened to her acting coaches over directors. Furthermore, she had been slow to fulfill her contractual obligations to Twentieth Century-Fox. Since signing her new contract in 1955, she had completed just two films for Twentieth Century-Fox, *Bus Stop* and *Let's Make Love*. The fact remained, however, that Marilyn Monroe had made Twentieth Century-Fox millions and was still popular with fans.

Fox appeared to be seeking more than to just rectify her behavior and collect on the movies she still owed them. It looked as though the company wanted to punish her for past behavior and her rebellion in 1955.

It is impossible to determine if Mickey Rudin would have been able to renegotiate any terms of the contract; the movie did not start filming on July 23 as the contract specified. It's quite possible he planned to negotiate. But there is little doubt Marilyn would have been devastated by what was presented to her. She was presented with a terrible choice—be sued in court for half a million dollars or agree to a humiliating contract.

Something's Got to Give, Cleopatra, and Fox

$\mathcal{T}$o fully understand what was happening on the *Something's Got to Give* set and the decisions made about the movie, one must factor in *Cleopatra*, the only other movie in production at Twentieth Century-Fox in 1962. The distress these two movies caused for the studio resulted from a perfect storm of dwindling audiences, poor cash flow, bad corporate strategy, and a crumbling studio system. When the turbulent lives of their leading ladies were layered over everything else, a company-wide crisis threatened the entire operation. There is no way around it: *Cleopatra* played a key role in the fate of *Something's Got to Give*.

Twentieth Century-Fox began experiencing financial distress in the 1950s when television started luring audiences away from movies in favor of at-home entertainment. To entice audiences back into theatres, in 1953 Fox debuted CinemaScope, a widescreen format that provided panoramic views television could not possibly compete with. Big changes came to Twentieth Century-Fox in 1956 when production head Darryl Zanuck resigned. He was replaced with Spyros Skouras, the man largely responsible for CinemaScope and its success.

In need of a large-scale epic, Twentieth Century-Fox entered into an agreement with producer Walter Wanger to begin work on *Cleopatra* as early as 1958. The original idea was to update the script from the 1917 version of *Cleopatra*, but because that was a silent film there was no dialogue. Soon, the script that was believed to only need some sprucing up was undergoing rewrites by multiple writers.

There was also the issue of casting. Several actresses were considered for the lead role, including Joan Collins, but the studio ultimately decided Elizabeth Taylor was the perfect candidate. Elizabeth Taylor had other ideas. She did not want the role and decided the best way to decline was to demand a ridiculous salary of one million dollars. It was an unheard-of sum at the time; no actor or actress had made anywhere near that amount of money for a single movie. But Twentieth Century-Fox was desperate and Elizabeth Taylor was shocked to learn that her absurd salary demand had been met. In addition to her fee of one million dollars, she was also granted 10 percent of the movie's profits.

Elizabeth Taylor was cast as Cleopatra in October 1959 but did not sign her contract until June 28, 1960. Things got off to a terrible start when director Rouben Mamoulian was still unhappy with the script even after five writers had worked on it.

In 1961, the epic movie sent its epic-sized crew to Pinewood Studios in London, the same place where Marilyn had filmed *The Prince and the Show-girl* five years prior. England's cold, damp weather didn't agree with Elizabeth Taylor, who was soon battling a life-threatening bout of pneumonia. Her illness required an emergency tracheotomy and hospitalization, followed by three months of recovery. Now unwilling to risk filming in England if the cold affected Elizabeth's health, Fox relocated production back to the Los Angeles lot. Rouben Mamoulian was replaced by Joseph Mankiewicz as writer and director. The leading men were also replaced with Rex Harrison now playing Caesar and Richard Burton playing Marc Antony.

In spring 1961, the large Fox backlot began undergoing a huge renovation that included leveling old sets and rebuilding towering new ones, including Alexandria and the slave market.

As crews diligently worked on the backlot sets, a new problem arose—there wasn't enough sound stage room to film the interiors. Television had come to Fox and this newer medium was occupying most of the sound stages. Production would have to move yet again. The backlot had been demolished and rebuilt for nothing, and the half-built sets were abandoned.

Production moved to Rome and was set up in Mussolini's old studio. Fox did not hire local Italian crews, which would have saved costs. Instead, they sent—and paid for—American crews to work and live in Italy during the filming. As crews began building new sets, they accidentally detonated abandoned World War II landmines, an incident that injured several and killed one. So many materials were required for building the sets that it caused a national shortage of supplies in Italy.

Principal photography finally began in September 1961. The original budget was $4 million. By November 1961, just two months after filming began, three countries had been involved and the budget had already ballooned to $15 million. The movie Fox had placed so much hope in was now draining precious finances. To help defray costs, Twentieth Century-Fox began selling off much of its land that made up the backlots. In total, 176 acres were sold and redeveloped into what is now called Century City, named for the studio that had once inhabited the property. Fox still maintained some of its property, but only around fifty acres remained.

If the cost, delays, crew casualties, multiple rewrites, recasting, and over-all filming troubles weren't enough, things were about to get worse, at least as far as publicity went.

By January, leading lady Elizabeth Taylor, who was married to Eddie Fisher, was having an affair with Richard Burton, who was also married. They had just started filming scenes together in January, so their affair started almost immediately. By January 26, Elizabeth Taylor was informing Mankie-wicz that she was in love with her costar. On February 17, she attempted suicide when Burton informed her he would not leave his wife. Soon the tab-loids were reporting the salacious affair, which turned into big news that the public couldn't get enough of. It was the latest chapter in Elizabeth Taylor's turbulent love life.

After her husband Mike Todd died in a 1958 airplane crash, she found comfort in the arms of his best friend Eddie Fisher—who was married to her friend Debbie Reynolds. Now the saga had taken another turn, with Eliza-beth cheating on Eddie with Richard Burton. The scandal was interna-tional news, but with the actual affair taking place in Rome, even the Vati-can got involved to condemn the adulterous couple. It was a boon for gossip columns, but a disaster for Twentieth Century-Fox, which now feared the negative publicity would impact ticket sales upon release. The scale of the coverage was so vast that in retrospect, many social historians pinpoint the filming of *Cleopatra* and the Taylor-Burton affair as the birth of modern celebrity.

On May 8, 1962, Cleopatra's triumphant procession into Rome, which required ten thousand extras, was filmed. This particular scene had been delayed for six months to utilize the longer days for more daylight.

Meanwhile, in Los Angeles, *Something's Got to Give* was also

Cleopatra was already a disaster during production when co-stars Elizabeth Taylor and Richard Burton began having an affair. The movie was over budget and behind schedule when the media broke the story about the couple's adulterous relationship. By Courier-Gazette, McKinney, TX. Photo from Twentieth Century-Fox / Wikimedia Commons

behind schedule and over budget. Like Elizabeth Taylor on *Cleopatra*, Marilyn on *Something's Got to Give* had frequently missed work due to illness. Finally, Fox executives were infuriated in May when Marilyn went to New York for a few days to sing "Happy Birthday" to President John F. Kennedy. Marilyn returned to work; she celebrated her thirty-sixth birthday on the set on Friday, June 1. Then she started calling in sick again.

Fox had to stop the financial bleeding somewhere. In many ways it would have seemed most logical to suspend production of *Cleopatra*, which was costing the company significantly more money. In fear of losing the tens of millions already invested in *Cleopatra* and spiraling with the logistics of pulling the enormous cast and crew out of a foreign country and getting everyone home (again), Fox chose the easier target. On June 8, 1962, Fox fired Marilyn and temporarily shut down production of *Something's Got to Give* with a $3 million loss. It was announced the company would quickly replace Marilyn Monroe with a new leading lady and get production started as quickly as possible.

With the light comedy suspended, *Cleopatra* was now the only Fox movie in production. The expenses for the *entire* company were now charged to *Cleopatra*, regardless of whether they had anything to do with the movie or not, further inflating the costs on paper.

In July, Darryl Zanuck returned to Twentieth Century-Fox to salvage the company and *Cleopatra*. To save expenses, he closed down the entire Los Angeles lot, not just *Something's Got to Give*. When the once-enormous studio went dark, many blamed Marilyn for putting the studio's employees out of work; she was devastated by the accusation.

Darryl Zanuck had never really liked or understood Marilyn, but he was a good businessman and knew she still had star power—and Twentieth Century-Fox needed money fast. When he resumed power at Fox that July, he started the process of hiring her back with the hope *Something's Got to Give* would finish quickly and make enough money to generate some cash flow, which had been the plan all along. Marilyn's death on August 5 dashed that hope.

The first edit of *Cleopatra* was finally ready for viewing in the late fall of 1962. It clocked in at an impossible five hours and twenty minutes. Mankiewicz proposed turning one movie into two, dividing up the story similar to how Shakespeare had—*Caesar and Cleopatra* and *Antony and Cleopatra*. Zanuck refused the idea and supplied $2 million more to cut two hours off the running time and finish the film once and for all.

On March 4, 1963, Fox reopened the lot on the same day *Cleopatra* completed production. The final cost of *Cleopatra* was an astonishing $44 million (1962 dollars) and the run time was still an exhaustive four hours and six minutes. At this point, a frustrated Mankiewicz completely disowned the movie after he and the studio could not align their respective visions for the project.

The movie finally opened on June 12, 1963, in general release. Multiple versions of the movie exist. First, a premiere version debuted at 243 minutes, which was then reduced to 222 the following week. The general release version was 194 minutes.

Contrary to what the studio had originally feared, the Taylor-Burton affair generated curiosity and interest among the public. Moviegoers were gobbling up tickets to the point they were selling out a month in advance. *Cleopatra* went on to be the highest-grossing film of 1963, but it still was not enough to cover the expenses of filming. By March 1966, *Cleopatra* had made $38 million, still short of the $44 million spent.

Twentieth Century-Fox remained in debt for years to come. The company released individual movies that were successful and made money, *The Sound of Music*, for example. But as a whole, the company didn't finally get out of debt until the release of *Star Wars* in 1977. *Cleopatra* itself didn't break even until 1973.

Today, the legacy of *Cleopatra* is mixed. Generally, it is not considered a great film, especially given the intention of creating a grand-scale epic. The movie is typically more famous for the behind-the-scenes drama than for cinematic achievements or expression.

Years later, Elizabeth Taylor said, "They had cut out the heart, the essence, the motivations, the very core, and tacked on all those battle scenes. It should have been about three large people, but it lacked reality and passion. I found it vulgar."

· 20 ·

The Coaches

*M*arilyn's good and bad points came together—and often clashed—during work. She made it a point to better herself and train hard at her craft but did so at the expense of alienating her colleagues. Her insecurities made it impossible for her to perform on the set without coaches standing just off to the side directing her, justifying their presence by insisting on retakes. The idea was the education provided by such instructors should give her confidence but the subtext was "You aren't good enough. You can't do this without me."

"She was a perfectionist, the way she wanted herself to be acting-wise, singing-wise or anything else," said Allan "Whitey" Snyder, her makeup man. "That's the only reason these coaches got to her and she worked with them so much because they thought she thought they could improve her so much. If she had just been her cute little self, she would have been so much better."

NATASHA LYTESS

Early in Marilyn's movie career, she began studying with acting coach Natasha Lytess, who went on to become one of the most pivotal (and controversial) figures in her life.

Marilyn first met Natasha in March 1948, after Columbia Pictures paired them for acting training, a routine task that turned into an anything-but-routine relationship.

At the time, Natasha Lytess was in her mid-thirties or so (there are varying years of birth) and hailed from Germany. Or was it Austria? It depends on who you ask. In the book *Marilyn Monroe: The Biography*, author Donald Spoto writes that Natasha sometimes claimed she was Russian to avoid anti-German sentiment.

What is known is that Natasha Lytess studied under revered German director Max Reinhardt, acted in the legitimate theatre, and, with novelist husband Bruno Frank, fled Europe after the Nazis rose to power. The couple settled in Los Angeles, where Natasha accepted bit parts in movies and gave birth to a daughter, Barbara.

Like many hopefuls, Natasha Lytess's acting career sputtered before finally stalling out in Hollywood. In Los Angeles, the theatre community was smaller than in Europe and New York, and likewise, her film parts soon dried up. Her thick accent and severe appearance did her no favors when it came to casting. Consequently, Natasha gave up her dreams of an acting career and began utilizing her stage and film experience to coach other performers.

In acting circles, Natasha appears to have been generally respected but not especially well liked. Some interpreted her as condescending and harsh, especially in her critiques of others' performances. Aspiring starlet Marilyn Monroe was no different and suffered Natasha's withering judgment when the coach assessed her acting as "inhibited and cramped."

In an article dated February 13, 1953, Hollywood columnist Armand ("Army") Archerd described Natasha this way: "Marilyn's mentor is Natasha Lytess, a prematurely gray, 34-year-old former actress, director and coach. Natasha is a slight, but tremendously dynamic Russian-born, German-educated woman and is now the power behind the throne in everything that Marilyn does in front of the cameras."

Exactly how these two women, seemingly such opposites, became integral parts of each other's lives is still rather mysterious in some respects. Natasha was older, European, sophisticated, dowdy, multilingual, and serious. In contrast, Marilyn had spent her entire life thus far in the greater Los Angeles area, spoke only English, was deeply sensitive, was a high school dropout, and was beautiful.

Still, Natasha managed to see raw acting talent in the twenty-one-year-old model-turned-actress, someone who could be molded into a great actress under her tutelage. Marilyn felt she had found someone from whom she could learn and improve her craft. In these respects, both women were correct in their opinions of the other.

Furthermore, if Marilyn was vulnerable after the death of her foster mother "Aunt" Ana Lower, Natasha was similarly so during this same time. After World War II ended, Natasha's husband left Los Angeles and returned to Europe, leaving her to raise their daughter alone. Natasha and Marilyn found comfort and a sympathetic ear in each other during devastating periods of their lives. It was in this environment that Marilyn and Natasha began both their professional relationship and personal friendship.

It was also not long after beginning their working relationship that Columbia Pictures cast Marilyn in a modestly budgeted B-movie titled *Ladies of the Chorus.* Unlike her brief, don't-blink-or-you'll-miss-her bit parts in *Scudda Hoo! Scudda Hay!* and *Dangerous Years, Ladies of the Chorus* was a starring role she was eager to sink her teeth into.

Considering its B-movie status, *Ladies of the Chorus* was a modest financial success at the box office. Unfortunately for Marilyn Monroe, it was not enough for Columbia to renew her contract. Once again without a job, Marilyn refused to give up on her dreams. She was determined to become a great actress and, in her mind, that goal required Natasha Lytess to obtain it.

With what little money she had, Marilyn scraped together a small amount to pay Natasha for private lessons. (It's possible some of these lessons were subsidized by actor John Carroll and his studio executive wife Lucille Ryman, who mentored and essentially sponsored promising young actors, of which Marilyn was one.)

Pupil and teacher began a rigorous training program that included acting techniques, breathing exercises, and diction lessons. Day after day, the two women worked on Marilyn's performance skills for hours on end. Marilyn gained confidence, but not everyone believed Natasha's techniques were sound. Critics would later point out the result was wooden movements on screen, unnatural mouth movements, and over-enunciation when speaking. Although Natasha had much to teach the young and naïve Marilyn, she was a tough taskmaster and showed little patience for her sensitive pupil.

Conversely, Natasha was also nurturing and loving when a situation called for it. With her worldly sophistication and extensive knowledge of theatre and literature, Marilyn often felt inadequate in her teacher's presence—a perceived inadequacy that only deepened her anxiety. Alex D'Arcy, Marilyn's costar in *How to Marry a Millionaire*, believed as many did—that Natasha exacerbated Marilyn's worst qualities: dependence, insecurity, neediness, and anxiousness.

Working with Natasha was more than a working relationship, however. An orphan who lived an unstable existence in her formative years, she would ingratiate herself into families, even if her attachments weren't always the healthiest situation for her. This is exactly what she did with Natasha and her daughter.

"Marilyn could go on by herself without any help, but she wants to learn, which is good," Natasha told Archerd. "Every young actor needs direction and guidance. She needs to build confidence. A great actor understands life. She is, of course, very young to understand it yet. Her life has not been happy up to now, anyhow. And don't tell me that her experience will help make a good actress out of her.

"The more pictures Marilyn does doesn't mean the experience will be good. Experience in films can be fatal to an actor. They can stagnate in the habitual ways they keep in picture after picture. They have to become natural instead of habitual."

Natasha also explained that Marilyn "was not a natural actress."

Marilyn took Natasha's harsh words to heart.

"There were days when I couldn't figure out why she kept me on as a student because she made me feel so shallow and without talent," Marilyn said later. "Very often it seemed that to her I was one of the hundred neediest cases."

But keep her on Natasha did, and Marilyn increasingly leaned on her acting coach, both professionally and personally. Natasha schooled her on great literature and nursed Marilyn's broken heart after her affair with vocal coach Fred Karger ended.

Natasha also weathered Marilyn's affair with Hollywood super-agent Johnny Hyde. Natasha's devotion was so total and complete it's generally believed that she, too, had fallen in love with Marilyn.

It's unclear how true or untrue this possibility is, and there has been much speculation about the nature of their physical relationship. The only two people who know for sure what happened are Marilyn and Natasha, but if Natasha developed feelings for Marilyn, she likely did not return Natasha's affection. The clue is in one of Natasha's statements from years later when she admitted: "I took her in my arms one day and I told her, 'I want to love you.' I remember she looked at me and said, 'You don't have to love me, Natasha—just as long as you work with me.'"

Regardless of whether or not there was a physical relationship, the friendship remained intense. In the fall of 1950, Marilyn once again moved in with Natasha and her daughter, but it wasn't always a quiet domestic life. Marilyn, who slept on the couch, wasn't the tidiest of houseguests, and her Chihuahua, Josefa, wasn't properly housetrained, which caused friction at home. Fortunately, Marilyn wasn't home all the time—she split her time between Natasha's modest house on Harper Avenue, Johnny Hyde's posh mansion on North Palm Drive in Beverly Hills, and, at times, a hotel room at the Beverly Carlton.

The arrangement didn't last long. Johnny Hyde, long battling a weak heart, suffered a series of heart attacks before finally succumbing in December 1950.

In the wake of Johnny Hyde's death, Marilyn's grief turned into a debilitating depression, culminating with Natasha finding her comatose with a mouthful of dissolving sleeping pills. Natasha later said she had saved Marilyn from a suicide attempt. Marilyn, in contrast, downplayed the incident and claimed Natasha had blown everything out of proportion.

Marilyn made her way back to Natasha's home in 1951, this time on North Crescent Drive. During this period Marilyn sold a fur coat—one of the few beloved presents from Johnny she had managed to keep—to help Natasha's financial woes at the time. Natasha also accompanied Marilyn on a trip to visit her long-lost father, which ended in Marilyn returning to the car in tears, saying that he refused to see her.

Even after his death, Johnny Hyde continued his gift-giving to Marilyn. His last and perhaps greatest present to Marilyn was securing for her a seven-year contract with Twentieth Century-Fox, which was activated on May 11, 1951.

Under the terms of the agreement, Marilyn was paid a salary of $500 per week for the first year. It was a boon for her financially. But she did not sign until one addendum was added to her contract—Natasha Lytess would be hired as an acting coach at Fox. The studio agreed, and Natasha was also provided a salary of $500 per week. Marilyn paid Natasha an additional $250 per week out of her pocket for private lessons, a move that made her coach considerably better paid than herself. Marilyn's fortunes, and consequently Natasha's fortunes, continued to improve.

Now with a permanent studio to call home, Marilyn's career had nowhere to go but up; still, her insecurities remained. Soon directors discovered that Marilyn Monroe on the set also meant Natasha Lytess on the set.

Marilyn developed the bad habit of looking off camera to Natasha for approval after a take, effectively usurping directors' authority. It was Natasha, not directors, she listened to, much to their frustrations. The result was Natasha's removal by directors from the set on numerous occasions, but Marilyn's refusal to appear in front of the camera without her coach always meant Natasha would eventually be reinstated.

While it's true Natasha wasn't making any friends on the set, at least some of the responsibility for Natasha's acrimonious relationships falls on Marilyn herself. Had she not looked to Natasha after takes or disregarded the directors' instructions in favor of Natasha's, filming would have gone more smoothly. Natasha's demanding, severe personality didn't exactly help matters, although it should be noted many of Marilyn's costars and directors disagreed with Natasha's acting advice.

Alex D'Arcy said, "Natasha was really advising her badly, justifying her own presence on set by requiring take after take and simply feeding on Marilyn's insecurity. 'Well, that was all right, dear,' she often said to Marilyn, 'but maybe we should do it one more time.'"

Many people encouraged her to drop Natasha, but Marilyn was incapable of performing without her. Screenwriter Nunnally Johnson, who wrote *How to Marry a Millionaire*, said Marilyn appeared to be under Natasha's "spell."

Natasha's intense overprotectiveness, once so comforting when Marilyn needed support, eventually began working against her. It was her overbearing behavior that would lead to a sour relationship with Joe DiMaggio.

Marilyn began dating Joe in March 1952 and soon found herself in the position of playing mediator between her new boyfriend and her closest companion. Marilyn later noted that Natasha was jealous of any man she dated, Joe especially.

"I disliked him at once," Natasha said of Joe. "He is a man with a closed, vapid look. Marilyn introduced us and said I was her coach, which made no impression on him. A week later I telephoned her and Joe answered: 'I think if you want to talk to Miss Monroe'—Miss Monroe!—'you'd better call her agent.'"

Natasha further told Marilyn that Joe "is the punishment of God in your life." It was a tad dramatic and did nothing to improve her position. In turn, the very private Joe resented Natasha's intrusive presence in his life with Marilyn.

Natasha had reason to be concerned—she probably sensed her place in Marilyn's life was threatened. After Marilyn married Joe in January 1954, Natasha was demoted from confidant to on-set coach. Natasha was losing her closest friend and, because she had quit her job at Columbia to work exclusively with Marilyn, she was in danger of losing her sole source of income.

And, as it turns out, the always-ambitious Marilyn had bigger and better plans for her career and they didn't include Natasha.

When Marilyn's marriage to Joe imploded later in 1954, Natasha was there to offer support and comfort. Marilyn repaid the kindness by demanding Twentieth Century-Fox give Natasha a raise. After almost twenty movies together it was becoming clear to Marilyn that absolutely no one she worked with liked Natasha Lytess.

Now unhappy with her contract at Fox, which kept her locked into a lower-paying salary, and separated from Joe, Marilyn had little reason to stay in California. To win the respect of the studio and have access to better roles, Marilyn stopped showing up for work. She secretly moved her life to New York, where she was hiding from the studio, and where she began studying at the Actors Studio under Lee Strasberg, just like she told Susan Strasberg she had intended.

One thing—she neglected to tell Natasha any of this. After Natasha had built her life around Marilyn, the actress vanished overnight, leaving Natasha alone in Los Angeles. Without Marilyn, she had no umbrella of protection at Fox, and the studio had no interest in keeping Natasha on the payroll.

Natasha later said, "In Marilyn's powerful position, she had only to crook her finger for me to keep my job at the studio. Had she any sense of gratitude for my contribution to her life, she could have saved my job."

But Marilyn wouldn't take Natasha's calls. When Marilyn returned to Los Angeles, she refused all communication when Natasha tried to get in touch.

Natasha once arrived unannounced where Marilyn was staying, only to have agent Lew Wasserman block the door and tell her, "Your engagement with the studio is none of Miss Monroe's concern." As Natasha left, she saw Marilyn watching from a second-story window without an expression on her face. They never saw each other again.

To make matters worse, Natasha had been diagnosed with cancer and was in physical pain. Relieved from her studio job, she now had to find other private students to support herself and her daughter. Natasha's confusion and hurt are understandable. That Marilyn so abruptly cut off all ties to someone who, for better or worse, had devoted herself so completely to her seems out of character. It is a strange anomaly in the story of Marilyn Monroe.

Before her death from cancer in 1964, Natasha said of Marilyn: "I wish I had one-tenth of Marilyn's cleverness. The truth is, my life and my feelings were very much in her hands. I was the older one, the teacher, but she knew the depth of my attachment to her, and she exploited those feelings as only a beautiful younger person can. She said she was the needy one. Alas, it was the reverse. My life with her was a constant denial of myself."

THE STRASBERG FAMILY

Marilyn first became aware of Lee Strasberg through Elia Kazan, whom she was dating at the time. Elia and Lee had known each other through the New York theatre scene for years, and both had been part of the groundbreaking Group Theatre, which Lee cofounded in 1931 with Cheryl Crawford and Harold Clurman. As early as the 1930s, Lee Strasberg demonstrated a divisive personality that drew praise for his genius and invited criticism from others who believed he was a charlatan and a bully.

"He was the force that held the thirty-odd members of the theatre together, made them 'permanent.' He did this not only by his superior knowledge but by the threat of his anger," Elia Kazan once said.

Elia's personal opinion of Lee over the years recognized both his talents and sliced through his hubris. Lee exhibited hints of brilliance and flashes of fine leadership, but he was also prone to arrogance and fury, all of which he used to his advantage.

"It must be said that in the Group's earliest years Lee Strasberg was, despite his abrupt manner, one of its great strengths," writes Richard Schickel in his book, *Elia Kazan: A Biography*. "The man didn't give a hoot about hits or flops. One almost gets the feeling that he didn't care all that much about the content of the plays he directed—except insofar as they were showcases for the thing he narrowly, passionately and forever cared about, which was his 'method.'"

The Group Theatre dissolved in 1941. It didn't last long, but many of the Group's writers, directors, actors, and teachers went on to extraordinary careers in American theatre and cinema. Clifford Odets, John Garfield, Franchot Tone, Frances Farmer, Phoebe Brand, Stella Adler, Robert Lewis, Sanford Meisner, Harry Morgan, Howard Da Silva, Morris Carnovsky and, of course, Elia Kazan, were just a few of the members honing their respective crafts in the Group Theatre environment.

Lee Strasberg's life changed immensely during his time with the Group Theatre. For one, he met and married his wife, Paula, who was a member of the Group. Next his career began focusing more on teaching rather than acting. One of his greatest strengths was his ability to hold an audience's attention, but the original plan was to have been an actor. He studied under Russian actress Maria Ouspenskaya and director Richard Boleslawski, who had worked with Konstantin Stanislavski in the Moscow Art Theatre.

It was Stanislavski's "system" of acting that evolved into the American version called the Method. "Strasberg was galvanized," Schickel writes. "He knew that his own future as an actor—he was a slight and unhandsome man—was limited. But he soon perceived that as a theoretician and teacher of this new 'system' he might become a major force in American theater."

By focusing on teaching, Lee found a unique niche in the theatre world. When Elia Kazan cofounded the Actors Studio in 1947, he invited his former mentor Lee Strasberg to lead a couple of workshops. Lee accepted the invitation over the protests of Paula, who argued that a genius of Lee's caliber should be paid for his services. But Lee's instincts proved correct. The short-term, unpaid assignment eventually parlayed itself into a long-term placement when Elia hired Lee to take the role of director in 1951—the same year Elia was seeing Marilyn on the West Coast.

The qualities Elia had observed in the Group showed themselves at the Actors Studio, but just as he had done in the past Lee Strasberg soon built a reputation as a formative teacher of the Method. Lee's version of the Method varied from others who also used Stanislavski's "system" of acting as a foundation. He wanted his students to focus on the psychological aspects of acting by delving into their pasts and using real events and emotions for their performances. Stella Adler, an actress from the Group and also Method instructor, found the Strasberg approach limiting, not to mention potentially unhealthy.

As director of the Actors Studio, Lee Strasberg built a reputation for himself and the academy as a preeminent destination for serious acting students. Through Elia Kazan, Marilyn would have had an insider's glimpse into the rise of the Actors Studio's prominence and importance as early as 1951. Her romance with Elia didn't last, but her interest in Lee Strasberg and the Actors Studio did. She began quietly formulating a plan to leave Los Angeles and study with the great Lee Strasberg at the Actors Studio.

As Susan Strasberg writes in her memoir, *Marilyn and Me: Sisters, Rivals, Friends*, when she and her mother were visiting the set of *There's No Business Like Show Business*, Marilyn pulled aside the younger Strasberg and whispered intensely, "I really admire your father, I've heard such wonderful things about him. He's so brilliant with actors, you must be so proud of him. . . . I'm going to come to New York and study acting with him. It's what I want more than anything."

It was the first time Marilyn had made her intentions known. In a 1972 interview, Lee said, "She always in that sense wanted to be an actress and therefore felt somehow unfulfilled. The more success there was, the more unfulfilled she was."

Marilyn began private lessons with Lee Strasberg in February 1955. Admittance into the Actors Studio required an audition, and she was not yet comfortable enough to participate in the public workshops. Working with Lee one-on-one at the Strasberg home allowed Marilyn to build relationships with the entire family. As was her pattern, Marilyn was soon part of the family—joining them for dinners, going on vacations, attending plays. In essence she functioned as a third sibling to Lee and Paula's children.

"The first time I met her, I remember she came out of the living room and Pop said, 'This is my son,' and my first impression of her was that she was different from most of the people who came to the house," remembered John Strasberg. "I watched all these people, trading their most human qualities, betraying themselves for success at all cost, to become rich and famous, and afterward, when it was too late, they realize they lost the best part of themselves along the way. But she, she was like me. When I looked into her eyes, it was like looking into my own, they were like a child's eyes. I was still a child. You know how children just look at you. My feeling was she had less ego, or was less narcissistic than most of the actors who never really bothered with me. She was just another person to me, another one from that world I felt cut off, excluded from. She was nicer, real simple, no makeup, and she really looked at me as if she saw me. It wasn't that I wanted people to look at me, but I knew the difference when she did. I knew everyone said she was the sexiest, most sensual woman in the world. Not for me. I thought there was something wrong with me for not feeling that from her. I felt it from other women who came to the house. I was pretty sexually frustrated then. She was so open, so loose, and her sensuality as such was so totally innocent, nothing dirty in it at all, and the first time it was just like talking to an ordinary person, only realer than most who came into the house in those days. She was quiet, too, I remember, like an animal is quiet, and I was like that, too, survival tactics. She seemed smart, but not in an educated way, instinctively, smart, nobody's fool."

Marilyn grew comfortable with the Strasbergs, both personally and professionally. At the heart of her relationship with them was Lee and Paula's belief in her acting abilities. Their encouragement gave her confidence, and along with it she eventually found the courage to join the workshops at the Actors Studios with the hope of pursuing more challenging parts.

Lee's approach to the Method was such that he believed anyone, with the proper training, could become a great actor and play parts originally thought beyond the person's capabilities. This could apply to trained actors, but also laypeople. This was exactly what Marilyn was looking for at this stage in her career.

"The idea of combating typecasting would have appealed to Marilyn, who was looking to rebuild her career and move beyond the dumb blonde roles and sex symbol image that was now working against her," Schickel writes. "If Lee Strasberg had a history of casting actors in roles other directors would not have considered, it may very well have buoyed Marilyn's belief that with discipline, rehearsal and training, her possibilities as an actress were limitless. Furthermore, the confidence in Marilyn's talent by someone as renown as Lee Strasberg would have made her feel accepted. By allowing her to become an extended member of the family, she would have felt accepted."

Marilyn's first movie after beginning classes with the Strasbergs was *Bus Stop* and her acting was noticeably more natural. *Bus Stop* also marked the start of a new dynamic on the set of Marilyn's movies. Paula was Marilyn's on-set acting coach, and it was she who helped Marilyn break down her scripts, learn lines, and develop exercises to help access characters for authentic performances. Lee remained in New York to continue teaching workshops but was available by phone when needed or on a trip if an emergency arose. Such was the case when Lee flew to England (at Marilyn's expense) during production of *The Prince and the Showgirl.*

Just as Lee's techniques were controversial in acting circles, he and his wife similarly experienced criticism for their place in Marilyn's personal life. As Marilyn had previously done with Natasha Lytess, she looked to Paula on the set for approval instead of the director. Marilyn's perfectionism and insecurity caused her to insist on multiple takes, and Paula did nothing to dissuade her from the need. Nearly everyone disliked Paula on the set; not only was she usurping control from directors, but she served as a gatekeeper to Marilyn herself. Behind her back, crew members made fun of her personality and her penchant for wearing only black. Her tendency to coddle Marilyn and mother her in professional settings didn't help matters. Ultimately, though, Marilyn shares much of the credit for creating the dynamic directors and crews so hated. Paula acted the way she did precisely because Marilyn wanted her to; and in fairness to Paula, if it weren't for her on the set guiding Marilyn's performance it's clear Marilyn wouldn't have performed at all.

In New York, Marilyn continued her education by attending workshops and private lessons with Lee. Directors and crew members had been unhappy with Paula Strasberg on the set, but another problem arose closer to home. Marilyn, now involved with Arthur Miller, found her new love, and her eventual husband had little patience for the Strasberg Method.

Marilyn converses with her drama coach Paula Strasberg while filming Something's Got to Give *in 1962. Marilyn's insistence on having coaches accompany her on the set caused enormous resentment with directors, crew, and other actors.*
Photofest

"From time to time in the following months I would stand at the back of the theatre watching sections of the performance, trying to understand what there was about it all that bothered me," he wrote in *Timebends*. "It was marvelously effective—although I could drive a truck through some of Lee's stretched-out pauses, which were tainting his performance with more than a hint of self-indulgence."

He wasn't alone. Lee Strasberg drew a lot of criticism from many directions, not least of all from Elia Kazan. It was Elia Kazan who had placed Lee Strasberg in charge of the academy and brought him to Marilyn's attention in the first place. Over the years, Elia's opinion of Lee teetered back and forth between admiration for his better qualities and frustration for his faults.

"He had a gift for anger and a taste for the power it brought him," Elia Kazan remembered of their time with the Group Theatre. "No one questioned his dominance—he spoke holy writ—his leading role in that summer's activities, and his right to all power. To win his favor became everyone's goal. His explosions of temper maintained the discipline of this camp of high-strung people. I came to believe that without their fear of this man, the Group would fly apart, everyone going in different directions instead of to where he was pointing. I was afraid of him too. Even as I admired him."

Criticisms aside, Marilyn trusted Lee Strasberg implicitly and believed her craft was improving. In many ways it was—but it came at a high price. Lee encouraged his students to enter analysis to gain insight into their pasts. When students can access their experiences—and traumas—they can use their authentic feelings and memories for more genuine performances. In Marilyn's case, this process appears to have hurt her more than it helped. In the 1950s, therapy was still developing. Psychiatrists helped Marilyn access her childhood traumas but were unable to provide her with tools to process and heal.

Marilyn had a natural inclination for depression and anxiety to begin with, and her symptoms intensified after she entered psychotherapy. In essence, instead of helping Marilyn, therapy was continually retraumatizing her. By the end of her life, Marilyn was seeing her psychiatrist daily, sometimes more than one session per day. It's important to point out this was also unintentional. Neither Lee nor her doctors intended to hurt her. As psychotherapy research further evolved and antidepressants were made available in the years following Marilyn's death, the process became much more helpful for patients. In the meantime, Marilyn diligently kept up her studies and analysis in the hope they would help her.

"He carried with him the aura of a prophet, a magician, a witch doctor, a psychoanalyst, and a feared father of a Jewish home," Elia Kazan remembered of Lee Strasberg. The word father is key. Marilyn looked to him as a father figure, someone more than just an instructor, but a protector who could help shape her life for the better. The authoritative demeanor he presented to others lent itself to interpretation as a savior of sorts. Because Lee and Paula allowed her to essentially become their third child, she placed herself in a position of looking to them for guidance and approval. Marilyn was generous with the biological Strasberg children—she gifted an original Chagall sketch to Susan and signed over her Ford Thunderbird to John. Susan later recalled that for as much as she grew to love Marilyn, there was also an underlying resentment. Lee could sometimes be an absent or cold father to Susan and John but rocked Marilyn to sleep and sang her lullabies when she was depressed.

Arthur Miller grew to resent the place Lee and Paula had in Marilyn's life. Arthur believed the sign of a good teacher was to make students feel confident enough to make them independent. In Arthur's opinion the Strasbergs kept their students reliant on them.

"You see, Strasberg pretended to have some secret key to heaven, and that's how he manipulated actors. In fact, you can do that with lots of people. Somebody assumes authority and nobody knows why. My reaction is just the opposite: I can't give authority that way to someone else, so I couldn't have peaceful relations with that person. Anyway, I thought Strasberg was a very destructive force. He tried to make himself indispensable to the actors, whereas a real coach should try to make them independent. Strasberg worked the opposite way."

Arthur further believed Paula fed Marilyn's insecurities on the set.

"She had a need for an older woman who could weave fantasies around her. But Paula was not helpful: she played the part of a guru, a power Marilyn had given to her, of course, because she was the wife and deputy of the great Lee Strasberg," Arthur said. "Occasionally, they [Marilyn and Paula] spoke with him on the phone, which increased her isolation from John [Huston] and all the others—except Paula. But Paula had nothing to give Marilyn that could help her, except to reaffirm her suspicions about others. That was her function, to confirm Marilyn's anxieties."

Marilyn's masseuse Ralph Roberts recalls one such incident during the filming of *The Misfits* when Marilyn was certain costar Eli Wallach was trying to position himself to have a better camera angle. "Paula and I were standing, looking into the room at the ranch house where they were filming the scene of Marilyn and Eli Wallach dancing. Eli was putting everything into the scene—one might almost say he was getting carried away with it all," Ralph remembered in his book. "Suddenly, Paula grabbed my arm, whispering, 'What on earth is he doing?'

"I looked again and wondered why she was so upset. It seemed a little heightened, but then he was supposed to be drunk. After 'cut,' Huston wanted another take. Marilyn walked over to us, 'Did you see what he's doing?'

"Paula replied, 'You must say something to John.'

"When I asked what was going on, Marilyn answered, 'He's leading me in such a manner that his face is always toward the camera. Doesn't he know that nobody is going to look at his face if the camera is focused on me wriggling my rear?'

"From that moment there was a definite coolness noticeable in her attitude toward Eli."

The Miller marriage collapsed for good during the filming of *The Misfits* in 1960. The Strasbergs supported Marilyn during the divorce process and in the aftermath of Clark Gable's death. On the day of his funeral, Marilyn was too distraught to attend. Marilyn stayed in New York and, at Lee's suggestion, spent the day at the Strasberg home. Ralph Roberts went with her. "Lee was wonderfully supportive," Ralph wrote. "There was much talk—wandering through the past, a discussion of the future work she was to do. We spent hours listening to symphonies and her favorite singer, Claudia Muzio."

In the company of the Strasbergs and Ralph, Marilyn felt safe and found comfort. After her day with the Strasbergs, Marilyn was able to gather herself enough to begin thinking of the future. On the way home, she told Ralph. "I feel completely drained. Lee is right. Clark lived the fullest life of anyone I've ever known. From the beginning to the very end. . . . I have to start going to the Actors Studio. I have to start putting my house in order."

Marilyn planned to build her life around work, and work meant the Actors Studio and the Strasbergs.

There are some reports that Marilyn may have been losing some of her faith in the Strasbergs. It's difficult to determine because she continued working with them until her death in 1962. What's clear is they made a few missteps in guiding her career. In 1961 the Strasbergs advised Marilyn against taking the part of Holly Golightly in *Breakfast at Tiffany's*. The 1958 novella by her acquaintance Truman Capote was purchased by Paramount Pictures and adapted into a screenplay by George Axelrod, the brilliant playwright behind *The Seven Year Itch*. Capote specifically requested Marilyn play Holly. Other than Holly's age, the description of her in the book perfectly describes Marilyn.

"She was still on the landing, and the ragbag colors of her hair, tawny streaks, strands of albino-blond and yellow caught the hall light. It was a warm evening nearly summer and she wore a slim cool black dress, black sandals and a pearl choker. . . . A pair of dark glasses blotted out her eyes. It was a face beyond childhood, yet this side of belonging to a woman. I thought her anywhere between sixteen and thirty, as it turned out she was two months shy of her nineteenth birthday."

Holly Golightly supports herself in New York by dating lonely men, and the Strasbergs were adamant Marilyn should not play "a lady of the night" type. The role eventually went to Audrey Hepburn and the movie itself is a classic of 1960s cinema. It's impossible to say how the movie would have been received with Marilyn in the lead role, but Capote himself disliked the movie.

Around the same time—early 1961—the Strasbergs were also responsible for Marilyn losing another role, this time for the television production of *Rain*. With television a growing market and movie scripts limited at Twentieth Century-Fox, Marilyn was open to expanding into another medium. In *Rain*, Marilyn would portray Sadie Thompson, a prostitute and free spirit on the island of Pago Pago. An impressive list of leading ladies had previously played Sadie, including Gloria Swanson in *Sadie Thompson* (1928), Joan Crawford in *Rain* (1932), and Rita Hayworth in *Miss Sadie Thompson* (1953). On Broadway, the great Jeanne Eagels played the part in the 1920s to great acclaim—a performance Lee Strasberg was familiar with.

Marilyn and NBC entered into negotiations to produce a television version of *Rain*. Marilyn requested Lee Strasberg as director and asked for $25,000 as his fee, along with $12,500 for Paula as her coach. Suddenly, the Strasbergs were in favor of Marilyn playing a prostitute and encouraged the production to move forward. NBC hired Frederic March to play Rev. Davidson and Rod Serling of *The Twilight Zone* to write the teleplay. The network allowed Marilyn to have a say when it came to hiring crew and approving the script, but talks stalled when she dug her heels in about the director. Lee Strasberg may have built a name for himself as an acting instructor but he was untested as a director. Marilyn insisted—no Lee Strasberg, no Marilyn Monroe. NBC executives were unwilling to let an inexperienced director take the helm of such a high-profile project. With negotiations at a standstill, NBC withdrew.

With *Rain* now off the table, Marilyn didn't begin her next project, *Something's Got to Give*, until 1962. Whether or not Marilyn was experiencing emotional distance when it came to her instructors, she did establish a physical distance in the form of moving back to Los Angeles. Technically, she was bicoastal because she maintained her apartment in New York. But Marilyn began spending an increasing amount of time in Los Angeles.

Production began on what would be Marilyn's last project, *Something's Got to Give*, in 1962. Once again, Paula was at her side on the set and once again, the presence of an acting coach and gatekeeper created tension among the crew and other actors. When Marilyn was fired, Paula returned home to New York; neither Paula nor Lee would see Marilyn alive again.

As Twentieth Century-Fox began contract negotiations to hire Marilyn back to finish *Something's Got to Give*, a draft of the new contract clearly indicates that Paula Strasberg would not be permitted on the set. "No employees of . . . hers will be allowed in the studio without the express consent of our studio."

As it turned out, the contract negotiations became moot once Marilyn passed away on August 5. Lee and Paula attended her memorial service together; Lee delivered the eulogy. A recording of Lee speaking that day exists and reveals that his voice is cracking with emotion and choking back tears.

Lee was surprised to learn that Marilyn had left the bulk of her estate to him in her will—before her death, he had no clue he had been included. Marilyn's estate was cataloged, boxed up, and put into storage for several years while the will went through the probate process. During that time, Paula passed away in 1966 at the age of fifty-seven from bone marrow cancer. In 1968, Lee married Anna Mizrahi, with whom he had two more children. Known primarily for teaching, Lee earned an Academy Award nomination for his portrayal of Hyman Roth in *The Godfather Part II*.

Marilyn's belongings weren't turned over to Lee Strasberg until a few years after her death. Lee died of a heart attack in 1982, with the estate then transferred to his widow, Anna Strasberg. She held onto Marilyn's belongings until 1999. In an interview with Scott Fortner, Anna said Marilyn left her belongings to Lee because she knew he would take care of them. In the process of managing the Marilyn Monroe estate after Lee's death, she said she tried to respect Marilyn's memory as Lee would have wanted. "I was guided by what I felt Lee would expect me to do—show her struggle to become a serious actor and protect her dignity," she said. Since 1999, Anna Strasberg has sold off the vast majority of Marilyn's estate, with some of the proceeds going to charity. She was getting older, she told Fortner, and it was time to downsize.

There are many strong opinions about Lee Strasberg and his teaching, and the place he and Paula had in Marilyn's life. Opinions aside, Lee Strasberg said of her in his eulogy, "For us, Marilyn was a devoted and loyal friend—a colleague constantly reaching for perfection. We shared her pain and difficulties, and some of her joys. She was a member of our family."

· 21 ·

The Method

$\mathcal{M}$arilyn Monroe learned about Method acting, Lee Strasberg and the Actors Studio from her one-time lover Elia Kazan. When Marilyn and Elia were seeing each other in 1951, he was in the process of installing Lee Strasberg as director of the Actors Studio in New York.

At the time, Elia Kazan had one foot in New York theatre and another foot in Hollywood movies. When he was in New York, he worked on strengthening the Actors Studio and part of the strategy was hiring Lee Strasberg, a man he sometimes spoke of glowingly and at other times he criticized bitterly. On his trips to Los Angeles, one of which was with Arthur Miller, he worked on establishing himself as a movie director. It's not much of a stretch to imagine him telling Marilyn about his career on the East Coast—theatre life, Stanislavski, Method acting, the Actors Studio, hiring Lee Strasberg, his collaboration with Arthur Miller. The blueprint for Marilyn's future was formed as early as 1951.

If Marilyn was adamant about one thing in her career, it was that she wanted to be a great actress. She wanted more than just being a movie star, a distinction she was unequivocally accomplishing by the early 1950s.

Becoming a member of the Actors Studio meant tapping into a lineage that had its roots in Russian theatre. Method acting as it is known today was inspired by Konstantin Stanislavski (January 17, 1863–August 7, 1938), an accomplished actor, director, and teacher who cofounded the Moscow Art Theatre in 1898 in Russia. As part of his work, Stanislavski began developing a "system" of acting that required actors to *experience* instead of *representing*.

Stanislavski subjected himself to self-analysis, which was in its infancy, to develop "psychological realism." In 1926, he began working on what would become *An Actor's Work*, a manual in the form of a fictional student's diary.

198

Once Stanislavski and his acting troupe came to the United States, his "system" evolved and the results depended on the instructor. The two most popular types of the American versions of Stanislavski's system became known as the Method, as taught by Lee Strasberg, who encouraged a psychological approach, and Stella Adler, who preferred the term "Modern Acting" and emphasized imagination. Lee believed tapping into one's own experiences and memories enabled actors to give a more authentic performance. He recommended students enter analysis as a means to mine their past.

"Not every actor Strasberg later directed bought into all this. 'Hocuspocus,' Morris Carnovsky called it," writes Richard Schickel in *Elia Kazan: A Biography*. "It must also be said that many an actor instinctively worked in this manner, without coaching. But Strasberg believed he could codify this system, a necessary precursor to teaching it to anyone who wanted to learn it."

In contrast, Stella Adler taught that reconnecting with memories took the actor out of the present, and therefore out of the performance. The internal emotional recollections, experiences, and traumas Strasberg's Method required, she further believed, were unhealthy. She advocated relying on the imagination and using external research. As she taught the "system," or Modern Acting or Method, this gave the artist more freedom and creativity. Actors achieve their performances more easily and can access a broader range than digging into their memories.

Stella was speaking from experience. As an actress under Lee Strasberg's direction at the Group Theatre, she found his Method difficult and too emotionally taxing. When she had the opportunity to meet the great Stanislavski in Paris, she confessed to him that she had grown to hate acting after being subjected to his theories. He invited her to study with him for a couple of weeks and during that time, she realized her interpretation of "the system" was closer to Stanislavski's, and it was her belief Lee Strasberg had gotten it wrong with his Method teachings.

As Lee taught the Method, actors draw upon their pasts to bring realistic elements and emotions to their performances. One of the exercises he taught was "effective memory," which requires actors to remember sensory details from emotional moments in their past to trigger those same feelings and then apply them to a performance. In theory, it leads to a more authentic performance.

Some believe Method actors can become too entrenched in their roles and potentially cause harm to themselves or their bodies. It could also be argued that when dredging up painful memories there is a risk of re-traumatizing the artist—which almost certainly happened with Marilyn. There have even been instances when actors have taken the Method too far and put themselves in extreme conditions as a way to identify with their characters or have lost the ability to compartmentalize their roles within real life. (In recent years, certain actors have become famous for not coming out of character during projects and, in effect, living as the character. It should be noted that Lee Strasberg advised against such behavior and would not have considered this Method acting.)

Potential damage to the psyche aside, there was another form of criticism aimed at the Method. More traditionally trained actors argued Method acting took away from the actual craft, which requires practice, technique, and skill. For example, Shakespearian actors argue that if one can perform Shakespeare—with the language, iambic pentameter, and the deep insight into human psychology—then an actor can accomplish any performance. Shakespeare relies heavily on imagination, as stage directions are minimal. Laurence Olivier's training was Shakespearian, and he had little patience for actors who took a different approach. His intolerance insulted Marilyn on the set of *The Prince and the Showgirl.*

What Olivier missed was that Method acting was much better suited to movie performances than he gave it credit for; his training took place on the theatre stage and required a completely different skill set. Movies require more nuanced performances because camera close-ups pick up subtle gestures. In contrast, theatre needs grand gestures, voice projection, and exaggerated facial expressions to bridge the physical gap between performers and audience members. Movies do not have to film in sequence, can call "cut!" if an actor needs to pause, and performances are spread out over weeks or months. That's not to say the performances aren't emotionally taxing, but the process is less ideal for theatre, which requires multiple performances every week. This is in addition to no retakes, memorizing the entire script, and staying aware of the audience so movements can be adjusted if needed.

Marilyn may have chosen one of the most respected drama schools in the United States, but not everyone appreciated the Method or agreed with the Lee Strasberg interpretation of it. Arthur Miller didn't believe Lee and his wife Paula helped Marilyn professionally and grew to dislike them personally. Her friend (and possible one-time lover) Marlon Brando is frequently associated with Method acting, the Actors Studio, and Lee Strasberg, but in actuality gave credit to Stella Adler for teaching him how to act. He did not consider himself a Method actor, did not like Lee, and resented the association with the Actors Studio.

Classes at the Actors Studio began with relaxation and concentration, then releasing any muscular tension, such as shaking out one's arms. (Marilyn was known to shake out her arms and hands before a scene.) In addition to effective memory, students performed scenes for one another and then listened to Lee for feedback. Other exercises included acting without sets or props, "overall sensation" to recreate the sensations of physical memories, and the "private moment," which was introduced in 1956. "The goal of the private moment was to conquer any remaining hang-ups an actor might have about performing in front of other people, and help them achieve 'public solitude,'" writes Isaac Butler in *The Method: How the Twentieth Century Learned to Act*. "To Strasberg's detractors, the private moment was nothing more than an excuse for exhibitionism and voyeurism. Although the vast majority of private moments were fairly mundane, nudity, mimed masturbation, and grand lachrymose displays were not unheard of."

And Lee Strasberg had a great many detractors, including other instructors and students. Many of his pupils went on to give acclaimed performances with accomplished careers. Others complained his instructions were difficult to understand and his feedback contradictory, not to mention unnecessarily vicious.

"From his very first session, Strasberg established anew his reputation for brutality," writes Butler in *The Method*. "He spoke with open disdain about Kazan's way of teaching, and, as the director Arthur Penn described it, he 'was a damn near despotic and frightening figure. There were ten gory years where Lee ruled with a capricious iron fist.' But Strasberg's appeal lay in the way he tailored his feedback to each individual actor and their needs, and in his remarkable eye for inauthenticity and cliché. Members of the Studio frequently compared him to a jeweler peering at them through some kind of magic loupe. But all of this also meant that, as Martin Balsam put it, 'he was impossible to please.' If you focused on emotion, he'd say you were neglecting action; if you were focused on action, he'd zero in on your feelings. 'We were all eager to please and our egos were so fragile,' Balsam said. 'It was murder.'"

Lee most likely spared the very sensitive Marilyn from the harshest parts of his personality. (Susan Strasberg once recalled overhearing her father lull Marilyn to sleep in their home by singing her Brahms' Lullaby.) Marilyn performed scenes in class like other students but typically kept quiet otherwise. With Lee's private lessons, she would have been able to receive one-on-one feedback.

Whatever negative feedback Lee Strasberg and the Actors Studio faced, Marilyn herself believed she had found the right place when it came to working on her craft. She felt safe in the environment, trusted Lee's and Paula's instructions, and took her studies seriously.

Marilyn's first film since training with the Strasbergs was *Bus Stop* in 1956, and her performance was indeed different than her previous ones. Her movements were more natural and she spoke with an Ozark accent appropriate to her character. It was indicative of a larger development in American acting. When movies began as silents, actors overemphasized their gestures to get their emotions across to the audience. When "talkies" arrived, actors spoke in a dialogue so formal and proper that it no longer sounded natural. Sometimes called the "Mid-Atlantic" or "Transatlantic" accent, it was an odd combination of British and upper-class American accents.

In the mid-century, with the influence of Stanislavski's system and the Method, acting was in the middle of a revolution. An increasing number of actors were evolving away from unnatural speaking voices and overly dramatic performances. The new way of approaching story and character was authenticity.

In an interview with Pete Martin for *The Saturday Evening Post* in 1956, Marilyn discusses her dedication. "'There's another thing I want to ask you,' I said. 'It's about something you said to a man in the Fox Studio legal department. You said, 'I don't care about money. I just want to be wonderful.' He didn't know what you meant by that.

"'I meant that I want to be a real actress instead of a superficial one,' Marilyn herself told me. 'For the first time I'm learning to use myself fully as an actress. I want to add something to what I had before. I want to be in the kind of pictures where I can develop, not just wear tights. Some people thought that they were getting their money's worth when they saw me in *The Seven Year Itch*, but in the future, I want people to get even more for their money when they see me. Only today a taxi driver said to me, 'Why did they ever put you in that little stinker, *River of No Return*?'"

In the late 1950s, journalist W. J. Weatherby asked Paula Strasberg about Marilyn and her acting career. "Actors should know themselves and their craft," she said. "There are too many unthinking, automatic performances. People patronize Marilyn. They think she's weak in the head and in her character. They don't know her. She's very intelligent and sensitive and a fast learner. She is never satisfied. She examines everything she does. Are you trying to tell me such intelligent behavior is wrong? If so, you're as bad as those moronic people in Hollywood, who underrated her for years."

The Actors Studio has provided a haven and solid education for some actors; others have found the Method impossible. Ultimately, it's a matter of opinion.

"The decade or so that had passed since the collapse of the Group had done nothing to soften Stella Adler's or [another instructor] Sanford Meisner's view of Lee Strasberg. Even though all three teachers were united in their belief in experiencing, Strasberg was, in Stella's and Sandy's eyes, a fraud who preached a theory of acting that was as unhealthy as it was unhelpful," writes Butler. "As they would tell their classes—or, when asked, reporters—Strasberg's internalized focus, along with his passion for true emotion, ruined actors."

· 22 ·

Television: The Medium
of a New Generation

*M*arilyn's rise to fame coincided with the television boom of the 1950s. At the beginning of the decade, only 20 percent of American homes had a television set. By the end of the 1950s, that number had grown to 90 percent. Marilyn herself appeared on TV only a couple of times, but the medium had a major impact on movies and her career in general.

In 1950, Marilyn appeared in a television commercial for Royal Triton Oil. In the ad, Marilyn portrays a young woman who just bought her first car, which she named "Cynthia." She says sweetly to a service station employee, "Put Royal Triton in Cynthia's little tummy." Then she looks directly into the camera and coos, "Cynthia will just love that Royal Triton!"

Movie studios were concerned about losing audience members to this new phenomenon, which didn't require leaving the house and, after the initial purchase, was free. To compete, studios began offering elevated experiences that television couldn't provide to lure the public back into theatres.

As the decade progressed, more movies were filmed in color, a distinct and obvious advantage over the black-and-white television picture. Beginning with Marilyn's breakout role, *Niagara* (1953), she was seen in glorious color. Her bright lips, platinum hair, and luminous skin glowed on the screen. A wardrobe was created in vivid colors to draw the eye directly to her.

Studios also experimented with technology, such as 3-D, stereophonic sound, and wide screens. In the case of Twentieth Century-Fox, the studio developed a wide-screen format called CinemaScope. The first two movies filmed in CinemaScope were *The Robe* and *How to Marry a Millionaire*, both of which were released in 1953.

To promote CinemaScope, Marilyn appeared on *The Jack Benny Show* on September 13, just days before *The Robe* opened. During a comedic sketch on the show, Jack Benny plays himself as a cruise passenger dreaming about how he wishes Marilyn Monroe or Jane Russell from *Gentlemen Prefer Blondes* (which had just come out in July) were on the ship with him. Marilyn appears and in her Lorelei Lee voice asks Jack to be a costar in her next film, which was, of course, *How to Marry a Millionaire*. She sings "Bye Bye Baby" before leaving the dream sequence.

Later in the show, Jack and Marilyn walk out hand in hand from behind the stage curtain and he announces, "Marilyn, this is your first appearance on television, isn't it?"

Smiling, Marilyn responds, "Yes, it is, Jack."

Jack goes on to ask Marilyn about her new film, to which Marilyn replies it's called *How to Marry a Millionaire* and it's in CinemaScope. When Marilyn says CinemaScope is complicated and theatres had to remove some seats to accommodate the bigger screen, he quips, "Well, in my picture they could have taken out *all* of the seats!" He then makes one of his trademark indignant Jack Benny faces as Marilyn and the audience laugh.

Marilyn's contract with Twentieth Century-Fox would not allow her to receive payment for appearing on television. Instead, *The Jack Benny Show* gifted her with a new black Cadillac convertible as "payment."

Her next appearance wasn't until April 8, 1955, when she appeared not to promote Twentieth Century-Fox, but instead to explain her rebellion against the company. For his show *Person to Person*, journalist Edward R. Murrow interviewed guests from a New York studio while his guests were in their own houses. Marilyn, Milton Greene, and his wife, Amy, gave their interview from the Greenes' Connecticut home.

During the interview, Marilyn discusses how she enjoys making musicals and comedies, but would like to expand into more dramatic parts, too. Milton and Marilyn talk about the formation of Marilyn Monroe Productions, and coincidentally the Greenes' phone rings. It allowed Milton to joke, "There's the telephone, Ed. That's another offer!"

Marilyn also discusses how important it is to have director approval and, more casually, how much she loves New York and Connecticut. She was visibly nervous as she spoke and Amy stepped in a few times to keep the interview going. It was her last appearance as a television guest.

In January 1961, newspapers reported that Marilyn was in negotiations to appear in an adaptation of *Rain* by Somerset Maugham for NBC. A movie star of Marilyn's caliber appearing in a television drama would have been big news, but the project stalled when NBC refused to hire Lee Strasberg as director.

Ultimately, television did erode movie ticket sales in the 1950s. Twentieth Century-Fox began losing money, leaving the studio vulnerable to more serious financial woes in the early 1960s.

· 23 ·

Theatre Life

Whether it was sitting in movies all day as a little girl, watching plays, or attending events, theatres in their various forms were central to the life of Marilyn Monroe. Because of her nearly obsessive need for retakes, Marilyn was best suited for acting in the movies, although early in her career she appeared in two plays, *Glamour Preferred* and *Stage Door*. She also appreciated theatre performances and rehearsed famous scenes on stage for classmates at the Actors Studio.

Interestingly, Marilyn's life story has gone on to inspire far more movies and theatrical performances than she actually appeared in.

THEATRES IN LOS ANGELES

[1] Fox Village Theatre | 961 Broxton Avenue, Los Angeles
Norma Jeane attended movies here as a child.

[2] La Reina Theatre | 14602 Ventura Boulevard, Sherman Oaks
Norma Jeane went to this air-conditioned movie theatre when living with the Goddards.

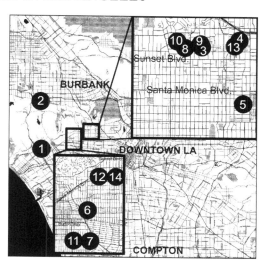

[3] **Las Palmas Theatre | 1642 N. Las Palmas Street, Los Angeles**
On June 16, 1948, Marilyn attended a performance of the musical *Lend an Ear* starring Carol Channing. Marilyn's name was mentioned for the first time in the newspaper for attending. Channing's success in *Lend an Ear* led to her going on to play the role of Lorelei Lee in *Gentlemen Prefer Blondes* on the stage. In a strange twist of fate, it was Marilyn who would play Lorelei in the movie version of *Blondes*. The Las Palmas Theatre is located just off Hollywood Boulevard and still stands but is now a nightclub.

[4] **Pantages Theatre | 6233 Hollywood Boulevard, Los Angeles**
The Pantages has been a staple of Hollywood since it opened on June 4, 1930. The decadent Art Deco theatre hosted the Academy Awards from 1949 to 1959 and it was here that Marilyn made her only appearance at the Oscars. On March 29, 1951, Marilyn presented the Oscar for Best Sound Recording to Thomas T. Moulton for *All about Eve*, the very movie she was there to represent. Today the Pantages remains a thriving venue.

[5] **El Centro Theatre | 804 N. El Centro Avenue, Los Angeles**
Established in 1946, one of the founding actors was Sydney Chaplin, son of legendary Charlie Chaplin. When Sydney and Marilyn were casually dating, she would sometimes accompany him to rehearsals. The building itself was constructed in 1910 and still stands but has long been empty. Coincidentally, it sits across the street from the orphanage where Marilyn lived as a little girl.

[6] **Coronet Theatre | 366 N. La Cienega Boulevard, Los Angeles**
Originally opened in 1947 by Russian dancer Freda Berkoff, the Coronet was a popular location for plays, movies, and art. According to Shelley Winters, she was a member of an acting troupe run by Charles Laughton at the Coronet. In later years, when Shelley claimed she and Marilyn shared an apartment in 1951, she invited Marilyn to participate in lessons with the other actors at the Coronet. Marilyn was so shy she struggled to speak loud enough for others to hear her. Eventually, Shelley said, she stopped inviting Marilyn. The Coronet building still stands but is now called the Largo.

[7] **Fox Wilshire Theatre (now the Saban Theatre) | 8440 Wilshire Boulevard, Beverly Hills**
Like many larger studios during the Golden Era of Hollywood, Twentieth Century-Fox owned a chain of theatres. The Wilshire Boulevard location served as Fox's primary venue for movie premieres, which is where the opening for *How to Marry a Millionaire* took place on November 4, 1953. As one of the first movies filmed in CinemaScope, Fox wanted to promote *Millionaire*

and the groundbreaking technology on a grand scale. Marilyn attended wearing a white gown accented with a satin sash designed for her by Fox costumer Travilla, who also dressed the three leading ladies in the film. Marilyn wore this same gown on *The Jack Benny Show* when she appeared to promote both the movie and CinemaScope, although this time with a taffeta sash in place of the satin one. Marilyn also attended the premiere of *Call Me Madam* at the Fox in 1953. As with the *Millionaire* premiere, Marilyn wore a Travilla gown to the event. This was a white version of the pink "Diamonds Are a Girl's Best Friend," dress but had a train instead of a large bow. (She wore the same dress to Walter Winchell's birthday party and the Cocoanut Grove that year.) Today the Fox Wilshire has been renamed the Saban, in honor of the couple who provided a $5 million grant for the building's restoration. The Saban was placed on the Federal and National Register of Historic Places in 2012.

[8] Paramount Theatre (now El Capitan) | 6838 Hollywood Boulevard, Los Angeles

Originally opened as the El Capitan on May 3, 1926, this was a legitimate theatre for performance and part of developer Charles E. Toberman's vision to create a theatre district in Hollywood. During the late 1930s, the theatre was struggling financially and began showing movies to stay afloat. Orson Welles famously held the premiere of *Citizen Kane* here in 1941 when no other theatre would risk the wrath of William Randolph Hearst. By 1942, the building was remodeled and reopened as the Hollywood Paramount. It was still operating under this name when Marilyn attended the premiere of the movie *Gigi* here on July 10, 1958. Disney purchased the theatre in the late 1980s, restoring much of the original interior and name.

Marilyn attended the premiere of Gigi *at the Hollywood Paramount in 1958. In recent years, the theatre has been restored and gone back to its original name, El Capitan.* Elisa Jordan

[9] Grauman's Egyptian Theatre | 6706 Hollywood Boulevard, Los Angeles
Opened in 1922, Sid Grauman built the first of his two Hollywood Boulevard theatres with an Egyptian theme as a response to the excitement surrounding King Tut's Tomb. The first premiere, *Robin Hood* starring Douglas Fairbanks, took place on October 18, 1922. Cecil B. DeMille's epic *The Ten Commandments* (1923) also premiered here. During the 1930s, Norma Jeane Baker walked from the house she shared with her mother to Hollywood Boulevard to sit all day in movie theatres, one of which was the Egyptian. Because movie theatres did not yet have concession stands in the 1930s, Norma Jeane stopped at the Pig & Whistle next door to purchase penny candy before heading inside. As Hollywood declined in the 1970s and 1980s, so too did the Egyptian, which did not enjoy the same lasting fame as its sister theatre, the Chinese. It finally closed in 1992 and was further damaged in the 1994 Northridge earthquake. The American Cinematheque, a nonprofit organization, purchased the theatre for $1 and began the painstaking and time-consuming job of restoring the theatre. Netflix purchased the theatre in 2020 to use as a venue for premiering movies to qualify for the Academy Awards.

[10] Grauman's Chinese Theatre | 6925 Hollywood Boulevard, Los Angeles
Possibly the most famous movie theatre in the world, Grauman's Chinese Theatre was the brainchild of promoter and all-around showman Sid Grauman. Building on the success of his Egyptian Theatre down the street, Grauman next dreamed of an elaborate Chinese-themed theatre. The Chinese Theatre broke ground in 1926 and opened on May 18, 1927, with a screening of Cecil B. DeMille's *King of Kings*. Known for the handprints and footprints of Hollywood's greatest stars in the forecourt, there are varying stories about how the tradition began. Regardless of how it started, fans soon were flooding the forecourt to place their own hands and feet into the prints of their favorite movie stars. One of those fans was Norma Jeane Baker. No doubt Norma Jeane took note of Jean Harlow's and Clark Gable's prints. As an adult, she returned as Marilyn Monroe to place her handprints and footprints in wet cement on June 26, 1953. It was a dual ceremony shared with Jane Russell, her costar in *Gentlemen Prefer Blondes*. Marilyn dotted the "I" in Marilyn with a rhinestone, which was soon pried loose by a thief. Today, Marilyn's handprints are the most visited in the forecourt—so much so that her prints have turned black from so many people placing their hands in her imprints.

The Chinese Theatre opened on May 18, 1927, and almost immediately became synonymous with Hollywood as a place and industry. Tourists come from all over the world to view the hand- and footprints of their favorite movie stars in the forecourt. As a little girl, Norma Jeane lived in the neighborhood and walked to the Chinese Theatre so she could wander in the forecourt and watch movies.
Elisa Jordan

[11] Bliss-Hayden Theatre | 254 S. Robertson Boulevard, Beverly Hills

An acting school and playhouse run by husband and wife team Lela Bliss and Harry Hayden, the Bliss-Hayden Theatre opened in 1936 and claimed Veronica Lake, Barbara Billingsly, Mamie Van Doren, and Kay Williams (later Mrs. Clark Gable) as former students. It was here in 1947 that Marilyn auditioned for—and won—a part in the play *Glamour Preferred*, which ran from October 12 to November 2. Marilyn shared the part with another actress and the two women alternated performances. (Ads for *Glamour Preferred* list the address as 244 S. Robertson.) Marilyn returned to Bliss-Hayden the following year to appear in *Stage Door*, which ran from August 15 to September 12, 1948. Bliss-Hayden was renamed the Beverly Hills Playhouse in 1954 and is still in operation.

[12] Players Ring Theatre (now the Coast Theatre)
8325 Santa Monica Boulevard, West Hollywood

Marilyn auditioned for a part at the Players Ring Theatre (then with the address of 8351) on March 12, 1950, in Los Angeles. There is no evidence she got the part. Since then, the building has gone through several name changes and an address number change.

[13] Huntington Hartford Theatre (now Ricardo Montalban Theatre)
1615 Vine Street, Los Angeles

Marilyn and Yves Montand, with whom she was having an affair, attended Josephine Baker's Follies at this theatre on April 26, 1960. Located on Vine, just off Hollywood Boulevard, this theatre is near the famous Hollywood and Vine intersection. It originally opened on January 19, 1927, as the Wilkes' Vine Street Theatre and was constructed in the Beaux-Arts style by Myron Hunt (who also designed the Ambassador Hotel) and H. C. Chambers.

[14] Marilyn Monroe Theatre | 7936 Santa Monica Boulevard, West Hollywood

Marilyn herself never stepped foot in the building named in her honor but bears her name as a tribute to her by the Lee Strasberg Theatre & Film Institute. The property itself was gifted to Lee by his third wife Anna in 1969, the same year he opened Strasberg Institute branches in New York and Los Angeles. The Marilyn Monroe Theatre has become a well-respected venue for plays in the Los Angeles area.

THEATRES IN NEW YORK AND ENGLAND

[15] Ziegfeld Theatre | 1341 Sixth Avenue, New York

Twentieth Century-Fox sent Marilyn to New York to watch the stage production of *Gentlemen Prefer Blondes* with Carol Channing in the role of Lorelei Lee. Although Channing made a name for herself playing Lorelei in live productions, Marilyn won the part for the 1953 movie version.

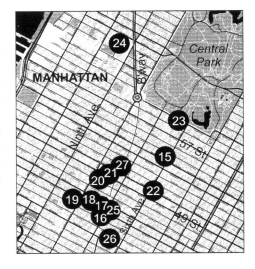

[16] Astor Theatre | 1537 Broadway, New York
As a benefit for the Actors Studio, Marilyn served as an usherette at the *East of Eden* premiere on March 9, 1955. The event sold out when it was announced Marilyn would be there. Arthur Miller attended with his sister, actress Joan Copeland. Marilyn returned to this theatre on December 12 of that same year for the premiere of *The Rose Tattoo*, where she was photographed with her friend Marlon Brando.

[17] Morosco Theatre | 217 West 45th Street, New York
With friend and business partner Milton Greene, Marilyn attended the premiere of *Cat on a Hot Tin Roof* on March 24, 1955. It was the latest work by playwright Tennessee Williams, who won the Pulitzer Prize for Drama that year. Elia Kazan directed.

[18] 46th Street Theatre | 226 West 46th Street, New York
On, June 7, 1955, Marilyn and Susan Strasberg attended a performance of *Damn Yankees*, which opened on May 5. The musical starred Gwen Verdon.

[19] Martin Beck Theatre | 302 West 45th Street, New York
In August 1955, Marilyn attended a performance of *Teahouse of the August Moon* to watch friend and Actors Studio classmate Eli Wallach.

[20] Coronet Theatre (now the Eugene O'Neill Theatre)
230 West 49th Street, New York
Marilyn attended the premiere of *A View from the Bridge* on September 29, 1955, a new one-act play by Arthur Miller. It ran for 149 performances and was considered unsuccessful.

[21] Ambassador Theatre | 219 West 49th Street, New York
Now a surrogate member of the Strasberg family, on October 5, 1955, Marilyn attended the premiere of *The Diary of Anne Frank*, starring Susan Strasberg. Marilyn was photographed proudly embracing Susan after her successful performance.

[28] New Watergate Theatre Club | 29 Buckingham Gate, London
After an unsuccessful 1955 run in New York, Arthur Miller expanded *A View from the Bridge* from one act to two. The revised version premiered on October 11, 1956, in London. In addition to Marilyn and Arthur, Laurence Olivier and Vivien Leigh attended opening night.

[29] Empire Theatre, Leicester Square | Leicester Square, London On October 29, 1956, after a Royal Command Performance of *The Battle of the River Plate*, Marilyn was presented to Queen Elizabeth II and Princess Margaret. Some of the other celebrities presented were Victor Mature, who stood to Marilyn's immediate right, Bridget Bardot, Joan Crawford, and Anita

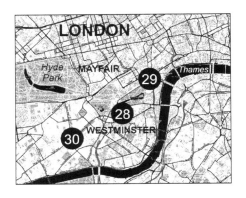

The Queen of England meets the Queen of Hollywood: One of the highlights of Marilyn's trip to the United Kingdom was being presented to Elizabeth II. Coincidentally, both women were the same age, having been born in 1926.
Photofest

Ekberg. A photograph of the Queen of England meeting the Queen of Hollywood has now become iconic.

[30] Royal Court Theatre | Sloane Square, London
After the success of the gritty American drama *A View from the Bridge* in London, a meeting was held on November 18, 1956, to discuss the current state of British theatre. The concerns were a lack of vitality in British drama, which had become "middleclass and bloodlessly polite," according to Arthur Miller's memoir, *Timebends*. Arthur was on the discussion panel, and Marilyn sat in the front row. Arthur later recalled how Marilyn was treated as a true acting professional throughout the evening and accepted as a member of the theatre community.

[22] Radio City Music Hall | 1260 6th Avenue, New York
The Prince and the Showgirl premiered here on June 13, 1957. Proceeds from the evening were donated to the Milk Fund for Babies charity.

[23] Barbizon-Plaza Theatre | 106 Central Park South, New York
Marilyn and Arthur saw his sister perform in the off-Broadway play *Conversation Piece* on November 18, 1957.

[24] New York Metropolitan Opera House | 30 Lincoln Center Plaza, New York
On February 10, 1959, Marilyn and Arthur attended *Macbeth*.

[25] Lowe's State Theatre (former location) | 1540 Broadway, New York
The premiere of *Some Like It Hot* took place here on March 29, 1959. It had just reopened after an $850,000 remodel that reduced the number of seats from 3,316 to 1,885, but they were wider and had more space between rows. It was also retrofitted to show CinemaScope and VistaVision movies. The color scheme of the luxe theatre was beige on gold.

[26] Henry Miller Theatre (now Stephen Sondheim Theatre) 124 West 43rd Street, New York
Marilyn and Montgomery Clift attended Yves Montand's one-man show on September 21, 1959. She went again the next night, September 22, with Arthur and their friends, Norman and Hedda Rosten.

[27] The Capitol Theatre (former location) | 1645 Broadway, New York
The premiere of *The Misfits* was here on February 1, 1961, which would have been Clark Gable's birthday. Marilyn was photographed on the arm of her friend and costar Montgomery Clift. Arthur Miller, who wrote the screenplay, was not in attendance as he and Marilyn were newly divorced.

IV

A HOUSEHOLD NAME

· 24 ·

Milton Greene

All I did was believe in her. She was a marvelous, loving, wonderful person I don't think many understood.

—Milton Greene

*M*ilton Greene was a boy wonder in fashion and celebrity photography. When he met Marilyn, he was just twenty-seven years old and already one of the most respected names in the industry. The original Monroe-Greene collaboration was a series of photos for *Look* magazine in 1953. Marilyn was thrilled with the results.

They kept in touch and their collaborations continued. While filming exterior shots in New York for *The Seven Year Itch* in 1954, Marilyn and Milton worked together again, including the Ballerina series.

Marilyn confided to Milton about the dissatisfaction she was experiencing with her career. She was serious about her intentions to move to New York, study at the Actors Studio, and position herself for better roles. He agreed with her assessment that the studio was not treating her fairly. Her salary was now too low for a star of her magnitude, and she deserved higher quality parts and dramatic roles if she wanted them. Milton encouraged her to challenge the studio and Hollywood's perception of her, and with his belief in what she aspired to, Marilyn's confidence soared. Their friendship soon transitioned into a business partnership, with Milton strategizing to fight Twentieth Century-Fox.

Milton told Marilyn it was in her best interest to set up her own production company, which would help her gain control over her career and future. He invited Marilyn to stay with his family, which included his wife, Amy, and their toddler son, Joshua. Marilyn quietly slipped out of Los Angeles with little more than the clothes on her back, arriving just in time to spend

Christmas 1954 with the Greenes. As was her pattern, Marilyn became an extended member of the Greene family. Marilyn loved children and adored little Joshua. Amy took her shopping for a New York wardrobe. As a former model, Amy possessed deep knowledge about fashion and elegant décor, which she shared with Marilyn.

When Marilyn first got to the East Coast, she kept a low profile and stayed out of sight for fear Twentieth Century-Fox would discover her location. Marilyn was officially on strike and as long as the company didn't know where she was, she had a strategic advantage.

Milton got to work with his lawyers to negotiate a new contract for Marilyn. As Arthur Miller recalled in his autobiography, "Her hopes were immense for this arrangement, which promised both decent roles and personal dignity. Naturally, the then powerful movie columnists were taking shots at Marilyn, the non-actor floozy, for the preposterous chutzpah of making artistic demands on so great and noble a corporation as Twentieth Century-Fox."

Twentieth Century-Fox was not about to let Marilyn go easily. She was now worth a tremendous amount of money and executives were in no mood to let such a valuable commodity slip out of their grip. Marilyn and Milton were similarly aware of her worth and knew they had leveraging power.

With the help of Milton and his legal team, Marilyn fought for—and received—a raise and approval when it came to directors, scripts, and cinematographers. Their partnership was split 51–49 percent in Marilyn's favor. This was a reversal from an earlier structure that granted Milton 51 precent and Marilyn 49 percent.

"I recalled her telling me months ago that she was putting off signing a contract that Greene and his lawyer had been pressing on her to set up her new company; it gave Greene fifty-one-percent control against her forty-nine," Arthur Miller wrote. "In return for his share he would bring in new recording and film projects that would not require her participation, but so far the new company's assets consisted only of her and her salary."

Once the contracts were ratified and gave Marilyn the controlling 51 percent interest, the launch of Marilyn Monroe Productions moved forward.

As the two business partners secretly set up Marilyn Monroe Productions, Marilyn simultaneously built a life in New York, living in hotels, studying at the Actors Studio, and attending the theatre. With her not working, Milton paid most of her bills, everything from lodging in the city to beauty treatments and clothes, to paying for Rockhaven Sanitarium where Marilyn's mother resided. To finally help curb expenses, instead of housing Marilyn in hotels he moved her into his apartment at 2 Sutton Place on the Upper East Side of Manhattan where he stayed when business required an overnight stay.

The friends and business partners officially announced the debut of Marilyn Monroe Productions on Edward R. Murrow's *Person to Person* television show. Murrow interviewed Marilyn, Milton, and Amy in their Connecticut home live on the air. Marilyn and the Greenes discussed the purpose of the company in terms of finding new projects and expanding Marilyn's career.

When Marilyn returned triumphantly to Los Angeles, Milton Greene was at her side. In a press conference at the airport, Marilyn talked about her upcoming role in *Bus Stop*, a dramatic part in a Joshua Logan movie, and how she had director approval. Marilyn and the Greenes moved temporarily to Cal-

An ecstatic Marilyn with her business partner Milton Greene at a cocktail party to announce the formation of Marilyn Monroe Productions in 1955.
Photoplay, April 1955 / Wikimedia Commons

ifornia, where they shared a large house on Beverly Glen Boulevard. During the week, Marilyn lived with the Greenes and filmed *Bus Stop* at Twentieth Century-Fox. On the weekends, she slipped away from the family home and stayed at the very private, very exclusive Chateau Marmont Hotel.

For the next two years, Milton photographed Marilyn constantly. There were dozens of photo shoots, not to mention behind-the-scenes pictures and candid shots at home. His photos are remembered as some of the finest pictures of her; she was always relaxed in front of the camera but the familiarity they had with each other created a synergy seldom found between artist and subject.

Arthur and Marilyn married during the summer of 1956 and Milton took photos of the traditional Jewish ceremony on July 1. Shortly thereafter, Milton accompanied Marilyn to England to film *The Prince and the Showgirl*.

As an executive producer, Milton was saddled with the business details of the shoot, such as overseeing elements of the production, finances, and legalities. In addition to his supervisorial duties, he had his hands full with a clash-of-the-titans-style feud on the set. On one side was Laurence Olivier, the leading man and director. On the other side was Marilyn Monroe, the leading lady, coproducer, and business partner. As the relationship between Laurence Olivier and Marilyn Monroe deteriorated, Milton was often stuck in the middle trying to negotiate two superpowers of the cinematic world.

Challenges arose closer to home, as well. As *The Prince and the Showgirl* continued filming, Milton's relationship with Marilyn went into decline. Glimmers of Marilyn's dissatisfaction with her partner began to show themselves during *Bus Stop* when Marilyn came to believe director Joshua Logan hated her and Milton wasn't doing enough to stand up for her.

In England, Marilyn's anxiety and stress were overwhelming; working with Laurence Olivier was a disaster and she felt disrespected; she had found Arthur Miller's diary opened to an unflattering passage about her; and she suspected Milton was purchasing English antique furniture, and shipping it home to America at the company's expense. (He always denied it.) She suspected ulterior motives when it came to Milton's movie-producing ambitions. Also, she accused him of not believing in her as an actress. In an interview with Norman Mailer, Milton said he turned down an offer for her to appear on a television series because he believed her value was in movies. "She felt that I didn't believe enough in her that she could make it as an actor," he said. "That's why she leaned toward Lee Strasberg. She felt after I turned down the TV series that I didn't believe in her as an actress."

To make matters worse, Arthur and Milton didn't get along. Milton resented Arthur's influence over Marilyn and worried that would extend to inserting himself into Marilyn Monroe Productions. Arthur believed Milton was using Marilyn. Navigating the relationship between business partner and new husband is a delicate process for anyone, but Marilyn was in no condition to balance the two most important men (at the time) in her life.

By the time *The Prince and the Showgirl* wrapped and everyone returned to New York, the relationship between Marilyn and Milton was nearly over. Marilyn offered to buy Milton out of their company for $500,000. He declined and instead asked for $100,000 and reimbursement for all the expenses he had incurred while setting up the company and supporting Marilyn.

As the holder of 51 percent of the company, Marilyn fired Milton in 1957 and began the process to legally remove him from ownership. Over several months, a settlement between the former partners underwent negotiations. On September 17, 1957, a proposed settlement was drafted.

Marilyn would pay Milton $50,000 for his stock in Marilyn Monroe Productions—five equal statements commencing for the year.

Marilyn would sell back her stock in Milton Greene Studios for $500, the amount she paid for it.

Milton would have no responsibility for any of the claims against Marilyn Monroe Productions:

Joseph Carr: $26,000 (disputed)
Irving Stein: $48,000 (disputed)
William Morris: $15,000 (settled at that figure)
MCA: $20,000 (not disputed)
Ermoyan: $15,000 (disputed)
Leonardi: $4,500 (now in courts)
Hollywood landlord: $700
Paula Strasberg: $10,000

It was a heavy debt, especially considering Arthur Miller amassed huge legal bills after HUAC subpoenaed him to testify. Marilyn began making payments to Milton, a debt she paid off in 1961. When finally finished, she told her friend Ralph Roberts, "It's one of the happiest days of my life! I just paid my last installment on Marilyn Monroe Productions to Milton Greene. A long time coming. I have my champagne ready to celebrate. Grab your vodka."

Over the years, the former partners remained respectful in their comments about the other. Marilyn told Ralph Roberts, "He and Amy took me under their wings when I first came to New York. He helped organize Marilyn Monroe Productions. It just didn't work out."

There has been much debate over whether or not the close friendship between Marilyn and Milton ever crossed the line into an affair. Marilyn didn't say, but Milton spoke to Norman Mailer about it in the early 1970s.

"We talked on the phone a lot. . . . Then I got married. . . . She was sad. . . . Amy knew I was friends with Marilyn. She didn't know about the sex. She said, 'Is that true?' And I said believe what you want to believe, Amy. Even if I was caught in bed by my wife, I'd say it wasn't true."

It's important to note that many men claimed to have bedded Marilyn over the years—so a confession of this sort doesn't necessarily mean it's true. Norman Mailer isn't the most reliable source of information on Marilyn Monroe either. His book about her is riddled with inaccuracies and outright falsities.

Milton and Amy Greene were married in 1953 and remained together until he passed away from lymphoma on August 8, 1985, in Los Angeles. The family scattered his ashes in the Pacific Ocean. Milton's legacy lives on through his son Joshua, who manages his father's body of work.

· 25 ·

The Men in Marilyn's Life

One of the great difficulties in researching the men Marilyn had romances with is that nearly every male within a fifty-mile radius of her claimed to have had an affair with Hollywood's favorite blonde. Some relationships were brief, such as Marlon Brando and Frank Sinatra, and others were around longer or meant more. She had some nice romances when she was younger, like with Bill Pursel, a regular guy who dated her briefly after she divorced Jim Dougherty. Marilyn dated and was hardly a prude, but she wasn't especially promiscuous, which is contrary to what many believe. Much of Marilyn's image focused on her sexuality, so it's easy to see how or why those who didn't know her came to such conclusions. Likewise, when others fabricate stories about her private life, her image makes such stories believable. Marilyn herself saw the double-edged sword that was her sex symbol image, and at times talked about the difficulty of being taken seriously as an actress. All this is to say—Marilyn was a fairly normal woman when it came to romance.

More than anything, Marilyn looked for security in a mate. As someone who hadn't felt loved, accepted, or safe for most of her life, Marilyn sought out those qualities. "Miller and DiMaggio were a lot alike," Norman Rosten told writer Maury Allen in 1975. "I don't want to say father figures. They were authority figures, also powerful men in terms of the public eye. DiMaggio was the king of baseball; Miller was a famous playwright. She gravitated toward power. This type of figure gives you security and absolution. With DiMaggio, she moved into a great circle of popular acceptance, into sports; with Miller, into the intellectual, literary world."

JAMES DOUGHERTY

Marilyn's first husband was born James ("Jim") Edward Dougherty on April 12, 1921, in Texas. He was the youngest of five children born to Edward and Ethel Dougherty, the children of English and Irish immigrants. During Jim's childhood, the family moved to Arizona, where they lived in a tent due to financial problems caused by the Great Depression. Eventually, the family moved again, this time settling in Van Nuys, California, where their neighbors included the family of Doc and Grace Goddard.

As a teen, Jim graduated in 1938 from Van Nuys High School; a fellow Van Nuys student was Jane Russell, who would one day costar with Marilyn Monroe in *Gentlemen Prefer Blondes* (1953).

In 1942, the Doughertys and the Goddards would transition from mere neighbors to family. Doc had accepted a job transfer to West Virginia. Although Doc's three children were moving to West Virginia with him and Grace, they concluded bringing their fifteen-year-old foster daughter Norma Jeane was cost-prohibitive. Grace's Aunt Ana Lower, who had taken custody of the young girl before, was now in poor health and unable to care full time for a teenager. To Norma Jeane's horror, it was looking as though she would have to return to an orphanage. This led Grace to approach neighbor Ethel Dougherty with an idea: Would Jim be willing to marry Norma Jeane?

Jim Dougherty was an ideal candidate. The Goddards and Doughertys knew each other, and Jim and Norma Jeane got along. He was a nice, handsome young man from a family of good people. He worked and owned a car.

In February, Ethel spoke with Jim, who was then twenty years old, and explained that Norma Jeane would have to move back to an orphanage with the Goddards leaving for West Virginia. Would he consider marrying her? Jim's initial reaction was less than positive. "Mom!" he cried. "She's a fifteen-year-old kid!"

His mother went on to emphasize that Norma Jeane would have nowhere to go except an orphanage, and they were just terrible places to live. As Ethel talked to Jim about her lack of options, he began to feel obligated. He also felt like he could save her—it wouldn't be the first time someone would try to save her. Finally, he agreed. Ethel was thrilled, and instantly said they could plan a June wedding. It was Jim's clue that this wasn't a spontaneous idea on his mother's part, but instead a plan. The wedding would take place after Norma Jeane turned sixteen and finished tenth grade in June.

After Jim agreed to marry his pretty young neighbor, the two began officially courting. He took her hiking in the Hollywood Hills and canoeing. According to Jim, the two fell in love right away.

When the Goddards left California, Norma Jeane temporarily moved back in with Aunt Ana to await her new life as a teen bride. The move meant

Norma Jeane married James "Jim" Dougherty on June 19, 1942, at the home of the Howell family. Photofest

another school, and she transferred from Van Nuys High School in the San Fernando Valley to University High School on the west side of Los Angeles. The sophomore's photo appeared in University's yearbook, the Chieftan, under the name Norma Jeane Baker. It was the same year her formal education came to an end.

Norma Jeane Baker, sixteen, and James Dougherty, now twenty-one, were married on June 19, 1942, at the home of family friends Chester and Doris Howell. The Howells' young twin daughters served as flower girls. Jim's older brother Marion was the best man. Norma Jeane's classmate, Lorraine Allen, was maid of honor. Aunt Ana made the wedding dress. After the ceremony, the attendees gathered in Hollywood for a reception at Florentine Gardens, where a waiter accidentally spilled soup on Jim's white tuxedo jacket.

As newlyweds, the Doughertys settled into a fun, playful relationship. Norma Jeane was, Jim later said, a virgin when they married and he made a point to be gentle with her. She tried her best to be a good wife, keeping the house clean and making healthy dinners for when Jim got home. Money was tight, so Jim's hunting skills helped put meat on the table. Norma Jeane would accompany him fishing but drew the line at going hunting. Although she was not a vegetarian (few people were in the 1940s), she was an animal lover and could not bear the thought of killing anything.

Norma Jeane had a good sense of humor and liked taking care of herself in terms of diligent grooming and perfecting her makeup. She equally cared for their dog, Muggsie, who she kept bathed and combed. Marion Dougherty was a frequent visitor and Norma Jeane doted on his children.

No relationship is perfect, and this includes the Doughertys. Jim noticed Norma Jeane had mood swings and sometimes slipped into depression. He took note that if she sensed his concern for her, she worked hard to bring up her mood. He also recounted comforting Norma Jeane after calling her father, Stan Gifford, who rebuffed her attempts to meet him.

Like a lot of young couples during the World War II era, wedded bliss was interrupted by a call to duty. Jim was working at Lockheed, a job considered "essential" and thus was granted a deferment. He was also considered a head of household due to his marriage. Still, the war effort needed more soldiers and Jim felt he might be drafted soon anyway, deferment or not. Worse, he was riddled with guilt. Most of the young men his age had already been drafted and were serving their country. Jim felt obligated to do his part.

When Jim finally told Norma Jeane his plans to enlist, she began to cry—but he was surprised at the intensity of her emotion. She wasn't merely sad; she appeared devastated. Norma Jeane wept and trembled at the idea of Jim leaving, and buried her face in his shoulder. It was more than just him leaving, he realized. Jim's enlistment triggered her memories of abandonment and fears of being left alone. As he tried comforting her (to no avail) she began pleading that they should have a baby. This way, she reasoned, with a baby she would always have a piece of him with her—especially if he died.

He wasn't going to die, he assured her, but he didn't want to leave her to care for a baby on her own. He promised they would start a family when he returned. In his later years, Jim admitted he understood her better as he aged—her insecurities, fears of abandonment, and need for a father figure. He sometimes wondered if he had made a mistake in denying her wish to get pregnant. He ultimately decided he came to the right conclusion but the thought stayed with him for years. With a baby, would she have gone on to be Marilyn Monroe? Or would have tried for a career in Hollywood anyway?

After his enlistment, Jim completed five weeks of basic training before moving to Catalina Island for further training. Norma Jeane was thrilled she—and Muggsie—could accompany him.

Catalina is twenty-six miles off the coast of Los Angeles, so although the move was not far, it was a bit isolated.

After training, Jim shipped out and once again Norma Jeane found herself alone. She moved in with her in-laws, who helped get her a job at Radioplane Company in Van Nuys. It was during her employment at Radioplane she was discovered by Army photographer David Conover, who took the nineteen-year-old's picture working on the OQ-3 for the war effort. Conover was impressed with how well Norma Jeane photographed and recommended modeling as a profession. As Jim was serving his country, he learned Norma Jeane was modeling after some fellow sailors hung up photos of Mrs. Dougherty. Incredulous, Jim informed them those photos were none other than his wife! Naturally, they didn't believe this bit of information but the photos were indeed Norma Jeane Dougherty. There was another issue. Norma Jeane was spending more money than she was earning. Modeling was expensive and she felt she needed to shop for clothing.

Mr. and Mrs. Dougherty on Catalina Island, where Jim was training in the Merchant Marine. Norma Jeane was experimenting with her look during this time and delighted in wearing clothing that showed off her figure. By Dell Publications, Inc. New York, publisher of Modern Screen / Wikimedia Commons

Jim wrote to Norma Jeane and informed her that although she could model while he was away, when he came home, she would have to settle back down into the life of a housewife. In a 1992 television interview, Jim said, "I thought it was fine. She could do it until I got home. But then it got deeper and deeper and she got more involved in it because I was gone so long."

Jim believed Norma Jeane was on board with the plan, but soon after received her reply in the form of a Dear John letter and divorce papers from Las Vegas. "It was like getting kicked by a mule," Jim said in an interview.

The Doughertys separated in 1946. According to Jim, Norma Jeane had a chance at a movie contract but the studio insisted their starlets not be married, for fear of losing an investment to pregnancy. "Back then," he said, "you didn't get pregnant unless you were married." Norma Jeane suggested that although they were getting a divorce, they could continue to be a couple when he returned from the war. Jim declined, and told her, "It doesn't work that way. I want a family."

When Jim returned home, he visited Norma Jeane at the apartment she shared with Aunt Ana on Nebraska Avenue, where he signed the final divorce paperwork. She also informed him that she was changing her name to Marilyn Monroe. Jim gave her a kiss, said good-bye, and started to leave when Norma Jeane noticed a redhead waiting in the car for him, which upset her and stoked her jealousy. "I don't know what you're upset for. You're divorcing me!" he responded. Norma Jeane replied, "She's not the person you should be out with."

That was the end of their marriage and they only spoke one more time after their divorce. Jim learned he had so many parking tickets under his name that he was at risk for arrest. Norma Jeane had never bothered to transfer their car into just her name, so her tickets piled up under his name by mistake. He called his former wife to straighten the mess out and was baffled by her deeper voice. "Do you have a cold?" he asked. No, she replied, she had been told that her voice was too high and she was working on lowering it.

Jim remarried in 1947 and his second wife, Patricia Scoman, was not thrilled that her husband's first wife became a famous movie star. The couple went on to have three daughters. "My second wife didn't even want our children to know that I'd been married to her," he said in 1992.

After Jim returned from the war, he joined the Los Angeles Police Department. The former Mr. and Mrs. Dougherty nearly encountered each other once again, when Officer Dougherty was assigned to crowd control at the premiere of *The Asphalt Jungle* in 1950. Mercifully, the starlet now known as Marilyn Monroe did not attend. Marilyn continued to keep a respectful distance from her former husband. "She knew that my second wife was extremely jealous. She didn't want to interfere with my family," Jim said in 1992.

Jim Dougherty was one of the first to learn of Marilyn Monroe's death on August 5, 1962. A police officer, who knew his colleague had once been married to Marilyn Monroe, arrived on the scene at her house in Brentwood and called Jim from inside Marilyn's home that morning. The call woke up both him and his wife. When he replaced the receiver on the phone's cradle, he told his wife, "Say a prayer for Norma Jeane. She's dead."

Jim's career as an officer with the Los Angeles Police Department was a long one. He was promoted to detective and helped create the Special Weapons and Tactics (SWAT) group in the 1960s and became the first training officer. In addition to his children, he worked with young people through the police department's partnership with the Boy Scouts.

Jim and Patricia divorced in 1972. He married his third wife, Rita Lambert, in 1974. After his retirement, the couple relocated to Rita's home state of Maine, where he taught at the Criminal Justice Academy. Jim and Rita remained married until she died in 2003. Jim Dougherty followed two years later in 2005 when he died of leukemia.

Later in life, Jim Dougherty gave occasional interviews and even wrote a book about his marriage to Norma Jeane. He was always quick to point out he never knew "Marilyn Monroe." He knew Norma Jeane. "If there is life after death, and I believe there is, there is so much I want to ask Norma Jeane/Marilyn Monroe. She left me with so many questions I never got answers to. I was there at the very end of Norma Jeane and the very beginning of Marilyn Monroe. I never got a chance to say goodbye to either woman. I wish I had."

ANDRE DE DIENES

Andre de Dienes was not the first photographer to take Marilyn's picture, but he was the first to build a lasting relationship with her, the first whose work got her a magazine cover, and the first to capture the transition from Norma Jeane to Marilyn.

Andor György Ikafalvi-Dienes was born on December 18, 1913, in Kézdivásárhely/Târgu Secuiesc, Kingdom of Hungary (now Romania).

After his mother committed suicide by throwing herself down a well on the family property, Andre left home at the age of fifteen. He traveled around Europe, mostly by foot, eventually buying himself a camera and working as a photographer for the Associated Press and *L'Humanité*, a Communist newspaper. A chance encounter in 1938 with the editor of *Esquire* led Andre to relocate to New York and the world of fashion photography. He found success in the field but considered the industry stifling.

When on his own time, he developed a passion for traveling and taking pictures of communities he believed were overlooked by mainstream America. He found beauty and warmth in African American neighborhoods and was especially passionate about photographing America's indigenous peoples. His other favorite subject matters were landscapes and female nudes.

He hired models for his photographic nude studies, and one of the agencies he worked with was Blue Book Models in Los Angeles. In 1945, Andre contacted Blue Book's owner Emmeline Snively to set up a photo shoot. Emmeline agreed to send a model for an interview to the Garden of Allah, a hotel at the bottom of the Sunset Strip known for catering to celebrities and artists, where he was staying. The model who arrived was nineteen-year-old Norma Jeane Dougherty. He was instantly smitten with the young woman.

"When Norma Jeane arrived at my bungalow later in the afternoon, it was as if a miracle had happened to me. Norma Jeane seemed to be like an angel. I could hardly believe it for a few moments. An earthy, sexy-looking angel! Sent expressly for me! The impact Norma Jeane had on me was tremendous," he wrote later in life. His memories were printed in a book after his death.

Andre de Dienes never did photograph Norma Jeane in the nude, but she quickly became his muse. The two went on a trip around the West and he photographed her in different types of terrain. "In the days that followed, I bought Norma Jeane various clothes to wear for my pictures and to keep her warm because it was December and my plans were to visit the desert, the mountains, everywhere in California, Nevada, Arizona, anywhere my fancy would dictate going. I removed the back seat of my big Buick Roadmaster automobile and laid down a sheet of thick foam rubber with blankets on top and pillows all around, so Norma Jeane could sleep whenever she wished during the long drives I was planning."

By the time they got to Death Valley, their first destination, Andre already had fallen in love with his model. "In the evening we got to Furnace Creek Inn, in the heart of Death Valley. I asked Norma Jeane whether she would like to sleep in the same cabin with me or whether she would prefer a separate one. Sweet, darling Norma Jeane calmly explained her sentiments to me—that she liked me very much, but she was only separated, not divorced, and she would feel better if she had own cabin."

During the trip, Andre took Marilyn to visit her mother, who then lived in Portland, Oregon. He later regretted not offering to take a picture of them together.

They finally did become a couple during their trip while in the Mount Hood area. There was one room left at the Government Lodge and she said, "Okay, let's take the room. Let's not worry anymore about anything."

According to Andre, the couple very quickly decided they would get married; she would move to Las Vegas for six weeks to get a divorce and they would tie the knot right after while still in the city. In the meantime, Norma Jeane went home to Los Angeles and Andre went back to New York. They kept in touch through letters and phone calls, often with her calling collect because she was broke.

Norma Jeane did indeed go to Las Vegas, but it wasn't until a few months later in the summer of 1946. Fate had other plans. "I phoned Norma Jeane in Los Angeles to tell her she could leave for Las Vegas and instructed her in which hotel to meet me," he wrote. "I told her how wonderfully happy I felt that at last we were getting married. Disaster struck me in those moments: in a sweet, apologetic voice, Norma Jeane said, 'Andre, please don't come, I can't marry you! I want to become an actress!' She said she had thought it over and her career was more important! She wanted to get into the movies! The news shocked me, but I took it calmly and told her I would come to Los Angeles anyway and that I would phone her when I arrived."

In Andre's story, the couple agreed to meet on the corner of Sunset and Vine, but when she didn't arrive after two hours, he went to her apartment unannounced and found her with another man. The two agreed to remain friends and Andre continued to photograph her over the years, including a stunning beach session at Tobay Beach in 1949 when she was on a media tour to promote *Love Happy.* He bought her a bathing suit and she frolicked in the sand for hours as he snapped away. He also photographed her in the early 1950s, but they drifted apart.

Andre de Dienes died in Los Angeles on April 11, 1985, and is interred just steps away from Marilyn Monroe in the locked Room of Prayer.

FRED KARGER

When Fred Karger was born in 1916, he made his debut with a Hollywood pedigree. His father, Maxwell Karger, was a founding member of Metro, later MGM, and his mother was Vaudeville performer Ann Conley of Ann & Effie Conley Sisters.

By the time he was employed at Columbia Pictures as a vocal coach in 1948, he was recently divorced and living at his mother's house with his young daughter, Terry. His sister, Mary, was also divorced and living in their mother's home with her children, Anne and Ben.

When Columbia assigned Fred to work with newly signed starlet Marilyn Monroe in March, it wasn't long before the professional relationship turned into something more. For her part, Marilyn quickly fell head over heels in love and, despite having been married once before, would forever after refer to Fred Karger as her first real love.

Soon enough, Marilyn was eager to become the next Mrs. Karger and confided to Natasha Lytess, "Freddy is the man of my dreams."

After their first date, Fred drove Marilyn home to drop her off but instead of directing him to where she lived, she pointed to a dilapidated hovel. This, she told him sadly, was her home and all she could afford. In reality, she lived at the Studio Club, a perfectly safe and clean dormitory for young women in the entertainment industry. But her ploy worked. Fred brought Marilyn to his mother's house and she made herself at home with the entire Karger clan.

Once entrenched with the Kargers, Marilyn dutifully pitched in with chores around the house, determined to prove she was wife and stepmother material. Ann and Mary immediately took to their houseguest. For Marilyn it must have seemed like a welcome relief from loneliness and the grief she was experiencing from recently losing her guardian, Aunt Ana Lower on March 14—just four days after meeting Fred. Ann Karger filled her need for a motherly older woman.

Marilyn's newfound security and happiness were short-lived. The Studio Club called Columbia to inquire about her whereabouts and soon Fred, furious, returned her to the club. Her ploy had backfired. She later said, "[Fred] said that because I lied about this, he couldn't trust me with anything. He didn't think I would be a good example to the children in his family. It made me feel pretty rotten."

Fred was in no hurry to tie the knot again anytime soon—and certainly not with Marilyn. Ten years his junior and not well-educated, Marilyn Monroe did not fit the proper wife and mother bill as far as Fred Karger was concerned.

"Most of his talk to me was a form of criticism," Marilyn later said. "He criticized my mind. He kept pointing out how little I knew and how unaware of life I was." He also told Marilyn: "You cry too easily. That's because your mind isn't developed. Compared to your figure, it's embryonic." Marilyn later said she felt like she couldn't argue because she had to look up "embryonic" in the dictionary.

Natasha Lytess encouraged Marilyn to end the relationship with Fred, but her advice fell on deaf ears. Marilyn continued trying to win him over, hoping he would love her as much as she loved him.

Here Marilyn was establishing yet another pattern she would frequently repeat: picking a man who was highly critical and emotionally unavailable. Many of Fred's actions were at once helpful and destructive. She began a rigorous study program after his negative comments regarding her lack of formal education. She made changes to her wardrobe at his suggestion. He paid for her to have cosmetic dental work performed on her teeth.

Despite all her efforts to please him, Fred remained distant. Consequently, the more remote and critical he became, the more it exacerbated her insecurities and desperate need for his love. By Christmas 1948, their romance was fizzling out, just a few months after it began. Years later, Marilyn was still making payments on an expensive gold watch she had purchased on credit for Fred, a continuing sad reminder of her failed first love.

In 1952, Fred Karger did finally take another Mrs. Karger—actress Jane Wyman, who would divorce Fred a few years later, then remarry and divorce him again. Marilyn was still smarting a few years after her breakup with Fred, as she showed up unannounced to Mr. and Mrs. Karger's wedding reception to congratulate the happy couple. Her friend Sidney Skolsky later said it was the "one bitchy thing" he had ever seen her do.

As for Ann and Mary Karger, they liked Marilyn so much their friendship with her outlasted her relationship with Fred. Fourteen years later they were among the handful of guests Joe DiMaggio, Inez Melson, and Berniece Miracle invited to Marilyn's funeral.

Fred Karger passed away on August 5, 1979—seventeen years to the day after Marilyn's passing.

JOSEPH SCHENCK

One of the most accomplished executives in early Hollywood, Joseph Schenck helped create the movie industry and shape it into the success it became. At one time, Schenck headed United Artists, then partnered with Darryl Zanuck in 1933 to cofound Twentieth Century Pictures, which later merged with Fox Film Corporation to form Twentieth Century-Fox. He was one of the founding members of the Academy of Motion Pictures Arts & Sciences, the organization responsible for the annual Oscars ceremony.

He was also a pivotal person when it came to guiding the early career of Marilyn Monroe. There has been much debate over whether or not the two had an affair. Powerful older men and young, ambitious women have coupled up since the beginning of time and Hollywood has always been an ideal place for such matchups. It can be difficult to say what happened in this case, and no one but Marilyn and Joe Schenck know for sure, but the evidence tilts in favor of a platonic friendship. Their private letters do not indicate much more than a mentor-mentee relationship and at times Schenck seems almost fatherly toward Marilyn.

Things started humbly for the movie mogul in Russia, where he was born on December 25, 1876. Under his birth name, Ossip Schenker, he immigrated to New York with his family in 1892. He got his first taste of the entertainment business as an employee of Fort George Amusement Park in New York. After learning the amusement park business, he and his brother Nicholas moved to California and purchased Palisades Amusement Park, where they began experimenting with the fledging movie industry. Dabbling in movies paid off, and Schenck partnered with Marcus Loew to operate the Loews chain of movie theaters.

It was through his movie industry connections that he met actress Norma Talmadge, whom he married in 1916. The following year, he helped her form Norma Talmadge Film Corporation, which went on to become a successful and lucrative company. They divorced in 1934 and he never remarried.

It was in the final days of his marriage to Talmadge that Schenck partnered with Darryl Zanuck in 1933 to create Twentieth Century, which merged with Fox two years later. Through this merge, Joe Schenck became one of the most powerful men in Hollywood but experienced a fall from grace in the early 1940s after serving a couple of months in prison. The conviction stemmed from perjury after paying bribes to mobsters Willie Bioff and George Browne, who threatened strikes by leveraging their connections to movie production unions. After returning home from prison, Schenck resumed a leadership position at Twentieth Century-Fox.

It was after his return from prison and reestablishing himself as a power player in Hollywood that he met a young starlet named Marilyn Monroe.

There are multiple versions of how the studio executive met and befriended a starlet in the beginning stages of her career.

One story says Schenck spotted her on the Twentieth Century-Fox lot. A second story says mutual acquaintance Pat DiCicco (former husband of Thelma Todd, who died under mysterious circumstances) brought Marilyn to a poker game at Schenck's estate. Finally, another story says she was invited to one of his regular Sunday lunches in his backyard. However they met, the unlikely friends appeared to have a strong kinship.

Around this time, Schenck invited Marilyn to stay in the guest cottage on his estate grounds. Not everyone in town believed the relationship remained platonic, although Marilyn herself spoke publicly about it and maintained they were strictly friends.

"Get this straight," she told Maurice Zolotow years later in an interview. "Mr. Schenck and I were good friends. He gave me encouragement when I needed it. He didn't do anything for me. He let Darryl Zanuck run the studio the way Mr. Zanuck wanted to run it. I know the word around Hollywood was I was Joe Schenck's girlfriend, but that's a lie. . . . I went to his house because I liked Mr. Schenck and I liked his food and it was better than the Studio Club food. I don't mean to imply the Studio Club had bad food. I mean, let's say, that Mr. Schenck's cook was just better than their cook."

It is not clear if Joe Schenck was aware of Marilyn's statements about dinner at his house, but he acknowledged she was a frequent dinner guest in an interview with writer Ezra Goodman. Goodman noted Joe Schenck was seventy-six at the time of their chat, had been ill, and spoke "slow and laboriously."

In response to Goodman asking about a dalliance with starlet Marilyn Monroe or if she looked up to him like a father figure, Schenck replied, "She used to come here quite often for dinner. I think she liked to eat. We have good food here. No, I never had any romantic thoughts about Marilyn and she never had any such thoughts about me. But it makes me appear very old if you say I'm a father."

Marilyn never said if she looked up to Joe Schenck in a fatherly way, but she did have a pattern of creating surrogate families and parental figures throughout her lifetime. Joe was at least a respected authority figure to her, if not a father figure. Given the late 1940s was a period of financial and career hardship for Marilyn, she may have taken respite in his protective guidance. It's also likely she just needed a square meal now and again.

Most tellingly, Joe Schenck appreciated Marilyn's determination to develop into the best version of herself and her desire to learn. "A girl doesn't have to be a actress [*sic*] to be a success," Schenck told Goodman. "A girl must be able to be herself, which she is capable doing. She had a very good reputation around the studio. She didn't run around with a lot of boys, which is natural, but not worthwhile doing. She always wanted to learn something. If she came to dinner and a good smart man was at dinner, I'd always put her alongside that man. She wanted to improve herself."

Joe Schenck's quote contradicts a commonly held belief that Marilyn was especially promiscuous during this time. It also reveals another pattern Marilyn created for herself: making friends with those who, at least from the outside, appeared more intellectual or somehow above Marilyn in social status. Because of her beauty, it is easy to overlook how Marilyn disarmed those around her with her quick wit and engaging, offbeat personality. She was funny, liked to read, enjoyed art and poetry, was passionate about acting, and sought out those from whom she could learn—and most were happy to share their passions for particular subjects. Something about Marilyn inspired Schenck to nurture her professionally and somewhat personally.

The two exchanged letters, and Marilyn kept her half of the correspondence, which provides a glimpse into their relationship.

In a letter postmarked December 9, 1948, and addressed to Marilyn at her Studio Club address, he writes:

Dear Marrylene, [*sic*]
    Am very pleased to know you have a good part in a picture. Stick to your work and you will make good. Make your career your first consideration. Am having a nice time in Miami. Leaving here for New York on the sixteenth. Expect to be home in two weeks. Write to me to Miami Beach all about everything.
Affectionately,
Joe

In a letter written on Twentieth Century-Fox letterhead (addressed to 1711 N. Stanley Avenue), he thanks her for remembering his birthday, which was December 25.

Dear Marilyne, [*sic*]
    Thanks for remembering me on my birthday. Wish you long health, long happiness and a measure of success for 1949.
Poor Joe

In a more mysterious note from Joe to Marilyn, which is undated and not on letterhead, he writes:

Dear Marilyn,
I am with you. I know you are right. Joe Schenck

Was it in response to a situation between Marilyn and Darryl Zanuck, with whom she didn't get along? Or something else? It is interesting to note that although Marilyn and Joe Schenck, a Twentieth Century-Fox executive, enjoyed a friendship, he did not seem to intercede on her behalf when it came to Darryl Zanuck.

Schenck did, however, call Columbia studio head Harry Cohn after Columbia dropped her and encouraged Cohn to give her another chance. Cohn responded by inviting Marilyn to accompany him on his yacht for an afternoon. When Marilyn replied she would love to join him *and his wife* for a day on the yacht, the excursion was called off and she never received another contract from Columbia.

Around this time—the late 1940s—Marilyn met Johnny Hyde and her life changed dramatically. She no longer needed a free meal and advice, as Johnny took control of her career. Marilyn did keep in touch with Schenck though, as she was photographed in 1950 with a Chihuahua he had gifted to her for her twenty-fourth birthday. In his honor, she named the dog Josefa, feminizing his name because the dog was female.

When Marilyn signed a new contract with Twentieth Century-Fox, which Johnny Hyde negotiated for her, it provided an opportunity for the two to stay in each other's orbit.

Joe Schenck suffered a debilitating stroke in 1957 and never fully recovered. Marilyn continued to check in on him when visiting Los Angeles from her new home, New York.

He died four years later in 1961, and Marilyn visited him shortly before his death.

Press agent Harry Brand wrote to Marilyn on Twentieth Century-Fox letterhead thanking her for a visit. Dated June 2, 1960, it reads:

Dear Marilyn:
Your visit to Mr. Schenck was very thoughtful and helpful.
It did a lot to cheer him up, and we all greatly appreciate it.
Best wishes.
Sincerely,
Harry

Whether or not the two engaged in a sexual relationship, one thing remains clear: They built a friendship based on respect that lasted for the rest of their lives.

JOHNNY HYDE

Often when I've done something I think is good, I say a little
prayer thanking him. I loved him. I wasn't in love with him, but
I loved him.

—Marilyn Monroe

During his career, Johnny Hyde became one of the most powerful—if not
the most powerful—agents in Hollywood. His clients included Rita Hayworth, Lana Turner, Betty Hutton, Mickey Rooney, Amos and Andy, and
Bob Hope, just to name a few. He is largely responsible for setting Marilyn
Monroe up for the major success she would experience; he was also deeply
in love with her.

Like Marilyn, Johnny started with very little and worked his way up
to the top of his career. He was born in Russia to a family of acrobats who
immigrated to the United States when Johnny was still a child. At the age
of twenty-one, the William Morris Agency hired him as a junior executive.

From the beginning, Johnny demonstrated that he was a brilliant executive and rose through the ranks at William Morris. He was great at talking
with people but tough when a situation warranted it.

With his tremendous success came other rewards, such as great wealth,
power in the entertainment industry—and beautiful women. Johnny had a
history of infidelity in marriages. When he met Marilyn, he was married to
his third wife, actress Mozelle Cravens, whom he had married in 1943. He
had two children with Mozelle, and two with his first wife, Florence Harper.
There are different stories as to how Johnny met Marilyn, but the most common version is that it took place on New Year's Eve 1948 at the Racquet Club
in Palm Springs.

Johnny Hyde didn't just help build careers; he created superstars and
Marilyn was his latest protégé. As it turns out, she would also be his last.
Johnny had a heart condition, and he knew he didn't have long to live.
Immediately, he dove into promoting Marilyn and trying to get her parts in
the best possible movies.

Johnny began devoting most of his time to Marilyn, both personally and
professionally. His wife finally had enough of his infidelities and the Hyde
marriage quickly fell apart. It's not like Johnny wanted to stay married anyway. From the moment he met her, Johnny wanted only Marilyn. He quickly
took ownership of Marilyn's career and bought out her contract with her first
agent, Harry Lipton. From that point on, he spent nearly all his working
hours on her behalf, often at the expense of his other clients.

When not negotiating deals, he escorted Marilyn out so she could be
seen at premieres, parties, and the best restaurants around town. "Johnny

Johnny Hyde was a top agent in Hollywood when he fell obsessively in love with Marilyn. A heart condition meant he didn't have long to live and he begged her to marry him. She declined because she didn't want to marry anyone for the wrong reasons. Photofest

knew everything that was going on in Hollywood," Marilyn told her friend and masseur Ralph Roberts in 1960. "He was one of the most influential and highly regarded agents in the business. He would have me sitting at his table at lunch, with everyone stopping to greet him, pass the time of day, and discuss what was going on around town. I don't think I ever said a word during any of these exchanges, but I sure learned a lot."

Marilyn moved into Johnny's Beverly Hills mansion, where they lived as a couple but to keep up appearances, Marilyn also maintained a room at the Beverly Carlton Hotel, which she used as her official address.

As part of his plan for furthering her career, Johnny paid for a plastic surgeon to implant a small piece of cartilage in her chin, which dissolved within a few years.

"I remember many times when he would say, 'Concentrate to learn to use your body as an instrument of expression, as well as a thing of beauty,'" she told Ralph Roberts. "'Acting is basically the fine art of gesture and gesture begins in a supple, agile body. And don't let the mind go untended.'"

Marilyn trusted Johnny implicitly and took his advice to heart, including his instructions to never fall victim to the casting couch. "Johnny very quickly and very firmly made it clear to me that such was the kiss of death," Marilyn told Ralph. "He said that every year, some young girl or man appeared on the scene, believing they were so irresistible, so wonderful in bed, that tomorrow morning they'd be waking up to their names in lights. Word spreads like wildfire about these. Once every decade, perhaps one does make it. But the percentages are 99-to-1 against."

Above all else, Marilyn appreciated Johnny's belief in her—her talent, her determination to succeed, and her future. "There's not one day that goes by that I don't think of him," she said to Ralph. "Some little silly incident will trigger off a whole flow of memories of him. Johnny sitting at Romanoff's talking about the things I was going to do. How, with my drive, my determination to be a top actress, nothing could stop me."

With Johnny's plan to make Marilyn a star set in motion and with her living at his home, there was just one order of business left—he wanted to marry Marilyn. For her part, Marilyn's feelings about Johnny were significantly more complicated than his feelings were for her.

Marilyn had grown to love Johnny deeply, but she was hesitant to get married again. For as much as Marilyn genuinely adored Johnny, she feared she wasn't *in* love with him. She was also keenly aware that if she married Johnny, others in Hollywood would consider her a gold digger. In reality, Johnny's money didn't mean much to her. She remained adamant about not marrying someone for the wrong reasons. Financial security wasn't enough to accept a proposal.

Johnny dangled the financial rewards of becoming Mrs. Hyde like a carrot in front of her and impressed upon Marilyn that he didn't have long to live. If she married him, he promised, she would inherit his vast wealth. Johnny even turned to Marilyn's friend and mentor, Joseph Schenck, for help. Could Joe talk sense to Marilyn and convince her to marry him? Marilyn continued to decline his proposals, although she did let him know she loved him very much.

There was another issue, which was her relationship with her acting coach Natasha Lytess. Marilyn spent her days with Natasha working on acting lessons, diction, and posture. Natasha was possessive of her student and developed sour feelings for the agent who now took up so much of Marilyn's time. Worse, Marilyn had moved out of Natasha's home to live with Johnny, taking all her belongings and—most importantly—her books with her. Natasha felt left out.

Despite the declined marriage proposals and difficulties with Natasha, Marilyn blossomed during her time with Johnny. His love and belief in her talent made her feel secure. The longer their relationship lasted, the more her confidence grew. He bought her nice clothes and jewelry, which were appreciated, but what Marilyn valued was how he felt about her.

Johnny's heart condition continued to plague him. He had a heart attack, which landed him at Cedars of Lebanon Hospital in Hollywood. His declining health only made him more determined to set Marilyn up for success before he died, and the work started to pay off. Johnny arranged for her to screen test for the John Huston-directed *The Asphalt Jungle*, a role she won, and got her a part in *All about Eve*, starring Bette Davis. They were small parts, but both movies were successful when they were released in 1950 and went on to become classics over the years. Small parts in the "right" movies can prove pivotal in a career.

Johnny also helped pave the way to roles in lower-profile movies, which still provided good exposure for her, including *A Ticket to Tomahawk*, *Right Cross*, and *Home Town Story*. With each movie she appeared in, her value in Hollywood went up. Again he proposed, and again she refused. She told Rupert Allan, "It would be ridiculous to pass myself off as Mrs. Johnny Hyde. I'd be taken less seriously than I am now."

She may have turned down his marriage proposals, but Marilyn cared for Johnny as his body weakened. Just as he had striven to care for her, it was now her turn to care for him. His final act of love was securing Marilyn a seven-year contract with Twentieth Century-Fox—he had ensured that she would have an income stream coming in after he died.

Johnny finally succumbed to his heart condition on December 18, 1950. Marilyn later told Elia Kazan that the Hyde family would not permit her to visit him in his hospital room. She stood outside his hospital door, helpless, as he called for her.

Johnny reportedly told his secretary Dona Holloway that his final wish was for Marilyn to be treated like a member of the family. The Hyde family was in no mood to follow these instructions. As soon as Johnny died, Marilyn was evicted from the home she shared with him. The Hyde family also refused to allow Marilyn to keep many of the gifts Johnny had given to her during their relationship.

It's reported that Johnny had intended to change his will and leave Marilyn one-third of his estate, even though she declined to marry him. If that was his intention, though, he never made it official. Johnny's original will was never changed and Marilyn inherited nothing—not that she had wanted anything.

Marilyn was devastated by Johnny's death. Part of her would grieve for him the rest of her life, but in the direct aftermath, Marilyn experienced a major depressive episode. Shortly after Johnny died, Natasha found Marilyn unconscious with sleeping pills foaming out of her mouth. Marilyn later brushed off the suicide attempt, but she was likely ill-equipped to handle her grief and in a moment of wanting her pain to stop, reached for something to help numb herself.

Johnny Hyde is interred in the Great Mausoleum at Forest Lawn Glendale in the Hall of Benediction, just steps away from where Jean Harlow also rests. The Great Mausoleum is private and closed to the public.

As years passed, Marilyn never forgot Johnny's love for her and never stopped heeding his advice. She gave him credit for her success and for mentoring her in such a way that she survived many of Hollywood's pitfalls. As she told Ralph Roberts, "From him, I learned the true story behind the scenes—the meanness, the pettiness, the arrogance, the egomania and, oddly, the envy that gnawed on so many of those in the power structure. The competitiveness. That is something that came hard for me. He said I had to develop it. That I had to explore all facets of myself, to learn which was the real me. I had to study all elements involved in the business. Not only to work with the top teacher of acting, to always aim for the top, but also, movement, mime, learn to be a 'presence.' Intangible, but absolutely necessary to learn—presence."

Just as Johnny loved Marilyn, in return she never stopped loving and appreciating him.

"He was the nicest person I ever knew," she told Ralph. "I miss him more than I would have ever thought possible."

ELIA KAZAN

Elia Kazan was one of the most groundbreaking and revered directors of his generation—and for a lot of cinephiles, of all time. Throughout his decades-long career, he was successful in both movies and on the stage and cofounded the famed Actors Studio. In the early 1950s, he also had a relationship with Marilyn Monroe.

In all likelihood, his time with Marilyn was not very long. However, during their time together, Kazan was a huge influence on her when it came to what would eventually become important aspects of her life: Arthur Miller, Method acting, the Actors Studio, and HUAC.

At first glance, a romance between Elia Kazan and Marilyn Monroe might seem unlikely. They were primarily based on opposite coasts, he was further along in his career than Marilyn, and he was married—although having a wife never seemed to matter to Elia when it came to pursuing other women. Still, the two found a lot of common ground. They bonded over feelings of insecurity, both having grown up as outsiders and underdogs. For his part, he loved beautiful women.

Born Elias Kazantzoglou on September 7, 1909, in Constantinople (now Istanbul) to Greek parents, the family relocated to the United States when Elia was three. His domineering, misogynistic father entered the rug business after arriving in America and expected his son to join the family business, but Elia had no interest. As he grew up, Elia was shy and awkward around other children. He had the distinct feeling of being an outsider—he was too American for his traditional parents but not American enough for other kids at school. Even while attending Williams College, Elia was rejected from every fraternity on campus. Unlike many of the well-off students he attended university with, Elia worked his way through school by waiting tables and washing dishes, sometimes serving the very students who had rejected him. That feeling of "otherness" lasted his entire life and was a guiding factor in how he lived as an adult.

While studying drama at Yale University, Elia met his first wife, Molly Day Thacher, a woman who represented everything he wasn't and had felt self-conscious about. Her roots were deeply American and she likely had ancestors on the Mayflower, one of whom helped found Yale. Molly's uncle was president of Yale University. To the awkward, working-class immigrant, Molly was the ultimate insider.

They met when she was dating Elia's best friend and college roommate. As someone who never felt handsome or like he belonged, he must have been thrilled when she chose him over his roommate. He finally experienced the excitement of winning over a highly regarded woman. Molly even cast him in one of her plays. "A deep and lasting artistic partnership was being born," he wrote in his memoir. "I came to rely on her judgement in scripts. She made up for my lax in taste and savvy. I gave her the energy and drive she needed. She loved me totally."

The once shy student who had always felt alienated was shocked to learn this exceptionally bright, all-American girl of Anglo-Saxon descent loved him. They married in 1932 and remained together until she died in 1963, but it was a complicated marriage, to say the least. Like his difficult childhood, which groomed him to present himself as an outsider, Elia's marriage was integral to who he was as a person because they were so intertwined. Molly had studied to become a playwright and her excellent taste in projects helped guide Elia's career. Instead of achieving her own goals, however, she often found herself in the position of having to support her husband and his career instead. She was also living in an era when that meant practically raising their four children mostly alone.

Elia would become infuriated with her at the slightest hint of her relying on him for anything, but depended on her insight and guidance throughout their marriage. Not only did she help support him financially, but Molly played a huge part in his success. For instance, she was single-handedly responsible for bringing the work of Tennessee Williams to her husband's attention, resulting in his making *A Streetcar Named Desire*. His close friend Arthur Miller also gave credit to Molly for encouraging him to keep the flashback scene in *Death of a Salesman* after he had been encouraged to cut it out. He acknowledged that taking Molly's advice helped save the play.

There were other problems with the marriage. In his youth, Elia Kazan had experienced the frustration of unrequited romantic feelings numerous times before blossoming into a successful man. After their marriage, Molly almost immediately noticed her new husband was unable to stay faithful. Unfortunately, he never curbed his lusty desires and he became a serial philanderer—often under very public circumstances. The affairs were humiliating for Molly. One of the many notable public affairs was with Marilyn Monroe, who at the time of her relationship with Elia was an upcoming starlet, and would soon rise to phenomenal fame.

Later in life, at times Elia Kazan would try to explain away his behavior when it suited him. In the case of infidelity, he blamed his father, who was so domineering he had to learn how to be deceptive. More likely, he was resentful of feeling unworthy during his earlier life, and he held a grudge.

"What I wanted most, I'd have to take—quietly and quickly—from others," he wrote in his book. "I specialized in taking women away from men, particularly those handsome young fellows who played leading roles in films. I found many women were working off the same kind of thing I was. They were getting back at squadrons of men and would go to extraordinary lengths to play out their grudges. Sometimes I thought they actually preferred breaking the marriage laws in their own bed and if an infant, the fruit of the union slept peacefully through it all in a gaily painted cot at one side or even in the bed with us, I got a special charge out of it. It proved what I needed to have proved twice over. Don't get mad at me. I'm not really worse than most of you. Admit it."

These days, Elia Kazan would likely be recognized as a narcissist, but back then little was understood about such conditions.

Elia Kazan's career got a break, albeit a modest one, when he landed an internship as a stagehand at the Group Theatre. Founded by Lee Strasberg, Cheryl Crawford, and Harold Clurman in 1931, the troupe's teachings were based on Konstantin Stanislavski from Russia. They selected a name with "group" in the title to emphasize collaboration among actors, writers, directors, and producers. The Group Theatre was an immediate success and became a highly influential entity and produced many successful actors, directors, and writers, including Clifford Odets, Stella Adler, Sidney Kingsley, Paul Green, John Garfield, Irwin Shaw, Harry Morgan, Franchot Tone,

Frances Farmer, Ruth Nelson, Howard da Silva, Sidney Lumet, John Randolph, Joseph Bromberg, Michael Gordon, and more.

It was here Elia Kazan received training that would lead to a distinguished career, taking him from an insecure stagehand to a brilliant director. There was one person who remained skeptical of the Group, however: Molly. It was a position Clifford Odets did not appreciate, especially because it came from a woman. Elia wrote about how his friend Odets, who had once advised him to "find a peasant," viewed women.

"Clifford was convinced that an artist should never marry, but if he did, it should be to a woman who'd keep house for him, cook for him, bear his children, then nurse and tend them, at the same time protecting her genius from all the distraction while he worked," he wrote. "In the company of the artist's peers, this perfect wife-creature would preserve a respectful silence. Clifford had noticed that Molly did not. Behaving 'like a man,' she'd join right in the conversation and as an equal. 'Who is she?' Clifford roared. 'What does she know about the theatre?' Molly had debated their every point of difference. Clearly she wasn't impressed with the Group and its reason for being. What Clifford didn't say was that she hadn't paid him the respect she would have given Beethoven. But gradually I'd become defensive; everything he'd said against her turned me toward her."

The Group was an ideal training ground for Elia and others, but it was not without its drawbacks.

Formed during the Great Depression, when many individuals were open to other forms of economy, some members showed an interest in Communism. This, combined with the Russian theatre influence and collective philosophy, would later arouse suspicion in the 1950s during the anti-Communism craze. Those associated with the Group would later be haunted by their affiliation with the organization.

Elia Kazan had attended some meetings but was nowhere near being a Communist. He was too selfish for anything too communal. He was more interested in artistic talent than political affiliations. "Only people as full of self-doubt as actors could go for it quite the way our bunch did."

Molly's instincts, as usual, had been correct. Elia left the Group Theatre and had much greater success than his fellow members, which is incredible given the talent that emerged from the troupe.

The Group disbanded in 1941, but despite lasting just ten years the ripple effects are still felt today. In 1947, Robert Lewis, Elia Kazan, and Cheryl Crawford founded the Actors Studio in New York. Building on what they started in the Group Theatre, the Actors Studio also took Stanislavski's teachings and further refined them, with their interpretation now known as

Method acting or the Method. While starting the school, Elia continued directing plays.

In the early 1950s, Elia's career in theatre was soaring but he began experimenting with directing feature films. The decision meant time away from the Actors Studio and more time in Los Angeles. In 1951, Lee Strasberg stepped in as the director once Elia began pursuing a film career.

Increased time on the West Coast meant more than just working on movies. Away from his wife, Elia was unhindered when it came to pursuing other women—and when he met an attractive starlet named Marilyn Monroe, he set his sights on her.

Elia Kazan met Marilyn on the set of *As Young as You Feel* in 1951 when he was visiting the director Harmon Jones. Elia was fast building a reputation as a great director. Marilyn was in the early stages of grief after the death of Johnny Hyde, and feeling vulnerable and alone. Shortly after they meet, Elia and Marilyn attended a screening of *A Streetcar Named Desire* on February 15, 1951. Soon, Marilyn also met Elia's good friend and partner Arthur Miller in a project called *The Hook*. She even accompanied Elia and Arthur to meet with Harry Cohn at Columbia for a meeting about *The Hook*.

The initial dalliance was brief, with Elia returning to New York on February 23. They picked up again when he returned in May and she served as his date for a dinner at Charles Feldman's house. Once again, Arthur Miller was in town and also present at Charles Feldman's house. Both Arthur and Marilyn would later recall an intense attraction during his visits to Los Angeles, despite the fact he was married and she was dating his friend. Arthur's marriage back home was crumbling, but he still worried his feelings for Marilyn would overwhelm him so he packed up and headed home to New York earlier than planned. Arthur was now able to stay in New York, where he was safe from his attraction to Marilyn—for the time being.

The deal for *The Hook* fell through when Arthur refused to change his script. Between heading home to his wife and refusal to compromise his work, as far as Marilyn was concerned she got a good look into his character; Arthur Miller was not a man who compromised his ideals.

Marilyn's affair with Elia Kazan was either brief or ended in the summer. He later claimed they continued to have a sexual relationship for the next ten years but this remains unlikely, as none of Marilyn's friends note the relationship lasting that long. Also, once he named others to HUAC he effectively became a pariah among his peers. On January 14, 1952, Elia Kazan was interrogated behind closed doors by HUAC. He refused to name others. It was not because of any loyalty to the Communist party, which he didn't have, but because he refused to put himself in a position where a studio might potentially dictate what kind of art he could make. On his way out, he was informed he would likely be called again.

In fairness to Elia Kazan, he was placed in a no-win situation. As movie studios began pushing artists to testify in front of HUAC and name names, he initially refused.

Pressure on Elia intensified. He was fresh off the success of *A Streetcar Named Desire*, a movie that increased his profile in Hollywood—and consequently with HUAC.

Elia Kazan never had much of an interest in Communism, but it was known he had ties to the Group Theatre, which *did* have members who joined the party. They also based their acting philosophy on a Russian and the Group has always emphasized working as a collective.

Elia was subpoenaed in February 1952 to testify in front of HUAC. It was his opinion that HUAC was looking to persecute famous artists to make a statement—and he was correct.

He had been expecting the subpoena and he was planning for it. He admitted to his brief membership in the Communist Party and discussed it freely, but he initially refused to name others who had the same affiliation.

The proceedings struck Elia as more performance than a search for the truth, but he understood the members of HUAC were still capable of ruining careers. *A Streetcar Named Desire* had been a Warner Bros. film, but as it turns out his next two projects—*Viva Zapata!* And *Man on a Tightrope*—would be Twentieth Century-Fox productions. Fox production head Darryl Zanuck and president Spyros Skouras pressured Elia Kazan to name others—or likely someone else would rat him out instead. If he didn't, they would end their working relationship with him.

Elia feared for his career and livelihood. He believed *A Streetcar Named Desire* paid the price for his troubles with HUAC. Although *Streetcar* won three major awards for Vivien Leigh (Best Actress), Karl Malden (Best Supporting Actor), and Kim Hunter (Best Supporting Actress), it lost other major awards, including Best Screenplay for Tennessee Williams, Best Actor for Marlon Brando (a student sometimes associated with the Actors Studio), and the "big two" for the Academy Awards: Best Picture (Charles Feldman, producer) and Elia Kazan for Best Director.

The ceremony took place on March 20, 1952. It's difficult to determine if *A Streetcar Named Desire* did lose out because of Elia's trouble with HUAC or if the votes were simply cast for others—either possibility is very real. Regardless, Elia felt as though he had been alienated once again.

As Elia Kazan juggled a career high with *Streetcar* and potentially career-ending threats from the government, in March 1952 Marilyn went on her first date with Joe DiMaggio.

In addition to coercion from Fox, Elia's wife Molly also insisted he name names, with the belief that if he told them what they wanted to know (and likely knew anyway) the government would see these artists had done nothing wrong, certainly nothing that would risk American safety.

There was no way out. The more Elia tried to avoid naming others, the more pressure HUAC applied and threatened jail. Twentieth Century-Fox refused to do business with him until his name was cleared.

On April 10, 1952, Elia Kazan finally conceded to pressure and testi-fied. By giving HUAC what it wanted, he reasoned, he would simply give the government information they probably already had and save his career. In addition to naming Arthur Miller for possible ties to Communism, he also named Lee Strasberg's wife Paula, Clifford Odets, Morris Carnovsky, and his wife Phoebe Brand.

He was right that his testimony saved his career, but the backlash was immediate and severe. His secretary quit. Theatre producer Kermit Bloom-garden and Arthur Miller both stopped working with him. Former colleagues avoided him. Marilyn, too, appeared to have become disenchanted with Elia Kazan.

Marilyn was already wrestling with an attraction to Arthur Miller, so Elia's betrayal of his friend would not have sat well with her. Her later close association with the Strasbergs would practically guarantee she would con-tinue to keep her distance.

With romantic partners, Marilyn found herself attracted to specific traits. She generally gravitated to older, accomplished men who were intel-lectual. With someone like Elia Kazan, Marilyn would have been attracted to his individuality and his exceptional knowledge of acting, theatre, and movies. She would have also found common ground in his struggle for acceptance and his fierce fight to rise from humble origins and build a career. When Elia Kazan bowed to pressure from HUAC and named colleagues as possible Communists or sympathizers, she would have seen it as a violation of his integrity. After she finally did begin a romance with Arthur Miller a few years later, Marilyn risked her career to stand by him in his fight *against* HUAC.

Testifying in front of HUAC and selling out his friends and colleagues violated his principles—and Marilyn's. She had bonded with him over stand-ing up for underdogs, and fighting the system when it was the right thing to do. Now he went back on his word. With his reputation in tatters, Elia Kazan released a public statement explaining why he had testified—it was ghostwritten by Molly.

After Marilyn's separation from Arthur, she ran into her former lover Elia Kazan on December 8, 1960, in New York. She whispered to her friend

Ralph Roberts to look over and "tell me what you think." Ralph replied with, "I think the man is in love with you."

Marilyn agreed. "That's the feeling I got. He did tell me years ago he loved me. We spent a great deal of time together in Hollywood. He even said he'd get a divorce if I would marry him. Then he introduced me to Arthur. I didn't think he really meant it. He was the catalyst who changed my life more drastically than any other single person I've ever known. He gave me courage to fight the system. He encouraged me to come to New York, study with Lee [Strasberg], and especially Paula [Strasberg]. 'She knows more about the film sense than anyone around,' he told me. But I agree—that was the look of a man in love."

Elia Kazan never did leave his wife. Molly passed away from a cerebral hemorrhage two days before her fifty-seventh birthday on December 14, 1963. She had endured more than twenty years of marriage to Elia Kazan, whose career she had helped shape and guide.

Elia Kazan's friendship with Arthur Miller was never the same after the HUAC testimony, but the former buddies healed their relationship enough to still work together occasionally. When Arthur Miller wrote about his relationship with Marilyn in a play called *After the Fall*, Elia Kazan directed its Broadway run from January 23, 1964, to its close on May 29.

JOE DIMAGGIO

Joseph Paul DiMaggio was the sixth of seven children born to Sicilian immigrants Giuseppe and Rosalia. Giuseppe came from a long line of fishermen and Rosalia's father encouraged him to move his family to California to make more money. Giuseppe worked in the United States for four years before he saved enough money to bring Rosalia and their oldest child, a daughter, to the United States. The DiMaggios settled in the San Francisco area, which was filled with Italian immigrant fishermen who arrived after the Gold Rush brought an influx of miners to the area.

When Joe was born on November 25, 1914, his father hoped his son would follow in his footsteps. Indeed, Giuseppe hoped all five of his sons would become fishermen. From an early age, however, Joe dreaded the awful smell of the dead fish he had to endure when helping to clean the boat. Instead, Joe and his older brother Vince spent a great deal of time playing baseball in San Francisco's sandlots. Giuseppe, a man normally of few words, was not shy about expressing his disappointment.

Not only did Joe not follow in his father's footsteps, but his teen years were also starting to look like he was directionless. He dropped out of high school and was working odd jobs when Vince helped get him the break he needed. Joe had been playing semiprofessional baseball but Vince had been playing professionally for the San Francisco Seals.

Vince managed to get Joe an opportunity to fill in for the Seals in the shortstop position. Joe DiMaggio made his professional debut in baseball on October 1, 1932, at the age of seventeen. His major league debut with the Yankees, with whom he would spend his entire major league career, took place on May 3, 1936. In the course of his career, Joe set a franchise record for hitting the most home runs by a rookie (that record stood for eighty years), led the Yankees to nine World Series championships, and went on a fifty-six-game hitting streak in 1941—a record that still stands.

Joe DiMaggio was already a legend during his active playing years with the Yankees. When he retired at the age of thirty-seven in 1951, he was considered one of the greatest baseball players to have ever lived. In his personal life, at this time he was divorced from actress Dorothy Arnold and had a young son, Joe DiMaggio Jr.

Joe DiMaggio spotted pictures of a beautiful blonde in a baseball-themed photo and wanted to know who the mystery woman was. He began asking around until he discovered her identity and requested a date with the starlet named Marilyn Monroe. Initially, she had no interest in meeting him and had to be persuaded into having dinner with him. Photofest

It was around the same time he retired that Joe spotted photos of a pretty blonde starlet holding a baseball bat and standing alongside Chicago White Sox players Gus Zernial and Joe Dobson. Curious, Joe began asking around about the attractive woman. If she was posing with ball players, surely she must love baseball and be familiar with the sport. Joe called Gus Zernial to find out the woman's identity and ask for her contact information. Gus was able to supply the name but did not have her phone number.

The man who finally acted as a go-between for Joe and Marilyn was David March, a business manager, who may have been trying to land Marilyn as a client. Joe knew David from hanging out at Toots Shor's Restaurant in New York. David contacted Marilyn on Joe's behalf to let her know a "nice guy" wanted to meet her. She did not seem interested, so David told her Joe DiMaggio wanted to meet her. He expected her to show some sort of excitement or enthusiasm when he mentioned *Joe DiMaggio* but she asked who he was.

Unfortunately for Joe, Marilyn Monroe didn't follow sports and had no clue who he was, his record-breaking career, or his legendary status. Instead, she pictured an obnoxious, ill-mannered "sports type" in a loud sportscoat. She declined to meet him.

David March pushed the issue, however, and Marilyn finally agreed to meet with Joe on March 8, 1952. The (sort of) blind date took place at Villa Nova, an Italian restaurant on the Sunset Strip. Because Marilyn and Joe had never met or spoken to each other, David agreed to have dinner with them as a means of easing any discomfort. He brought along an actress named Peggy Rabe to make it an official double date.

Marilyn tended to run late anyway, so coupled with the fact she wasn't excited about the date, arrived two hours late. Joe patiently waited for her. Although Marilyn had pictured an abrasive loudmouth, she could not have been more wrong about her dinner companion. Joe DiMaggio was quiet, respectful, and dignified. Far from wearing a loud checkered sports coat, he wore a gray flannel suit. Joe greeted Marilyn but was quiet most of the date so Marilyn wasn't sure what to say to him. She talked mostly to David March.

If Joe was not what she expected in a sports figure, he was also distinctly different from the other types of men she had encountered in Hollywood. She may not have been instantly smitten, but she was certainly intrigued. She was also delighted to point out that one of the polka dots on Joe's tie knot was exactly centered and asked if he had planned it.

Joe was never much of a conversationalist but when he did speak, he noticed Marilyn listened intently. In one version of the story, Mickey Rooney was at the restaurant and walked over to talk baseball with Joe, disrupting the date and the conversation at the table. Men stopping by the table to speak with Joe was a regular happening when at dinner, as Marilyn quickly learned.

Marilyn later told Ben Hecht, "I found myself staring at a reserved gentleman in a gray suit, with a gray tie and sprinkle of gray in his hair. There were a few blue polka dots on his tie. If I hadn't been told he was some sort of ball player, I would have guessed he was either a steel magnate or a congressman.

"The other men talked and threw their personalities around. Mr. DiMaggio just sat there. Yet somehow he was the most exciting man at the table. The excitement was in his eyes. They are sharp and alert.

"Then I became aware of something odd. The men at the table weren't showing off for me or telling their stories for my attention. It was Mr. DiMaggio they were wooing. This was a novelty. No woman has ever put me so much in the shade before.

"But as far as I was concerned, Mr. DiMaggio was all novelty. In Hollywood, the more important a man is the more he talks. The better he is at his job, the more he brags. By these Hollywood standards of male greatness my dinner companion was a nobody. Yet I have never seen any man in Hollywood who got so much respect and attention at a dinner table. Sitting next to Mr. DiMaggio was like sitting next to a peacock with its tail spread—that's how noticeable you were."

After dinner, Marilyn offered to drive Joe back to his hotel. He didn't live in Los Angeles, so he was staying at the Knickerbocker Hotel in Hollywood and had taken a taxi to the restaurant.

For their next date, Marilyn and Joe dined at a lower-profile Italian restaurant so they would have more privacy. Then they went for a drive by the beach on Pacific Coast Highway.

Soon, the pair began seeing each other regularly and Joe even visited Marilyn on the set of *Monkey Business*, a movie costarring Cary Grant and Ginger Rogers. Marilyn had a small part as a sexy secretary but her career was on the brink of major stardom.

On March 17, Marilyn, who previously had no interest in baseball, attended a charity game to watch Joe play at Gilmore Field, where CBS Studio is now located in Hollywood. It was the only opportunity she would ever have to watch him play baseball.

On the surface, there were a lot of differences between Marilyn and Joe. Marilyn had experienced a lonely childhood and moved around a lot; Joe had grown up in a large family still deeply rooted in their Italian origins and traditions. Joe's strong ties to his Old World family also meant he expected women to focus on the home and family. In contrast, Marilyn was a career woman who openly celebrated her natural sexuality. Joe had just ended his career at a time when Marilyn's was just ascending.

There were, however, deeper connections. Each had a failed marriage. Both came from working-class origins and rose to the pinnacle of their chosen careers, resulting in a level of celebrity experienced by very few. Neither one had finished high school and was self-conscious about the lack of formal education. Their respective success placed them in situations requiring they interact with all types of people, including those whose education and socioeconomic standings were drastically different than their humble beginnings. They also both wanted children, or in Joe's case, more children. In the meantime, Marilyn adored his son, Joe Jr.

As the couple continued dating, they tried to keep a low profile. Just as Marilyn had an aversion to "sports types," Joe similarly had negative feelings about "Hollywood types." Neither one of them liked the party scene or nightclubs, which helped keep their romance private. They were occasionally seen out together but more often than not, when Marilyn had to make an obligatory public appearance, she went alone or with friend Sidney Skolsky. When Marilyn and Jane Russell placed their hands and feet in wet cement at Grauman's Chinese Theatre in June 1953, Joe was not on hand to witness the honor. He did, however, attend a quieter celebratory dinner after the ceremony at Chasen's in Beverly Hills.

What Joe liked most of all was watching television. Initially, Marilyn found this activity pleasant enough but as time passed she needed a little more intellectual stimulation. She also tried cooking Italian meals, such as spaghetti, for Joe but she was never much of a cook and didn't enjoy the experience.

Joe and Marilyn's blossoming romance coincided with Marilyn's transition from starlet to star. The year 1953 saw three movies, *Niagara*, *Gentlemen Prefer Blondes*, and *How to Marry a Millionaire*, all released to considerable success. That same year Marilyn traveled to Canada to film *River of No Return*, an experience so negative that Joe flew to the set location to comfort her.

It was also a time of major change.

Marilyn was never one to be satisfied with just being a movie star. She was determined to become a great actress and now with some professional success behind her, she began to assert her authority at the studio. When Twentieth Century-Fox presented her with another musical comedy, *The Girl in Pink Tights*, she refused the script and was suspended by Fox.

With her work schedule cleared, Joe suggested they get married and she could accompany him to Japan for a work trip. Japan would double as a quiet honeymoon. Marilyn had no problem accompanying Joe in Japan, but was unsure if they should get married. Joe would not hear of it. If they were traveling together, they should be married. When he visited her in Canada, he pointed out, he stayed in a separate hotel.

Joe and Marilyn were married on January 14, 1954, at the courthouse in his hometown of San Francisco. The press besieged the courthouse, where Marilyn and Joe politely smiled and kissed for the cameras before speeding off in a car driven by Joe. Shortly thereafter, the newlyweds left for Japan. It would not be the quiet honeymoon Joe had imagined.

The Japanese public was crazy about baseball but they were crazier for Marilyn Monroe. Enthusiastic fans yelled for her and chanted her name. Without trying or meaning to, Marilyn became the star and focus of the trip. It was a bad sign.

While in Japan, the Army asked Marilyn if she would be interested in singing for the troops in the Korean War, an offer she was honored to receive and readily accepted. After a short tour of Korea, she returned exhilarated by the experience and tried to share it with Joe. "You never heard such cheering!" To which he dismissively replied, "Yes, I have."

The newlyweds spent a lot of time in San Francisco, where the movie star tried to turn herself into a dutiful housewife. She loved being a member of the large DiMaggio family and they loved her in return. She had fantasized about being an ideal wife for Joe, but the reality was she simply didn't have the right personality to enjoy standing over a stove all day or catering to a husband.

When she returned to Los Angeles to make *There's No Business Like Show Business*, Joe had the misfortune of visiting the set on the day she filmed the "Heat Wave" dance number. Seeing Mrs. DiMaggio dressed in a skimpy outfit, gyrating around, and singing suggestive lyrics did not go over well with Mr. DiMaggio.

Marilyn's next movie was *The Seven Year Itch*, a sexy comedy that had to be toned down for film from its original run on the Broadway stage. Most of the movie was filmed in Los Angeles soundstages at Twentieth Century-Fox, but some outdoor scenes in New York were filmed in September 1954. Among those scenes was the night Marilyn

Marilyn and Joe married at the San Francisco City Hall on January 14, 1954. Because both of them were divorced, the couple was unable to wed in the Catholic church, as Joe had done for his first marriage.
Macfadden Publications New York, publisher of Radio-TV Mirror / Wikimedia Commons

stood over a subway grate while a fan underneath blew her pleated white skirt up around her waist, exposing her legs and panties.

The public street was filled with reporters, news photographers and onlookers hooting and yelling. Writer Walter Winchell persuaded Joe to head down to the shoot with him, and the results were disastrous. Joe was livid with the scene playing out before him. The unruly crowd cheering as his wife's skirt billowed up over and over again proved too much for him. Infuriated, he left and waited for Marilyn's return to the hotel.

It is unknown what exactly happened when Marilyn arrived at the hotel. There was an argument of some sort, but stories have circulated for years that Joe may have lost his temper to the point of physically striking her. Furthermore, according to the stories, Marilyn had bruises on her body that required covering with makeup so she could film the following day.

However, a newspaper article from the day after she filmed the skirt scene indicates Marilyn was posing for photographs with Philippe Halsman. The photo shoot included pictures of Marilyn wearing a spaghetti-strap cocktail dress and jumping (she jumped a few times over the years for Halsman, who liked asking celebrities to jump in photos). "Just before she left, Halsman asked her to jump for him, since he is fond of photographing famous people in mid-air," the newspaper article reads. "Marilyn cooperatively jumped; her legs didn't show and Halsman asked her to jump again. Again they didn't show. 'Marilyn,' he complained, 'can't you jump and express your whole personality?' Confused, she protested, 'But Philippe, I don't know how to.'

"Photographer Halsman was understandably frustrated. Earlier that day (from 12 to 3 a.m.) America's Number One Sex Queen had stood in front of a midtown New York restaurant and allowed her skirt to be blown nearly waist-high by the breeze from a subway pavement grill, while cheering thousands ogled her legs during the making of a scene from *The*

Joe and Marilyn were all smiles at the premiere of The Seven Year Itch, which was the movie that ended their marriage. The event was held on June 1, 1955, which was also Marilyn's twenty-ninth birthday.
Twentieth Century-Fox / Photofest / © Twentieth Century-Fox

Seven Year Itch. Now every time she jumped for him, no legs registered in his camera."

Other pictures from that photo shoot with Halsman show plenty of Marilyn's skin, legs included. No bruises are visible on her arms, back, chest, face, or legs. There is no evidence of cuts or swelling. She doesn't appear to be hiding any parts of her body or wearing clothing to cover up, nor does she complain of any pain. She was able to jump for Halsman multiple times.

Joe physically abusing Marilyn has still not been proved for certain, but what was certain is the marriage was over. Shortly after the skirt scene was filmed, Marilyn returned to Los Angeles and the couple separated. The marriage turned out to be very different than what Joe wanted or expected. He had anticipated Marilyn would give up her career and become a traditional wife, staying home full time and cooking meals. Marilyn had finally achieved the career she had always dreamed about when she was a little girl and wasn't about to give it up now.

On October 6, 1954, the day they announced their breakup, Joe left the house he shared with Marilyn in Beverly Hills. Marilyn and her lawyer, Jerry Giesler, met with the press in front of the house and spoke to the press. More specifically, Jerry Giesler did the talking while Marilyn stood tearfully by his side. A few weeks later, on October 26, Joe appeared to be having second thoughts about their impending divorce and called Sidney Skolsky to ask if he thought Marilyn might change her mind. She didn't. Just two days later, Marilyn testified in court and was granted a divorce, which would take effect in 1955. Sidney attended court with her.

"We rented a lovely cottage in Beverly Hills and settled down to married life. Everything went fine for a while, until Joe started complaining about my working all the time. He even would find little things to upset him after a while. It got so that we didn't even talk to each other for days. I began living in one part of the house and Joe the other. It was now too much to take. When I did the film *The Seven Year Itch*, he said my dress flying scene, my exposing my legs and thighs, even my crotch—that was the last straw. When I married Joe in 1954, he had already retired from baseball, but he was a wonderful athlete and had a very sensitive nature in many respects. His family were immigrants and he'd had a very difficult time when he was young. So he understood something about me, and I understood something about him, and we based our marriage on this. But just 'something' isn't enough. Our marriage wasn't very happy, and it ended in nine months."

The marriage may have been over, but it wasn't a clean break. Around the holidays Marilyn moved to the East Coast, and the former couple was occasionally seen out together.

In January, Marilyn, Joe, Joe's brother Dominic, and his wife Emily were photographed outside a restaurant in Boston. As Marilyn's interlocutory divorce decree had been granted in October, reporters were quick to ask if they were reconciling. Joe turned to Marilyn and asked, "Is it, honey?" Marilyn's answer was not what he wanted to hear. "No," she told reporters. "Just call it a visit."

Joe and Marilyn stayed with Emily's family, the Fredericks, in Wellesley. The press hounded the former couple. Reporters noted he granted autographs to youngsters who were waiting on the porch and when asked where Marilyn was, he replied she was staying with friends. Newspapers published a photo of Joe peeking out from behind the Fredericks' front door. During the same trip, reporters followed Joe to Dominic's industrial plant in Lawrence. Here, too, reporters asked Joe if there were plans for a reconciliation with Marilyn. In his typical stoic way, Joe responded, "There is none."

On January 26, Joe and Marilyn drove back to New York in a borrowed car. On the way home, while stopped at a red light on 2nd Avenue and 125th Street, Marilyn anticipated Joe's induction to the Hall of Fame. "I want to be the first to congratulate you," she said. "I know you're going to make it." Joe told sports writer Jimmy Cannon in an interview at the Madison Hotel, "She pecked me on the cheek after she congratulated me."

While still at the intersection, a man driving a truck yelled out "Congratulations!" to Joe. "Anyway, I thought he said that," Joe told Cannon. "He just yelled. He was going pretty good. I was just driving leisurely."

They turned on the radio and during a news segment, Joe and Marilyn learned he had indeed been inducted into the Hall of Fame. "I know two people who are happy," Marilyn told him. "I'm happy and little Joe [Joe DiMaggio Jr.] will be happy."

There were other evenings out, including Jackie Gleason's birthday party in February and—remarkably—the premiere of *The Seven Year Itch*, the very movie that was the proverbial straw that broke the marriage camel's back. It was also Marilyn's birthday, and after the premiere they celebrated by having dinner.

They continued to drift apart and by 1956, Marilyn was dating Arthur Miller. They didn't see each other again until after her divorce from Arthur and the circumstances responsible for bringing them back together were unpleasant.

Joe and Marilyn didn't enter each other's orbit again until 1961 when Marilyn was hospitalized against her will in a lockdown mental health facility. Terrified and infuriated, she managed to make a call to Joe and begged for help. Joe soon arrived and threatened to take the building apart "brick by brick" unless Marilyn was released into his custody. Marilyn was discharged.

Marilyn checked into a hospital better suited to her needs, followed by a trip with Joe to Florida, where he was a batting instructor for spring training. While in Florida, Marilyn watched baseball practice and the two made time for relaxing on the beach. Their friendship blossomed and their relationship was much happier than it had been years earlier.

"I've always been able to count on Joe as a friend after that first bitterness of our parting faded," she said. "Believe me, there is no spark to be kindled. I just like being with him, and we have a better understanding than we ever had."

The sentiments she voiced in public are backed up by her private comments. Marilyn ended a telegram to Joe dated September 22, 1961, with "LOVE YOU, I THINK, MORE THAN EVER."

Whitey Snyder also noticed. "Joe DiMaggio was the best friend Marilyn ever had," he said. "They were no good married, but that's the way it goes with thousands of men and women."

As Marilyn got her life together following her hospitalization and split from Arthur Miller, Joe was around to lend support. He visited her after gallbladder surgery and helped with a down payment on a house—the first one she bought on her own. She was excited about the prospect of purchasing her own home and wanted Joe to give his thoughts before finalizing the deal.

In a postcard from May 1962, Joe wrote:

Dearest Marilyn,
    Have a short stop over here in Copenhagen enroute for the "long underwear country." Should be there in about three hours.
    Spent nine days here in 1950. Wonderful country. The famous Tivoli Park was one of my favorite places.
    Love, Joe

In a telegram for her thirty-sixth birthday, Joe wrote, "HAPPY BIRTHDAY HOPE TODAY AND FUTURE YEARS BRING YOU SUNNY SKIES AND ALL YOUR HEART DESIRES AS EVER—JOE."

It would be Marilyn's last birthday. When she passed away on August 5, Joe stepped forward to arrange Marilyn's memorial service, along with her half-sister Berniece Miracle and business manager Inez Melson. Photos of a grief-stricken Joe DiMaggio at her service on August 8 appeared in newspapers.

After Marilyn passed away, Joe arranged for a half dozen red roses to be delivered to her crypt three times per week. The order was filled by Parisian Florist in Los Angeles. Joe kept the flower deliveries going for twenty years—Parisian never raised the price on him.

Joe was a private man and generally kept to himself, although he did speak about Marilyn to Earl Wilson in 1973. He was horrified by the rumors she had been murdered and believed she had taken too many pills by accident. "I've always refrained from talking about it," he said. "But I don't think she took those pills by intent. I don't believe it was suicide. Accidentally, yes."

After Joe's death, many of his personal items were auctioned off—including a portrait of Marilyn that had been hanging in his home. He never married again.

ARTHUR MILLER

She has more courage, more intimate decency, more sensitivity and love for humanity than anyone I ever knew in my life.

—Arthur Miller

Arthur Miller was born in 1915 in Harlem the middle child of Isidore Miller, an immigrant from Radomysl Wielki, Galicia (now Poland), and his mother was a native New Yorker also of Polish descent. Isidore owned a women's clothing manufacturing business that at one time employed four hundred people, but he lost everything in the Depression. To help the family make ends meet, Arthur delivered bread before school while still in his teens. The family's financial duress and the lasting impacts of coming of age during the Great Depression made a lasting impression on how Arthur viewed life, politics, and socioeconomics, all of which were major themes throughout his work.

As a boy, Arthur felt lost between his siblings, Kermit who was older and the better student, and Joan who was the baby. He rode his bike around the city alone to escape the family dynamics.

As Isidore Miller worked to rebuild his failed business, Arthur and Kermit pitched in to help. In addition to helping their father and the family business, the brothers traded off attending college. Kermit attended for a year, then Arthur at the University of Michigan.

During his sophomore year of college, Arthur won a prize for a play called *No Villain*, which explores Marxist theory and portrays a once-successful family who has lost everything with a son away at university. Upon Arthur's win, Kermit sacrificed his education and agreed to let Arthur finish his degree; Kermit would help run their father's struggling business. It was a tremendous act of love Arthur felt he could never repay, and it caused him to experience considerable guilt. Later, the brothers discovered their father had lied to them. Isidore Miller had stashed a little bit of money away but didn't want his sons to know because he wanted them to be part of the family business. Had they known about the extra money, both sons would have been able to complete their schooling. Arthur never fully recovered from the betrayal.

At the beginning of World War II, both Miller brothers volunteered for service. Kermit was accepted into the Officer Candidate School and Arthur was rejected due to a knee injury from high school football. Again, he was plagued by guilt.

Isidore's business and success never recovered and he struggled to learn how to live again. As Arthur began a serious writing career, he channeled many of his unresolved feelings about his father into his work. *All My Sons* was his first important play, followed by *Death of a Salesman*, which won the Pulitzer Prize for Drama and Tony Award for Best Play.

Arthur had found financial and critical success; he was also married to his college sweetheart, Mary Slattery, but he continued to struggle emotionally. He took long walks around the city to clear his head.

"My walks, it gradually seemed to me, were in themselves indicative of some personality failure," he recalled in his autobiography. "I loved the city, was feverishly curious about all the lives lived in it, but moved through it alone, unconnected. My shyness tortured me. Life was always elsewhere. And yet, paradoxically, out of my aloneness I was communicating my feelings to thousands of strangers every week in the theatre."

At least part of what he was experiencing was guilt; he had made a conscious effort to champion underdogs and examine the dynamics of American society. The shift in his status was something he was unequipped to deal with and didn't fully understand. "I'd spent my life on the outside and now I was on the inside, where all the dangers and the wild animals live."

Arthur first met Marilyn when he and Elia Kazan came to Hollywood in 1951 to pitch *The Hook*, a screenplay Arthur had written about corruption on docks.

Miller and Kazan went to the set of *As Young as You Feel* at Twentieth Century-Fox, where he noticed Marilyn quietly weeping. He later learned it was over Johnny Hyde.

They met again a few days later at the Beverly Hills home of producer Charles Feldman, who was hosting Arthur during his trip. Feldman threw a dinner party, and when Marilyn showed up he noticed how shy she appeared.

During his stay at the Feldman house, Arthur discovered he was unable to write while staying in Hollywood. He found while in Los Angeles "impossible to concentrate" on his work. Once again, he was uncomfortable with the trappings of success and ostentatious signs of wealth. "As I sat at a glass table beside Feldman's swimming pool, the waterfront kept vanishing into the sun sparkling on the eggs Benedict, the very effort to conjure it up whispering of fraud. A Filipino houseman provided coffee and whatever else I could imagine eating. I finally gave up and lay staring at the birdless foliage wondering if this was what being 'in' meant. It was a question I would never be able to answer; it may be that Hollywood is merely a living Escher drawing with no inside at all, only an outside, since everyone I met regarded himself as an outsider perpetually passing through, like politicians in Washington."

According to both Miller and Kazan, Marilyn tagged along and posed as a secretary when they pitched *The Hook* to Harry Cohn at Columbia Pictures. (She proved to be a huge distraction when Cohn recognized her.)

After the meeting, Elia, Arthur, and Marilyn went to a bookstore where Marilyn looked for a copy of *Death of a Salesman*.

"The three of us wandered through a bookstore, Marilyn wanting to find *Salesman*. When I turned to hand her a copy I had found on the drama shelf, I saw out of the corner of my eye a man, Chinese or Japanese, staring at her from the next aisle while masturbating in his pants. I quickly moved her away from the man, whom she had not seen. She was wearing an ordinary blouse and skirt, not at all provocative, but even here, with her attention on other things than herself, the air around her was charged."

Miller was already starting to feel an attraction and decided he needed to get out of Los Angeles and away from Marilyn as soon as possible. "I could not place her in any world I knew; like a cork bobbing on the ocean, she could have begun her voyage on the other side of the world or a hundred yards down the beach."

Miller, Kazan, and Cohn made a tentative deal that they wouldn't make any money unless Columbia made money. Later, when Cohn requested Miller change the corrupt union bosses into Communists, Miller withdrew his script. If asked to lie about who the "bad guys" were, then he didn't want any part of the deal. The content of his work was more important to him than landing a movie deal.

Arthur's character and integrity were contributing factors in switching Marilyn's affection from Elia to Arthur. Under pressure from HUAC, Elia Kazan saved his career and named others as suspected Communists. Arthur Miller, on the other hand, fought HUAC.

There was another thing she liked about Arthur—his appearance. It was no secret that Marilyn idolized two men during her life. One was Clark Gable; the other was Abraham Lincoln, the American president who symbolized honesty, integrity, and doing the right thing at all costs. To her, Arthur Miller must have seemed like the closest thing to Lincoln she would ever meet.

"She liked to tease Arthur on his 'Abraham Lincoln' side: a tall, serious man who smiled very little when she was so bubbly," said Patricia Rosten, daughter of Norman and Hedda Rosten. The entire Rosten family was close to both Marilyn and Arthur. "This great intellectual was everything she loved in a man. Everything about her leaned towards reading and writing. Marilyn was first of all a cerebral person. But at the time, people did not detect this aspect of her personality as her beauty was dazzling."

Their romance wasn't quite ready to bloom. Arthur stayed in New York with Mary and Marilyn went on to marry Joe DiMaggio, but they couldn't forget one another. "I no longer knew what I wanted, certainly not the end of my marriage, but the thought of putting Marilyn out of my life was unbearable," he wrote.

Marilyn and Arthur didn't become a couple until she moved to New York. His marriage was on the rocks and miserable; she was coming out of a challenging marriage with Joe. The initial attraction they had felt—and tried to resist—in 1951 never went away. Now free to explore a possible romance, they were madly in love right away. Unlike Joe, Arthur was supportive of her career ambitions and took her acting aspirations seriously.

"I don't know how to say it, but I was in love with him from the first moment," Marilyn said. "I'll never forget the one day he said to me I should act on the stage and how the people standing around started to laugh. But he said, 'No, I'm very serious.' And the way he said that, I could see he was a sensitive human being and treated me as a sensitive person, too. It's difficult to describe, but it's the most important thing."

The press joked about the relationship and referred to them as "the hourglass and the egghead," but it was an unfair assessment of the couple. Arthur was a playwright and was surrounded by actors, writers, and artists, including his sister, who was an actress. Marilyn was an actress, and although had little stage experience was serious in her studies and had a deep interest in technique and reading about acting and theatre. She had a large library, loved to read, and was quick-witted. Together, they created a life filled with a circle of friends that included writers, artists, and actors.

"The very inappropriateness of our being together was to me the sign that it was appropriate," he said in an interview in the 1980s. "We're two parts, however remote of this society, of this life. It was sensuous and life-loving it seemed, while in the center there was a darkness and a tragedy that I didn't know the dimensions of at that time. And the same thing was true of me. So it wasn't that crazy."

Their ideals were tested when Arthur received a subpoena to testify before HUAC. For the committee's public image of representing truth, justice, and the American way, it had a way of seeking out high-profile people to call. Arthur Miller didn't receive attention until his relationship with Marilyn went public, even though Elia Kazan named him as having possible Communist ties during his testimony.

While speaking to a news crew in 1956, Arthur told reporters he hoped to have the HUAC issues cleared up so he could go to England with the woman he hoped to marry. It could only be Marilyn Monroe, which caused a stir. Almost immediately, reporters camped out at Marilyn's apartment until she came downstairs to make a statement.

There have been rumors that at the moment, Arthur used Marilyn to better his position with HUAC, and Marilyn was completely unaware of any marriage plans until he announced them to the press, which trapped her into marrying him. A letter dated May 17, 1956, from Arthur to Marilyn revealed a much different story. They had clearly been making plans to get married and Arthur had already been to Reno to obtain a divorce from Mary so he could wed Marilyn. His affectionate nickname for her was Gramercy 5.

> Dear Heart; My Own Wife; My Very Own Gramercy 5; Sweetheart:
> I am enclosing a letter I got today from the first woman I ever knew in my life. My mother. Now maybe you will understand where I learned to write and to feel. I know I am liable to get very sentimental and maudlin about this, but today is one of the most revelatory days of my life. I could write many pages even a volume, about what this letter brings to my mind. I think that had I died without ever receiving it, I should never have known some unbelievably simple but important things.
> You see, Poo, I often try to tell you that you mean things to me beyond your body, beyond your spirit, beyond anything you can know about yourself, and it is hard for another person to understand what she—or he—really signifies to one who loves her. I will try to tell you a few of the things you mean to me, and which became absolutely clear to me when I got this letter today. (I got it today, Thursday, by the way, because I was in Reno for my passport business, and picked up my mail at the post office.)
> First let me say what I feared. They are very conventional people. That doesn't mean they're stiff—far from it. But they believe in family virtues, in wives being wives and husbands being husbands. They are not especially scandalized by infidelity, but neither do they forget that the big happiness is family happiness. Above all, they know how to love their children, and truly, if I ever needed anything they would die to get it for me. At the same time, my father could take advantage of me and my brother, if we let him, but he would do that as a father's privilege; which sounds strange, but when he was a young man it wasn't until he was twenty-five or so that his father let him keep his own paycheck. Everything went into the family pot. It was the European way. So I rebelled in many ways against both of them and for many of the usual reasons, but the time came when I began to write successfully, when once again we were friends. I had established my independence from them; they understood it, and we created the necessary adult distance between ourselves, my parents and I, and yet a friendship of grown people, more or less.

In recent years, though, a terrible thing began to happen. As my situation with Mary worsened, I found myself turning against my parents. It was hard to speak with them, especially when she was present, because somehow a sense of hypocrisy overwhelmed me. I knew my mother could never reach her, and yet the poor woman was bewildered, thinking it was her fault. And when, occasionally, there was a happy and easy hour, I would sit there saying to myself, "What will happen when I break this up? They will turn against me." They simply worship my children, and if I left the marriage, surely they would come down on my head. The guilt, you see, was mine, because I knew Mary would never move to break it up, and I know in my heart that I would not end my days married to her. So I always came to my parents' house feeling fake and a liar, and it turned me against them . . .

Now I receive this letter. (All the above thoughts came as a result of receiving it.)

I sat in the public square outside the post office in Reno reading it and my whole life suddenly seemed so marvelously magical. I had saved it! Darling, I had done the right, the necessary, the gloriously living thing at last! For suddenly I saw many questions answered, and many weights lifting off my heart.

It is not that I would hesitate to marry you if they disapproved. Truly, sweetheart, that was not it. It was that somewhere inside me I wanted their love to flow toward both of us because it would give me strength, and you too. It is not that they are my judges, but the first sources of my identity and my love. I know now that I could enjoy seeing my mother. She becomes a pest after too long with her, but that's another thing. And it is not her, so much not her corporeal, real being, but what she represents that I can now hold up instead of trampling on it. It is my own sexuality, do you see? I come to her with you, and to my father, and in effect I say—I am a lover. Look, I say, look at my sweet, beautiful, sexy wife. I can see my father's pleasure at the sight of you—if only because he loves clothes, having been in that business all his life, and he will go mad seeing how you wear them! And if it will only be possible—I can see us with Bob and Jane and all of us joined with one another in joy. I see blue, clear air for the first time in my life when I think of myself and my wife and my children in the house of my parents. . . .

Every time I had trouble with Mary, the worst threat she thought she could make was to go to my parents and tell them I had been unfaithful. . . . She simply cannot conceive that my mother will accept you and my marriage, with you because you are a sexual being, and therefore I am, and parents are by their nature, in her mind, the punishers of sexuality not its helpers and allies. . . .

Wife, Dear, Dear Woman—I have been thinking crazy thoughts. For instance, a wedding with maybe fifty people. Maybe in Roxbury, maybe somewhere else in a big house. And Bob and Jane there. And just a little bit of ceremony. Not fancy, but maybe my old friend Reverend Melish, a courageous and wonderful fighter for fine causes; or a Rabbi of similar background—I know one. Or maybe just somebody who can marry people. I want to dress up, and I want you dressed up; I want all my past looking on, even back to Moses. I want the kids to see us married, and to feel the seriousness and honorableness of our marriage, so that nothing Mary can say to them will ever make them believe we have sneaked away to do this, or that I have hidden myself and what I wanted to do. And I want this for their sakes as much as for my own pride and my joy; so that they will see their Grandma and Grandpa full of happiness—and crying too, of course. (Isn't it strange?—I didn't have my parents to my first marriage, which was in Cleveland. It could have been arranged, but I felt better not to have them there. That time I felt untrue, you see? This time I feel true, and if the world wanted to come I would embrace them all.) Do you see why I say I am proud of you?

You have given me back my soul, Darling. And thank god I knew it always; always and always since the hour we met, I knew there was something in you that I must have or die. And the revolution it implied for me was so much more than uprooting my household, my life; facing my own damning curse for depriving the children **of me—as** I thought of it then, and so on. The revolution was of another sort. It meant that I must face myself and who and what I am. It meant that I must put down those fearfully protective arms of reticence and blushing and all that stupidity, and put my arms around the one I loved and face the startling, incredible, simply glorious fact, that I am a tender man and not the fierce idiot I have tried—and failed—to become. How could you have known that, Darling? How I bless you that you knew it! I am near tears this minute at the miracle you are to me. How happy I will make you! What beautiful children I will give you! Oh, I will watch over you, and pester you, and worry about you.

I feel something today that marks it, like an anniversary, or more truly, my real day of birth. I have reached a kind of manhood I never really knew before. I tell you dear, I am afraid of nothing in this world. The soul of my talent is coming up in me as it has been these past six months, but now I feel it like bread in my hands, like a taste in my mouth. Because I am touching its source and not turning away from it anymore. Believe in me, Darling—I am certain enough of myself to tell you that. And worry nothing about yourself.

You are beyond all danger with me because I love you like life itself. Truly, you are my life now. Your husband, Art [in Miller's hand] "Some more --------------- PS . . . If we got married before you had to leave, I could then come and live openly with you and we could maybe tour around on your free time and have some fun. The problem is the lack of time before you have to leave. I'll be back from Michigan on the 17th. The kids, by our agreement, have to be back with Mary by the 2nd, in order to have a week's time—(a little less)—to prepare for camp, shopping, etc. Assuming I have a divorce by June 1 or a few days after—as is now planned—we would either have to do it between June 1 and June 15th; or between June 17th and July 7th. . . . The whole problem is to juggle the time I have with them, and the time you'll be around to attend the ceremony. Don't worry about it, though. I'm just warning you, however,—you'll be the most kissed bride in history when my family is there. I'll have to fight the bastards off. I'm going to put up a sign, "ONE KISS TO A RELATIVE!" (Don't worry, there won't be that many.) How I love you. My heart aches when I think of you being so tired. But you'll perk up here right off, dear wife. OH, AM I GOING TO MAKE LOVE TO YOU, BEGINNING WITH THE SOLES OF THE FEET AND GOING DUE NORTH, UNTIL SLU-U-U-SH!-RIGHT INTO GRAMERCY PARK! The World's Luckiest Man Since Adam

    Art

Marilyn and Arthur married in a civil service on June 29, 1956, and again on July 1 in a traditional Jewish ceremony. Marilyn converted to Judaism to show her commitment to their relationship.

The marriage got off to a difficult start just weeks after their weddings in England when Marilyn spotted a negative diary entry in Arthur's private journal about her. The exact content is unknown but it had something to do with his disappointment in how she was behaving. Anyone's feelings would have been hurt, but Marilyn was especially sensitive and saw any sort of disapproval as a betrayal. She was having a miserable time balancing her movie obligations, Laurence Olivier's personality, and a weakening relationship with Milton Greene. Arthur and Milton resented each other's influence on Marilyn, and Paula Strasberg was always fluttering around to mother Marilyn like she was a child. Eventually, Lee Strasberg was summoned from New York like the father figure he was to help with Marilyn.

There were also happy moments on the trip—Arthur's play *A View from the Bridge* opening in London and Marilyn meeting Queen Elizabeth II—but everyone was eager to get home.

Marilyn and Arthur settled into a domesticity that included an apartment in the city, a country house, and a canine companion in the form of a basset hound named Hugo. For the first two years of their marriage, much of their focus was on trying to conceive and preparing a legal defense for Arthur's HUAC testimony. Money grew tighter as legal bills mounted and Marilyn was unable to work. Hollywood was keeping its distance from her while awaiting the result of the trial. All this caused considerable stress on them as individuals and as a couple.

The HUAC situation worked out in favor of Arthur, which was good news for both of them in terms of their careers surviving. The bad news was they needed money.

Financial salvation came in 1958 in the form of *Some Like It Hot*, a movie Marilyn wanted to turn down but begrudgingly agreed to because she needed to get back to work. Another dumb blonde role, she lamented, after everything she had done to distance herself from that type of character. But Arthur disagreed. He read the script and assured her that no, this was no ordinary movie with a ditzy, sexy blonde. *Some Like It Hot* was brilliantly written with smart, funny dialogue and this was a movie she would want to be part of.

Arthur accompanied Marilyn on location in California and was frequently spotted on the set. The couple was thrilled to discover that she was expecting again, but Marilyn was troubled during production. Arthur was consumed with his wife and unable to work on his writing at all. Shortly after production, Marilyn lost their baby. It was the last time she was pregnant and it was becoming clear she was unable to carry a baby to term. She sank into a depression as she mourned the loss of a family she desperately wanted.

Marilyn didn't work again until 1960 when she accepted a role in the movie *Let's Make Love*. It was a mediocre script at best, but Marilyn owed Twentieth Century-Fox movies and she was behind in her obligations. Marilyn was unhappy with the script and her wardrobe, and she was correct in both assessments. The future for *Let's Make Love* looked abysmal. A writers' strike prevented the studio from getting help for the script, so Arthur volunteered to smooth it over. It was a gesture for his wife, but it backfired. She had looked to him as a man who stood up for the working classes, the underrepresented, and for doing the right thing. By helping with the *Let's Make Love* script, even though he did not seek or accept credit, she saw it as crossing a picket line.

"During the shooting of *Let's Make Love* and *Some Like It Hot* I had all but given up any hope of writing; I had decided to devote myself to giving her the kind of emotional support that would convince her she was no longer alone in the world—the heart of the problem, I assumed," he wrote in *Timebends*. "I went so far as to do some rewriting on *Let's Make Love* to try to save her from a complete catastrophe, work I despised on a script not worth the paper it was typed on. It was a bad miscalculation, bringing us no closer to each other. She seemed to take for granted what for me had been a sacrifice of great blocks of time, and if it was plain that her inner desperation was not going to let up, it was equally clear that literally nothing I knew to do could slow its destructive progress."

One of the few things Arthur finished was a script for *The Misfits*, a movie he had written for Marilyn as a vehicle to show her dramatic skills.

During the filming *Let's Make Love*, Arthur traveled to Ireland to meet with John Huston about directing *The Misfits*. While he was away, Marilyn began an affair with her costar Yves Montand. Arthur didn't speak of it, but the affair took a toll on their marriage, which lasted just long enough to get *The Misfits* going. During production, the Millers moved into separate hotel rooms.

"He introduced me to the importance of political freedom in our society," Marilyn said after their divorce.

"All the time I was married to Arthur—four years—our life was set in a definite pattern. Summers in Connecticut—no deviation. Winters in our New York apartment. Then back to Connecticut.

"He's a wonderful writer, a brilliant man. But I think he is a better writer than husband. I'm sure writing comes first in his life. . . .

"We're on friendly terms—we're friendly enough. It's not like fighting a dual."

The Miller marriage was plagued by infertility, HUAC, financial woes, and infidelity. Marilyn grew to feel inadequate, which may have started the day she found his journal entry.

"I wish I'd had a longer formal education," she told W. J. Weatherby. "Sometimes when Arthur and his friends were talking, I couldn't follow. I don't know much about politics. I'm just past the goodies and the baddies stage. The politicians get away with murder because Americans don't know anymore about it than I do. Less even. Arthur was always very good at explaining, but I felt at my age I should've known. It's my country and I should know what they're doing with it."

Shortly after their divorce was finalized, Arthur ran into a photographer who had been assigned to *The Misfits*. Inge Morath worked for Magnum, a photography agency that rotated photographers in and out of the movie's production.

By all accounts, there was no connection between Arthur and Inge on location. She was busy working and he had his hands full with everything happening on a very troubled set. With Arthur now divorced and Inge also single, the two began a relationship that quickly turned into a marriage. Almost immediately, Inge was expecting a baby and heavily pregnant at the time of Marilyn's death. The following month, she delivered Rebecca, a healthy baby girl. In 1966, she delivered a son, Daniel, who was born with Down syndrome. Daniel was institutionalized and there is no mention of him in Arthur's autobiography.

A 1968 entry in his journal reads, "I found myself not doubting the doctor's conclusions, but feeling a welling up of love for him. I dared not touch him, lest I end by taking him home, and I wept." In the 2018 documentary

Arthur Miller: Writer, written and produced by Rebecca, she notes that he offered to do an on-camera interview about Daniel, but as she explains in the movie, "I had the opportunity to finish this film in the nineteen-nineties, but I didn't know how to finish the film without talking about my brother, and I didn't know how to do that. I told my father this, and he offered to do an interview about it. I put it off. I put it off for a long time. I had children, and I started making other films, and he died."

As Arthur worked through his marriage to Marilyn, he did what he always had done—turned to drama to sort out his feelings. In his 1964 play *After the Fall*, a thinly disguised *roman a clef*, Arthur writes of Quentin whose failed marriage to the beautiful but self-destructive Maggie has him doubting if he wants to commit to Holga. Quentin's friend Mickey betrays his integrity by naming names.

Marilyn had felt violated during production of *The Misfits* because private conversations she'd had with Arthur surfaced in the script as dialogue. *After the Fall* was clearly and recognizably written about Marilyn. It's doubtful Arthur would have released it had Marilyn lived, but she would have been horrified had she known. *After the Fall* is one of Arthur Miller's lesser works. It takes place in Quentin's head and much of it is stream of consciousness. Critics complained it was disjointed; fans were livid at the invasion of Marilyn's privacy. If not for the association with Marilyn Monroe, it would probably be largely forgotten.

Arthur and Inge were married for forty years. She passed away in 2002; Arthur followed three years later in 2005. He died fifty-six years to the day *Death of a Salesman* premiered on Broadway.

YVES MONTAND

When Yves Montand was cast as the lead in *Let's Make Love*, he had to learn his lines phonetically because he didn't yet speak English well enough. Yves was cast after nearly every leading man in town had turned down the role of Jean-Marc Clement, a billionaire who is being satirized in a play.

Marilyn had attended Yves Montand's one-man show in New York in 1959, and recommended him to Twentieth Century-Fox. In need of an actor to fill the part, the studio offered him the job. He was an accomplished singer and actor in Europe, so although he was unknown to the American audience, he was not without talent and proven success. Early in the production, Marilyn told a reporter, "Next to my husband and along with Marlon Brando, I think Yves Montand is the most attractive man I've ever met."

Yves Montand and his wife, actress Simone Signoret, arrived in Los Angeles for filming and were housed at the Beverly Hills Hotel. Their bungalow was right across from Marilyn Monroe and Arthur Miller, and the two couples quickly became friends. The wives often took turns cooking for the foursome; Arthur and Simone engaged in long, intellectual conversations. One such evening was captured on film by photographer Bruce Davidson, who quietly snapped pictures while trying to remain inconspicuous to his subjects.

Marilyn and Simone also bonded over hair treatments. At her own expense, Marilyn paid for Pearl Porterfield—Jean Harlow's hairdresser—to travel from San Diego to Beverly Hills every week to color her hair. Marilyn's hospitality always included a buffet lunch for Pearl to snack on while working. Simone was a welcome guest when Pearl was over and the two actresses would get their hair done at the same time while listening to stories of Old Hollywood.

It was while Arthur was out of town that the dynamic between the couples began to shift. As it turns out, during one of his absences, Simone also had to leave for a while. Their respective absences created an opportunity for their spouses to take up with each other. Soon, the Monroe-Montand affair became the worst-kept secret at the studio, then in Hollywood. Gossip columnist Hedda Hopper, never Marilyn's biggest fan, gleefully reported on the adulterous relationship.

Arthur didn't speak of the relationship but Simone, who took the news about as well as anyone possibly could, wrote about it in her autobiography. It was not the first time her husband had strayed, and she managed to maintain a dignified understanding of his ways.

"I was very sad. But I wasn't surprised.

"A half-hour later, the hotel manager told me that he had just refused to rent rooms to journalists from Paris who had asked him where I could be found. I am grateful to this gentleman. He helped me to avoid shining the limelight on an incident that the press had unmercifully hammered away at two years earlier.

"That same press had latched on to the four of us—Marilyn, Montand, Miller and myself—in order to make us play parts we had never learned in a play we hadn't read. It's a pity that they never saw us live as we did for four months. They knew nothing about the quiet lives of the four people in Bungalows No. 20 and 21. If they had, they would have seen nothing resembling the blonde heartbreaker, or the moody dark man, or the bookworm, or the admirable wife standing on her dignity, which were the labels they pasted on us."

Oddly enough, the sexual chemistry the Monroe-Montand relationship produced off-screen did not translate to the movie itself. *Let's Make Love* was a flop, thanks to a poorly written and executed script and lack of connection (at least onscreen) between the leading actors. The romance between Marilyn and Yves was short-lived but had a lasting impact on the Millers. Ultimately, the affair contributed to what was fast becoming a troubled marriage.

The Montand marriage survived, just as it had with Yves's other indiscretions. During the production of *The Misfits*, Marilyn traveled from northern

Their movie was not successful, but the off-screen relationship between Marilyn and Yves Montand became romantic when their respective spouses left Los Angeles while Let's Make Love *was in production.*
By Twentieth Century-Fox—eBayfrontback / Wikimedia Commons

Nevada to Los Angeles, officially to detox from pills. Another underlying reason was one last time to see her lover before he returned to France.

After their affair ended, Yves gave an interview in English and said, "I think she's an enchanting child, a simple girl without any guile." The tone of the quote was hurtful, and Marilyn never saw him again. It's difficult to determine if this was because of his quote or simply because she was in the United States and he was in France. In fairness to Yves Montand, he was not speaking in a language he was fluent in, and it's possible he misspoke or gave the wrong impression.

Still, it seems Marilyn left a lasting impression on him. In his autobiography, he wrote:

"The public and many of my friends thought I was mainly flattered by the relationship. I was certainly flattered. But to a much greater degree, I was touched. Touched because it was beautiful and it was impossible. Not for a moment did I think of breaking with my wife, not for a moment; but if she had slammed the door on me, I would probably have made my life with Marilyn. Or tried to. That was the direction we were moving in. Maybe it would have lasted only two or three years. I didn't have too many illusions. Still, what years they would have been!

"But the way that Simone chose to behave meant that the question never arose."

· 26 ·

The Hook and *On the Waterfront*

$\mathcal{T}$*he Hook* was the screenplay that originally brought Arthur Miller to Los Angeles, making it responsible for bringing him and Marilyn together. His close friend Elia Kazan had offered to direct the film if a studio agreed to produce it. Arthur and Elia pitched the movie together in Hollywood, and it was during his trip to L.A. that Arthur met Elia's current mistress, a young starlet named Marilyn Monroe.

Originally written in 1947, *The Hook* was based on the true story of Pietro "Pete" Panto, a dockworker who attempted to expose deplorable working conditions and that Joe Ryan, the head of the International Longshoremen's Association, was corrupt. On July 14, 1939, the twenty-eight-year-old Panto mysteriously disappeared and his dead body wasn't discovered until eighteen months later in 1941.

It is suspected that crime boss and hitman Albert Anastasia ordered the murder, but, not surprisingly, was never indicted. The actual killers are believed to be Mendy Weiss, Tony Romanello, and James Feraco of Murder Inc., an organized crime syndicate with a deep influence in New York. A chief witness, Abe Reles, died on November 12, 1941, when he either jumped or fell from the room where six police officers were guarding him. Reles was a mobster but believed to have been ready to inform on Anastasia. Like Anastasia, no one else was indicted either.

Set in the Red Hook district of Brooklyn, *The Hook* tells the story of longshoreman Marty Ferarra in a fictionalized version of Panto's story. From the beginning, the screenplay had trouble finding a studio willing to produce it.

In his autobiography, *Timebends*, Arthur writes, "I put myself to work on *The Hook*, the screenplay about Panto's doomed attempt to overthrow the feudal gangsterism of the New York waterfront. After reading the script, Kazan agreed to direct it but felt we must first go to Hollywood together and try to get the backing of a major studio. Kazan was then under contract to Twentieth Century-Fox, but they would have nothing to do with this grimy story and its downbeat ending. So we decided to approach, among others, Harry Cohn, president of Columbia Pictures and himself a tough graduate of the Five Points district of the lower Manhattan waterfront who would likely know what the script was about."

Having come from that part of New York, Cohn was the best studio executive to approach. He would have been the most likely to have understood the script and the characters Arthur and Elia were trying to portray. Marilyn, posing as a secretary, attended the meeting with Arthur Miller, Elia Kazan, and Harry Cohn.

"He could hardly keep his eyes from Marilyn; trying to recall where he had seen her, he marched around in front of her hitching up his pants like a Manhattan cab driver getting ready to fight," Arthur recalled. "His face has receded from memory, but not his flowing brutality and candor as he peered at her, growling, 'I t'ink I know whose goils you were,' while she sat there in her special agonized mixture of amusement and shame."

The meeting continued until his memory finally jagged. Cohn pointed a finger at Marilyn and exclaimed, "I remember you!" Cohn had invited Marilyn to come aboard his boat but she said she would only go if Mrs. Cohn joined them. Miller recalled this "grievous insult that for a moment passed a reddened blush of anger over his forehead."

When it came to the actual script, Cohn proved to be a tough sell.

"'This picture won't make a dime,' Cohn aggressively announced once he had settled himself behind his desk," Arthur wrote. "But he kept hearing messages through the air, it seemed, and would interrupt himself to punch a button and yell into the intercom to his secretary beyond the closed door. He knew every yard of the studio complex and what was happening everywhere and sent commands and questions down the barrackslike halls as we went on talking about our picture. 'But I come from back there, though,' he said jabbing a hairy finger down at the script, 'and I know the whole story. But it won't make a dime, but I'll go in with yiz, pervided yiz don't take any money unless it makes money. And I'll back it because'—he turned and pointed at Kazan—'I want you to make a picture for me after this.'"

A tentative deal was put in place, but it wasn't yet a firm commitment. Cohn wanted his labor relations employee to look the script over because it was a story about unions. He also wanted to check with the FBI.

Arthur returned to New York and waited for Elia to call with the terms of an agreement from Columbia. It took longer than expected, and when Elia finally did call, he informed Arthur that Cohn wanted changes. The biggest change Cohn wanted was to turn the corrupt union guys and their gangster muscle into Communists.

"Roy Brewer, the head of all the Hollywood unions, had been brought into the matter—by the FBI, presumably; he had read the script and said flatly that it was all a lie, that he was a personal friend of Joe Ryan, head of the International Longshoreman's Association, and that none of the practices I described took place on the piers," Arthur wrote in *Timebends*. "Finally, he informed Cohn that if the film was made he would pull all the projectionists across the country out on strike so that it could never be shown. The FBI, moreover, regarded it as a very dangerous story that might cause big trouble on the nation's waterfronts at a time when the Korean War was demanding an uninterrupted flow of men and materiel. In effect, unless Tony Anastasia was turned into a Communist, the movie would be an anti-American act close to treason."

To Arthur, the demands were "idiotic" and if he changed the bad guys from racketeers to Communists he would be embarrassed to show his face on the waterfront again. That day, he sent a wire to Harry Cohn at Columbia to withdraw his script. The following morning he received a telegram in response: "ITS INTERESTING HOW THE MINUTE WE TRY TO MAKE THE SCRIPT PRO-AMERICAN YOU PULL OUT. HARRY COHN."

Arthur remained steadfast in his decision. He was unwilling to change the characters or screenplay, as it would take away from his original intent.

"The studios then were still in full command, and the notion of the writer's control over his script—or, for that matter, the director's over his film—was simply beyond discussion. I took for granted that we were heading into a struggle in the coming days, but the prize was worth it: a truthful film about a dark cellar under the American Dream. Everything was contradictory, inside me and without. And with Kazan, too, my relation was complex."

Elia Kazan's path in Hollywood turned out to be very different than Arthur Miller's. Both men enjoyed unparalleled success during their lifetimes, but Elia proved to be more adaptable to the demands of studios.

In 1954, Elia Kazan released *On the Waterfront*, generally considered to be his response to his HUAC testimony, and likely inspired by his initial participation in *The Hook*. At the very least, *On the Waterfront* was likely inspired by *The Hook* in terms of making a movie about corruption on the docks.

The two screenplays were different enough for *On the Waterfront* to get produced, but unlike *The Hook*, in this new movie the man who testifies is the hero. In other words, Elia Kazan glorifies the man who tells on others.

The Hook was not the only inspiration for *On the Waterfront*. The movie is based on a twenty-four-part series of articles from 1948 called "Crime on the Waterfront," for which journalist Malcolm Johnson was awarded the Pulitzer Prize. The articles were adapted into a screenplay written by Budd Schulberg, who was also already working on a waterfront story. Like Elia Kazan, Budd Schulberg had testified as a "friendly" witness in front of HUAC and was motivated to portray the snitch as a hero.

In *Waterfront*, dockworkers and corrupt bosses are still the center of the plot, but in this version, union boss Johnny Friendly (Lee J. Cobb) forces Terry Malloy (Marlon Brando), into luring longshoreman Joe Doyle onto a rooftop, where he is pushed to his death. Terry is shaken and guilt-ridden because he hadn't known a murder plot was planned. In fear for their lives, Terry and the other dockworkers refuse to testify.

After finally being persuaded to testify against Johnny Friendly, Terry loses union work. Every day, Terry shows up at the docks ready to work and he remains unchosen by bosses. Unrepentant, he taunts Friendly that he is proud of his testimony. As a response, Friendly provokes Terry into attacking him, after which his goons beat Terry until he is almost dead. Now the longshoremen rally around Terry and show support by refusing to work unless Terry can work, too. Terry rallies and drags himself into the warehouse, followed by the other dockworkers. Friendly is defeated and the "good guy" (the snitch) wins.

Unlike *A Streetcar Named Desire*, where Elia Kazan believed he had been frozen out of Academy Awards because of his HUAC testimony, *On the Waterfront* won Best Picture, Best Director, and Best Actor—the very same awards *Streetcar* had been shut out of just a few years before when he initially refused to testify.

Elia Kazan's professional career was at a pinnacle, but many in his personal circle distanced themselves from him, in some cases permanently. He claims his sexual relationship with Marilyn continued for the next several years, but this remains highly unlikely. It was around the same time he chose to testify in front of HUAC that she began dating Joe DiMaggio—an American hero. When her relationship with Joe concluded, she started a relationship with Arthur Miller—who had *not* named names.

The one-two punch of Elia Kazan's HUAC testimony and *On the Waterfront* severely damaged the friendship between him and Arthur. There was a bit of reconciliation in 1964 when theatre producer Bob Whitehead carefully navigated the complex relationship of the drama titans who stood on opposite sides of HUAC and had both loved Marilyn Monroe. With Whitehead's help, Arthur and Elia reunited for a production of *After the Fall*, the play written about Arthur's marriage to Marilyn. In addition to characters based on Arthur and Marilyn, there was also a character based on Elia, who directed the play.

· 27 ·

Mr. Miller Goes to Washington: A Playwright, An Actress, and HUAC

> I don't believe and I never did that a man has to become an informer in order to practice his profession freely in the United States.
>
> —Arthur Miller

$\mathcal{A}$rthur Miller had always suspected HUAC subpoenaed him because of his high-profile relationship with Marilyn Monroe. It sounds like a paranoid notion, but his suspicion is not without merit. By the time he received his subpoena in 1956 his relationship with Marilyn went public and was headed for marriage. Prior to dating Marilyn, Arthur Miller had managed to avoid much of the scrutiny that had troubled or outright ruined many of his peers, including friend and collaborator Elia Kazan.

Arthur Miller had long positioned himself as someone who championed the working class and underdogs, so attracting the attention of HUAC seems inevitable. Compared to other artists, however, Arthur's luck, at least for a while, was better. Most likely, those behind HUAC were seeking higher-profile names.

Unlike his old buddy Elia Kazan, who had attended a couple of Communist party meetings in the 1930s before quickly losing interest, Arthur Miller didn't bother to attend meetings until the late 1940s. From early on in his career, Arthur had decided he wanted to use his talents to explore social issues and, hopefully, bring about some positive change in the world.

Upon experiencing financial success, Arthur was feeling pangs of guilt from profiting off telling the stories of the downtrodden. Was this why he attended a couple of Communist meetings? Regardless of the reason, he didn't show interest in the movement and quickly ceased going. He later said the meetings consisted of people drunkenly discussing literature.

As the anti-Communist movement turned into a frenzy by the early 1950s, Arthur began looking for a way to express his cynicism. He found inspiration in the Salem witch trials, a series of trials that pressured witnesses to name others as possible witches, resulting in the hangings of innocent people, mostly women. During the same time frame of his research, Arthur's friendship and working partnership with Elia Kazan, who did name others to HUAC, fractured. Arthur disagreed with Elia testifying and was unsupportive of the decision. HUAC seemed to have a special interest in targeting Hollywood, and Elia had made the transition from theatre to film. It was likely a major factor in why he had received considerably more pressure than Arthur.

Infuriated with Arthur's lack of understanding, Elia's wife Molly faulted the notion of using the witch trials as a metaphor for Communism. Witches did not actually exist, Molly told Arthur, but Communists did. Technically speaking, she was not wrong and it was a criticism others shared when *The Crucible* debuted to mixed reviews in 1953. What they missed was the underlying theme of paranoia. The metaphorical contagion was more important to the plot than the literal accusations.

It's difficult to exaggerate the threat of being accused of Communism in the years following World War II. In addition to individuals who had lost their livelihoods, reputations, friends and family, a more general sense of conformity permeated over the United States. Those who did not follow social and cultural expectations were seen as outsiders and in the more extreme cases, such as Communism accusations, at risk of losing everything.

The government was watching and collecting data on many artists, Arthur Miller among them. His leftist reputation made him a person of interest, but it wasn't until he moved to Reno, Nevada, in 1956 to establish residency and obtain a divorce so he could marry Marilyn Monroe that he finally received a subpoena. He was immediately suspicious of HUAC's intentions. In his past he had spoken up for the working class, signed petitions for change, written a play that drew comparisons between the witch and HUAC trials—nothing happened. Once his name was associated with Marilyn Monroe, he was called to testify.

Arthur applied for a passport to accompany Marilyn while filming *The Prince and the Showgirl* in England. His application was declined upon further investigation due to suspected ties to Communism.

Arthur was scheduled to testify on June 21, 1956. Before he left for Washington, Twentieth Century-Fox studio head Spyros Skouras called long distance on the telephone. "He had called from Hollywood to ask Marilyn if he could stop by as soon as he got to New York," Arthur wrote in his autobiography. "I knew what this meant, of course, since the president of Twentieth Century-Fox was not in the habit of making such flying visits, not to see Marilyn, at any rate, when the studio was still at odds with her. He would be trying to get me to avoid a possible jail term for contempt of Congress. Not that I mattered to him, but if the rumors that we were going to marry were true, the patriotic organizations might well decide to picket her films. Such were the times. If there were any surprise by his phoning, it was that he had not done so earlier."

Marilyn had proved to be a rebellious star, but she was still a valuable commodity to Twentieth Century-Fox. Skouras asked if she was in love, she said yes and gave an indication that they would likely marry. "'Gah-bless-you-won'erful,' he said, patting her hand with fatherly benediction; if it was really love and marriage, especially the latter, then God had entered the case and the fooling around was over."

The Millers went to Washington, D.C. in 1957 for his appearance in front of the House on Un-American Activities Committee. The experience nearly ruined both their careers and left the couple needing money to pay Arthur's legal bills.
Credit: Photofest

As expected, Skouras tried to impress upon Arthur that he needed to work with Congress. It was no longer just his career to worry about, but Marilyn's, as well. As Fox had once offered to help Elia Kazan, so, too, was the company now offering to help Arthur Miller.

"I know these congressmen very well, Artr, we are good friends," Skouras told him. "They are not bad men, they would take you privately in executive session, you understand? No necessity to be in that public at all. I can arrange this if you tell me."

In other words, if Arthur testified and named names, Fox could arrange for a more private testimony and spare him a public trial. With Marilyn still in the room and showing her support, Arthur told Skouras it "was out of the question. . . . I can't do it."

Skouras finally gave up and left the apartment, but not before drawing a comparison between Arthur and Socrates, who was condemned to death after accusations of corrupting the minds of others. "How the rage hit me or what exactly triggered it I never could recall later, but in his persistence I felt myself cornered; it was as though he was trying to exercise control over my work, and it was intolerable. I got off only a sentence or two, but he quickly caught the idea and held up both his hands and went to his coat, which was lying over the back of a chair, and incredibly sure I heard him mutter, 'You are a Socrates.' He embraced Marilyn again, but now with a real sadness, and I walked him out to the elevator."

During his testimony, members of HUAC questioned Arthur for several hours at the House's office building. When asked to name Communist sympathizers, he declined. Although he did not name names, he also did not plead the Fifth Amendment, which would have granted him some immunity. Instead, he relied on the First Amendment and offered to speak freely about his own past. "I want you to understand that I am not protecting the Communists or the Communist Party. I am trying to, and will, protect my sense of self. I could not use the name of another person to bring trouble to him. I will be perfectly frank with you about anything relating to my activities, but I cannot take responsibility for another human being. My conscious will not permit me to use the name of another person."

Shortly after his meeting with HUAC, Arthur and Marilyn married on June 29 in a civil service. A traditional Jewish ceremony followed on July 1. On July 10, HUAC recommended charging Arthur Miller with contempt for not naming names. His troubles with the government were far from over, but he was at least granted permission to fly to England with Marilyn on July 13.

On February 18, 1957, the Federal Grand Jury officially charged Arthur Miller with two counts of contempt of Congress. He entered a plea of not guilty on March 1 and the trial began on May 13. Marilyn not only accompanied her husband to Washington, D.C., but she expressed her support of him to the press. "I would like to say that I'm fully confident that in the end my husband will win this case," she said to news cameras. She also answered questions from reporters and confirmed she hadn't been working recently when asked how the trial had affected her career. She ended the press conference by saying, "We hope to go back to our normal life."

The Millers returned to New York, where they awaited a verdict. Soon they learned the judgement was guilty of contempt of Congress. Arthur was fined $500 and sentenced to thirty days in jail, which he promptly appealed. The appellate court sided with Arthur and overturned his conviction.

As it turns out, Arthur's suspicions that his association with Marilyn Monroe—a Hollywood movie star of the highest magnitude—may have brought him added attention had merit. During the process, a lawyer informed Arthur that if Marilyn agreed to take a photo with Francis E. Walter, who served as chairman of HUAC from 1951 to 1963, charges against him would be dropped. Arthur not only declined, he laughed at the absurdity of the request when it was presented to him.

Arthur Miller was successful, but it had been a harrowing experience and the legal bills left the couple in financial distress. Marilyn hadn't been working and their savings were depleted.

The one silver lining to the HUAC debacle is that Marilyn accepted *Some Like It Hot* after the trial and appeal concluded. They needed the money, but the movie won her a Golden Globe for Best Performance in a Comedy or Musical and in 2000 the American Film Institute voted it the No. 1 comedy on its AFI's 100 Years . . . 100 Laughs list.

· 28 ·

Korea

I never felt like a star before in my heart. It was so wonderful to look down and see a fellow smiling at me.

—Marilyn Monroe

One of the highlights of Marilyn's career and life was an unexpected opportunity that came at an unexpected time—when she was offered the chance to sing for U.S. troops stationed in Korea while she was on her honeymoon in Japan.

After Marilyn married Joe DiMaggio on January 14, 1954, later on January 29, the newlyweds set off on an extended honeymoon to Japan. Joe had already been scheduled for the trip, during which he would train six different Japanese baseball teams over a twenty-four-day promotional tour.

These two superstars were now not only appearing together in Japan but making their first appearances as husband and wife. There was, however, an unexpected twist during the trip. During press conferences, most of the questions were directed to Marilyn instead of Joe even though the trip was centered around him. Photographers pushed forward and clamored to get pictures of the famous platinum blonde whenever she appeared.

When Marilyn sat in the stands to watch a game Joe was coaching in Hiroshima, the crowd lost interest in what was happening on the field and began watching her every move on the sidelines. For a proud man like Joe DiMaggio, the experience must have been unnerving.

During the visit, Gen. Charles Wilkes Christenberry presented an offer to Marilyn on behalf of Gen. John E. Hull, Commander in Chief of the Far East Command: Would Marilyn be willing to entertain troops stationed in wartorn Korea? Marilyn was surprised at the request but honored she had been asked and eagerly accepted.

The Army set Marilyn up with a band, which would be called Anything Goes, and a rehearsal was hastily set up. She sang songs from her movies, such as "Diamonds Are a Girl's Best Friend" and "Bye, Bye Baby." She also sang Cole Porter's "Anything Goes" and George Gershwin's "Do It Again," which was changed to "Kiss Me Again" to make the lyrics less suggestive.

During rehearsals, Marilyn practiced singing while moving on stage and making sure the microphone picked up all her vocals. Similar to the perfectionism she showed on movie sets, Marilyn asked to go over the songs again and again. The hard work she had put into training at the studios paid off for her stage show. Unlike movie production, though, Marilyn was about to embark on live performances and there would be no retakes if mistakes were made. She worked diligently to get everything right. Piano player Al Carmen ("Gus") Guastafeste recalled in his book *A Different Side of Marilyn*, that at lunchtime she requested, "Gus, can we do it another time if you don't mind, and then we'll go eat."

The request for one more time turned into an hour and a half before they finally broke for lunch. Gus obliged because he recognized she was insecure and was relying on him to help her performance.

When it came time to leave for Korea, Joe saw her off at the airport. Also at the airport were baseball player Lefty O'Doul and his wife, Jean, who were on the tour of Japan. So Marilyn wouldn't have to travel alone with strangers, Jean served as her companion for the Korean tour. Marilyn was assigned a nurse, Lt. Olive Palmer, who would tend to her during the trip if any health issues should arise.

Marilyn's four-day tour began on February 16 and encompassed ten shows. They traveled to each location by helicopter, and then to and from the stage by jeep.

Clothing for Marilyn and Jean was an issue. Neither had packed appropriate clothes for the frigid Korean weather. The army issued both women boots, socks, pants, shirts, and sheepskin-lined leather jackets to help keep them warm while traveling.

Marilyn's performances were another problem altogether. She hadn't planned on singing outdoors in the cold, so her stage wardrobe was limited to what she had packed for social events in Japan. But the show must go on and Marilyn dressed up as the glamorous movie star she was by donning a cocktail dress. Made for her by designer Ceil Chapman, the plum-colored, form-fitting dress was made of crepe and featured spaghetti straps, tiny sequins, and bugle beads sewn in a vermicular pattern. She literally sparkled on stage.

"There were 17,000 soldiers in front of me, and they were all yelling at me at the top of their lungs. I stood smiling at them. . . . Standing in the

One of Marilyn's happiest memories was singing for the troops serving in the Korean War. The trip was unexpectedly offered while she was in Japan with Joe DiMaggio on their honeymoon, so she had to make do with the clothing already in her suitcase. She performed wearing a cocktail dress in freezing rain and frigid temperatures.
Unknown author or not provided—U.S. National Archives and Records Administration / Wikimedia

snowfall facing these yelling soldiers, I felt for the first time in my life no fear of anything. I felt only happy."

Every time she took the stage, soldiers gave her a resounding ovation and cheered throughout the performance. Determined to entertain the troops, Marilyn performed in her cocktail attire in freezing weather, rain, and even snow.

In his book, Gus recalled that Marilyn never complained about the difficult conditions. Instead, she talked only about how difficult the soldiers' conditions were so she was happy to entertain them. She signed autographs, blew kisses, waved from helicopters and jeeps, spoke to soldiers on the ground, and ate in the mess hall with everyone else.

The weather did affect Marilyn's health, however. She had always been susceptible to colds, viral infections, and sinus issues, and soon she was exhibiting the signs of illness. It didn't take long for her sickness to deepen into pneumonia.

During her short, whirlwind tour, Marilyn performed in front of more than one hundred thousand troops. She returned to Japan exhilarated from the experience. "You never heard such cheering!" she exclaimed when she saw Joe upon her return. "Yes, I have," he replied.

Despite Joe's chilly response, the trip to Korea remained one of Marilyn's fondest memories. In the news footage of Marilyn performing, she looks radiant as she sings on stage. "For the first time in my life, I had the feeling that the people seeing me were accepting and liking me," she later said.

· 29 ·

The Wrong Door Raid

$\mathcal{M}$arilyn Monroe and Joe DiMaggio officially separated in October 1954, but it was far from a clean break. They continued to visit each other, talk, and generally stayed in each other's lives. Joe made no secret of the fact that he wanted a reconciliation, but Marilyn's mind was made up. She was no longer interested in marriage.

Joe's old jealousies got the better of him, and he became certain Marilyn must be seeing another man. She was close to her vocal coach Hal Schaefer, but it's unclear if the two engaged in something more than friendship. Joe wanted answers. To be certain and satisfy his curiosity, he hired private investigators Barney Ruditsky and Phil Irwin to follow Marilyn. On the evening of Friday, November 5, 1954, Ruditsky and Irwin called Joe and informed him they had found Marilyn in an apartment with Schaffer. Ruditsky and Irwin would wait at the apartment if Joe wanted to come right over and confront his estranged wife with her lover.

Wasting no time, Joe, his friend Frank Sinatra, and the detectives gathered in front of a small apartment building at 8122 Waring Avenue in West Hollywood. The four men (and possibly more) burst through the front door in a dramatic display of anger and indignation—and came face to face with a terrified Florence Kotz. The thirty-seven-year-old woman lived alone and had retired for the night, only to be startled awake by strange men storming into her home.

As it turns out, the building was correct but the apartment was not. The commotion and noise were loud enough to alert the people in the other apartments that something was terribly wrong. That included Marilyn, Sheila Stuart (another of Hal's singing students and the resident of the apartment), and possibly Hal himself, depending on who's telling the story. What's clear is that in the initial ruckus, Marilyn realized what was going on—and who was involved—and hurried out of Sheila's apartment to her car for a quick getaway before she could be spotted.

Joe DiMaggio, Frank Sinatra, and the detectives were left standing in Ms. Kotz's apartment with the proverbial egg on their faces. Instead of catching Marilyn with a lover, the police were called out to take a report, which turned into a protracted legal battle. Florence Kotz filed a lawsuit against Joe DiMaggio for $200,000; he eventually settled the suit for $7,500. The friendship between Joe and Frank immediately cooled and was never the same after that night.

Had it not been for the tabloid magazine *Confidential* getting ahold of the story in 1955, the public may have never known about what became known as the "Wrong Door Raid."

According to Ralph Roberts, in Marilyn's version of the story Hal was indeed there. She reminisced about the Wrong Door Raid one night out to dinner at the Villa Capri in Hollywood. "Did you ever hear about the time when Joe and I were separated. I had a sick friend, Hal Schaefer, a wonderful coach and pianist at Fox. One night I took him some chicken soup, not knowing Joe had hired a private detective to follow me. The detective called Joe, who was here [the Villa Capri]. Frank wanted to join. They came roaring up. The detective pointed, 'She went thataway!' They burst in the door, much screaming and shouting. They broke into the wrong apartment—the apartment of a lady who had just retired for the evening, and who joined in the screaming. I scrambled out the back window, over the back fence, and heard sirens whirling as I drove away. It really was funny. But it taught me one thing: always have an exit, however innocent or innocuous the situation."

· 30 ·

See You in Court

*M*arilyn was a law-abiding citizen, but sometimes in life legal matters come up. Here's a look at Marilyn's court appearances.

September 13, 1946
After waiting six weeks in Las Vegas, Nevada, Norma Jeane Dougherty was granted a divorce from her husband, James Dougherty.

Early 1950s
Marilyn was sued for unpaid phone bills at North Crescent Drive. The matter was settled out of court.

June 26, 1952
Marilyn testified before Judge Kenneth Holaday in the case of Jerry Karpman and Morrie Kaplen, who were selling Marilyn's nude calendar photo through a mail-order business.

May 21, 1954
Marilyn was charged with reckless driving after rear-ending a car belonging to a man named Bart Antinora. The accident took place at the confusing six-street intersection of Sunset Boulevard and Beverly Drive; Joe DiMaggio was the passenger. Antinora sued Marilyn for $3,000 and was awarded $500 on his claim. (Antinora later portrayed a slave in *The Ten Commandments*.)

Marilyn and her attorney Jerry Giesler at the Santa Monica courthouse for her divorce from Joe DiMaggio. When Marilyn was nervous or concentrating, she frequently poked her tongue through her lips, as seen here. By Los Angeles Times / Wikimedia Commons / CC by 4.0

October 27, 1954

Marilyn and her attorney Jerry Giesler appeared at the Los Angeles County Superior Court—Santa Monica (1725 Main Street) for her divorce case against Joe DiMaggio. Judge Orlando Rhodes granted an interlocutory divorce on the grounds of mental cruelty.

October 31, 1955

Judge Elmer Doyle granted the final divorce decree for the DiMaggio marriage. Marilyn was living in New York by this time.

February 28, 1956

Marilyn appeared at the Municipal Court in Beverly Hills located at 9355 Burton Way to settle a ticket she had received for driving without a license on November 21, 1954. Marilyn had moved to New York without paying the ticket before she left, which eventually led to a warrant for her arrest being issued. When she returned to Los Angeles in February 1956 to film *Bus Stop*, she finally appeared in court. Judge Charles J. Griffin fined her $55, and chastised her by saying, "Laws are made for all of us, rich or poor, without race or creed or whether your name happens to be Miss Monroe or not, and this kind of acting won't win you an Oscar."

June 29, 1956

Marilyn and Arthur Miller were married in a four-minute civil ceremony at the Westchester County Courthouse in White Plains, New York, at 7:21 p.m.

January 20, 1961

Judge Miguel Gomez Guerra granted a divorce on the grounds of incompatibility of character in the Miller marriage. Marilyn traveled to Juarez, Mexico, with friend and publicist Patricia Newcomb on the day of President Kennedy's inauguration so news of her divorce would get buried in the newspaper coverage.

Other Homes in Marilyn's Life

*M*arilyn lived in several homes, and the way she moved had a profound influence on her. But some houses she didn't live in also played an important function in Marilyn's life. The following are some places connected to Marilyn, although she never lived in any of them.

[1] 2331 Alta Avenue, Louisville, Kentucky

When Marilyn's mother, Gladys, separated from her first husband Jasper Baker, he kidnapped their two children and returned to his home state of Kentucky. Gladys followed him in hopes of getting custody of her young son and daughter back. During her time in Kentucky, she stayed with a family and worked as a nanny to a little girl named Norma Jean. It's generally believed Gladys liked the name Norma Jean and later gave it to her own daughter a few years later, although with a slightly different spelling. Gladys was unable to regain custody of her children and returned home to Los Angeles.

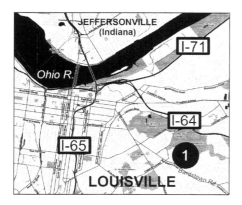

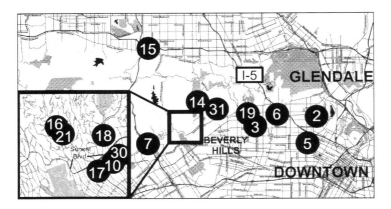

[2] 1211 Hyperion Avenue, Los Angeles
Gladys and her best friend Grace shared this house starting in 1923.

[3] 831½ Formosa Avenue, West Hollywood
Stan Gifford, Norma Jeane's biological father, lived here in the 1920s.

[4] 206 E. Rhode Island Street, Hawthorne
Norma Jeane's grandmother, Della Monroe, lived here in the 1920s. The house was across the street from Wayne and Ida Bolender, who became Norma Jeane's first foster parents. Gladys moved here in spring 1927 to care for her ailing mother.

[5] 237 Bimini Place, Los Angeles
Gladys and Grace shared another apartment in 1927.

[6] 6228 De Longpre Avenue, Los Angeles
Gladys and Grace shared this apartment in 1929.

[7] 432 South Bentley Avenue, Los Angeles
Norma Jeane and Jim Dougherty married here on June 19, 1942, at the home of the Howell family, who had once lived down the street from the Knebelkamps, a former foster family. (Enid Knebelkamp was Grace's sister.)

[8] 3654 Cicotte Street, Detroit

Teenage Norma Jeane Dougherty visited her half-sister Berniece Baker Miracle for the first
time in 1944 at the Miracle
family home in Detroit.

[9] Dalt Hotel, 34 Turk Street, San Francisco

After her breakdown, Gladys
lived in sanitariums on and off
for the rest of her life. She had a
few periods in the 1940s during
which she attempted to create a
life for herself away from hospitals. In 1945, she lived briefly
in Portland, Oregon, and lived
with Grace, Aunt Ana, Marilyn, Berniece, and granddaughter Mona Rae in Los Angeles
in 1946. In 1948, Gladys relo-

cated to San Francisco and lived in the Dalt Hotel. In a letter postmarked
June 4, 1948, Gladys wrote to Grace asking about the death of Aunt Ana.
She closed the letter with,

> By the way, how is Norma Jeane getting along? Love & all that goes with
> it.
> Gladys P. Baker
> P.S. I've gotten myself into debt up here & it is the first time I've been in
> debt & hope to soon pay it off. Goodness I sure don't like to be in debt at
> this day & age & time. So pray for me.

[10] 702 North Crescent Drive, Beverly Hills

On December 31, 1948, Marilyn attended a New Year's Eve party at producer Sam Spiegel's house. There she possibly met Johnny Hyde. (Another
story has their meeting at the Racquet Club in Palm Springs.) Johnny quickly
fell madly in love with the young starlet and began devoting himself to promoting her career.

[11] 2743 North Indian Canyon Drive, Palm Springs

The Racquet Club was a popular resort with celebrities who spent weekends and vacations in Palm Springs. Marilyn was also a visitor and was photographed poolside with Johnny Hyde. Some believe Marilyn and Johnny met at the Racquet Club.

[12] 21663 Pacific Coast Highway, Malibu

The home of Allan "Whitey" Snyder, Marilyn's long-time makeup artist and close friend, was built in 1950. Marilyn sent him Christmas cards to this location.

[13] 1333 East Menlo Avenue, Hemet, California

The Red Rock Dairy Farm was owned and operated by Charles Stanley Gifford. At various points in her life, Marilyn traveled out to Hemet to connect with her biological father.

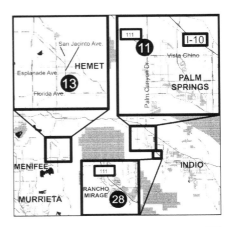

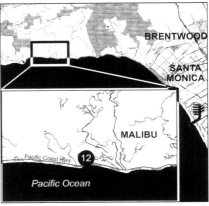

[14] 2000 Coldwater Canyon Drive, Los Angeles

Marilyn attended a party at Charles K. Feldman's house, where Arthur Miller was staying during his visit to Los Angeles in 1951. Their attraction to each other was so powerful Arthur left California.

[15] 4839 Saloma Avenue, Sherman Oaks

When Marilyn and Joe DiMaggio were dating, they often visited the home of Joe's friend Vic "Chic" Massey. The house has since been razed.

[16] 1225 Benedict Canyon Drive, Beverly Hills

Known as Green Acres, this lavish estate belonged to former silent movie star Harold Lloyd. After retiring from movies, Lloyd took up photography and in 1953 spent a day photographing Marilyn on the grounds. In the most famous pictures, she is lounging by the swimming pool.

[17] 725 Rodeo Drive, Beverly Hills
Marilyn attended a party at Gene Kelly's house in the fall of 1953. A game of charades was going on, but Marilyn spent the evening speaking to photographer Milton Greene, who was in town with his wife Amy on business. Marilyn's first photo session with Milton was on September 2.

[18] 1005 Rexford Drive, Beverly Hills
The home of Clifton Webb, Marilyn attended a party here in fall 1953 with friend Sidney Skolsky as her escort. Having trouble fitting in and feeling comfortable among Hollywood's A-list guests, Marilyn confided to Judy Garland that she was scared. Judy replied, "Honey, we're all scared."

[19] 1327 North Vista Street, Los Angeles
Vocal coach Hal Schaefer's apartment where he attempted suicide on July 28, 1954.

[20] 72 Solimar Beach, Ventura
Hal Schaefer's Ventura home, where he recovered from his suicide attempt, was where Marilyn visited him often during his recovery.

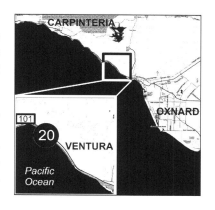

[21] 1708 Tropical Avenue, Beverly Hills
Newlyweds Marilyn and Joe stopped by Hedda Hopper's house for an interview before leaving for New York to film *The Seven Year Itch* exteriors.

[22] 127 East 78th Street, New York City
One-time home of Milton Greene and his family.

[23] 59 East 64th Street, New York City
Home of lawyer Frank Delaney, who helped find loopholes in Marilyn's Twentieth Century-Fox contract. His efforts made

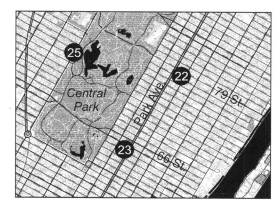

her a free agent. On January 7, 1955, Frank Delaney's townhouse hosted a party announcing Marilyn Monroe Productions.

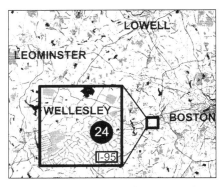

[24] 56 Woodcliff Road, Wellesley, Massachusetts

Marilyn stayed here for a few days while visiting with Joe DiMaggio. The house belonged to Mr. and Mrs. Fredericks, the mother- and father-in-law of Joe's brother Dominic. The recently divorced couple attracted an enormous amount of attention while visiting Massachusetts for a few days in January 1955. For one thing, they were traveling together and they had only just been granted their divorce in October. Rumors were circulating that Joe would be inducted into the Baseball Hall of Fame within days. (Joe and Marilyn heard the good news on their drive back to New York.) Marilyn herself was also making headlines. In addition to her announcing the launch of her own production company, Twentieth Century-Fox reported she was suspended for not showing up for work on the movie *How to Be Very, Very Popular*. Joe and Marilyn were newsworthy both on their own and together. At one point, newspaper reporters showed up on the porch of the Fredericks's house and photographed Joe cautiously answering the door. He gave autographs to a couple of fans, but when reporters asked where Marilyn was, he said, "She's not here." He said she was staying with friends but wouldn't elaborate.

[25] 135 Central Park West, New York

The Langham building where the Strasberg family lived. Marilyn took private lessons from Lee here and became a surrogate family member.

[26] 84 Remsen Street, Brooklyn

Marilyn was a regular visitor to the Brooklyn home of friends Norman and Hedda Rosten, whom she met through Arthur Miller. The Rostens were among her closest friends and Hedda even worked in a secretarial role for Marilyn. During her years on the East Coast, Marilyn said she had fallen in love with Brooklyn and it was her wish to retire there.

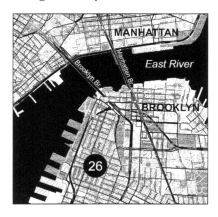

[27] 902 Franklin Street, Santa Monica

Dr. Ralph Greenson's house, where Marilyn visited for psychiatric sessions and socializing. As she had done throughout her lifetime, Marilyn ingratiated herself with the Greenson family. She was a regular visitor and even spent her last Christmas at the Greenson home. The house was originally built in 1946 by John and Eunice Murray, but within less than a year they could no longer afford the payments. Ralph Greenson purchased the house in 1947 for $16,500. Marilyn fell in love with the Franklin Street house's Mexican architecture and, when she decided to buy her own home, wanted one with the same style. She selected a house just a few minutes away from Franklin Street. In a strange twist of fate, Mrs. Murray accompanied Marilyn to Mexico on a trip specifically to purchase authentic Mexican furnishings for her new house—which was based on Mrs. Murray's former house.

[28] 70375 Calico Road, Rancho Mirage

Nestled in the Thunderbird Heights gated community, this Palm Springs-area home was where Bing Crosby spent weekends and leisure time when not in Los Angeles. The house is at the center of significant controversy, for a couple of reasons. First, President John F. Kennedy spent the weekend of March 24–25 at this estate, but it was not his original destination. Frank Sinatra, a Democrat and longtime supporter of President Kennedy, spent a significant amount of money readying his Palm Springs house for the president's expected stay. He even went so far as to build a helipad.

Younger brother and U.S. Attorney General Robert Kennedy had different ideas. He was on an anti-mafia crusade and it would look terrible if President Kennedy stayed with a man known to have friends in the mafia. President Kennedy agreed and instead stayed at the home of Bing Crosby—Frank's rival and a *Republican*, at that. Frank, who believed his campaigning had helped get Kennedy elected, felt this was a huge betrayal, and never spoke to any of them again. (Jacqueline Kennedy was not present because she was representing the United States in Pakistan that weekend.)

The second part of the controversy comes with the others who stayed at the Crosby estate that weekend, namely Marilyn Monroe. Marilyn did spend some time there that weekend. It was an ideal weekend for her to get away, as her new home in Los Angeles was undergoing plumbing work and the water was shut off. She washed her hair at Dr. Greenson's and then left for Palm Springs on Saturday, March 23. It is generally believed that *if* something happened between Marilyn and the president, it would have been this weekend at the Crosby estate. It's the only time they could have possibly been alone together. But Marilyn wasn't there the entire weekend and may not have even been there overnight, although she was there for dinner. On

Sunday, March 24, she spent the day with Norman Rosten, who was visiting from New York, and her former husband Joe DiMaggio—away from the Crosby estate. She then returned to Los Angeles for a Monday meeting about *Something's Got to Give.*

President Kennedy's schedule that weekend is as follows:

Friday, March 23
11:00 a.m. Alameda Naval Air Station
11:45 a.m. Lawrence Berkeley Radiation Laboratory
1:40 p.m. Charter Anniversary Ceremony, University of California at
   Berkeley
4:08 p.m. Vandenberg Air Force Base
Evening: Dinner at Bing Crosby's estate
Saturday, March 24
11:00 a.m. Meeting with former President Dwight D. Eisenhower

[29] 625 Palisades Beach Road, Santa Monica

Home of Peter Lawford and Pat Kennedy Lawford where friend Marilyn was a frequent guest. Pat Lawford's brothers, President John F. Kennedy and Senator Robert Kennedy were also visitors when they were in town. On November 18, 1961, John Kennedy attended a Democratic fundraiser dinner held in his honor at the Hollywood Palladium. Later that night, he attended a dinner at his sister's house in Santa Monica. On that night, Marilyn was a dinner guest at Dr. Greenson's house. The following day, Pat Lawford hosted a luncheon on November 19, 1961, for her brother with other guests present. That same day, Marilyn met with photographer Douglas Kirkland to review proofs of their recent photo session. Then she went to dinner at the Lawford house.

It's difficult to say if Marilyn and President Kennedy crossed paths at the Lawfords' home. They were not officially there at the same time, but it's not impossible they ran into each other. When the president was in town, the Lawford house was a hub of activity and events. If the two did happen to see each other at the Lawford home, there would have been many guests present and they would have never had an opportunity to be alone.

In the summer of 1962, Marilyn did a photo shoot with George Barris close to the Lawford family home. She wore a bikini and frolicked on the sand and in the waves. As the sun set and the temperature dropped, she wrapped herself up in a green beach towel, a short white robe, and finally a sweater she had bought in Mexico. The house was originally built in 1936 by Louis B. Mayer. The house was rented by John Lennon, Ringo Starr, Keith Moon, and Harry Nilsson in 1974 during what became known as Lennon's "lost weekend." The last pictures of Lennon and Paul McCartney together were taken at this house. It still stands but has been extensively remodeled over the years.

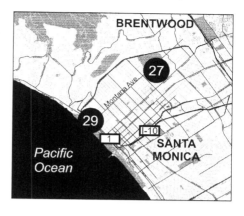

[30] 711 North Rexford Drive, Beverly Hills

This is the rented home of *Something's Got to Give* producer Henry Weinstein, who threw a party here in January 1962. Marilyn attended, as did Carl Sandburg.

[31] 1506 Blue Jay Way, Los Angeles

Marilyn posed for a series of photos at the home of Tim Leimert, a friend of photographer George Barris, on June 30, 1962. This same street would be immortalized a few years later in the song "Blue Jay Way" by the Beatles.

· 32 ·

On the Town: Restaurants, Bars, and Nightclubs

*M*arilyn was never what you would call a "foodie" or a "scenester." Like anyone, she enjoyed an evening out now and then, but overall didn't put too much effort into making appearances at fancy restaurants, trying trendy menu items or dancing all night at clubs. She preferred staying home with a good book or studying for an upcoming part. Her career made appearances necessary, but generally she stayed home. When it came to eating out, Marilyn was equally as comfortable dining in an exclusive restaurant as she was in a local watering hole.

CALIFORNIA

[1] Barney's Beanery | 8447 Santa Monica Boulevard, West Hollywood

Opened in 1927 on what was the original Route 66, this authentic roadhouse has become a landmark known for serving chili, burgers and beer at reasonable prices. Because of its central location, it has long been a magnet for celebrities, struggling artists, and working-class folks looking for a casual, hearty meal. Clara Bow, Rita Hayworth, and Marilyn's childhood idol, Clark Gable, were all known to have stopped in.

During the years she wasn't making much money, Marilyn was known to eat here, including the day

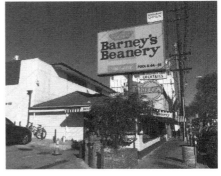

Barney's Beanery on the old Route 66 has been a staple of Los Angeles since 1927. Marilyn was known to eat here during the years when money was tight. Elisa Jordan

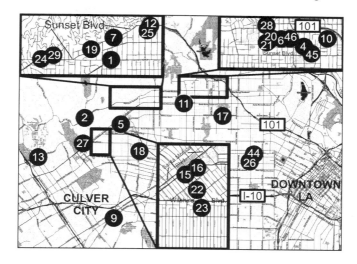

she posed nude for Tom Kelley. After her photo session, Marilyn slid into a booth at Barney's for a comforting bowl of chili.

[2] Beverly Hills Hotel | 9641 Sunset Boulevard, Beverly Hills

The Beverly Hills Hotel has been the center of high society since it opened in 1912. When the movies came to town around the same time, Hollywood royalty Douglas Fairbanks and Mary Pickford chose Beverly Hills as their home. The rest of Hollywood's elite soon followed and the luxury hotel was able to provide the exclusivity they craved. The hotel offers more than one dining option but the Polo Lounge is by far the most famous.

Marilyn is closely tied to the Beverly Hills Hotel. She lived at the hotel on more than one occasion, attended parties, accepted awards at ceremonies and, of course, dined here often.

[3] Blue Fox | 659 Merchant Street, San Francisco

While on a weekend break from filming *The Misfits*, Marilyn, Paula Strasberg, Ralph Roberts, May Reis, Agnes Flanegan and her husband, and Pearl Porterfield had dinner at this San Francisco restaurant. The hostess was a relative of Joe DiMaggio and joyfully threw her arms around Marilyn when they saw each other.

[4] Brown Derby | 1628 Vine Street, Los Angeles

The Brown Derby had multiple locations around the Los Angeles area, including one right in the heart of Hollywood. Located on Vine, not far off Hollywood Boulevard (the famous intersection of Hollywood and Vine), Marilyn and Joe had Thanksgiving dinner here in November 1952 with Joe's friend Bernie Kamber.

[5] Chasen's | 9039 Beverly Boulevard, West Hollywood

Opened in 1936, Chasen's sat on the border of Beverly Hills and catered to a very exclusive crowd. This was a place to see and be seen, so Johnny Hyde liked taking his protégé Marilyn Monroe to dinner here so the "right" people saw her around town. Marilyn returned on June 26, 1953, with Jane Russell after placing their hands and feet in wet cement at Grauman's Chinese Theatre to celebrate. They were accompanied by their respective dates: Joe DiMaggio and Jane's husband, football great Bob Waterfield. Movie star and future President of the United States Ronald Reagan proposed to actress Nancy Davis here. Their booth is now on display at the Ronald Reagan

Since closing in 1995, Chasen's restaurant has been repurposed into a high-end grocery store. Fortunately, a small section of the original restaurant has been preserved. Elisa Jordan

After placing her hands and feet in wet cement at the Chinese Theatre, Marilyn celebrated at Chasen's restaurant. Joe didn't attend the public ceremony, but did accompany her to the quiet dinner afterward. Photofest

Library. Chasen's closed in 1995, but the exterior was preserved, along with a small section of the dining room. The building is now a high-end grocery store.

[6] Cinegrill Lounge (at the Roosevelt Hotel) | 7000 Hollywood Boulevard, Los Angeles

The Cinegrill is located within the Roosevelt Hotel, where Marilyn posed in a 1951 photo shoot. Contrary to popular belief, there is no evidence Marilyn lived at this hotel, although she did eat at the Cinegrill.

[7] Ciro's | 8433 Sunset Boulevard, West Hollywood

Opened in January 1940 by William Wilkerson, who also owned *The Hollywood Reporter* and the popular Café Trocadero and La Rue, Ciro's became one of the most popular nightclubs on the Sunset Strip in the 1940s and 1950s. Not only was it exclusive and known for its world-class entertainment, dinner and dancing, showing up at Ciro's was an excellent way to get some free publicity because Hollywood gossip columnists were also regular patrons. Marilyn came here many times, including with Joe DiMaggio, who wasn't known to enjoy high-profile locations, and most famously for Walter Winchell's birthday party in 1953. That evening Marilyn was photographed with *How to Marry a Millionaire* costar Betty Grable and wore a white version of the pink strapless "Diamonds Are a Girl's Best Friend" dress in *Gentlemen Prefer Blondes.*

[44] Cocoanut Grove | 3400 Wilshire Boulevard, Los Angeles (former location)

Touted as "the world-famous Cocoanut Grove," the nightclub within the Ambassador Hotel attracted entertainment's top talent for decades. A national radio show was broadcast from the club in the 1930s; Paramount Pictures even went so far as to recreate the famous venue for a movie called—naturally—*Cocoanut Grove.* Guests were treated to live music, dancing, and dinner. In the early 1940s, Jim and Norma Jeane Dougherty were photographed sitting at a table enjoying an evening out. Jim, gazing lovingly at his wife, wore his Merchant Marine uniform and Norma Jeane wore a large corsage on her dress and an elegant hat. Marilyn Monroe returned to the Cocoanut Grove for a party in 1953 and again to accept her Golden Globe award for Best Actress in a Musical or Comedy, which she received for *Some Like It Hot.*

Over protests from historians, the Ambassador Hotel—along with the Cocoanut Grove—were demolished in two phases—the first in September 2005 and the second in January 2006.

[8] DiMaggio's | Fisherman's Wharf, San Francisco

Joe DiMaggio's ties to San Francisco ran deep. Brothers Tom and Dom, along with Joe's close friend Reno Barsocchini, ran DiMaggio's, which served an assortment of pasta and seafood. Joe and Marilyn had dinner here on December 31, 1953, only about two weeks before they got married.

[9] Ferris Webster's Retake Room | 3918 Ince Way, Culver City

In October 1949, Marilyn, Johnny Hyde, and director John Huston had drinks here to celebrate Marilyn winning the role of Angela in *The Asphalt Jungle.*

[10] Florentine Gardens | 5951 Hollywood Boulevard, Los Angeles

Opened in 1938, Florentine Gardens was a popular Italian restaurant and nightclub throughout the 1940s. Marilyn, then still Norma Jeane, held her wedding reception here in June 1942 when she married James Dougherty. The building still stands but has undergone several incarnations over the years.

[11] Formosa Café | 7156 Santa Monica Boulevard, West Hollywood

Situated across from the lot where *Some Like It Hot* was filmed in 1958, Marilyn was known to occasionally cross the street for meals and drinks during production. Because of the proximity to studios, the Formosa, as locals call it, has long been a celebrity hangout. In addition to the high-profile clientele, the Formosa is famous for its Chinese food and prominent appearance in *L.A. Confidential* (1997). Originally opened in 1939, the Formosa served guests out of a converted Red Car trolley. It's still there and visible from the exterior, but the restaurant has been expanded since 1939.

Originally opened in a Red Car trolley, the Formosa has been serving Los Angeles since 1939. The interiors for Some Like it Hot *filmed across the street, and Marilyn was known to pop over for meals during production.* Elisa Jordan

[12] Greenblatt's Deli | 8017 Sunset Boulevard, West Hollywood

Opened in 1926—the same year Marilyn was born—family-owned Greenblatt's Deli fed Angelenos Jewish comfort food for nearly ninety-five years. Marilyn was known to come in for pastrami sandwiches. According to the owners, who handed down the business to younger generations, Marilyn used to quietly come in and go unrecognized by other patrons after her return to Los Angeles from New York. The exception was when she arrived one day with Joe DiMaggio, who was back in her life, and others noticed the very famous former couple. The location of Greenblatt's has changed since Marilyn dined there. From the 1920s to the 1980s, Greenblatt's sat on the northwest corner of Sunset and Laurel, across from Schwab's Drugstore. The deli moved to the space next door in the 1980s and the Laugh Factory now occupies the former Greenblatt's spot. Greenblatt's closed during the COVID-19 pandemic.

[13] Hi-Ho Drive-in Café/Mrs. Gray's Inn | Wilshire Boulevard and Westwood Boulevard, Westwood

Hi-Ho Drive-in opened in the 1930s and by the end of the decade was called Mrs. Gray's Inn. Located within the Westwood Village neighborhood near UCLA, it was also close to where the Knebelkamps and their neighbors, the Howell family, lived during the 1930s. Norma Jeane and foster sister Bebe Goddard used to hang out here. By the 1950s the name had changed again to Truman's Drive Inn and then closed for good in the late 1960s. A high-rise building now occupies the site.

[14] Holiday House | 27400 West Pacific Coast Highway, Malibu

Opened in 1949, Holiday House sat overlooking the water and was a popular watering hole for movie stars, including Frank Sinatra, Shirley MacLaine, Lana Turner, Cornel Wilde, and David Niven, among others. In the early 1950s, Marilyn had lunch with director Nick Ray here. Today the property has been downscaled and a restaurant named Geoffrey's now occupies the spot.

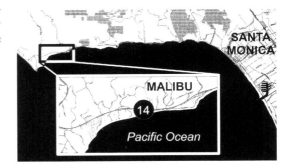

[45] Hollywood Palladium | 6215 Sunset Boulevard, Los Angeles
During her brief time in Las Vegas, Marilyn dated a gentleman by the name of Bill Pursel. He helped her drive home to Los Angeles before returning to Las Vegas, and the two remained on friendly terms. In 1948, Pursel registered at Woodbury College in Burbank and he resumed his friendship with Marilyn. By this time, she was deeply in love with Fred Karger, but they met on occasion for lunch. In the book *Marilyn Monroe: Private and Undisclosed,* Pursel told author Michelle Morgan that one night the former couple went dancing at the Hollywood Palladium, where he observed clarinet player Woody Herman was noticeably distracted by Marilyn's beauty during his performance. Marilyn, whose back was to the stage, had no clue she had caused such a reaction.

La Scala
[15] 9455 Santa Monica Boulevard, Beverly Hills
[16] 460 North Canon Drive, Beverly Hills
Originally opened in 1956, this upscale Italian eatery has been a staple of Beverly Hills for decades. Marilyn ate here on her last birthday, June 1, 1962, after making an appearance at Dodger Stadium, where she threw out the first pitch. The receipt for the meal indicates enough food for another person, possibly even two other people, to have been present. La Scala has moved a couple of times since it first opened.

[36] Lefty O'Doul's Restaurant & Cocktail Lounge
333 Geary Street, San Francisco
During the filming of *The Misfits*, Marilyn visited San Francisco for a weekend getaway with friends. While there, she dropped by Lefty O'Doul's restaurant to say hello to her old friend, whom she knew through Joe DiMaggio.

[17] Lucey's Restaurant | 5444 Melrose Avenue, Los Angeles
Lucey's opened in the 1920s and was a safe place to imbibe during the Prohibition era. The structure itself was a two-story Spanish style, which was popular at the time. Its proximity to studios in Hollywood made it a prime hangout for celebrities and industry types over the years. In April 1951, friend Sidney Skolsky arranged a meeting between Marilyn and producer Jerry Wald to discuss the part of Peggy in *Clash by Night*.

Right in the heart of Hollywood, Marilyn and Joe DiMaggio were known to dine at Miceli's Italian Restaurant.
Elisa Jordan

[46] Miceli's | 1646 North Las Palmas Ave., Los Angeles
Steps off Hollywood Boulevard, Miceli's has been serving Italian comfort food since 1949. During their relationship, Marilyn and Joe were known to eat here. Fun fact: When the Pig & Whistle—where she bought penny candy as a little girl—closed, Miceli's bought the wooden booths, which pictured pigs playing whistles. These booths are still at Miceli's today. Extra fun fact: When Lucille Ball needed to learn how to toss pizza dough for the "Visitor from Italy" episode of *I Love Lucy,* she came to Miceli's for training in 1956.

[18] Ming Room | 358 South La Cienega Boulevard, Los Angeles
When Marilyn and Joe were dating, they became regulars at this Chinese restaurant, a place where fans didn't bother them and the staff was discreet. The Ming Room was owned and operated by Los Angeles–born actor Bruce Wong, who also owned Chinese Village Café at 745 N. Main Street, in the Chinatown section of downtown. Wong sold Chinese Village Café right before his death in 1953.

[19] Mocambo | 8588 Sunset Boulevard, West Hollywood

The Mocambo opened on January 3, 1941, and had a Latin American theme that included an aviary with live exotic birds. As was popular for the era, the nightclub regularly featured live entertainment and big band music. Frank Sinatra first performed as a solo act at the Mocambo in 1943. Marilyn was known to attend events at the Mocambo many times, and stories have circulated that she got Ella Fitzgerald a singing gig in the segregated club if she promised to show up for every performance. This story, however, cannot possibly be true as the Mocambo wasn't segregated and Marilyn was in New York at the time of Ella's engagement at the Mocambo. (For the full story, see the Myths chapter.)

[20] Musso and Frank Grill | 6667 Hollywood Boulevard, Los Angeles

As one of the most popular and legendary restaurants in Hollywood, nearly every Old Hollywood star (and probably in New Hollywood) has dined at the fabled eatery. Marilyn, like everyone else, came here many times throughout her life, including with her friends from the Actors Lab and dates with Joe DiMaggio.

Musso and Frank opened in 1919 and is the oldest continuously running restaurant in Hollywood. Legend says Mary Pickford and Douglas Fairbanks Sr. returned from Italy with the recipe for fettuccine Alfredo, which the chefs at Musso and Frank dutifully prepared for them. It was the introduction of the dish to the American public. Musso and Frank is such a part of Hollywood history and culture that it was featured prominently in the 2019 movie *Once Upon a Time . . . in Hollywood* by Quentin Tarantino.

[21] Pig & Whistle | 6714 Hollywood Boulevard, Los Angeles

When Norma Jeane lived in Hollywood as a little girl, she walked to the Chinese Theatre and Egyptian Theatre to watch movies. When going to the Egyptian, she stopped next door at the Pig & Whistle to purchase penny candy before the feature. Because of its location, the Pig & Whistle became a celebrity hangout, but closed in the late 1940s. After the closure, the building went through a series of incarnations, including retail stores and other restaurants. In 1999, the Pig & Whistle restaurant was restored to the location and opened for business in the original location. The restaurant was forced to close during the COVID-19 pandemic and was unable to reopen.

Romanoff's
[22] 326 N. Rodeo Drive, Beverly Hills
[23] 140 S. Rodeo Drive, Beverly Hills
Marilyn and Johnny Hyde used to eat here during their relationship. It was close to where they lived in Beverly Hills and was Marilyn's favorite restaurant. Romanoff's was the site of a party thrown by Twentieth Century-Fox in Marilyn's honor after filming for *The Seven Year Itch* wrapped. She danced with her childhood hero Clark Gable on this occasion. The restaurant moved to a new address in 1958, and it was at this location that Marilyn attended a party in honor of Billy Wilder.

It was said that Romanoff's was owned by an eccentric man who claimed to be from exiled Russian royalty. It closed in the 1970s.

[24] Scandia | 9140 Sunset Boulevard, West Hollywood
Scandia was a popular, exclusive Scandinavian restaurant on the Sunset Strip at the southeast corner of Doheny. Marilyn was known to eat here in the early 1950s. The sleek, mid-century building was torn down in 2015 to make way for a high-rise hotel.

[25] Schwab's Drugstore | 8024 Sunset Boulevard, Los Angeles
Opened in 1932, Schwab's Drugstore on Sunset Boulevard was a hub of entertainment business activity from the 1930s through the 1950s. In the days before social media and the internet, Schwab's was the place industry insiders, young hopefuls, journalists, and everyone else hung out and exchanged gossip, networked and chose to "be seen." As was common for the era, the drugstore sold pharmaceuticals and also served ice cream and food over a counter. Schwab's gained national fame when entertainment reporter Sidney Skolsky, who used the place as his office, started publishing a column called "From a Stool at Schwab's" for *Photoplay* magazine.

Schwab's became synonymous with Lana Turner after it was reported she was "discovered" sipping a Coca-Cola at the drugstore's soda fountain. (She was indeed discovered at a soda fountain, but it was the Top Hat Café on Sunset Boulevard, across from Hollywood High School, where she was a student.)

In the 1940s, starlet Marilyn Monroe became one of the young Hollywood hopefuls who made it a point to drop in at Schwab's frequently. A rumor persists that she first heard about the *Love Happy* part at Schwab's. What is certain is Marilyn befriended Sidney Skolsky, who went on to become one of her biggest champions and most trusted allies.

Schwab's was demolished in the 1980s to make way for a larger shopping structure. It is reported that actress and comedienne Harriet Nelson was so upset the Hollywood landmark was torn down that she looked the other way when driving by the former site.

[26] Tiffany Club | 3260 West 8th Street, Los Angeles
As one of the most popular and respected jazz clubs on the west coast, the Tiffany Club hosted some of the greatest musical acts of the day, including Louis Armstrong, Charlie Parker, Billie Holiday, Chet Baker, and Ella Fitzgerald. While recovering from gynecological surgery in November 1954, Marilyn attended multiple performances at the Tiffany to watch Ella Fitzgerald. The two women were photographed together at the club and this photo is often mistakenly attributed to the Mocambo Club instead of the Tiffany.

[27] Trader Vic's | 9876 Wilshire Boulevard, Beverly Hills
Located in the Beverly Wilshire Hotel, Trader Vic's was a Polynesian-themed restaurant that opened in 1955 and instantly became a popular celebrity hangout. Marilyn was known to eat here on several occasions.

[28] Villa Capri | 6735 Yucca Street, Los Angeles
Joe DiMaggio loved hearty Italian food, so it is no surprise he selected Villa Capri as the location for his fortieth birthday party. On November 13, 1954, just weeks after their separation, Marilyn joined Joe and his brother Dominic at the Villa Capri to celebrate Joe's milestone birthday. Marilyn gifted her estranged husband a gold watch, which he wore for years until it was damaged beyond repair after a car accident. The Villa Capri opened in 1950 by Pasquale "Patsy" D'Amore, who had found previous success with restaurants Casa D'Amore on Cahuenga Boulevard and Patsy D'Amore's Pizza at the Farmer's Market on 3rd Street and Fairfax Avenue. Frank Sinatra was a close friend of Patsy's and because the Villa Capri was so close to the Capitol Records building, it became a hot spot for the company's executives and musicians. Joe and Frank were eating at Villa Capri in 1954 when private detectives alerted them that they had tracked Marilyn to an apartment and she might be with a lover—only to be mistaken. Marilyn returned to Villa Capri in September 1961 with Ralph Roberts, and lamented about how she and Joe had liked to dine here. She also talked about how life was coming full circle now that both Joe and Frank were reentering her life, and recounted the disaster known as the Wrong Door Raid.

James Dean ate dinner here on September 29, 1955, the night before he died in an accident while driving to a race in Salinas. The building was razed in 2005.

[29] Villa Nova (now the Rainbow Bar and Grill)
9015 Sunset Boulevard, West Hollywood

One of the most storied restaurants in Hollywood, Villa Nova opened in the 1930s and was an immediate success with industry folks and movie stars. Director Vincent Minelli was part owner and proposed to Judy Garland in one of the booths. On March 8, 1952, Joe DiMaggio met Marilyn here on a blind date. David March and his date, Peggy Rabe, were also present. Ownership changed in 1972 and the building was renamed the Rainbow in honor of Judy Garland's most famous song. Since then the restaurant has catered to a rock-and-roll crowd as elite as the Old Hollywood crowd it used to serve.

Marilyn and Joe DiMaggio met at the Villa Nova restaurant on the Sunset Strip for their first date in 1952. Now called the Rainbow Bar & Grill, the building remains intact although now caters to a rock 'n' roll crowd.
Elisa Jordan

Remnants of the Villa Nova are still present at the top of the stairs in the Rainbow Bar & Grill.
Elisa Jordan

Von's Midway Drive-In | Hemet
Marilyn and Joe DiMaggio ate here when they drove out to Hemet in an attempt to meet her father.

NEW YORK

[30] Copacabana | 10 East 60th Street, New York
After announcing the launch of Marilyn Monroe productions, Marilyn took a group of friends to see a Frank Sinatra show at the Copacabana in 1955. There is also a joke in *All about Eve* that Marilyn's character, Miss Casswell, is a graduate of the Copacabana School of the Dramatic Arts.

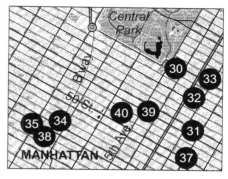

As one of the most influential nightclubs in American history, the Copacabana casts a long shadow when it comes to popular culture. It's been portrayed in such movies as *Goodfellas, Tootsie, Raging Bull, Carlito's Way*, and *The French Connection*. Barry Manilow's song "Copacabana (At the Copa)" became a cultural touchstone in the 1970s.

[31] El Morocco | 154 East 54th Street, New York
El Morocco was one of the first places Marilyn ever experienced in New York, a city she would grow to love. During her publicity tour for *Love Happy* in 1949, she stopped at El Morocco. She returned in September 1954 with Joe DiMaggio when they were in town for her exterior scenes in *The Seven Year Itch*. It would be one of the last times they appeared in public as a married couple.

[32] Four Seasons | 99 East 52nd Street, New York
As one of New York's most elite restaurants, the Four Seasons elevated fine dining standards for the modern generation. It is known for introducing the concept of seasonal menus to the United States, serving American wines, and being the first eatery of its kind to print menus in English. When Marilyn moved to New York, she visited this icon of the city often. This location closed in 2015.

[33] Gino | 780 Lexington Avenue, New York
Marilyn ate here during her New York years. It was an Italian restaurant that was a popular hangout with the likes of Frank Sinatra, Ed Sullivan, Gregory Peck, Ralph Lauren, and Jackie Onassis.

[34] Howard Johnson's | 1551 Broadway, New York
When Marilyn moved to New York, she dove into the theatre scene by attending plays regularly. Located in the heart of New York's Times Square neighborhood, this Howard Johnson's was an easy place to pop in for a classic Americana meal, especially after a play. It remained a staple of the neighborhood until 2005 when it was razed.

[35] Jim Downey's Steakhouse | 705 8th Avenue, New York
Located in the Times Square neighborhood and catering to theatre patrons, Downey's was known for a mural depicting famous stage actors; Marilyn was added after appearing during a curtain call for *Teahouse of the August Moon*. Now long gone, Downey's was mentioned in two episodes of *Mad Men*, showing the relevance it had during the 1950s and 1960s.

[37] Manny Wolf's Chop House | 797 3rd Avenue, New York
Manny Wolf's was a classic New York establishment dating back to 1897. Before being turned into a restaurant, the building served as a buggy whip factory. The business was still part of New York culture when Marilyn visited in the mid-1950s. Since 1977, the restaurant located here has been called Smith & Wollensky.

[38] Sardi's | 234 West 44th Street, New York
Perhaps one of the best-known restaurants in New York, Sardi's has been in this location since 1927. Sardi's has been a popular place to drop in before or after seeing a show in the theatre district since it opened. In addition to its legendary cultural status, it is famous for the caricatures of celebrities lining the walls. When Marilyn became a regular theatregoer during her stay in New York, she was known to grab meals here on occasion.

[39] The Stork Club | 3 East 53rd Street, New York
Originally opened in 1929 at another location, the Stork Club resided on East 53rd Street from 1934 to 1965, where it became an institution of New York society. The Stork Club attracted presidents, royalty, socialites, the very wealthy, and movie stars. In September 1954, when Marilyn traveled to New

York to film exterior scenes for *The Seven Year Itch*, she was photographed smiling and laughing with her husband Joe DiMaggio at the Stork Club. Little did they know their marriage was about to end.

[40] Toots Shor's | 51 West 51st Street, New York

Named for its owner, Toots Shor, Marilyn was known to attend functions at this restaurant during her relationship with Joe DiMaggio, who had been a regular for years. The atmosphere was masculine and Toots Shor's unofficially served as a de facto men's club—an establishment where men could enjoy hard liquor and a hearty steak. Although Toots Shor's touted itself as a saloon specializing in unpretentious American fare, it was also known to attract a celebrity (mostly male) clientele. Toots Shor himself was especially welcoming to baseball players, and he catered to the great Joe DiMaggio in particular. Joe liked to come in after Yankees games to unwind and hang out with the guys. When he didn't want to be bothered, Toots personally ensured autograph seekers left him alone. For a reserved and ferociously private individual like Joe, the respite from strangers would have put him at ease and guaranteed his loyalty to the establishment and his buddy Toots.

After Joe and Marilyn separated in the fall of 1954, they attended Jackie Gleason's birthday party together at Toots Shor's in February 1955. Photos from that evening show the former couple smiling and relaxed in each other's company. A few months later, they returned to Toots Shor's on June 1. They arrived after attending the premiere of *The Seven Year Itch* and stopped here to celebrate Marilyn's twenty-ninth birthday. After making an appearance at such a public spectacle as a movie premiere, Joe may have chosen to celebrate here because they could be left alone and it's where he was most comfortable.

Joe and Toots maintained a friendship for years, but it ended abruptly when Toots made the mistake of mentioning Marilyn's name. Joe allowed very few people into his inner circle, and those close to him knew better than to bring up the former Mrs. DiMaggio. Why Toots chose to breach this tacit understanding is unknown, but he reportedly made the infraction worse by speaking poorly of Marilyn. In an instant, the friendship between Joe DiMaggio and Toots Shor was over.

Meanwhile, as years went on business at Toots Shor's declined. Key sports teams, like the Dodgers and the Giants, left New York, and sports fans—and athletes—were integral to the saloon's success. After selling his lease, Toots moved to a new location on 52nd Street in 1960. He was forced to close in 1971 after authorities locked Shor out of his own restaurant for unpaid taxes.

OTHER CITIES

[41] Corey's Café | 402 Fremont Street, Las Vegas

While staying in Las Vegas to obtain her divorce from Jim Dougherty, Marilyn met a young man named Bill Pursel while he was talking to a friend outside the house where she was living. In the book *Marilyn Monroe: Private and Undisclosed,* he tells author Michelle Morgan how the two introduced themselves, and he asked the pretty young woman if she would like to go for a walk. She agreed, and they eventually ended up at Corey's Café on Fremont Street, where they continued to chat.

[42] Flamingo Hotel & Casino | 3555 South Las Vegas Boulevard, Las Vegas
Opened on December 26, 1946, by mobster Benjamin "Bugsy" Siegel, the Flamingo ushered in a new era of glamour to the dusty desert town of Las Vegas. In the fall of 1947, Marilyn and other young actors posed for photos by the Flamingo's swimming pool. In the decades following, the Flamingo has been entirely rebuilt and none of the original structure remains.

[43] Locke-Ober | 2 Winter Place, Boston
In January 1955, Marilyn and Milton Greene arrived in Boston to meet with a potential contributor to the newly founded Marilyn Monroe Productions. Unexpectedly—or perhaps expectedly—Joe DiMaggio also arrived in town and just so happened to show up at their hotel. Marilyn promptly deserted the trip's original mission in favor of Joe.

On January 24, Marilyn, Joe DiMaggio, his brother Dominic and wife Emily, and her parents, Mr. and Mrs. Albert Fredericks, dined out in a private room at Locke-Ober, a Boston restaurant that dated back to the mid-1800s.

[47] Scott's | 18-20 Coventry Street, London
Opened in the 1850s as an oyster house, Scott's is one of the oldest restaurants still operating in London. Scott's has long been a destination restaurant and is part of English culture. Over the years, Scott's saw the likes of author Ian Fleming, actor Charlie Chaplin, and Prime Minister Winston Churchill

dining at the upscale eatery. Fleming was such a regular that his character James Bond also visited the restaurant in the novel *Diamonds Are Forever.* (Scott's serves a martini that is shaken, not stirred in honor of the fictional spy.) It is also mentioned in the 1963 movie *The Great Escape.* When Marilyn spent a few months in England in 1956 to film *The*

Prince and the Showgirl, she joined the ranks of the legendary figures who dined here.

On August 24, Marilyn visited London for a day, which included shopping and lunch. The day was anything but peaceful or relaxing, as fans were eager to catch a glimpse of Hollywood's most popular blonde. Marilyn quite literally stopped traffic. Newspapers reported that eight policemen were called to stop cars and control the crowd of hundreds of fans, which consisted mostly of teenage girls. The commotion and media coverage were evidence of Marilyn's influence and acclaim not just in the United States, but on a global scale.

Dressed in a smart black fur-trimmed jacket and sunglasses, Marilyn started her day in London by shopping on Regent Street in the West End. For lunch, she was taken to the celebrated Scott's, where she ate liver and bacon and had a double gin and tonic.

Scott's moved to a new location in Mayfair in 1967, where it has remained since. In November 1975, the restaurant gained the unfortunate distinction of having been bombed by the Irish Republican Army. After an extensive refurbishment in 2006, Scott's continues to thrive as one of London's finest and best-loved restaurants.

[48] The Country Inn | 416 South B Street, Virginia City, Nevada

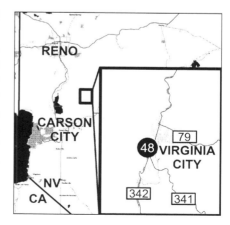

During the filming of *The Misfits*, Marilyn ate in the garden of the Country Inn. Owner Edith Palmer made Marilyn, Ralph Roberts, May Reis, and Dorothy Blass feel at home during the very difficult production in the hot desert. "It became a haven for her," Ralph Roberts said. Today the property is known as Edith Palmer's Country Inn with the original 1860s house serving as a bed and breakfast.

· 33 ·

Animal Companions

$\mathcal{M}$arilyn loved animals and had a variety of pets throughout her lifetime. From the time she was a little girl, Marilyn had an affinity for them. When she was a teenage bride, her husband Jim Dougherty even reported that he came home one day to find his wife trying to coax a cow into their home to get it out of the rain. He recognized her heart was in the right place but informed her that a family home was no place for a farm animal.

There is a maxim that warns against working with children and animals because they will steal the scene. Marilyn, on the other hand, loved working with children and animals. From her earliest modeling days, she posed with all sorts of animals, most commonly dogs. When it came to having pets as an adult, Marilyn typically had good intentions but was not always the most attentive guardian. To be fair, Marilyn's career was not conducive at all to sharing a life with pets. Her days at the studio were long and kept her away from home for extensive periods. As a result, her animal companions were sometimes given away.

TIPPY

While living with Wayne and Ida Bolender, Norma Jeane had a black-and-white dog named Tippy. Norma Jeane and Tippy had a close bond, with the dog following her to school in the morning and waiting for her to return in the afternoon. Then the two walked home together. Norma Jeane suffered serious trauma in her young life when Tippy was shot and killed by a neighbor, who was angry the little dog dug in his yard.

314

MUGGSIE

During her marriage to James Dougherty, they had a collie named Muggsie. The family of three—Norma Jeane, Jim, and Muggsie—moved to Catalina Island together for Jim's Merchant Marine training. While Jim was working during the day, Norma Jeane and Muggsie went for walks around the island. After Norma Jeane started modeling, her schedule changed. Gone were the regular hours of working at Radioplane. Instead, she picked up jobs as they were assigned, and often these were long days. Furthermore, to improve her chances of getting hired, Norma Jeane took classes at her modeling agency, which also kept her away from home. As her career picked up and she booked more modeling assignments, Muggsie stayed mostly with the Dougherty family. Muggsie passed away, and Jim later said it was from a broken heart.

JOSEFA

For Marilyn's birthday on June 1, 1950, Twentieth Century-Fox executive Joseph Schenk gave her a female Chihuahua. Marilyn named her Josefa, after Schenk. Josefa lived with Marilyn at both Natasha Lytess's apartment and the house in Beverly Hills she shared with Johnny Hyde. It was at the Beverly Hills house that Earl Leaf photographed an entire series of Marilyn playing with Josefa in the backyard. Marilyn never properly housetrained Josefa, making her a pint-sized nuisance for others who had to share homes with her. Marilyn must have given Josefa away because the little dog disappeared from her life sometime in 1951.

Marilyn playing with her Chihuahua Josefa in the yard of the house she shared with Johnny Hyde. Josefa was a twenty-fourth birthday present from Joseph Schenck at Twentieth Century-Fox.
Photofest

EBONY

While Marilyn and Arthur were married, they purchased a horse named Ebony, who roamed around the couple's yard in the country.

SERAFINA

The Millers got a Siamese cat in 1959.

PARAKEETS

While married to Arthur Miller, they had three budgies (more commonly known as parakeets) named Butch, Clyde, and Bobo.

HUGO

Hugo, the dog Marilyn and Arthur shared, was a black and brown basset hound with white feet. They doted on Hugo, who traveled with the couple between their apartment in bustling New York City and their much quieter farmhouse in Connecticut. Hugo belonged to both Millers, although his 1959 New York City license names Arthur Miller as his legal owner. Similarly, records for boarding Hugo from Southdown Kennel in Roxbury, Connecticut, also named Arthur Miller as owner. Some of these boarding dates coincide with Marilyn's filming schedule in California and Nevada for *Some Like It Hot*, *Let's Make Love*, and *The Misfits*.

When Marilyn and Arthur separated, Hugo stayed with Arthur, who kept the Roxbury farmhouse, a location with plenty of land for a dog to run around.

Marilyn's half-sister Berniece visited her in New York in 1961 as Marilyn recovered from gallbladder surgery. She recalled accompanying Marilyn to the Roxbury house to help pick up the remaining belongings left behind in Connecticut. Also along for the journey was Maf, Marilyn's new puppy who played and romped in the yard with Hugo while the sisters gathered Marilyn's things.

MAF

Marilyn's last pet was a small, fluffy white dog gifted to her by Frank Sinatra. She named him Maf, short for Mafia, a joke alluding to Frank Sinatra's alleged underworld connections. Maf's breeder was Maria Stephen Gurdin, Natalie Wood's mother. Maf's parents were Andre du Bois (father) and Shoo Shoo (mother). He was born on January 16, 1961, right around the time her divorce from Arthur Miller was finalized.

Marilyn's canine companion in the final years of her life was Maf, a gift from Frank Sinatra. After Marilyn's death, Maf was adopted by Gloria Lovell, Sinatra's secretary.
Photofest

There seems to be some discrepancy about which breed Maf was. On his New York dog license, dated July 18, 1961, Maf is listed as a poodle. For his Los Angeles dog license, dated July 9, 1962, his name was listed as "Mafia" and his breed was Maltese. He accompanied Marilyn to her final home on Fifth Helena in the Brentwood neighborhood of Los Angeles, where Marilyn allowed him to sleep on a fur coat Arthur Miller had gifted her.

Like Josefa, Maf was never adequately housetrained and was known for having occasional accidents indoors. When Marilyn was fired from Twentieth Century-Fox in June 1962, Maf was a close companion at home. To save her career, Marilyn began granting interviews and arranging photo sessions—including one in which she is holding Maf.

Among the many heartbreaking photos taken on the morning of Marilyn's death, the ones of a police officer walking Maf out of the house for the last time are some of the most poignant. Maf was given to Frank Sinatra's secretary, Gloria Lovell, who kept him until he died in 1974.

· 34 ·

Religion

$\mathcal{T}$hroughout her lifetime, Marilyn was exposed to various religions but was never a devout practitioner of anything in particular. Most of her exposure to religious and spiritual matters came from other people.

BAPTISM

According to some stories, baby Norma Jeane was possibly baptized at Angelus Temple, the first church founded by the International Church of the Foursquare Church in the Echo Park neighborhood of Los Angeles. The church's leader was Aimee Semple McPherson, known as Sister Aimee, who was a celebrity evangelist in the 1920s and 1930s. Sister Aimee was a pioneer when it came to utilizing media to build her congregation and seek donations. In many ways, she was a forerunner to what are now called megachurches.

As the story goes, Norma Jeane's grandmother, Della Mae, wanted the baby girl baptized and took her here for the service, possibly even performed by Sister Aimee herself. The church is located at 1100 Glendale Avenue in Los Angeles and still holds services. In another version of the story, Norma Jeane was baptized at the Hawthorne Foursquare Church located at 5411 West Broadway Boulevard in Hawthorne, which was just a few blocks away from where her first foster parents, the Bolenders, lived. Della Mae was also in the neighborhood—she lived across the street from the Bolenders. (The address number has changed since the 1920s. The original address was 4503 West Broadway.)

UNITED PENTECOSTAL CHURCH

For the first seven years of her life, Norma Jeane lived with Wayne and Ida Bolender, who were devout members of the United Pentecostal Church. During her time with the Bolenders, Norma Jeane was also brought up in the faith. As members of the church, the Bolenders did not participate in such activities as movies, theatre, dancing, gambling, drinking, tobacco, drugs, or cursing. Norma Jeane was taught to pray every night before bed.

BAPTIST

Nancy Bolender, one of the other children Wayne and Ida later adopted, said that although Ida had once been a member of the United Pentecostal Church, the Bolenders were, in fact, Baptist. According to her, the family attended church on Sundays and Wednesday evenings.

CHRISTIAN SCIENCE

Of all the religions Marilyn was exposed to, Christian Science was probably the one she had the most lasting connection to. Founded by Mary Baker Eddy in the late nineteenth century, Christian Science gained considerable popularity in the early twentieth century. When Marilyn, then still Norma Jeane, was growing up, her beloved guardian Ana Lower was a devoted practitioner of Christian Science. She encouraged Norma Jeane to read the Bible and gifted her a copy of Eddy's *Science and Health with Key to the Scriptures*.

Christian Science emphasizes philosophical idealism, which minimizes materialism and encourages the idea that reality and the mind are associated. It was Ana Lower who taught Marilyn that she could accomplish anything she set her mind to, a philosophy she utilized for the rest of her life. Her ability to focus on accomplishing goals was one of her greatest strengths.

The other side of this idea is that prayer is often the best solution for medical conditions, so seeking treatment from doctors is limited. When Marilyn began menstruating in adolescence, she started experiencing the excruciating pain associated with chronic endometriosis. Ana showed the young girl considerable love and empathy for her condition, but prayer never cured her agony. When she grew up, Marilyn sought the help of doctors for endometriosis and other medical issues she was experiencing.

When Marilyn was an adult, photographer and lover Andre de Dienes once noticed she had a Christian Science prayer book in her bag while traveling. Still, Marilyn was never one to fully commit to any single religion enough to practice regularly.

Marilyn was not the only family member with a connection to Christian Science. Her mother Gladys became fixated on Christian Science after her breakdown. It is common for those diagnosed with schizophrenia to use religion as a coping mechanism. Gladys devoted her life to reading the Bible and studying Christian Science literature.

CATHOLICISM

When in a relationship with Fred Karger, his mother Ann once recommended to Marilyn that she seek spiritual guidance from Saint Victor's Catholic Church at 8623 Holloway Avenue in what is now West Hollywood (then unincorporated Los Angeles). The Catholic church was near the Karger home a few blocks away. Ann believed a visit to the sanctuary would help ease Marilyn's broken heart after her relationship with Fred was not working out the say she wanted. Marilyn did not find the solace or peace she had hoped for and soon returned home. The current church on this spot is not the original one that was standing in 1948 when Marilyn visited.

Marilyn's second marriage was to Joe DiMaggio, who was raised in the Catholic faith. When she married Joe in 1954, they were wed at the San Francisco courthouse. They were not permitted to marry in the church because both he and Marilyn had been divorced and the faith does not recognize divorces.

HOLLYWOOD CHRISTIAN GROUP

Jane Russell was especially kind to Marilyn on the set of *Gentlemen Prefer Blondes*. She innately understood that Marilyn's anxiety was related to deeply rooted insecurity. To put Marilyn at ease, Jane befriended the starlet, making her feel more comfortable and walking with her to the set. Jane's friendship extended to inviting Marilyn to the informal Bible studies she hosted at her home. Marilyn attended once, but ultimately did not continue.

JUDAISM

When Marilyn fell in love with Arthur Miller, she began the process of converting to Judaism so they could marry. Her conversion was made official on July 1, 1956. Her certificate of conversion was signed by Arthur, Milton Greene, and Rabbi Robert Goldberg, who also performed Arthur and Marilyn's traditional Jewish wedding on that same date.

Arthur was not an especially religious man but was moved when she took his faith seriously and wanted to convert for him.

MEMORIAL SERVICE

Marilyn's memorial service was performed by Rev. A. J. Soldan, a Lutheran minister from the Village Church in Westwood. It was a nondenominational service.

The sermon was based on the quotation, "How fearfully and wonderfully she was made by the Creator." Readings were made of Psalm 23, chapter 14 of the Book of John, and excerpts from Psalms 46 and 139. The Lord's Prayer was also read.

V

THE END

· 35 ·

Goodbye, Norma Jeane:
Marilyn's Funeral

$\mathcal{A}$lmost immediately after Marilyn passed away, a newspaper headline trumpeted that her body went unclaimed at the coroner's office. As with many things concerning Marilyn—and her death in particular—the story was untrue, but that hasn't stopped it from being repeated over the years as though it were fact. The reality of Marilyn's memorial service is much different and, in fact, reveals she was well taken care of by people who loved her.

Marilyn died on the morning of August 5, and her funeral followed just three days later on the morning of August 8 at 11 a.m. Her body was claimed immediately and memorial arrangements began the day she died.

SUNDAY, AUGUST 5

Berniece Baker Miracle learned her half sister passed away on the morning of August 5. She was distressed the media announced Marilyn's death publicly before notifying her. Shortly after learning of Marilyn's death, the Los Angeles County Coroner's Office sent a telegram to Berniece. As she was next of kin, the office needed her permission to release Marilyn's body to Joe DiMaggio. Berniece approved the request, then promptly sent a message to Joe himself letting him know she would arrive in Los Angeles as soon as possible. Although clunky by modern standards, telegrams were the fastest way to communicate in 1962. Even telephoning someone could be challenging because long-distance charges were cost-prohibitive for many people.

In an era before credit cards were common, Berniece had limited options for catching a flight quickly. It was Sunday and banks were closed. To book a flight required withdrawing the money from a bank in person. The Miracles had just arrived home to Florida from vacation and were low on money. Berniece scrambled to scrape together money and soon booked a flight. She

The double doors where Marilyn's body was wheeled out at Westwood Memorial as they appear today. A portico has been added since 1962. Elisa Jordan

sent a telegram to Joe letting him know she was unable to book the midnight flight from Florida to California but managed to arrange for the next one, allowing her to arrive early the next morning.

While Berniece was trying to book a flight, Marilyn's body was autopsied and then released to the custody of Joe DiMaggio, who was able to arrive in Los Angeles quickly. Joe identified Marilyn's body and arranged for her remains to be taken to Westwood Memorial.

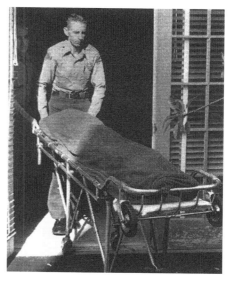

On the morning of August 5, Marilyn's body was wheeled out from Westwood Memorial and taken to downtown Los Angeles for a post-mortem exam. This photo is frequently misidentified as her house. Channel 5 Broadcasting / Photofest © Channel 5 Broadcasting

MONDAY, AUGUST 6

On Monday morning, Joe DiMaggio arrived at Westwood Memorial to continue with arrangements. Also present were Milton Rudin, Marilyn's Los Angeles attorney, and Aaron Frosch, her New York attorney, who had flown in from the East Coast.

When Berniece arrived in Los Angeles early on Monday, she was horrified to find the press waiting for her. As soon as she touched down at the airport, reporters began snapping photos and asking questions. She was never able to figure out how they knew she was coming.

Berniece went immediately to Westwood Memorial and was ushered into an office where Joe, Milton, and Aaron were already attending to arrangements. Together, Joe and Berniece selected a bronze casket with champaign-colored lining for Marilyn. In her book, Berniece noted that at $3,500, the casket was "medium-priced."

The next step was choosing a dress for Marilyn to wear for her viewing and interment. Berniece didn't have a car in Los Angeles, so Inez Melson drove her to Marilyn's house in Brentwood.

At Marilyn's home, Berniece went through two closets filled with clothing—one in Marilyn's bedroom and another closet in a guest room. She wanted Marilyn to wear color so she settled on an apple green dress with long sleeves by Pucci, an Italian designer Marilyn was especially fond of wearing the last couple years of her life.

Berniece and Inez also gathered some things they thought the mortuary staff might need when dressing Marilyn, including safety pins, a set of falsies, a wig, a sheet, and some other dresses in various sizes as backups. The mortuary staff had informed Berniece that Marilyn's hair had been damaged during the autopsy, and recommended a wig might be helpful to make Marilyn look better during the viewing. The falsies were because Marilyn had lost a significant amount of weight in 1961, and Berniece wanted to make sure she could fill out her clothing while lying in repose. All the items were delivered to the mortuary by nightfall on Monday.

Marilyn did indeed require a wig—and it was styled by none other than her hairdresser Agnes Flanagan. As it turns out, the falsies were not used. The woman dressing Marilyn at the mortuary inserted them into Marilyn's bra, but was unhappy with how they looked—she didn't look like Marilyn Monroe. After the autopsy, Marilyn's body had sustained some damage due to the procedure, and because of the Y-incision her chest was not as it had been in life. The woman preparing her was determined to make sure Marilyn Monroe looked like Marilyn Monroe. She removed the falsies from Marilyn's bra and stuffed it instead. Satisfied with her work, she said, "Now *that* looks like Marilyn Monroe!"

TUESDAY, AUGUST 7

Berniece and Inez went to Parisian Florist on Sunset Boulevard where Marilyn had been a customer during her life. They purchased three sets of floral arrangements for the funeral. Berniece ordered a blanket of flowers to cover the casket, as this is the traditional tribute from family members. They also ordered an arrangement in the shape of a cross from Inez and her husband Pat, and roses from Joe.

Following the flower selection, Berniece and Inez went back to the mortuary and received a tentative itinerary for the service; Lee Strasberg had been selected to give the eulogy after Joe's first choice, Carl Sandburg, had to decline due to poor health. A guestlist had already been started by Inez for the service; Berniece requested the additions of Grace's widower, Doc Goddard, and his new wife. She also added Sam and Enid Knebelkamp.

The guestlist was intentionally kept small. Stories of celebrities arriving at the service and being turned away are not true. There was a definite guestlist of invitees and if a celebrity had shown up only to be barred admission, the newspaper reporters, photographers, or fans with cameras would have captured the scene on film.

Only a select few were invited to Marilyn's service in an effort to keep things private, but reporters, photographers, and fans crowded around the cemetery.
Channel 5 Broadcasting / Photofest © Channel 5 Broadcasting

Joe, Berniece, and Inez released a joint statement to the press explaining their decision to keep things small:

> We could not in conscience ask one personality to attend without perhaps offending many, many others. And for this reason alone we have kept the number of persons to a minimum. Please, all of you, remember the gay, sweet Marilyn and say a prayer of farewell within the confines of your home or church.

It's also important to note that the chapel at Westwood Memorial is small and doesn't have space to seat a large number of people.

That same day, Marilyn's longtime makeup artist and close friend Allan "Whitey" Snyder made good on a promise that he would do Marilyn's makeup for her funeral. With the help of some alcohol hidden in a flask, he completed his mission. It was also his birthday.

When Marilyn's makeup, hair, and wardrobe were complete, pink tea roses were placed in her hands. They were a gift from Joe DiMaggio.

During the first two days Berniece was in town—Monday and Tuesday—she was completely overwhelmed by the intensity of the media coverage. Emotionally drained, grieving, and in need of spiritual guidance, she sought the help of a minister who might be able to assist her. She didn't know anyone in Los Angeles, so she looked through the phone book and finally called Rev. Floyd Darling of the First Southern Baptist Church in Santa Monica. Rev. Darling agreed to come over and ended up being the steadying presence Berniece needed to help get her through the next couple of days.

That night, Joe DiMaggio sat with Marilyn for hours; those who were close enough to overhear said he repeatedly told her, "I love you, I love you." At some point, Joe returned to the Miramar Hotel to rest, shower, and change.

WEDNESDAY, AUGUST 8

Berniece met with Joe and his son, Joe Jr., in the lobby of the Miramar Hotel on the morning of the service. In the book *My Sister Marilyn*, "Both Berniece and Joe are too distraught to engage in small talk, but Joe is cordial and kind, introducing Berniece to Joe, Jr., the courteous young man in uniform standing quietly at his father's side. The young man takes Berniece's hand and she looks up into a face whose features are a near mirror of Joe's grieved expression."

Westwood Memorial sent a limousine to pick up Berniece; at the cemetery, Rev. Darling greeted Berniece as she exited the vehicle and stayed by her side during the service.

Marilyn's service was set for 11 a.m. on Wednesday. As expected, hordes of onlookers, fans, photographers, and reporters surrounded Westwood Memorial that day. For crowd control, security was provided by local police, a private security company, and Twentieth Century-Fox.

Westwood's chapel was new in 1962, and Marilyn's was likely only the second service to be held there. Before everything began, Berniece went up to the open casket and whispered, "I love you" to her sister.

The service was conducted by Rev. A. J. Soldan, a Lutheran minister of the Village Church, a nondenominational congregation in Westwood, and the official pastor for the California Peace Officers' Association.

As planned, Lee Strasberg gave the eulogy. Judy Garland's version of "Over the Rainbow" was played for the attendees, as well as selections by Tchaikovsky and Gounod.

After the service, Marilyn's casket was closed and loaded into a 1962 Cadillac Funeral Coach for the short procession to her crypt. Mourners gathered in front of her crypt for final prayers, and then Marilyn was laid to rest.

The attendees included:

Joe DiMaggio (former husband and friend)
Joe DiMaggio Jr. (Joe's son)
Agnes Flanagan (hairdresser)
Aaron Frosch (lawyer)
Erwin ("Doc") and Anna Goddard (foster father and Grace Goddard's husband; Anna was his wife after Grace passed away)
Lotte Goslar (dance instructor)
Dr. Ralph Greenson and Family (psychiatrist)
Sydney Guilaroff (hairdresser)
Ann and Mary Karger (friends)
Rudy Kautzky (chauffeur)
Enid and Sam Knebelkamp (foster parents)
Inez and Pat Melson (business manager and her husband)
Berniece Miracle (half sister)
Eunice Murray (housekeeper)
Pat Newcomb (publicist)
Pearl Porterfield (hairdresser; also Jean Harlow's hairdresser)
May Reis (secretary)
Milton Rudin (lawyer)
Ralph Roberts (friend and masseuse)
Allan "Whitey" Snyder (makeup artist; his wife and daughter also attended)
George Solotaire (Joe DiMaggio's best friend and friend of Marilyn)

Lee and Paula Strasberg (acting coaches)
Florence Thomas (maid)

Westwood Memorial was a modest, small cemetery when Marilyn was placed there in 1962. Since her interment, it has become a popular cemetery for celebrities, entertainment executives, and the wealthy.

Two of Marilyn's foster mothers, Grace Goddard and Aunt Ana Lower, were already laid to rest at Westwood. Westwood was likely selected because Grace and Ana helped raise Marilyn, and it was a way to place her with the closest thing she had to mother figures. A third foster mother, Enid Knebelkamp, was also placed in the family plot after she passed away in 1974.

Every year on August 5 the Marilyn Remembered Fan Club holds a memorial in the chapel where Marilyn's service took place in 1962. The service includes speakers, "Over the Rainbow" by Judy Garland, and a recording of Lee Strasberg delivering his eulogy.

Joe DiMaggio and his son Joe DiMaggio, Jr. at Marilyn's funeral on August 8, 1962.
Channel 5 Broadcasting / Photofest © Channel 5 Broadcasting

A photo of Marilyn's crypt today.
Elisa Jordan

· 36 ·

Health, Doctors, and Medical

*T*hroughout her lifetime, Marilyn was prone to several medical ailments. For that reason, medical bills would consistently be one of her biggest expenses.

Beginning in adolescence, Marilyn developed painful menstrual cramps, which was later diagnosed as endometriosis.

During a normal menstrual cycle, the lining of the uterus thickens in anticipation of pregnancy. When a woman's egg is not fertilized, the uterus sheds the inner lining of blood, mucous, and tissue through the vagina.

For a woman with endometriosis, tissue grows outside the uterus so when it is time to shed the lining, instead of the normal process it becomes trapped. The results are severe pain, bleeding between periods, distended belly (sometimes colloquially called "endo belly" these days), scar tissue in the fallopian tubes and—for Marilyn, the most devastating of all—extreme difficulty conceiving a child.

Marilyn had several surgical procedures to relieve the symptoms of endometriosis and help increase her chances of conceiving a child. This is a stark contrast to rumors she had multiple abortions. Marilyn's desire to start a family was such that she declined the recommended solution of having a hysterectomy. Today, there are much better treatments for women living with endometriosis, including improved fertility technology, although hysterectomies are still frequently performed.

Approximately one in ten women are diagnosed with the condition, making it a common ailment. As with a lot of people diagnosed with chronic, painful illnesses and women experiencing difficulty conceiving, depression can also become a factor. Such was the case with Marilyn, but she also had a genetic predisposition to the condition. Marilyn battled depression and anxiety for much of her life, likely a combination of difficult childhood circumstances and heredity.

From the mid-1950s until the end of her life, Marilyn saw psychoanalysts regularly. She began going initially as part of her studies at the Actors Studio, and continued both in the hopes of improving her acting and finding relief from depression and anxiety. Treatment at the time included barbiturates prescribed by a doctor. Beginning in 1960, she got massages multiple times per week from Ralph Roberts to help her sleep better. By the last year of her life, she was seeing her psychiatrist almost daily, sometimes twice a day.

Finally, from an early age Marilyn was prone to colds, sinus infections, and bronchial illnesses and there were ongoing struggles with her health. The orphanage she lived at during childhood reported her tendency to catch colds.

DR. HERMAN BEERMAN

Dr. Beerman delivered Norma Jeane on June 1, 1926.

Norma Jeane was born at Los Angeles General Hospital on June 1, 1926, in the charity ward. The old maternity building has since been torn down and what was once the administrative building remains. It now houses the Los Angeles County Medical Examiners Office. Elisa Jordan

DR. MARCUS RABWIN

Dr. Rabwin assisted Dr. Leon Krohn during Marilyn's appendectomy in 1952.

DR. LEON KROHN

469 North Roxbury Drive, Beverly Hills

Dr. Krohn was Marilyn's longtime gynecologist on the West Coast. He graduated from Northwestern University Medical School in Chicago in 1930 and became licensed in the state of California in 1937. Dr. Krohn maintained a private practice in Beverly Hills and was associated with Cedars of Lebanon Hospital, where he worked his way up to the Chief of the Gynecology Department.

Dr. Krohn removed Marilyn's appendix in 1952 and became a trusted confidant for both medical and personal matters, especially as she struggled with infertility. Dr. Krohn was present at the DiMaggio-Monroe house on Palm Drive in Beverly Hills in October 1954 when the couple announced their separation to the press. Joe DiMaggio stayed at Dr. Krohn's house after moving out of the home he shared with Marilyn.

The following month, on November 7, Dr. Krohn performed a gynecological surgery on Marilyn related to chronic endometriosis at Cedars of Lebanon Hospital.

Not long after her surgery, Marilyn left California to pursue the next phase of her life in New York. Marilyn saw other gynecologists for routine checkups, infertility, and endometriosis treatment, but Dr. Krohn remained her West Coast doctor. He attended to her, for instance, when she was pregnant and filming *Some Like It Hot* in California. During this time, his office was located in Beverly Hills at 469 North Roxbury Drive, a neighborhood now referred to as "the Platinum Triangle."

When Marilyn returned to Los Angeles in 1961, Dr. Krohn again tended to her. He had recently moved to an office just a couple of blocks away from his previous one at 9735 Wilshire Boulevard, still in the Platinum Triangle.

In May 1961, Dr. Krohn performed another surgery on Marilyn related to endometriosis at Cedars of Lebanon Hospital, where he had previously operated on her.

Dr. Krohn refuted the rumors Marilyn had abortions and said she never had one.

DR. MICHAEL GURDIN

416 North Bedford Drive, Beverly Hills
Marilyn visited Dr. Michael Gurdin in July 1958 to discuss the mild flatness that had developed under her chin after her bovin cartilage implant had been absorbed. In her records, he wrote, "I cannot palpate any cartilage subcutaneously." In 1962, Marilyn returned for a possible broken nose. She told Dr. Gurdin she fell in the shower, although some believe she was covering another story. The injury caused her to miss a meeting with Twentieth Century-Fox, and she was officially fired the following day.

DR. C. RUSSELL ANDERSON

416 North Bedford Drive
Marilyn's dermatologist was in the same building as Dr. Gurdin, the plastic surgeon.

DR. MARIANNE KRIS

Dr. Marianne Kris was a pioneering psychoanalyst and teacher from Vienna, Austria. She was born on May 27, 1900, to a pediatrician doctor, who was a friend of Sigmund Freud. Dr. Kris's childhood exposure to the work of her father and Freud appears to have shaped her life and career as an adult. She became a psychoanalyst and specialized in children and family matters.

From 1925 to 1927, she had psychoanalytic training in Berlin with Franz Alexander. With her husband, Ernst Kris, she joined the Vienna Psychoanalytic Society in 1928. Anna Freud was a trusted friend and close collaborator.

Dr. Kris left Vienna in 1938 for London, where she joined the British Psycho-Analytical Society before finally settling in New York. In 1944, she became a member of the New York Psychoanalytic Society. She worked as an analyst but also established herself as a respected teacher. In addition to training analysts for the complexities of treating children, she also worked with social workers and schoolteachers for training nonphysicians.

In 1957, Marilyn began seeing Dr. Kris, who had an office in the building where the Strasbergs lived. When Marilyn finished *The Misfits* and was struggling with her physical and mental health, Dr. Kris recommended Marilyn check into a hospital for rest and treatment. Marilyn agreed, but unknown to her, Dr. Kris checked her into the Payne Whitney Psychiatric Clinic, a lockdown facility for seriously disturbed patients.

Payne Whitney was not what Marilyn expected, nor was it the appropriate treatment for her. Ralph Roberts recalls picking Marilyn up at Payne Whitney, a ride home in which Dr. Kris was also present. During the drive,

Marilyn released an angry tirade at her doctor, and it became very clear that Marilyn would never return to Dr. Kris (although some people erroneously say Marilyn continued to see Dr. Kris). According to Ralph Roberts, after dropping off Marilyn at home, Dr. Kris reportedly said, "I did a terrible thing. I didn't mean to, but I did a terrible, terrible thing."

Despite this, Dr. Kris was named in Marilyn's will. The will had been drawn up in January 1961, one month before Marilyn's stay at Payne Whitney. According to Marilyn's half-sister, Berniece, Marilyn was unhappy with her will and had plans to change it at the time of her death. This story has merit because a telegram from Marilyn to Joe DiMaggio dated September 22, 1961, reads:

> Dear dad darling airplane developed engine trouble plus all oil ran out of same plane so we had to turn back and land back in LA. Leaving again on another plane at 5 p.m. arrive New York 1pm. When plane was in trouble I thought about two things you and changing my will. Love you I think, more than ever.
> Mrs. Norman

Mrs. Norman was one of Marilyn's aliases when trying to protect her privacy.

Marilyn never did get around to changing her will, so Marianne Kris received money "to be used by her for the furtherance of the work of such psychiatric institutions or groups as she shall elect," the will read.

Remembering Marilyn's love for children, Dr. Kris gave that money to a child therapy center at the London Tavistock Center Clinic to fund the Monroe Young Family Centre, which still exists. It is, perhaps, the one bright spot of the entire story.

DR. HILLIARD DUBROW

Dr. Dubrow attended to Marilyn on August 1, 1957, when she was rushed by ambulance to the hospital for a miscarriage. It was discovered the fetus, about five to six weeks along, was an ectopic pregnancy—meaning the baby was developing in the fallopian tube and not the uterus. This is a complication for women with endometriosis, as scar tissue builds up in the fallopian tubes. When an ectopic pregnancy occurs, the fetus is unable to survive and surgery is required. It is a medical emergency and potentially life threatening for the mother. Dr. Dubrow performed the procedure and assured Marilyn it was safe to try for another baby. She left the hospital on August 10.

Dr. Dubrow had a distinguished career. He graduated from Brown University in 1932 and Bellevue Hospital Medicine School in 1936. He had once served as director of gynecology at Doctors Hospital (later called Beth Israel North), was an attending obstetrician-gynecologist at Lenox Hill Hospital, and also maintained a private practice. From 1980 to 1990, Dr. Dubrow was a clinical associate professor of obstetrics and gynecology at the New York Medical College. He was a clinical professor of obstetrics and gynecology at the Cornell Medical College from 1982 to 1988.

DR. OSCAR STEINBERG

Dr. Steinberg was a gynecologist who cared for Marilyn when she lost a baby in late 1958, not long after wrapping production on *Some Like It Hot*. Her misfortune was announced to the press in December. Dr. Steinberg also performed a surgery on Marilyn in 1959 to try to unblock her fallopian tubes, a complication of endometriosis.

DR. MORTIMER RODGERS

Dr. Rodgers performed a corrective genealogical surgery on Marilyn on June 23, 1959, at Lenox Hill Hospital. Dr. Rodgers was a highly respected doctor in his field. He served as director of gynecology obstetrics at Lenox Hill from 1955 to 1962 and was president of the hospital's medical board for the 1959–1960 term.

DR. NATHAN HEADLEY

After working through freezing temperatures while filming *Bus Stop*, Dr. Headley treated Marilyn for bronchitis and a viral infection.

DR. ROBERT ROSENFELD

Marilyn came down with an illness while filming *There's No Business Like Show Business* in 1954, which Dr. Rosenfeld treated.

DR. LEE SIEGEL

Dr. Siegel was an internist for Twentieth Century-Fox from 1955 to 1971, a position enabling him to become the personal physician for many of the studio's top talent, Marilyn included. During the filming of *The Seven Year Itch*, Dr. Siegel treated Marilyn for a lung infection and prescribed sleeping pills as her marriage to Joe DiMaggio crumbled in 1954. He later treated her for bronchitis while she filmed *Bus Stop* in 1956 and again in 1962 when she battled sinusitis during *Something's Got to Give*. In total, Dr. Siegel practiced medicine in Los Angeles for fifty-five years.

DR. MARGARET HERZ HOHENBERG

After Marilyn's move to New York in 1955, she entered psychoanalysis. Lee Strasberg recommended students undergo analysis to better understand their emotions, which in turn would lead to better performances. Marilyn's childhood was another factor in seeking out therapy. The trauma experienced in her youth led to attachment issues, anxiety, and depression. In everyday life, these manifested in showing up late, inability to maintain long-term relationships, fear of abandonment, and need for approval. In February 1955, Marilyn began seeing Dr. Margaret Herz Hohenberg, who also treated Milton Greene.

Dr. Hohenberg was originally from Hungary and had studied at the University of Vienna, in Budapest, Prague, and Israel. In the 1930s, she moved to London and then the United States. When Marilyn became her patient, Dr. Hohenberg maintained a medical practice in her home, located at 155 East 93rd Street on the Upper East Side of Manhattan in the Carnegie Hill neighborhood. Marilyn had sessions three to five times per week, depending on her class schedule at the Actors Studio.

After Marilyn left for England during the summer of 1956 to film *The Prince and the Showgirl*, it became clear she needed assistance. Flight records indicate Dr. Hohenberg left for England on August 28 to attend to her patient.

After Marilyn's partnership with Milton Greene dissolved, so, too, did her relationship with Dr. Hohenberg. In a letter dated April 2, 1957, Dr. Hohenberg wrote to Marilyn:

Dear Marilyn:
I am sending you your file for the sessions you had during March.
I hope you are getting along in your new analysis, yet I want to repeat what I said last time over the phone: Whenever and for whatever reason you may want to see me again—you will be always welcome.
With kind regards,
Margaret Hohenberg

As it turns out, Marilyn did seek out Dr. Hohenberg again in 1962. In a medical bill dated August 1, 1962, Marilyn was charged $420 for services over the phone in the months of June and July. The balance from May was also $420, bringing the grand total up to $840.

This indicates that Marilyn was regularly having sessions with Dr. Hohenberg via phone in the last months of her life while at the same time continuing to see Dr. Ralph Greenson in person on an almost daily basis.

DR. BERNARD BERGLASS

Originally from Poland, Dr. Berglass arrived in the United States in 1938 and practiced medicine in New York. He was one of Marilyn's physicians and performed a surgical procedure on her at the time of her ectopic pregnancy in 1957. His office was located at 57 East 88th Street in Manhattan.

DR. PHILLIP BERNARD

After Marilyn moved to New York in 1955, Dr. Bernard worked as her physician. He wrote prescriptions for sedatives and barbiturates, which was a common practice at the time.

DR. HYMAN ENGELBERG

Born in New York City, Hyman Engelberg graduated from Cornell University with his bachelor's and medical degrees at the young age of twenty-two. He worked as a doctor in World War II, then completed his residency at Cedars of Lebanon Hospital in Los Angeles after the war. He went into private practice in Beverly Hills, where he became acquainted with psychiatrist Dr. Ralph Greenson.

Dr. Engelberg became Marilyn's personal physician toward the end of her life. He worked closely with Dr. Greenson and there have been varying reports about how the doctors were handling Marilyn's prescription drug addiction. It's generally believed Greenson was trying to ween Marilyn off, and Dr. Engelberg continued to prescribe medications for her.

In an interview from the 1990s, Engelberg went on record as saying Marilyn had bipolar disorder (then called manic depression), a condition characterized by extreme mood swings. This is the only mental health diagnosis made public from any of her doctors. Historians have only his word to go on, but the medications she was taking at the end of her life were the kind prescribed for anxiety and depression. Such medications are now considered dangerous for their addictive qualities, and have long since been discontinued.

Treatments for depression and anxiety (and bipolar disorder) have improved considerably since Marilyn sought help. Today antidepressants, medications targeting specific conditions, trauma therapy, and talk therapy have all made major strides in treating mental health.

In the last months of her life, Engelberg gave Marilyn "vitamin shots," which were a type of amphetamines; she received one just a few days before she died. It was enough time for her skin to heal, as no needle marks were found on Marilyn's body during the autopsy.

After Greenson was called to Marilyn's house on August 5, 1962, Engelberg rushed over and pronounced her dead. In the aftermath of

Marilyn's death, investigators questioned Engelberg about the prescriptions he had written for Marilyn.

> Investigator: There were apparently quite a volume of pills that were discovered at her death, at her bedside.
> Engelberg: Yes.
> Investigator: Were they all prescribed by you?
> Engelberg: No. Only one had been prescribed by me. I had prescribed Nembutal to help her sleep, but there certainly were lots of other pills I had not prescribed.
> Investigator: Chloral hydrate specifically?
> Engelberg: I knew nothing about any chloral hydrate. I never used chloral hydrate.
> Investigator: So you wrote her a prescription for Nembutal only?
> Engelberg: That was it. It's the only prescription I wrote for sedatives.

In the decades following Marilyn's death, the prescriptions Engelberg had written for Marilyn surfaced and he had indeed prescribed chloral hydrate. In today's world, such information would have been found almost immediately and Engelberg would have been investigated for medical malpractice (at the very least), as he had not only lied to investigators but it was his prescriptions—Nembutal and chloral hydrate combined—that killed Marilyn. In addition to Nembutal and chloral hydrate, he prescribed Seconal, Tuinal and Valmid to help Marilyn sleep. In the ninety days leading up to Marilyn's death, Engelberg prescribed somewhere between eight hundred and nine hundred pills. Among the prescriptions were 25 Nembutal on July 31 and then a refill on August 3, totaling 50. After Marilyn's death, he told authorities Dr. Siegel from Fox had prescribed Nembutal on August 3.

It's worth noting that at the time of Marilyn's death, Engelberg was going through a difficult time personally and dealing with a divorce, which many believe left him distracted when it came to caring for Marilyn's health.

RALPH GREENSON

During the last couple years of Marilyn's life, Dr. Ralph Greenson had a profound influence on her. He was no stranger to celebrity patients, which included Marilyn's own friend Frank Sinatra. In an only-in-Hollywood scenario, Ralph Greenson was the inspiration for the novel *Captain Newman, M.D.*, the 1961 book by his friend Leo Rosten. The book was loosely based on Greenson's experiences in World War II, and was adapted into a movie in 1963 starring Gregory Peck as the doctor.

Born Romeo Samuel Greenschpoon in 1911 in Brooklyn, New York, the man later known as Ralph Greenson had a twin sister, Juliet, who grew up to be a pianist. He earned his undergraduate degree from Columbia University in New York before attending medical school in Switzerland. In Switzerland, he met his future wife, Hildi, and underwent analysis by Wilhelm Stekel, who was known as one of Sigmund Freud's "most distinguished pupils." (A further connection to Freud was his close professional relationship to Anna Freud, an analyst herself and youngest daughter of Sigmund Freud.)

Greenson served in World War II and later built a reputation for working with war veterans suffering from what is now called post-traumatic stress disorder, or PTSD. Ralph Greenson built a medical practice in California, working with private clients and serving as a clinical professor of psychiatry at the UCLA School of Medicine. Greenson believed in a balanced medical practice of analysis and medication. He was known as a prolific researcher and writer on psychology.

It's a little unclear how Greenson became Marilyn's doctor, but his approach with her was a little unorthodox, especially by today's standards. He invited Marilyn into his home so she could observe a normal family, almost as though he were trying to re-parent her into being a healthy adult. Marilyn became like an extended member of the Greenson family, coming over for family dinners, holidays, and social gatherings.

In the final year of her life, she had appointments with Greenson almost daily, sometimes more than once a day. Meanwhile, Greenson's brother-in-law Milton Rudin became her attorney; his colleague Dr. Engelberg became her physician; friend Henry Weinstein became a producer on *Something's Got to Give*; and he pushed Marilyn to hire Mrs. Murray as her companion.

Much to Marilyn's horror, in October 1961, Greenson insisted Ralph Roberts, her friend and masseuse, go home to New York because she was becoming too dependent on him. Ralph was with Marilyn almost constantly—he chauffeured her to doctor appointments every day, drove her on errands, gave her massages so she could sleep at night, and accompanied her to social gatherings. He was heartbroken when he was asked to leave, but left Los Angeles and flew back to New York as requested.

"Three nights later the phone rang," Ralph wrote in his unfished memoir. "A subdued voice whispered: 'Rafe [Marilyn's name for him], I am sorry. More sorry than I think I have ever been. The look on your face has haunted me. It has all been a dreadful nightmare. Dr. Greenson was emphatic that you return to New York. I fought it all during those sessions. He said you were what he called a "leak" in the analysis. Having you around was dissipating his effectiveness. I told him you never countered any of his advice—in fact, you were most supportive. However, I do want to do anything to get out of this quagmire. He didn't forbid my calling you. It isn't the same. Will you go along with me?'

"I choked out, 'Yes. You know that.'"

With Ralph Roberts now on the East Coast, Mrs. Murray filled many of the duties he had once done for her.

Greenson encouraged Marilyn to purchase her own home as a way to build a foundation for herself. She selected a Mexican-style home similar to the Greenson home, just minutes away. Mrs. Murray, naturally, was a big part of the process. She helped Marilyn look for the house, accompanied Marilyn to Mexico to purchase authentic furnishings and helped decorate.

Dr. Ralph Greenson was Marilyn's final psychiatrist and known for working with high-profile people.
Channel 5 Broadcasting / Photofest © Channel 5 Broadcasting

After Marilyn's trauma from placement in Payne Whitney, Greenson decided against hospitalization and opted instead to create a type of semi-hospitalization for Marilyn as an outpatient. This included seeing her every day, inviting her over to his house, and asking Mrs. Murray to spend the night when he believed Marilyn needed someone to keep an eye on her (even though Eunice Murray was not a trained nurse or medical professional).

Opinions on Greenson tend to be mixed. Some see him as a doctor doing the best he could for his patient with the tools available to him at the time. Antidepressants were not yet available to help alleviate symptoms and psychoanalysis has since fallen by the wayside in favor of more helpful therapy. Others see him as someone who violated professional boundaries and as an opportunist who was enamored with the idea of treating celebrities. With Greenson so deeply involved in both her personal and professional life, it's difficult to ascertain how his treatment was helping Marilyn become more independent or cope with her childhood traumas.

Since Marilyn had begun analysis in the mid-1950s, it appeared that her pain only increased. Her sleep was disrupted, her depression deepened, and a pill addiction—prescribed by doctors—worsened, resulting in troubled relationships and difficult behavior on and off movie sets. While Greenson cannot be held accountable for the doctors who treated Marilyn before him, she was not showing improvement under his care. Those close to Marilyn at the time began suspecting she was growing distrustful of Greenson.

Greenson and Engelberg worked in concert to help her, or at least tried to, but it appears they didn't always communicate well with one another. When Marilyn died, Greenson discovered Engelberg had written prescriptions he didn't know about. On Marilyn's nightstand an empty bottle for twenty-five one-hundred-milligram Nembutal pills dated August 3 from Engelberg was found, as were ten pills remaining from a bottle of fifty five-hundred-milligram chloral hydrate pills from Greenson on July 25 and refilled on July 31.

In a letter Greenson wrote to Marianne Kris, he confided, "I was her therapist, the good father who would not disappoint her and who would bring her insights, and if not insights, just kindness. I had become the most important person in her life. I also felt guilty that I put a burden on my own family. But there was something very lovable about this girl and we all cared about her and she could be delightful."

"Marilyn was the fairest game of all for such manipulation: impressed by learned and paternal men who seemed to offer protection; thrice divorced and uncertain of her own worth, acceptability, talent and capacity for love; about to have her own home for the first time—she mutely accepted what Greenson made of himself for her: the all-providing savior figure every heathy and unneurotic therapist dreads to become," writes Donald Spoto in *Marilyn Monroe: The Biography.* "Everything that happened between Monroe and Greenson from that spring to her death suggests a perilous obsession. 'She was a poor creature I tried to help,' he said later. 'and I ended up hurting her.' These were perhaps the truest words he could have chosen to summarize their association."

HOSPITALS

Throughout her life, Marilyn was prone to illness, most notably severe endometriosis, which required hospitalization on multiple occasions. She was also susceptible to colds, viral and sinus infections, and depression, a trait that ran in her family. Here are some hospitals associated with Marilyn and her family members.

Patton State Hospital | 3102 Highland Avenue, Patton, California
Otis Elmer Monroe, Marilyn's maternal grandfather, died at Patton State Hospital on July 22, 1909, of "general paresis," or severe dementia. He was forty-three. His wife Della told their children, Gladys and Marion, their father had gone crazy. Otis's illness, however, was not hereditary. The cause of his illness was bejel, or endemic syphilis, which was caused by the unsanitary living conditions while working for the railroad in Mexico.

Norwalk State Hospital | 11401 Bloomfield Avenue, Norwalk
Marilyn's maternal grandmother, Della Mae Monroe, died at Norwalk State Hospital on August 23, 1927, from myocarditis while in a manic depressive psychosis. In the mid-1930s, Marilyn's mother Gladys was also placed here for her mental illness, schizophrenia.

Los Angeles General Hospital | 1100 Mission Road, Los Angeles
Gladys Monroe Baker Mortenson gave birth to her third child, a daughter named Norma Jeane Mortenson, on Tuesday, June 1, 1926, at 9:30 a.m. The delivery took place at Los Angeles General Hospital in the charity ward. The attending physician was Dr. Herman Beerman.

Over the years, Los Angeles General Hospital was repurposed by the city and turned into the Los Angeles County Medical Coroner's Office. The structure was severely damaged in the 1994 earthquake and parts of the building, including the old maternity ward, were torn down. The former administration building, however, was saved and still stands after considerable restoration and retrofitting. Although the building is no longer a hospital, the top of the front steps still read "Los Angeles General Hospital" on the tiles.

Cedar Lodge Convalescent Hospital
2030 Griffith Park Boulevard, Los Angeles
Santa Monica Rest Home for Ladies
2828 Pico Boulevard, Los Angeles
Marilyn's mother Gladys was a patient at both Cedar Lodge and Santa Monica Rest Home for Ladies after she was found crouching under a staircase at home in January 1934.

Los Angeles General Hospital | 1200 State Street, Los Angeles
Not to be confused with the hospital where Norma Jeane was born, this new Los Angeles General Hospital opened in 1933. Gladys was transferred here before moving on to Norwalk State Hospital in the mid-1930s.

Norwalk State Hospital | 11401 Bloomfield Avenue, Norwalk
In the mid-1930s, Gladys was placed in a state hospital for her mental illness. It was familiar to her because her mother, Della, died here in 1927.

Cedars of Lebanon Hospital | 4833 Fountain Avenue, Los Angeles
Originally opened in 1930, Cedars of Lebanon was a centrally located hospital in the heart of Hollywood. Marilyn had a long association with Cedars of Lebanon, beginning with visiting Johnny Hyde in 1950 during the heart failure that would ultimately lead to his death.

Marilyn herself also stayed here on many occasions for various ailments.

March 1, 1952: After complaining of severe stomach pains on the set of *Monkey Business*, Marilyn visited a doctor at Cedars of Lebanon. Her extreme pain turned out to be appendicitis. Director Howard Hawks would not permit her to have an appendectomy until the shooting was finished, so her surgery was delayed.

April 28, 1952: With filming on *Monkey Business* complete, she checked into the hospital and had her appendix removed.

April 14, 1953: She had a gynecological surgery performed, most likely having something to do with her endometriosis.

November 7, 1954: Marilyn had a gynecological procedure performed due to her endometriosis. Although separated from Joe DiMaggio, he was seen coming and going during visits to his newly estranged wife. Clark and Kay Gable, who had recently met Marilyn at *The Seven Year Itch* wrap party, sent Marilyn flowers during her stay in the hospital. There is famous news footage of Marilyn trying to hide her face from a crush of paparazzi while leaving Cedars of Lebanon after this stay. Marilyn, recovering from her procedure and without her hair styled and makeup on, tries to protect her privacy by pulling her coat lapel over her face and turning away from the cameras toward a corridor wall.

September 12, 1958: During the filming of *Some Like It Hot*, Marilyn checked into Cedars for exhaustion. Some people, however, believed the stay was for a drug overdose.

May 26, 1961: Another gynecological surgery related to Marilyn's endometriosis.

July 20, 1962: Marilyn had a gynecological surgery related to her endometriosis. In later years, this stay will give rise to the rumor that Marilyn had an abortion and the father was likely one of the Kennedy brothers. Marilyn, however, had not been pregnant since 1958.

In 1961, Cedars of Lebanon began the process of merging with another hospital, Mt. Sinai, to become Cedars-Sinai. Construction on a new hospital complex began in Beverly Hills in 1972 and opened to the public in 1976. In 1977, the Church of Scientology purchased the now-empty Cedars of Lebanon hospital building and refurbished it. The exterior has been painted blue and now has a Scientology sign affixed to the front, but otherwise looks mostly the same as it did while still a hospital.

Saint Vincent's Hospital | 2131 W 3rd Street, Los Angeles

During the production of *Bus Stop*, Marilyn came down with a serious viral infection that required a stay at this hospital from April 5–9, 1956. Shortly thereafter, a relapse required her to stay off the set from April 16–24.

Lenox Hill Hospital | 100 E 77th Street, New York

Dr. Mortimer Rodgers performed corrective gynecological surgery on Marilyn on June 23, 1959, at Lenox Hill Hospital.

Westside Hospital | 910 S Fairfax Avenue, Los Angeles

During the production of *The Misfits*, Marilyn suffered a breakdown in the Nevada heat. She left the desert to check into this private hospital on August 27, 1960, to recover and detox from prescription pills. According to Ralph Roberts, an emotional breakdown and pill habit were not the entire story. When Marilyn arrived at the hospital, she was also diagnosed with heat exhaustion and continuing complications from endometriosis. She returned to the set on September 5.

Payne Whitney Psychiatric Clinic | 525 E 68th Street, New York

When her psychoanalyst, Dr. Marianne Kris, recommended rest and recuperation in early 1961, Marilyn agreed. It was a dark time for Marilyn: her third marriage had just ended in divorce; reviews of her latest movie, *The Misfits*, were less than stellar; she believed Kay Gable blamed her for Clark Gable's fatal heart attack; she had miscarried more than once; she had struggled with fertility and painful endometriosis; she had trouble sleeping; and the medications doctors prescribed had become a habit. Many believe Dr. Kris feared her patient might be suicidal.

On February 5, 1961, Dr. Kris checked Marilyn into the Payne Whitney Psychiatric Clinic (now the Weill Cornell Medical College) with the promise she would rest and heal in private. Marilyn used the name Faye Miller as a precaution to protect the privacy she craved.

To Marilyn's surprise—and horror—she found herself in a lockdown psychiatric ward for seriously disturbed patients. Marilyn, deeply depressed though she was, hardly belonged in a padded cell.

Furthermore, finding herself in a psychiatric ward for severe mental illness exacerbated Marilyn's deepest fear: that she would go crazy like her mother. Gladys had tried to live independently a few times, but she was unable to care for herself. Marilyn, on the other hand, functioned quite well in the world, despite her depression. Instead of helping Marilyn, her stay at Payne Whitney backfired.

Desperate to discharge herself, she began trying to send notes outside to plead for help. At one point, she wrote, "I'm locked up with these poor nutty people. I'm sure to end up a nut, too, if I stay in this nightmare. Please help me."

Marilyn was smart enough to understand she needed help but well enough to know she didn't need to be incarcerated in a lockdown psychiatric hospital.

On February 8, the Strasbergs received a letter from Marilyn begging for help in getting her out, but they were unable to assist.

Marilyn managed to get a message to the one person she knew would—and could—help: Joe DiMaggio. Immediately, DiMaggio dropped everything and flew to New York. Some unfortunate person at Payne Whitney had to endure the irate DiMaggio as he thunderously demanded to release Marilyn into his custody or he would take apart the clinic "brick by brick" to retrieve her. Not surprisingly, they released her.

Columbia Presbyterian | 630 W 168th Street, New York

After the fiasco of Payne-Whitney, Joe DiMaggio arranged for Marilyn to check into Columbia University Presbyterian Medical Center, where she stayed from February 11 to March 5, 1961. Publicist John Springer told reporters, "She is here for a complete physical check-up. She's had a hell of a year. She had been exhausted, really beat down. More than anything else, this was just meant for her to go in and have a chance to rest and recuperate a little. It has been blown up all out of proportion."

Joe DiMaggio visited every day and upon checking herself out, accompanied him to Florida for Yankees spring training and then to a resort in Florida. There, Marilyn was able to relax and get away from the pressures of Hollywood and New York with Joe by her side.

Manhattan Polyclinic Hospital | 341-351 W 50th Street, New York

Marilyn stayed at this hospital twice. The first time was in December 1958 following a miscarriage. She was approximately four to five months along, and the doctors were able to determine the fetus had been a boy. This was Marilyn's final pregnancy.

She checked in again on June 28, 1961, and was diagnosed with cholangitis. She had surgery the following day to remove her gallbladder. She checked out on July 11.

· 37 ·

Inner Circle

$\mathcal{M}$arilyn wasn't known for having a large circle of friends. Many of the people closest to her were either employees or in some way business associates. Even Hedda Rosten, who was a personal friend, was hired at one point to help Marilyn in a secretarial or assistant type role. Much of this has to do with trust—Marilyn was fiercely protective of her privacy and as a person who had bounced around in foster homes as a child, she had difficulty connecting with people. She was never the type to go out for lunch and shopping in the afternoon with other women. Much of her adult life centered around her work, in one way or another.

In fairness to Marilyn, it's not so unusual for high-level celebrities to surround themselves with people who work for them or to keep their social circles small. Pulling back the layers of a celebrity's life is like peering into an ecosystem that keeps lives and careers moving at an almost unnatural pace. A select group that can be relied upon becomes invaluable. As is usually the case, not everyone was worthy of the trust Marilyn placed in them, but others were loyal to her even after she died.

INEZ MELSON

Of Marilyn's employees and close friends, Inez Melson had one of the longest associations with her. Inez had an accounting background and began working with Marilyn in 1951 or 1952. Soon, Inez was deeply involved in Marilyn's life and functioning similarly to a personal assistant. In a letter dated November 2, 1953, Marilyn informed executives in writing that Inez was now officially her business manager.

Gentlemen,

Please be advised that I have made arrangements with Mrs. Inez C. Melson whose address is 9128 Sunset Blvd., Los Angeles 46, to take over the management of my affairs.

All salary due me will continue to be picked up by my agent. Please direct all statements, correspondence, etc. concerning my affairs to me in care of Mrs. Melson.

Very truly yours,

Marilyn Monroe

Marilyn granted power of attorney of her mother to Inez, who visited the elderly woman on Marilyn's behalf for years. Inez paid Gladys's bills at Rockhaven Sanitarium and took her on shopping trips and lunches. The arrangement made Inez, in a roundabout way, part of the family, at least in a legal sense. At any rate, she was deeply involved in Marilyn's world and even testified in the Monroe-DiMaggio divorce case in 1954.

When Marilyn died in 1962, Inez was one of three people to make arrangements for the funeral—the other two being Joe DiMaggio and Marilyn's half sister, Berniece Miracle. Inez represented Gladys, Marilyn's next-of-kin, but was also the person most familiar with the inner workings of Marilyn's life and finances.

Inez's work continued following Marilyn's death. She spent years sorting out Marilyn's finances, helping document her belongings, sorting through legalities, itemizing outstanding bills, and caring for Gladys. It was not an easy job. Taxes and bills ate up the estate immediately after Marilyn died, leaving no money. The probate process took years.

Inez passed away in 1985. She had seen through the drawn-out process of Marilyn's will, which lasted until the 1970s. Marilyn's estate was finally able to pay out Marilyn's bequests about a decade after her death. Inez continued to serve as Gladys's guardian until the mid-1960s, when Berniece moved her mother to Florida where she lived.

But that is not the end of Inez Melson's connection with Marilyn Monroe. Controversy surfaced years later when Inez's nephew, Mill Conroy, began working on a book consisting of the contents of Marilyn's private file cabinets, which had been in the possession of Inez, and then her heirs. Why did Inez keep the file cabinets?

In a letter to Joe DiMaggio dated September 6, 1962, Inez expresses suspicions about the will. Specifically, she mentions attorney Aaron Frosch and his secretary, and the Strasbergs, who are not directly named in her letter.

In the letter, she mentions to Joe,

On January 14th, 1961, the date on which our baby purportedly executed her will, she had car rental charges as follows:

4½ hours—8:45—1:15 (From Paul A. Reilly, Inc.

2½ hours—4:45—7:15 (528 E. 73rd Street, N.Y. 21

I have a reason for wanting to know if the car was used and if so, where did she go but if I write directly, it might create a situation. Do you know anyone who could obtain this information quietly? Those hours appear on the bill and I know the rental agency would have a record of where she went. I know it sounds like a "Perry Mason" television script but I am (between thee and me) very suspicious about that will and my only interest lies in the protection of future care of Mrs. Eley [Gladys]. If you can help me, fine—if not, I will see what I can do elsewhere since I appreciate how you feel.

I have pretty well constructed what happened on that day and I find it impossible to see why Mr. Frosch had to be a witness along with his secretary. I know that you will understand how very discreet I must be about this.

It's difficult to say, but it is possible Inez's concerns had some merit. Berniece wrote in her book that Marilyn resented her will and felt pressured to sign it before going into Payne Whitney. "They tried to rush me into signing a will just before I went into the hospital," she told Berniece. "They kept insisting. . . . My secretary and my attorney stuck a will under my face to sign as I was going out the door. It was already made. I was furious! I told them I was not going to sign it! I stood and argued."

The secretary Marilyn referenced might be Aaron Frosch's secretary; it was Frosch and his secretary Louise White who signed the will as witnesses. Berniece later said she was "haunted" by the fact that Marilyn was so angry about her will, and that it was never changed.

Inez had itemized Marilyn's estate but shipped at least one of Marilyn's file cabinets to her home. When some of Marilyn's items were auctioned off after her death, another filing cabinet was purchased under the name Walter Davis—Inez Melson's nephew.

The cabinets were kept at Inez's home until she died in 1985, at which time ownership transferred to her sister-in-law Ruth Conroy. The cabinets stayed in Ruth's possession until she died in 2001 when her son Mill Conroy inherited them.

It is widely reported that there were two file cabinets belonging to Marilyn Monroe's estate. In actuality, there were three. Mill quietly sold off the contents of the first cabinet a little at a time over years. When Mill began a book project about the remaining contents of Marilyn's personal papers, the estate became aware of the existence of the remaining two cabinets and filed a lawsuit. Because the estate did not know of the cabinets' existence after Marilyn's death, no consent was ever given to sell them—to Inez Melson or anyone else. The court ruled in favor of the estate and the two remaining cabinets were transferred to Lee Strasberg's heir, his wife Anna Strasberg. The book project that had been underway was completed and released as *MM–Personal: From the Archives of Marilyn Monroe* in 2011.

It's impossible to say why Inez kept the cabinets, but she was known to be fiercely protective of Marilyn. Even after Marilyn died in 1962, Inez helped plan the funeral, attended to Marilyn's personal affairs and finances, tried to sort out the estate and, of course, oversaw the care of Marilyn's mother. Inez could have been protecting Marilyn's privacy by hiding Marilyn's private papers.

Inez had a right to be suspicious of people like Aaron Frosch, which her letter to Joe DiMaggio in 1962 illustrates. In his book *Icon: The Life, Times, and Films of Marilyn Monroe*, volume 2, author Gary Vitacco-Robles notes that Frosch did not renew Marilyn Monroe Productions' distribution rights for *The Prince and the Showgirl*, causing Marilyn's estate to lose revenue. Also, "Frosch failed to pay Rockhaven Sanitarium in entirety for Gladys's care and made numerous management errors in his financial favor. In 1981, Marianne Kris sued Frosch for plundering the estate, validating Cherie Redmond's mistrust in him while Marilyn was alive."

After several years in storage, the remaining contents of Marilyn's file cabinets were opened, itemized, and sold off via auctions.

EUNICE MURRAY

Dr. Ralph Greenson originally met Eunice Murray when he bought the Santa Monica house she and her husband had built in the 1940s. The Murrays separated shortly after they sold their house and their divorce was finalized in 1950. Murray continued to stay in touch with Dr. Greenson because of her deep emotional attachment to the Franklin Street house. Eventually, Mrs. Murray asked Greenson if he had any work for her because she was in desperate need of an income after her divorce. Greenson agreed to hire Mrs. Murray and place her in the homes of some of his most challenging patients as an alternative to hospitalization. She faithfully reported back to him what she saw.

In 1962, Mrs. Murray was paired with Marilyn as a companion, housekeeper, and caretaker. Marilyn's experience at Payne Whitney had been deeply traumatic for her, and Dr. Greenson was trying to create an environment in which he could treat her at home instead of in a hospital setting again.

Mrs. Murray—which is what Marilyn called her—assisted Marilyn around the house, cooked for her, and accompanied Marilyn to Mexico to

Eunice Murray worked as a housekeeper, cook, gofer, driver, and companion for Marilyn. To avoid hospitalizing Marilyn, Dr. Greenson instead placed Mrs. Murray in the home as a way to keep an eye on her. It was Mrs. Murray who discovered there was a problem in the early morning hours of August 5 and alerted Dr. Greenson to rush over to Marilyn's house. Pictured here is Mrs. Murray getting into her car on the morning Marilyn died. The man behind her is her son-in-law Norman Jeffries, who did handyman work for Marilyn.
Channel 5 Broadcasting / Photofest © Channel 5 Broadcasting

shop for authentic furnishings and décor. The trip was probably therapeutic for both women. Marilyn was decorating the first house she had purchased on her own and was thoroughly enjoying the experience. Mrs. Murray was able to relive some of the excitement of building and furnishing her own Mexican hacienda-style house, which Dr. Greenson now owned.

As instructed, Mrs. Murray kept an eye on Marilyn and reported back to Dr. Greenson. When he was especially concerned about Marilyn's mental state, he would ask Mrs. Murray to spend the night in the guest room. This is likely what happened when Mrs. Murray spent the night on Saturday, August 4, 1962. It was Mrs. Murray who became alarmed when she noticed Marilyn's bedroom light was still on in the middle of the night and a phone cord was still under the door. She alerted Dr. Greenson, who came over to the house and found Marilyn dead.

As it turns out, Mrs. Murray wasn't keeping an eye on Marilyn for just Greenson. When Marilyn's FBI file was released after her death, one of the informants was a woman identified as "Eunice Churchill" (Churchill was the last name of one of her in-laws). In the files, Eunice Churchill is identified as an "interior designer" who is traveling in Mexico with Marilyn while shopping for furniture. In the files, "Eunice Churchill" informed the FBI that Marilyn still has some leftist leanings that "rubbed off" on her during her marriage to Arthur Miller. Although Marilyn indeed met with Frederick Vanderbilt Field while in Mexico, it was a friendly social meeting and hardly a political one. Marilyn's objectives in Mexico were buying furnishings and a mini vacation.

PATRICIA NEWCOMB

As an employee of the Arthur P. Jacobs Co. Inc., a public relations agency, Pat Newcomb worked at a company known for representing a who's who of Hollywood, including Marilyn Monroe.

Pat handled Marilyn's press for *Bus Stop* in 1956, but there had been some sort of falling out. Rupert Allan became Marilyn's primary press agent for the next few years until he left to work for Princess Grace in 1960. Pat was reassigned to Marilyn in time to handle her divorce from Arthur Miller. From this point on, Pat worked closely with Marilyn, and in many ways functioned as not just a professional associate, but a best friend.

She handled the press for Marilyn and also accompanied her to photo shoots, appearances, and private outings. With May Reis, Pat was by Marilyn's side when she left Columbia Presbyterian in 1961; she also traveled in 1962 with Marilyn to Mexico, where Marilyn spoke to the press during a trip to buy furniture for her house. Pat was present at the 1962 Golden Globe Awards when Marilyn won for world's favorite star, and at both the rehearsal and performance of Marilyn singing "Happy Birthday" to President Kennedy.

When Marilyn was trying to salvage her career after Twentieth Century-Fox fired her in the summer of 1962, Pat helped arrange interviews and photo sessions. In a typed memo dated July 11, 1962, from the Arthur P. Jacobs agency files, Pat writes:

Redbook story—August issue
Vogue layout—September issue
Cosmopolitan—Cover and inside spread November issue
The *Esquire* cover is pending your availability. The *Playboy* story awaits our decision.
I will pick you up tomorrow (Thursday) at 5:30 to go to the beach to complete the Cosmopolitan layout. If possible, we would like to do the interview with you following the pictures, and it would only take an hour.
Love,
Pat

Pat was one of the last people to see Marilyn alive, having spent the night at the Fifth Helena house on Friday night. Marilyn, a chronically troubled sleeper, was angry that Pat had slept soundly until noon. Mrs. Murray fixed hamburgers for lunch, which Marilyn and Pat ate, and the two were on good terms once again. Pat left when Dr. Greenson arrived for a session with Marilyn at her home. Around 4 a.m. the following morning, Pat's phone woke her up to the news Marilyn had died. When she arrived at Marilyn's house shortly thereafter, a grief-stricken Pat called the reporters gathering on the driveway "vultures."

Much has been made about Pat being spotted on a boat with the Kennedy family shortly after Marilyn's death—and that's true. She was on a yacht with the Kennedy family on Sunday, August 12, 1962. Some writers have implied the Kennedys brought her into their fold as a way to keep her quiet . . . whatever they wanted to keep her quiet about. However, Pat already had a history with the Kennedy family, dating back to before she had met Marilyn.

Pat was born in Washington, D.C., to a father, Carman Newcomb, who was close friends with George Skakel—the father of Ethel Skakel, Robert Kennedy's future wife. George Skakel amassed a fortune in the coal industry, and in the 1940s purchased investment properties in Southern California. In 1946, when Pat was a teenager, Skakel asked Carman Newcomb if he would move to California and oversee the land. The Newcombs relocated to the Golden State, where Pat finished high school and attended Mills College. While pursuing her bachelor's degree, she took journalism classes from Pierre Salinger, who hired Pat as a research assistant in 1952 after she graduated. Her job was helping research a project about teamster union corruption. The opportunity provided an introduction to Robert Kennedy, who was also investigating union corruption and mafia ties.

Salinger turned the research into a series of articles on union corruption for *Collier's* in the 1950s, which ended up changing the direction of his life. His young assistant Pat Newcomb was able to introduce him to Robert Kennedy, who hired Salinger as legal counsel for the Senate Select Committee on organized crime. From there, Salinger began work as a press secretary for then-Senator John F. Kennedy, which led to a pivotal spot in his presidential campaign. After John Kennedy was elected, he hired Salinger as his official presidential press secretary. Salinger was an integral part of the Kennedy family's inner circle, and he had Pat Newcomb to thank for the initial introduction.

Although a coincidence, Pat was the perfect press agent to accompany Marilyn to the Democratic fundraiser where she sang "Happy Birthday" to President Kennedy. She would have understood the inner workings of the event and its family members.

Marilyn was already in a similar social circle as the Kennedys because of her friendships with actor Peter Lawford and his wife, Pat Kennedy Lawford, the president's sister.

After Marilyn's death, Pat left for Maine, where she interacted with the Kennedys, then went on an extended trip to Europe starting in late August. She didn't return until February 1963. She successfully carried on her career, working at various times for Natalie Wood and Robert Kennedy. After Robert Kennedy's assassination, she went to work for Fox, before starting her own company and also working as a vice president for MGM.

In the 1970s, Pat spoke a little about Marilyn, but after being misquoted and burned by unethical journalists, made it a point to mostly avoid the topic.

LENA PEPITONE

From 1957 up to Marilyn's death in 1962, Lena Pepitone worked as Marilyn's maid in New York. The native Italian married an American soldier during World War II and moved to the United States, where she became a naturalized citizen in 1944. In 1979, Lena wrote the book *Marilyn Monroe Confidential*, which has been widely criticized for its scathing tone and inaccuracies.

CHERIE REDMOND

Marilyn's last personal secretary was Cherie Redmond, who went to work for Marilyn in January 1962. Marilyn's attorney, Milton "Mickey" Rudin recommended Cherie as an excellent secretary. At the time she began working for Marilyn, Cherie was in her early fifties and had experience as an employee for celebrities. In the 1950s, she worked for Hecht-Hill-Lancaster, a production company cofounded by actor Burt Lancaster, and served as a personal assistant and accountant for composer Leo Robin. Marilyn hired her, but put her foot down on certain matters—unlike with her other employees, she refused to become Cherie's friend or even permit her in the house.

According to Eunice Murray, Cherie did indeed turn out to be an excellent secretary and was well worth the $250 per week Marilyn paid her. Like Marilyn's other secretaries, Cherie tended to business matters, kept Marilyn's schedule, handled mail, made phone calls, and helped with Marilyn's taxes. It's unclear why Marilyn distanced herself from Cherie Redmond, who was a loyal employee. Cherie had even tried to call attention to attorney Aaron Frosch, who she didn't trust. Years later, Cherie's instincts proved correct about the lawyer, who had mismanaged Marilyn's estate.

MAY REIS

If one were to describe May Reis and her commitment to Marilyn, the word loyalty would fit perfectly. May had originally been an employee of the Actors Studio from the late 1940s until 1952. She was working directly for Elia Kazan at the time, and May resigned in protest when he named names to HUAC.

May began working for Arthur Miller sometime around 1955, and during Miller's marriage to Marilyn, she worked for both. May had the arduous task of trying to keep Marilyn organized. May handled the mail, screened phone calls, read scripts that had been sent over, and served as a liaison between Marilyn and business associates. When Marilyn was on set, so was May.

There is some disagreement about whether or not May continued working for Marilyn after her divorce from Arthur or if she simply remained a devoted friend. Either way, May was almost always close at hand when it came to Marilyn and knew every detail of the movie star's daily life.

May was at Marilyn's side in 1961 when she left Columbia Presbyterian Hospital; a few days later, she accompanied Marilyn to the funeral of Augusta Miller, Arthur's mother. When Marilyn went to Madison Square Garden to rehearse singing "Happy Birthday" for her performance in front of President Kennedy, May went with her.

May was one of the few people who attended Marilyn's funeral on August 8, 1962. For her friendship and loyalty, Marilyn left May $10,000 in her will. In 1964, May went to work for Barbra Streisand.

RALPH ROBERTS

One of Marilyn's closest friends and confidants in the last years of her life was masseur Ralph Roberts. Like Marilyn, he had been taking acting classes and dreamed of an acting career. To support himself, he gave massages. He first gave Marilyn a massage in November 1959 at the Beverly Hills Hotel. Within the next year, he was part of her inner circle. She loved calling him "Rafe," the British pronunciation of his name.

While on the set of *The Misfits*, Ralph became indispensable to Marilyn, to whom he gave regular massages to get her through the day and to sleep, but more than that he was a steadfast friend without judgment.

His proximity to Marilyn during this time meant he saw the toll her crumbling marriage was taking on her and Arthur. He was with her for lunches and much of her free time. He was continuously on the set watching filming and even landed a small part as the medic who attends to Perce (Montgomery Clift).

After *The Misfits* wrapped, he maintained his close friendship with Marilyn. When not giving her massages, he often drove her around to appointments or on errands. When she moved back to Los Angeles, Ralph helped with the transition and also relocated, at least for a while.

Ralph drove Marilyn to her doctor appointments, picked her up at the hospital after she had a gynecological procedure, accompanied her to dinners with friends, and of course, massages. They shared a common love of books, and frequently discussed what they were reading and philosophical topics.

Things changed in October 1961 when Marilyn's psychiatrist, Dr. Ralph Greenson, told Marilyn to send Ralph Roberts home to New York. The reasoning, he told Marilyn, was that she had become too dependent on him. Both Marilyn and Ralph Roberts were upset with the order but complied.

Ralph returned to New York, but Marilyn continued to call three to four times per week. When Marilyn returned to her apartment in New York for visits, they made a point to meet up. He also visited in the summer of 1962 and gave Marilyn her last massage on August 2 at her home on Fifth Helena. Even after Dr. Greenson had tried to separate them, Marilyn and Ralph remained devoted to one another. Ralph Roberts was one of the few who was invited to Marilyn's very small, private memorial service.

NORMAN AND HEDDA ROSTEN

Through her marriage to Arthur Miller, Marilyn met the Rostens, who had a long history with Arthur and his first wife, Mary. When her marriage to Arthur ended, she continued her friendship with the Rosten family.

Born on January 1, 1913, Norman Rosten was a New York–born poet and playwright who met Arthur Miller while both were attending the University of Michigan. Like Arthur, Norman returned to New York after college and began a writing career. He settled in Brooklyn with his wife Hedda and wrote poetry, plays, and articles for the *New Yorker*.

Norman's wife, Hedda, was also a graduate of the University of Michigan. At school, she had studied psychology, also an interest of Marilyn's. Hedda had been college roommates with Mary Slattery, then Arthur's girlfriend and later wife, and through Arthur and Mary, she met her future husband.

After graduation, Hedda took a job as a social worker at the Hartford Retreat, but she was a product of her generation and marriage came before career ambitions. Arthur later noted that she was a devoted wife and mother, but still called her a "half-willing bride." She was also solitary and her background made her insightful, especially when it came to Marilyn. She once told Arthur, "You are both very guilty." When he asked for further explanation, she said, "You both have the same conscience. . . . You can't accept what you don't think you deserve; you take exception to each other when it was supposed to be perfect. So you're punishing yourselves."

Hedda was supportive of Marilyn, a safe space and a person to confide in. Marilyn hired Hedda as a personal secretary and she became just as good of an employee as she was a friend. Marilyn had spoken about going to parties and no one talking to her—men were afraid of conversing with Marilyn for fear of angering their wives. The women were threatened by Marilyn's beauty and feminine sexuality. Hedda Rosten, in contrast, felt no such threat when it came to her friend Marilyn. The two women became a good team, with Hedda understanding how to work with Marilyn better than most. For as supportive of Marilyn as she was, she was far from a yes woman and gently pushed back on Marilyn when the situation warranted it.

Perhaps out of all her friends, Norman Rosten captured the dichotomy that was Marilyn's personality. After her death, he wrote a small but insightful book about her and always spoke about his friend in a loving, but honest, manner. The Rostens understood there were both light and dark sides to her, and met her where she was at, loving and appreciating Marilyn as she was. "As a summer weekend houseguest, she was fine and fitted in with the family," he said. "Cheerful and cooperative. She helped cook, prepared spaghetti and clams and always volunteered to do the dishes. She was proud of her dish washing and held up the glasses for inspection. She played badminton with a real flair, occasionally banging someone on the head (no damage). She was just herself, and herself was gay, noisy, giggling, tender."

For as much as he and his wife loved her, he also acknowledged Marilyn was not always easy to be around. "She was a difficult woman, you know. We liked her and we said the nicest things about her and she deserved them; but she was troubled and she brought that whole baggage of emotional difficulties of her childhood with her."

The Rostens became an integral part of Marilyn's life. Hedda traveled with Marilyn to England for *The Prince and the Showgirl*. And as she often did with friends who had children, Marilyn grew to love the Rostens' daughter, Patricia.

After her divorce from Arthur, Marilyn remained close to the Rostens. Hedda tried to help keep Marilyn organized; Marilyn showed her poetry to Norman, who encouraged her to continue writing. At times, Marilyn bonded with Norman over their depressive tendencies. In 1961, Marilyn shared with Norman a short poem she had written:

> Help Help
> Help I feel life coming closer
> And all I want to do is die

In all likelihood, the Rostens are among the last people to speak with Marilyn. On August 3, she received a vitamin injection (filled mostly with amphetamines) from her internist, Dr. Hyman Engelberg; later that day, Marilyn called the Rostens and spoke with them for thirty-two minutes. She seemed upbeat and was speaking quickly, at times jumping from subject to subject. She encouraged the couple to visit her in Los Angeles, and even offered to heat the pool if that would entice them. If they both couldn't come, she said, what about Hedda visiting? She also sent her love to Patricia, who was a teenager at the time.

In Marilyn's will, she bequeathed $5,000 to Patricia for her college education. However, the Rostens did not receive the money until the 1970s.

SAM SHAW

Photographer Sam Shaw originally met Marilyn in 1951 around the time she was dating Elia Kazan. Sam recalled times when the three of them drove out to the Twentieth Century-Fox ranch in Malibu and on the way home stopped at a roadhouse for food, beer, and dancing to the jukebox.

"Everybody knows about her insecurities, but not everybody knows what fun she was, that she never complained about the ordinary things of life, that she never had a bad word to say about anyone, and that she had a wonderful, spontaneous sense of humor," he was quoted as saying in Donald Spoto's book.

Twentieth Century-Fox and producer Charles Feldman hired Sam to document the making of *The Seven Year Itch*, which was filmed primarily in a Los Angeles soundstage. Sam is sometimes credited with the idea of filming the skirt-blowing scene on a public street; if he did, it was a brilliant idea. Either way, he was most certainly there that night, and many of the most famous photos of Marilyn from that evening are courtesy of Sam Shaw. The DiMaggio marriage broke up after that fateful night in New York, but Sam Shaw remained friendly with both former spouses.

When Marilyn moved to New York shortly after her separation from Joe, Sam was one of the first friends she had in the city. He helped her with accommodations when it came to finding hotels to live in before settling into a permanent residence and, of course, Marilyn loved spending time with the Shaw family. Sam had two little girls, Edith and Meta, who Marilyn doted on and took to the circus.

Marilyn and Sam remained in touch over the years, and he documented her romance and relationship with Arthur Miller. He also captured some of the most tender photos of her at home in nature and frolicking on the beach in Amagansett, New York.

SIDNEY SKOLSKY

As one of Hollywood's top gossip columnists, Sidney Skolsky knew just about every celebrity in town during his writing career of fifty-plus years. He had a newspaper column, wrote for *Photoplay*, had a television show in the 1950s, authored books, and even worked on screenplays and as a producer. Schwab's Drugstore on the corner of Sunset Boulevard and Crescent Heights in Hollywood was an unofficial hub of the entertainment industry and Sidney had helped make it so legendary—his *Photoplay* column was called "From a Stool at Schwab's." His office was inside Schwab's, and entertainment insiders and hopefuls alike were regulars.

During her rise to stardom, Marilyn befriended Sidney and he soon became not only an ally but a trusted friend. In 1952, when news broke that Marilyn had posed nude early in her career, Sidney helped her write a statement and navigate the delicate, potentially career-threatening situation. His guidance and support helped save her reputation and career. Marilyn's trust in Sidney was total, and she confided many of her deepest secrets to the writer.

That same year, Marilyn began dating Joe DiMaggio, a man with no interest in the Hollywood scene. Marilyn had little interest in the parties and appearances that came along with celebrity, but on occasion, duty called and she was obligated to attend events. More often than not, Joe opted out on many of these outings and Marilyn's escort was her pal Sidney. When Marilyn and Joe split up, Joe called Sidney to see if there was any way he could win her back. Marilyn's mind was made up, and Sidney sat with her during the court proceeding to finalize their divorce.

During Marilyn's marriage to Arthur Miller, she made it a point to visit Sidney during her trips to California. Sidney later noted that while Marilyn was in town filming *Let's Make Love*, he had dinner with Marilyn almost every night—unless Arthur was also in town. On those nights, Marilyn ate with Arthur.

Just as Sidney weathered Marilyn's divorce from Joe, Sidney remained her rock after the marriage to Arthur ended. Marilyn moved home to Los Angeles after a few years on the East Coast, and the two friends resumed their close bond. Despite their friendship, when Marilyn passed away, Sidney was not invited to her funeral.

HAZEL WASHINGTON

Originally hired by Twentieth Century-Fox in the mid-1950s, Hazel was Marilyn's maid on and off in Los Angeles. At times she functioned almost like a personal assistant. Hazel signed for deliveries, was on the set in Los Angeles, and even traveled on occasion with Marilyn, such as on location filming for *Bus Stop* and *The Misfits*.

· 38 ·

Making Myths

$\mathcal{W}$ith someone as famous as Marilyn Monroe, there are bound to be stories with mistakes. Some of the misinformation is accidental. Other times it's the work of sloppy research. Frequently, these stories have been invented to sell books, magazines, movies, and television shows. Regardless of how they started, some of these myths about Marilyn have been so widely repeated they are now accepted as fact by the general public. The list of untrue stories about Marilyn are too numerous to cover in total, but these are some of the most common ones.

Myth: Marilyn's IQ was genius level.
Truth: Marilyn's IQ was never tested.

Myth: Marilyn was of Mexican descent.
Truth: Marilyn was of European descent, specifically of Scottish and Irish descent on her mother's side. This misconception stems from the fact that her mother Gladys was born in Mexico. Marilyn's grandparents, Otis and Della Mae Monroe, were Americans living in Mexico while Otis worked for the railroad. They did not stay long and soon returned to the United States—Los Angeles, to be exact.

Myth: Marilyn was the model for Tinker Bell in Walt Disney's *Peter Pan* (1953).
Truth: Margaret Kerry was the live-action model for Tinker Bell. There are photos of her portraying Tinker Bell in various scenarios for artists to observe and create sketches from, which in turn became scenes in the movie. Margaret also served as a model for one of the mermaids in the Mermaid Lagoon sequence. In 2016, Kerry published a memoir called *Tinker Bell Talks!*

Animation historian Mindy Johnson wrote an entire book called *Tinker Bell: An Evolution*, which describes how the beloved Disney character came to be.

Myth: Marilyn had six toes on her left foot.

Truth: This story starts with Joseph Jasgur, who photographed a young Norma Jeane on Zuma Beach in 1946. The photo in question depicts Norma Jeane (not quite yet Marilyn) wearing a bathing suit and standing on sand in her bare feet. The angle of the photo makes it look like the fifth metatarsal bone at the base of Marilyn's little toe on her left foot is extra prominent. Jasgur pushed the "sixth toe" story decades after working with Marilyn (and, of course, after her death), most likely to create interest in his photos and a book he published.

Marilyn was a pinup model early in her career and regularly appeared in bathing suits. Keen observers can clearly see ten perfectly formed toes in all her photos. Furthermore, photos of toddler-age Norma Jeane playing on the beach in the late 1920s also prove she had ten toes her entire life.

In the years after Marilyn died, photographer Joseph Jasgur claimed to have a picture of Marilyn with six toes on her left foot. Photos of her as a toddler, however, reveal ten perfectly formed toes. ARCHIVIO GBB / Alamy Stock Photo

Myth: Marilyn had twelve abortions (or multiple abortions, depending on the story).

Truth: There is no evidence Marilyn had any abortions. Marilyn had an extreme case of endometriosis, which made it very difficult for her to conceive. Her longtime gynecologist, Dr. Leon Krohn, went on record to say, "She never even had one. Later, there were two miscarriages and an ectopic pregnancy requiring emergency termination, but no abortion."

Myth: Marilyn had a same-sex affair with Joan Crawford.

Truth: That story comes directly from John Miner, who served as Los Angeles County Deputy District Attorney from 1959 to 1970. Miner claimed to have been present at Marilyn Monroe's autopsy, but his attendance has not been proved. In 1962, autopsy attendees were not required to sign in as part of the procedure's permanent record. John Miner also claimed to have interviewed Dr. Ralph Greenson after Marilyn's death, but there is no proof this interview took place. According to Miner, he was conducting an investigation into Marilyn's death and during his meeting with Dr. Greenson, he listened to tapes of Marilyn speaking to her doctor. Such tapes have never surfaced, but Miner claimed to have taken "near verbatim" notes on what Marilyn said and during this conversation, confesses to a lesbian affair with Joan Crawford.

In addition to no evidence of this recording existing, the two women did not travel in the same social circles. Neither woman's friends ever indicated they knew each other outside of brief interactions over the years. In 1953, when Marilyn accepted an award for Fastest Rising Star of 1952 while wearing a gold lamé dress with a plunging neckline, Joan was quoted in Bob Thomas's column saying, "The publicity has gone too far. She is making the mistake of believing her publicity. Someone should make her see the light. She should be told that the public likes provocative feminine personalities, but it also likes to know that underneath it all, the actresses are ladies."

Marilyn issued a response through columnist Louella Parsons. "Although I don't know Miss Crawford very well, she was a symbol of to me kindness and understanding to those who need help. At first, all I could think of was WHY should she select me to blast? She is a great star. I'm just starting. And then, when the first hurt began to die down, I told myself she must have spoken to Mr. Thomas impulsively, without thinking."

Myth: Marilyn got Ella Fitzgerald hired at the segregated Mocambo Club on the Sunset Strip after agreeing to attend every performance. By attending the performances, she promised the club owners, the press would show up and the Mocambo would receive a lot of publicity. Ella herself even wrote about the event in *Ms. Magazine* and her autobiography.

"I owe Marilyn Monroe a real debt. It was because of her that I played the Mocambo, a very popular nightclub in the '50s. She personally called the owner of the Mocambo, and told him she wanted me booked immediately, and if he would do it, she would take a front table every night. She told him—and it was true, due to Marilyn's superstar status—that the press would go wild. The owner said yes, and Marilyn was there, front table, every night. The press went overboard. After that, I never had to play a small jazz club again. She was an unusual woman—a little ahead of her times. And she didn't even know it."

Truth: Marilyn was a fan of Ella Fitzgerald and supportive of her career, but there is no evidence Marilyn attended Ella's shows at the Mocambo. The most likely scenario is that Ella herself mixed up some details as a genuine mistake rather than lying. The Mocambo Club was *not* segregated, as African American performers are depicted in 1950s-era advertisements for upcoming shows. By the mid-1950s, Ella's career was going well, but she encountered two challenges when it came to live performances. One, because she was African American there were some clubs that would not book her. Two, Ella Fitzgerald did not have a sexy or glamorous image like many of her peers.

Hollywood historian April Vevea's research reveals there is a connection between Marilyn and Ella, but it's not what has previously been believed. Ella Fitzgerald began her run at the Mocambo Club in Los Angeles from March 15–25, 1955; *Jet Magazine* covered the event extensively and Marilyn does not appear in the photos or text of the article. Judy Garland, Frank Sinatra, Eartha Kitt, Bob Hope, Jeff Chandler, Dinah Shore, singer Ella Mae Morse, and fashion designer Don Loper were all mentioned in *Jet's* coverage. During the same time frame of Ella's performances at the Mocambo, photojournalist Ed Feingersh was following and documenting Marilyn in New York City for *Redbook Magazine*.

There is a photo of Ella and Marilyn together from November 1954 that is often attributed to the Mocambo engagement but the photo was actually taken at the Tiffany Club, a jazz club in a different area of Los Angeles. The Tiffany was one of the West Coast's premiere jazz clubs and had always welcomed racially diverse performers and audiences.

Marilyn attended more than one of Ella Fitzgerald's performances at the Tiffany Club in November 1954. In 2016, a memo to Marilyn from her business manager Inez Melson dated February 15, 1955, came up for auction. It references a party Marilyn promises to throw if Ella got booked at the Mocambo. Inez had talked with Jo Brooks, the wife of Jules Fox, who was Ella's press agent.

The memo reads:

Jo Brooks is husband of Jules Fox who is a publicity agent, handling publicity for Ella Fitzgerald. A few months back, Miss Monroe visited the Tiffany Club on West 8th Street where Ella Fitzgerald was playing. Miss Monroe said when this happened, she would like to give a party for Miss Fitzgerald.

Miss Brooks wanted to know if Miss Monroe was serious about giving a party. I told her that I did not think that Miss Monroe would be in town that date but I would tell her about Miss Fitzgerald's opening.

Around this same time, a blurb by Dorothy Kilgallen read: "Ella Fitzgerald at Mocambo, Marilyn Monroe, a big Ella fan, agented the booking." Marilyn was indeed out of town on the dates Ella Fitzgerald performed at the Mocambo and, therefore, unable to throw a party. It's quite possible that Marilyn's promise to host a party helped get Ella the Mocambo gig, which would explain the "agented" reference in the newspaper.

Although Marilyn was in New York and couldn't attend Ella's Mocambo residency or host an event, Ella got a party courtesy of Frank Sinatra.

The story of Marilyn Monroe helping Ella Fitzgerald get a booking at the Mocambo Club began in the August 1972 issue of *Ms. Magazine*, which featured a tribute to Marilyn on the tenth anniversary of her dying. Ella wrote about the incident and likely (although not proven) simply mixed up the Mocambo and Tiffany, which were only a few months apart; remembered the promise for a Mocambo party incorrectly; or some sort of combination of the two. In 1972, she would have been trying to recall events from seventeen years prior.

Regardless, even if the story is not quite as Ella Fitzgerald recalled it, she made clear that Marilyn was supportive of her career and came out to watch her perform.

Myth: While filming *The Prince and the Showgirl*, Marilyn grew very close to a young man named Colin Clark, who worked as the third assistant director. While having a difficult time during production, Marilyn found friendship and solace with the recent Eton graduate, who was in his mid-twenties at the time. During the course of filming, Colin Clark was one of the few people on the set she trusted and continued to draw him closer to her. This culminated in Clark showing Marilyn around England for a week. Like most men in her presence, Clark became smitten with Marilyn.

Truth: Colin Clark wrote two books about Marilyn Monroe: *The Prince, the Showgirl and Me*, and *My Week with Marilyn*. The books, presented in diary format, were turned into the movie *My Week with Marilyn*, starring Eddie Redmayne as Colin Clark and Michelle Williams as Marilyn Monroe.

The Prince, the Showgirl and Me was published in 1995 and recounts his time as a gofer on the set of *The Prince and the Showgirl* in 1956. Clark's second book, *My Week with Marilyn*, followed in 2000. Like *The Prince, the Showgirl and Me*, the second installment recounts Marilyn's time in England while filming *The Prince and the Showgirl*. Unlike the first book, however, *My Week with Marilyn* is an account of his nine private days with Marilyn Monroe.

Clark's books are not without their controversies. Those familiar with Marilyn's time in England have long been suspicious of Clark's memories, saying much of his diaries blur the line between fiction and fact.

Perhaps the biggest question is simply this: If Colin Clark published his diary in the form of *The Prince, the Showgirl and Me*, then why did he deliberately leave out an entire week—a week spent with the world's most famous movie star at that? He later said he had "forgotten" but if one is publishing a diary, several days' worth of writing does not merely disappear. Why are there no photos of him escorting Marilyn, the most famous and photographed woman in the world at the time, around England?

There are other concerns. People have noted the dates in Clark's diary don't always match the dates and accounts in the production logs for *The Prince and the Showgirl*.

While in England, Marilyn was accompanied by a large entourage, none of whom recalled a close friendship with anyone on the set, let alone a young crew member who took off with her for nine days.

Furthermore, why was a celebrity of Marilyn Monroe's stature spending a week with the set's gofer? And at that, a gofer so closely tied to Sir Laurence Olivier, with whom Marilyn had one of the worst working relationships of her entire career. (Clark's parents were close friends with Olivier and his wife, actress Vivien Leigh. After *The Prince and the Showgirl* wrapped, Clark became Olivier's assistant. With Olivier's help, Colin Clark went on to carve out a career in television.)

Other than getting him a job working for Laurence Olivier, Colin Clark's family clearly influenced him numerous ways, as well. Clark's father was famed art historian Sir Kenneth Clark, who built a reputation running museums and hosting the television documentary series *Civilisation*. Colin Clark's older brother, Alan Clark, was a noted Tory politician, historian, and writer.

The reason for Colin Clark's desire for fame or credibility are most likely rooted in his family's significant accomplishments.

In his autobiography, *Younger Brother, Younger Son*, Colin Clark wrote, "I was proud of my family, but they cast too deep a shadow. I wanted to be left to my own devices. Brains aren't everything. My father and Alan both had more than me, but I didn't envy them a bit. There is enormous happiness to be found in not wanting to be the best, or have the most, or shout the loudest."

Indeed, it wasn't until Colin Clark published *The Prince, the Showgirl and Me* that his name achieved considerable recognition. That undoubtedly increased again with the book's sequel, *My Week with Marilyn*, as he was even more closely tied to Marilyn Monroe.

Colin Clark passed away in 2002, nine years before his books were turned into a movie.

· 39 ·

Public Schedules

The Trouble with Getting Two Icons in a Room

$\mathcal{B}$oth Marilyn and John Kennedy had very public schedules, so it's fairly easy to place them in their respective locations on any given day. It has generally been repeated that Marilyn and John Kennedy were in the same place at the same time just five times. With information coming to light, even some of those can now be scrutinized more closely. Let's take a look.

1. The April in Paris Ball at the Waldorf-Astoria in New York in 1957. More than 1,300 guests paid $100 for the charity gala held in honor of the Duke and Duchess of Windsor. Marilyn attended with Arthur Miller. John Kennedy, then still a senator, attended with his wife, Jackie. It is unclear if Marilyn and John Kennedy met that evening, but both couples were photographed extensively that night and no photos of the two meeting have surfaced. Senator Kennedy was a rising star in politics at the time but nowhere near the celebrity status he would obtain a few years later. At this time, Marilyn was by far the more famous of the two. Some reports indicate photographers turned their cameras away from the Duchess to snap pictures of Marilyn as soon as she arrived.

2. November 19, 1961: The story is Marilyn and President John Kennedy were guests at a luncheon at the Santa Monica beach house of Peter and Pat Lawford. At the time, actor Peter Lawford was married to the president's sister, Pat.

   This remains unconfirmed. The day before, President Kennedy attended a fundraiser at the Hollywood Palladium, then went over to his sister's house in the evening. On that night Marilyn was confirmed to have been a dinner guest at Ralph Greenson's home in Santa Monica.

On November 19, the day of the luncheon, Marilyn was confirmed to have been going through pictures from a recent shoot with photographer Douglas Kirkland. She did go over to the Lawford house later in the evening, but it's not known if John Kennedy was still present. If they did cross paths, it would have been a situation where many guests were present and they were not alone.

3. December 5, 1961: Wealthy socialite Josephine "Fifi" Fell hosted a large dinner party at her Manhattan townhouse in honor of President Kennedy. For years, it was believed Marilyn was indeed present. As more of Marilyn's paperwork has come to light recently, it has become clear that Marilyn was in Los Angeles that entire week.

In the book *Marilyn Monroe: A Day in the Life*, author April Vevea reveals that Marilyn had appointments with Dr. Hyman Engelberg at her Los Angeles home on December 1, 2, and 4. On December 5, she wrote to Marlon Brando suggesting they partner on a production company. She could not possibly have attended. For that matter, President Kennedy couldn't have attended either. During the day in Washington, he met with the Governor and First Lady of Guam, had a meeting with Secretary of Labor Arthur J. Goldberg and Secretary of Commerce Luther H. Hodges, received a visit from students in conjunction with Foreign Student Day, met with the Ambassador of Costa Rica, and met with Charles L. Bacon, the National Commander of the American Legion. In the afternoon, he left for New York to attend the Football Hall of Fame dinner, where he was for the entire night.

Some sources have claimed the dinner at Fifi Fell's took place in February but there is no evidence that can place either one of them at her home during that month.

4. March 24, 1962: President Kennedy spent the night at Bing Crosby's estate in Palm Springs. JFK arrived in Palm Springs on Saturday and was driven through town in a convertible. He spent the afternoon meeting with former President Eisenhower at his home; after their meeting, the two presidents posed for press photos outside. That evening, Crosby hosted a dinner for more than a dozen guests in honor of the president. Those in attendance included Peter and Pat Lawford, Conrad Hilton, and Marilyn. The following morning, President Kennedy attended Mass at Sacred Heart Catholic Church with two hundred other worshippers. That evening, approximately three thousand spectators gathered to watch the presidential party leave the Palm Springs airport at approximately 11 p.m. Before leaving,

President Kennedy personally thanked Capt. Lloyd Watson of the highway patrol, Capt. Robert Presley of the Riverside County Sheriff's Office, Capt. Lawrence Brooks of the Indio Sheriff's Substation, and Palm Springs Police Chief Gus Kettmann for the exceptionally high level of security displayed during his trip.

This is one of the few times Marilyn Monroe and John Kennedy could be placed in the same room at the same time. Although it has generally been accepted that Marilyn was an overnight guest at Crosby's estate, that is possible but still *not* confirmed. Marilyn was in Palm Springs that weekend—it was the same weekend she had plumbing updated in her new house in Los Angeles. She spent Saturday morning at the home Ralph Greenson, where she washed her hair because her plumbing was turned off, then drove to Palm Springs that day and attended the dinner at Bing Crosby's estate. On Sunday she spent the day with Joe DiMaggio and friend Norman Rosten. Both Marilyn and the president had very full weekends planned and most of those hours did not involve the other.

May 19, 1962, was one of the most memorable nights in twentieth-century American history—in large part because of the conspiracy theories surrounding Marilyn Monroe and President Kennedy. Although the event at Madison Square Garden has often been referred to as a "birthday party," it was a fundraiser for the Democratic Party. The president's birthday was on May 29, so as part of the evening, his birthday was celebrated. Marilyn sang "Happy Birthday" and a revised version of "Thanks for the Memories." Then a giant birthday cake was brought out onto the stage.

It has been noted many times, as though to draw an inference of some sort, that First Lady Jacqueline Kennedy was not present. Mrs. Kennedy not being present at Madison Square Garden is correct; she was not in attendance. To infer anything, however, would be a mistake. Mrs. Kennedy rarely participated in fundraisers and it was completely in character that she was not there. She was in Virginia at an equestrian event.

An after party took place at the home of Arthur Krim, president of United Artists, and his wife Mathilde. Marilyn, John Kennedy, and his brother Robert Kennedy were all in attendance—as were dozens of other people. There is a photograph of Marilyn chatting with the brothers at the party and it remains the only known photo of Marilyn with either brother.

Marilyn's guest that night was Isidore Miller, Arthur Miller's father. Marilyn and Isidore remained close even after her divorce from Arthur, and she paid for his trip to New York. Arthur's mother had recently passed away,

Dozens of attendees crowded into the Manhattan townhouse of Arthur and Mathilde Krim after the Democratic Fundraiser at Madison Square Garden on May 19, 1962. Diahann Carroll treated guests to a private singing performance. Marilyn can be seen watching at the far right. An unidentified woman is leaning in between Marilyn and her former father-in-law Isidore Miller, who was her guest for the evening.
Cecil Stoughton. White House Photographs. John F. Kennedy Presidential Library and Museum, Boston

and Marilyn gifted the trip and visit to him as a way to cheer him up. By all accounts, Marilyn was very attentive to her former father-in-law that evening, hardly leaving his side except to sing on stage.

· 40 ·

Robert Slatzer and Jeanne Carmen:
They Never Knew Marilyn

$\mathcal{T}$wo of the most prominent proponents of the conspiracy theories surrounding Marilyn's death involve so-called close confidants of Marilyn named Robert Slatzer and Jeanne Carmen. Both practically made careers out of being interviewed for talk shows, news programs, and documentaries. Both ended up with book deals and Slatzer even sold the rights to his story for a made-for-television movie. Each claimed to have inside knowledge of Marilyn and her relationships with the Kennedys. The problem is there is no proof anywhere to confirm their stories.

Myth: Marilyn was secretly married for a couple of days to Robert Slatzer in 1952.
Truth: There is no evidence to support the claim Robert Slatzer was married to Marilyn Monroe at any time. Evidence very clearly proves they were never married and didn't know each other outside of meeting once.

Slatzer was a writer whose press pass allowed him access to the *Niagara* set in New York in 1952. He met Marilyn, who posed for a couple of photos with him.

According to Slatzer, however, the two fell in love and eloped a few months later. On Friday, October 3, he said, they traveled to Mexico and were married the following day on Saturday, October 4. Upon their return to California, Twentieth Century-Fox studio head Darryl Zanuck demanded they annul their marriage, as Marilyn was now too valuable as a sex symbol to be a married woman. As a faithful employee, Marilyn insisted on following orders. She and her new husband drove back to Mexico, located the judge who married them, and bribed him to burn their marriage license.

There are several problems with Robert Slatzer's story, however. For one thing, Marilyn was dating Joe DiMaggio when she was filming *Niagara* and the relationship was getting serious.

Next, Slatzer claimed they drove to Mexico on October 3, but Marilyn made a public appearance that evening at a party in honor of *Photoplay* Editor-in-Chief Ruth Waterbury. She was photographed by the press at the event.

On October 4, the day Slatzer alleges they were married in Mexico, Marilyn went shopping in Beverly Hills, which a canceled check to Jax clothing store for $313.13 proves. (A check to Schwab's Drug Store on Sunset Boulevard dated October 1 further proves she was in town all week.)

Slatzer also claimed he was one of Marilyn's closest confidants, but none of Marilyn's inner circle ever heard her mention him, no one saw him around her, and her telephone and address books do not list him.

To complicate matters, Slatzer planted his name in a couple of newspaper items after meeting Marilyn on the *Niagara* set. In Dorothy Kilgallen's column dated August 16, 1952, she reports, "A dark horse in the Marilyn Monroe romance derby is Bob Slatzer, former Columbus, Ohio literary critic. He's been wooing her by phone and mail and improving her mind with gifts of the world's greatest books."

Another newspaper clip dated January 6, 1953, reads: "Marilyn Monroe gives the boys trouble even when she's not around. The other night when she was attending a press party, two of her most ardent suitors—Joe DiMag, of course, and Bob Slatzer—wound up cooling their heels at her house. The dialogue that ensued was frosty, but they both left at the same time."

Yet another article appeared in a May 1957 tabloid magazine *Confidential* with juicy details of a sexual encounter between Marilyn and Robert Slatzer during the time of her courtship with Joe DiMaggio a few years prior. When this article was printed, she was married to Arthur Miller and she was reportedly furious. (Tabloid magazines, it should be noted, frequently pay sources. It is likely Robert Slatzer was paid for his "tips" to gossip columnists and tabloid magazines.)

In the early 1970s, Slatzer pitched an article about Marilyn dying in a political conspiracy involving the Kennedys, who were also her lovers (Martin Luther King Jr. was also a lover, he claimed) to journalist Will Fowler. Fowler declined, but Slatzer later published a book about his claims in 1974.

After his book was released, Slatzer frequently served as a source for journalists writing about Marilyn, appeared in documentaries and was interviewed as a guest on talk shows—often paid for his time.

Will Fowler, the journalist who declined Slatzer's story in the early 1970s, later said, "Slatzer made a career out of being a pretender. Selling gullible talk show producers who don't do their research very well with the deception that he was married to Marilyn. He was never married to her. He met the star only once in Niagara Falls. . . . He never met Marilyn before or since."

Myth: Jeanne Carmen claimed she was Marilyn's neighbor and best friend, and because of her close relationship to Marilyn, was a witness to her affair with Robert Kennedy. She says she was a visitor at Marilyn's house on a day when Robert Kennedy was also present. When Jeanne arrived and saw the Attorney General, Marilyn ran into the room and began kissing him passionately. The three—Marilyn, Jeanne, and Robert Kennedy—also enjoyed nude romps at the beach. Marilyn wasn't recognized because she wore a wig. Jeanne also claimed Marilyn called her on the night of her death and begged for sleeping pills, but she could not come over. She regretted this deeply, as she may have been able to save Marilyn's life had she been at her friend's house.

Truth: Like Robert Slatzer, years after Marilyn died Jeanne Carmen began making the rounds as a (paid) source for stories about Marilyn Monroe.

There are several problems with Jeanne Carmen's stories. As with Robert Slatzer, none of Marilyn's confirmed inner circle had even heard of Jeanne Carmen, let alone recall her physical presence near Marilyn. The name Jeanne Carmen does not appear in any of Marilyn's telephone or address books. There are no letters, birthday cards, holiday cards, photos of them together, or any other evidence indicating they knew each other.

The story about the pills is easily debunked—photos of Marilyn's bedroom on the morning of her death show she had access to several bottles of pills, all prescribed in her name. She did not need anyone to bring pills to the house.

As time went on, Jeanne Carmen's stories expanded and got more ridiculous to include her own affair with Robert Kennedy, and affairs with Elvis Presley and Frank Sinatra. All were dead by the time Carmen made her claims.

· 41 ·

Death Myths

Conspiracy theorists point to several things when it comes to Marilyn's death in order to prove she was murdered or died under mysterious circumstances. Most stories or accusations are cleared up fairly easily. Ironically, two of the biggest conspiracy proponents, Robert Slatzer and Milo Speriglio, were the individuals who pushed to have Marilyn's death reinvestigated in 1982— ironic because the new investigation concluded what they did not want to hear. Marilyn's death was indeed a "probable suicide" and there was nothing nefarious about the original investigation. Many of the policies since 1962 had been updated or improved over the years, but everything had been conducted in accordance with the standards of the time. The 1982 investigation was even more thorough than the first and utilized newer technology, only further proving the original conclusion had been correct.

THE STOMACH WAS EMPTY

Claim: Marilyn's stomach was empty, so there is no way she could have swallowed enough pills to have killed her. There would have to be pill residue left in her stomach.
Secondary Claim: The tissue samples taken during the autopsy were stolen or mysteriously disappeared to prevent analysis.
Fact: As noted in the official autopsy record: "The stomach is almost completely empty. The contents is brownish mucoid fluid. The volume is estimated to be no more than 20 cc. No residue of the pills is noted. A smear made from the gastric contents and examined under the polarized microscope shows no refractile crystals."

First, the fact that Marilyn swallowed enough pills to kill her without any remaining residue in her stomach is proof to many that her death was not caused by oral ingestion of pills. In reality, not having pill residue in her stomach simply means she was able to digest them. Some stories theorize Marilyn was injected with the drugs that killed her, but Dr. Noguchi has always maintained he went over Marilyn's body with a magnifying glass looking for needle marks and found none.

"Marilyn Monroe had been a heavy user of sleeping pills and chloral hydrate for years," Dr. Noguchi wrote in his book *Coroner*. "Her stomach was familiar with those pills, and they were digested and 'dumped' into the intestinal tract. In my experience with pill addicts, I expected to see no visible evidence of pills—a fact that only proved they were addicts, not that they were murder victims who had been injected."

Marilyn's stomach contents have long been a source of controversy. Dr. Noguchi took samples of the contents of Marilyn's stomach. The samples, however, were never tested and later thrown away. Untested and discarded samples from Marilyn's stomach seem suspicious now, but in 1962 this was in keeping with standard procedure. The amount of drugs found in Marilyn's blood (8 mg% [mg/dl] of choral hydrate and 4.5 mg% of Nembutal) and liver (13mg% of Nembutal) revealed that Marilyn had died from an overdose, so the contents of her stomach were not needed and therefore discarded. This is no longer standard procedure; these days all tissues samples are tested to prevent confusion.

NEMBUTAL STAINS IN THE DIGESTIVE TRACT

Claim: Nembutal pills leave yellow stains/discoloration in digestive tracts when ingested orally. Marilyn's digestive tract showed no signs of such discoloration, so she could not have swallowed the Nembutal found in her system.
Fact: As Dr. Noguchi later explained, Nembutal does not leave yellow stains in those who take the drug orally. He also noted this concern must have been raised by a layperson unfamiliar with Nembutal. "As a medical examiner I had come to know this pill very well. It seemed to be one of the favorite drugs for those who wanted to commit suicide. And I pointed out that if you take a yellow Nembutal and touch it to your lips to moisten it, then rub your finger over the wet pill, you'll find that the yellow color does not rub off. Nembutal is made with a capsule whose color does not run when it is swallowed."

MARILYN MUST HAVE BEEN GIVEN AN
ENEMA FILLED WITH DRUGS

Claim: With the empty stomach and lack of Nembutal stains in the digestive tract, surely Marilyn was given an enema filled with drugs to create the high levels found in her blood and liver.

Fact: The stomach and Nembutal have been debunked earlier, but let's go further. The autopsy notes, "The colon shows marked congestion and purplish discoloration." The purplish discoloration that was noted has led to theories that Marilyn was killed via enema. However, according to the Los Angeles County Medical Examiner, this does not mean anything other than a purplish discoloration was observed and noted. In and of itself it means nothing.

The very next line of the report reads, "The fecal contents is light brown and formed." If Marilyn had been given an enema, it seems unlikely she would have had a formed stool in her lower intestine.

The enema theory was promoted by Deputy District Attorney John Miner, who claimed to have been present at Marilyn Monroe's autopsy. However, it is unknown if John Miner was actually in attendance. Dr. Noguchi was focused on completing the procedure and does not recall who was present. In 1962, the Los Angeles County Medical Examiner's Office did not require a written record of those attending an autopsy. Today, keeping such a record is mandatory.

THE AMBULANCE

Claim: Marilyn was transported via ambulance, then returned to her house, and placed back in bed.

Secondary Claim: The ambulance attendant witnessed Marilyn's doctor inject her with a syringe to the heart, killing her.

Fact: The ambulance story has many variations, almost too many to count. One of the more common stories is that an ambulance was called while Marilyn was still alive. Marilyn died on the way to the hospital, so the ambulance turned around and she was placed back in bed.

There is no record of an ambulance being called. A man by the name of James Hall sold a story to *Globe* claiming that he was part of the ambulance team that found Marilyn. His story changed at various times and he wanted money from the investigators to tell his story, just as he had done with the *Globe*.

The 1982 investigation reveals:

> In the November 23, 1982, edition of the *Globe*, a weekly tabloid published in West Palm Beach, Florida, the headline article states that a former ambulance driver by the name of James Hall alleges that he saw Marilyn Monroe murdered.
>
> Mr. Hall first contacted the Los Angeles District Attorney's Office on 8/11/82. Thereafter, under a code name "Rick Stone," he telephonically contacted this office several times. Ultimately, he attempted to sell information to the District Attorney's Office relating to his alleged observations at the death scene on the morning of August 5, 1962, at Marilyn Monroe's home. These conversations were recorded.

After comparing Mr. Hall's ("Stone's") statements concerning his observations with the physical and documentary evidence available to us, we informed Mr. Hall that we were not interested in making a money payment for his information, but that we would be more than happy to interview him in person and perhaps pay for a plane ticket should he wish to meet with our investigators in a mutually agreed-upon location. Mr. Hall claimed to be in fear for his life and was very evasive concerning his identity and other particulars. Ultimately, he telephonically told us that he had changed his mind and would not charge us any money for his information and "would get back to us." He never got back to us. Thereafter, apparently he gave interviews with various representatives of news publications. No other information concerning him surfaced until the publication of the *Globe* article.

The statements attributed to Mr. Hall in the *Globe* article differ in various particulars from statements he gave to us.

Mr. Hall's statements to the press and to us can be analyzed without reference to internal contradictions and inconstancies by simply looking at the physical evidence and by reference to interview material.

According to the *Globe* article, Hall says that he received a call to go the Monroe residence by his ambulance dispatcher somewhere between 3:00 and 4:00 in the morning. He said he found Monroe naked and comatose, lying face up on the bed. He claims he removed her to the floor and attempted to revive her by means of closed chest massage—which attempted he terminated when a person calling himself Miss Monroe's doctor entered the room and took charge. According to Hall, the doctor ultimately plunged a giant syringe filled with a brownish fluid into her heart, after which she quickly died while on her back on the floor.

In our conversation with Mr. Hall on August 13, 1982, he told us that he arrived at the Monroe residence somewhere between 4:00 a.m. and 6:00 a.m. The version of the story printed in the *Globe* allows time for Hall to have been there prior to the arrival of any of the doctors. However, he also told us that after his attempts to revive the body, all of which covered a short time span, and after the conduct of the person with the syringe, still within a short time frame, he and his partner packed up their gear and left. At the time he was leaving he observed a police unit or units on the scene.

There are several significant problems with this story:

(1) The Los Angeles Police Report states that Miss Monroe was pronounced dead at 3:50 a.m. by her personal physician, Dr. Engelberg, who was present with her psychiatrist, Dr. Greenson, at that time, and that the Police Department was called at approximately 4:25 a.m. Although time discrepancies have surfaced as a result of former Sgt. Clemmon's [sic] allegations that he was told that the body was discovered much earlier, under any credible version of the facts, Miss Monroe had been pronounced dead between 3:00 and 4:00 a.m.

Ignoring the discrepancies between the time sequence Hall gave the District Attorney's Office and that which is attributed to him in the *Globe*, Hall consistently stated he observed a police car, or police cars, at the scene when he was leaving. Since police records indicate that the dispatcher received the call at 4:25 a.m., it would be impossible for any police unit to get there before a few minutes after 4:25 a.m. This leads to the conclusion that if Hall had been there, he could not have left there before approximately 4:30 a.m.

More significant, however, is the unchallenged official report that the body was in a condition of rigor mortis at the time she was pronounced dead at 3:50 a.m.

Rigor mortis is a condition of stiffening of the body caused by chemical and physical changes after death. Although scientific studies cannot pinpoint the exact timetable for the onset of rigor mortis, it is scientifically known that rigor mortis is not instantaneous—it is a process which on the average takes two to four hours to begin under typical circumstances. It is scientifically observed that generally rigor mortis peaks from six to eight hours after death (again, subject to many variables—ambient temperature, previous physical condition of the subject, and several other factors) and then gradually diminishes, leading to a relaxed state of muscle tissue. Thus, given this physical phenomenon Miss Monroe must have been dead for several hours before 3:30 a.m., and prior to the earliest arrival time Mr. Hall claims.

(2) Miss Monroe died while in a prone position; that is, she died lying on her face. Absent unusual circumstances, the pattern of lividity in dead bodies constitutes strong evidence in determining the position a body was in at the time of death. Lividity, as described to our investigators, is a process by which blood drains to the lowest point in a deceased person after death due to the joint effect of the pull of gravity and the cessation of the blood pumping mechanism of the body. Thus, a person who dies on his back and remains in that position for some period of time will have a definite pattern of lividity on the back and other places on the back side of the body. A person who dies on his face will have a distinct pattern of lividity on the front side of the body, such as the chest, face, etc. All this presupposes that the surface upon which the person died and remained until discovery was relatively level, such as a bed, floor, etc. In addition to the rigor mortis observed in Miss Monroe's body, Noguchi and others observed a pattern of lividity on her face and chest. Also observed was congestion about the eyes, which correlates to the lividity found on the front side of her body. Under all accepted medical theories, the phenomenon associated with the draining of blood and other liquids to the lowest part of the body is strong evidence of the position of the body at the time of death. Hall's statement concerning finding her alive on her back, then seeing her murdered while still on her back, is directly contrary to the physical evidence observed by others.

(3) Hall alleges that he saw this "doctor" plunge a large syringe into the heart of Miss Monroe and that Miss Monroe thereafter expired. The particular location he describes is within the area carefully examined by Dr. Noguchi, whose examination was witnessed by others. If Miss Monroe had been dead at the time of this alleged injection, the careful examination previously described would most probably have revealed the presence of the needle mark and possibly the presence of both foreign fluid and of internal tissue damage in the region of the heart. Conversely, if, as Hall alleges, the doctor gave her a fatal shot while she was alive, we should expect to see a hemorrhagic track following the path of the needle through the subcutaneous tissue and we should likely observe further damage associated with this traumatic intrusion into the heart cavity. No such tell-tale damage was present.

Minor streaks of lividity were also found on her back. These minor traces disappeared upon touch. This finding is consistent with the normal practice of transporting bodies from the death scene to the mortuary or Coroner's Office on the decedent's back, which to a minor extent reverses the gravitational flow of blood toward the lowest point in the new position of the body, i.e., the back side. This new movement of body fluids is much less marked, however, because a blood thickening process has begun which prevents a significant free-flow of the fluid.

(4) Miss Monroe died, according to the toxicological reports, from a lethal dose of pentobarbital in combination with a high dosage of chloral hydrate. If the mysterious "doctor" had given Miss Monroe a fatal shot of pentobarbital, leading to her rapid death as described by Hall, the level of pentobarbital in her blood would have been elevated, perhaps as much as three or four times higher than it was; conversely, the level in her liver would not have been as high as it in fact was because her body would not have had time to metabolize the "hot shot."

(5) Since Mr. Hall's statements have surfaced another person, a Mr. Ken Hunter, has been located who claims to have been an ambulance driver who responded to the Monroe residence in the early morning hours of August 5, 1962. He reports that he arrived at the scene in the morning hours with his partner, whom he believes with reasonable certainty to have been a Mr. Murray Liebowitz, and entered the Monroe residence within one or two minutes after their arrival. He observed Miss Monroe in the bedroom, on her face or side. He reported to us that Miss Monroe was obviously dead and exhibited signs of lividity as blue in color. He did not touch the body so that he reached no conclusions concerning the presence of rigor mortis. He reports that after he and his partner made the cursory observations of the body, they both left the scene. He reports that police officers were at the scene at the time he and his partner left.

While at the residence, he did not observe anyone enter Monroe's bedroom other than his partner.

Mr. Hall's declarations concerning his conduct and observations at the scene of death are not credible.

WAS MARILYN'S HOUSE BUGGED?

Claims: One of the stories about Marilyn's house is that it was bugged to obtain information about her affairs with the Kennedy brothers. There are even some men who claim to know who hid the wires in her house or have heard the tapes. Stories further allege that in the years following Marilyn's death, a family living in her house did some remodeling and workers found the old wiring from the electronic bugging devices. The leftover wiring was found in the crawl space between the ceiling and the roof. This would prove, of course, that Marilyn had been bugged and followed because of her association with the Kennedys and possibly the Mafia.

Facts: First, for all the talk of audio tapes of Marilyn and President John Kennedy or Attorney General Robert Kennedy having sex, no one has ever been able to produce one. Second, it is impossible for any wiring to have been found in the crawl space—because Marilyn's house did not have a crawl space.

According to Gary Vitacco-Robles, author of *Cursum Perficio: Marilyn Monroe's Brentwood Hacienda*, Marilyn's house had cathedral ceilings; with the construction of most cathedral ceilings, the walls extend up into where the attic or crawl space would normally go. Sheetrock or plaster is applied to the underside of the roof rafters. In the case of Marilyn's house, when she submitted a bid to purchase the home, she noticed roof repairs were needed and adjusted her offer accordingly. With no crawl space or attic to act as a buffer, roof repairs would have been even more imperative to prevent damage.

The 1982 investigation further addressed the issue of wiretapping in Marilyn's home. The following is taken directly from the report.

> Was Marilyn Monroe's house bugged via an electronic listening device or telephone wiretap and did this secret eavesdropping reveal a romantic relationship between Attorney General Robert Kennedy and Marilyn Monroe?
>
> *Response*: The allegation that the Marilyn Monroe residence had been bugged (or wiretapped) comes from three sources. Each will be treated separately.
>
> *The Bernard Spindel Matter*
> Bernard Spindel in the 1960s was a rather notorious illegal wiretapper. In the mid-sixties, Manhattan District Attorney Frank Hogan's detectives staged a raid on Spindel's home in a town outside New York City and seized his files and various tape-recordings. The purpose of the raid was to secure evidence against Spindel for illegal wiretapping. Sometime after the seizure of the tapes pending the outcome of the pretrial motions and trial, Spindel, in a motion to the court in New York, alleged that at least some of these tapes contained material relating to the circumstances surrounding the death of Marilyn Monroe. Spindel allegedly had been working for

Jimmy Hoffa in an effort to secure embarrassing information on Robert Kennedy so that Kennedy would stop his investigation of Hoffa. Later, according to an attorney presently on the staff of the Manhattan District Attorney's Office, Spindel backed down in his request to have the contents of the tapes made public.

Spindel apparently had been laboring under the misunderstanding that the investigators in the District Attorney's Office had not heard the tapes. His asserted desire to have the tapes made public appears to have been a ploy. Our investigators successfully tracked down the investigator who supervised the district attorney's investigation of Bernard Spindel in the 1960s. He reported to us that the tapes were in fact heard by District Attorney staff investigators and that none of the tapes contained anything relating to Marilyn Monroe. The supervising investigator, Mr. Bill Graff, who is now Chief Investigator with the US Environmental Protection Agency, reports that Spindel was "a known boaster" and frequently alluded to having knowledge of a number of secrets.

Spindel died in 1968 after having served a prison sentence for his illegal wiretapping crimes.

Spindel had boasted to various people that he had secret tapes on Bobby Kennedy and Marilyn Monroe. No such materials were ever found.

Milo Speriglio

Mr. Milo Speriglio is a private investigator associated with the Nick Harris Detective Agency in Van Nuys, California. He was interviewed by our investigators on various occasions concerning information he might have relating to the death of Marilyn Monroe. One particular area of our interest was the allegation that secret tapes existed which in some way pointed to criminal conduct associated with Miss Monroe's death.

Mr. Speriglio told our investigator that in August of this year he received a telephone call from an informant who stated that he, the informant, had previously been associated with Bernard Spindel and also had worked with a Mr. Mike Morriesey who is presently an attorney in practice in Washington, D.C. Mr. Speriglio tape-recorded his conversation with the informant. A copy of the tape-recording of the informant's statements was provided to our investigators and the tape has been listened to on several occasions. Much of the tape if [*sic*] of poor quality and certain segments are unintelligible. However, the essence of the information the informant relayed was that while working for Jimmy Hoffa, Bernard Spindel had made a tape-recording on which could be heard the sound of a slap followed by the sound of a body striking the ground. The informant further stated that a phrase was heard on the tape regarding "what should be done with the body." Allegedly this recording is of Marilyn Monroe's death. The informant apparently was seeking to sell his information.

Attempts by Speriglio and another person working with Speriglio to track down the alleged tape-recording have been unsuccessful. Speriglio reports to this office that the person who allegedly could corroborate the existence of the tape, Mr. Morriesey, had denied any knowledge of the tape.

Based upon other information secured during our threshold investigation, it is our view that any allegation concerning the existence of such a tape-recording must be viewed with extreme skepticism. The physical evidence associated with the autopsy reports and interviews with Dr. Noguchi and Mr. Miner fail to support any finding that Miss Monroe had suffered trauma at or about the time of her death. The minor bruising observed on her body was typical of minor bruises often observed on female patients and normally observed during close examination of deceased persons.

In addition, as previously discussed, there is no evidence that Miss Monroe suffered a rapid death associated with a hypodermic injection or other rapid-acting lethal instrumentality. All known existing evidence causes us to believe that the story is a fabrication.

Joseph Mankiewicz

One of the critics of the police investigation, Robert Slatzer, now alleges that a woman reported to him that a source had told her that a small electronic microphone had been found at the residence of Marilyn Monroe many years after the events of 1962. Our investigators were able to track down one Joseph S. Mankiewicz, who related to us that during 1977 (15 years after Marilyn Monroe's death) he had been hired by a San Fernando contractor to haul debris from a vacant residence on Fifth Helena Street. He had been advised that the residence had once been owned by Marilyn Monroe. Nearby neighbors advised that the residence he was working on had once been owned by Marilyn Monroe. Mankiewicz initially stated that a person, probably a supervisor for the contracting firm, told him that a telephone repairman had discovered wiring in the attic which was not telephone wiring. Mankiewicz later stated to our investigators that the telephone repairman allegedly found wires mixed into the telephone lines which were not telephone company wires.

In October of this year our investigators contacted the Security Manager for General Telephone Company, Santa Monica Office, and requested assistance from the telephone company in examining the telephone wiring that was at that time in the former Marilyn Monroe residence. Our investigator then accompanied a field supervisor to the residence. The supervisor, Mr. Dwayne Gortner, inspected the telephone wires in the residence and noticed they had been completely changed in 1971. He inspected the electrical work and lines and discovered no eavesdropping devices or suspect wiring.

The supervisor reported to our investigators that the residence could have been previously equipped with multiple telephone lines. "When new occupants moved in, telephone lines may have been disconnected but the wires may have remained at the telephone pole. New or inexperienced telephone repairmen may not have recognized the disconnected lines as telephone equipment." [Author's Note: Marilyn's house did have two telephone lines.]

Published stories relating to the discovery of bugging devices apparently have their genesis in the third-hand hearsay statements Mr. Mankiewicz attributes to a telephone repairman, who spoke to a contractor, who in turn spoke to Mankiewicz relating to conditions which existed in 1977. According to our investigation, this was six years after the lines had been completely changed in 1971. The rewiring of the house in 1971 occurred nine years after Miss Monroe's death. The net effect of the purported "discovery" is of no evidentiary value.

LIONEL GRANDISON, THE DEATH CERTIFICATE, AND THE RED DIARY

Claim: Coroner's Aide Lionel Grandison was coerced into signing Marilyn's death certificate, despite his belief that there were problems and inaccuracies with the paperwork concerning Marilyn's death.

Second Claim: Lionel Grandison saw a red diary that came into the coroner's office with Marilyn's possessions on the morning of August 5, 1962. Marilyn's private notations about the Kennedy family, members of the mafia, and highly classified secrets were in the diary—which mysteriously disappeared from the coroner's office and was never seen again.

Facts: This story originally appeared in Robert Slatzer's book, *The Life and Curious Death of Marilyn Monroe.* Later, Lionel Grandison, a former employee of the coroner's office, was one of those who perpetuated the red diary story over the years.

He claimed he refused to sign the death certificate because the investigation was incomplete, and Chief Coroner Dr. Theodore Curphey forced him to sign the document. Grandison did indeed sign Marilyn's death certificate; however, he did not have the authority to challenge anyone or refuse to sign the document. Grandison's title at the coroner's office was Deputy Coroner's Aide, a job in which he performed routine paperwork. Even if he had declined to sign the death certificate, his position was so low that one of his superiors or Dr. Curphey himself could have signed in his place.

In the 1982 investigation, it is reported:

> Mr. Grandison reported that he saw associated with Miss Monroe's property a scrawled note and a red diary. He alleges that both items disappeared from the Coroner's Office shortly after the autopsy was performed. Grandison claims to have briefly examined the diary and noted that it contained the names of government figures and perhaps matters relating to sensitive government operations. Our investigation points to the conclusion that Mr. Grandison is in error, for the following reasons:

(1) The records prepared at the time and kept by the Coroner's Office show that no property was recovered from the victim. The property report in our possession is a photocopy of the original; so it is impossible to state categorically that it has not been surreptitiously altered to reflect the failure to recover property. However, there is no indication of any tampering with the document. Absent information that the Coroner's Report was changed, the document has evidentiary weight.

(2) Dr. Noguchi was interviewed concerning the diary and states that he saw no such item as part of the Monroe property.

(3) Those associates closest to Miss Monroe at or about the time of her death, such as Pat Newcomb, Mrs. Murray, and her masseuse, state that they never saw such a diary.

(4) Mr. Grandison admits that prior to his public statements concerning the existence of the diary, he had previously read Slatzer's book, "The Life and Curious Death of Marilyn Monroe," published in 1974. The story of the red diary first publicly appeared in Slatzer's book. Slatzer claimed to have seen it and to have discussed with Miss Monroe the contents of her diary, including references to Robert Kennedy, Fidel Castro, the C.I.A., etc. Excluding Mr. Grandison's belated statements concerning the diary, Slatzer is the only source alleging the existence of the document.

Mr. Grandison was discharged from the Coroner's Office a short time after the Monroe autopsy for misconduct involving the theft of the property from dead bodies. A review of the court documents associated with his discharge and the criminal charges stemming from his conduct demonstrates that there is solid documentary substantiation for the allegations against Mr. Grandison.

According to the court records, on November 19, 1962, Mr. Grandison appeared in Department 109 of the Superior Court in Los Angeles and pled guilty to the one count of forgery. On December 21, 1962, he received a sentence of Proceedings Suspended with five years probation with an order that he spend the first six months of his probationary period in the County Jail. He was also ordered to make restitution through the Probation Department. He successfully completed his probationary period on December 14, 1967, and his original sentence was reduced to a misdemeanor pursuant to Section 17 of the California Penal Code.

(5) The systematic keeping of a diary and the mental discipline associated with daily recording of important events in one's life are personality traits inconsistent with the mental state of Marilyn Monroe during the last few months of her life. Her closest associates seriously doubt that Marilyn Monroe had the emotional strength to maintain any sort of diary during this period. She suffered from a variety of physical and emotional problems that caused her to be disorganized and in almost daily need of psychiatric support to accomplish ordinary tasks.

(6) Former LAPD Sgt. Jack Clemmons was the first police officer on the scene. He was ushered into the Monroe residence by Mrs. Murray and

was present until the arrival of other police officers on the morning of Miss Monroe's death. He arrived at the house at approximately 4:30 a.m. Three persons were there when he arrived: Mrs. Murray; Dr. Greenson, Miss Monroe's psychiatrist; and Dr. Engleberg, her physician.

Mr. Clemmons states he saw no such note or red diary. Although he did not perform a search for these items, the allegation that they were later picked up at the scene and delivered ultimately to the Coroner's Office by someone, would imply that they were readily available or actually near the body at the time the body was recovered by the mortuary people. In other words, Mr. Clemmons didn't see a red diary and he was in a good position to have seen such a document.

(7) The alleged existence of the red diary has particular meaning under the conspiratorial theory raised by critics who claim that since the diary contained explosive information it relates directly to the motivation to murder Marilyn Monroe.

Unfortunately, this scenario doesn't hold together. Under it, those who some might consider as suspects in her death e.g., her physicians and her housekeeper, were with her at the time of her death or shortly after and therefore had the greatest access to her personal documents, including the alleged diary. They are likely to have been the same persons who turned over the diary to the authorities from the Coroner's Office or to the mortuary employees had such a diary existed. It doesn't make sense to imply that those who were closest to Miss Monroe were responsible for her death and then to allege that these same people turned over to outsiders the very information they sought, by killing her, to suppress.

Even if one assumed that a stranger or a Coroner's employee discovered a diary at the death scene and then passed it on to the authorities, one would also have to assume that the "conspirators" were incredibly inept to allow such a discovery.

Lionel Grandison's statement concerning the existence of the diary at the Coroner's Office (and also a scrawled suicide note) is inconsistent with evidence available at this time and is not supported by credible corroborating information.

THE WASHER AND DRYER MYSTERY

Claim: According to Jack Clemmons, the first Los Angeles police officer to arrive at Marilyn Monroe's house on the morning of August 5, 1962, Eunice Murray had the washing machine running at the time of his arrival. This was suspicious, he said in interviews years later. What was she washing? At some point, this evolved from Mrs. Murray doing laundry to Mrs. Murray specifically washing sheets. The implications pointed to one of the possibilities of Marilyn's death, which was murder via enema. She would have expelled the enema in bed, the conspiracy dictates, soiling the sheets. Mrs. Murray would have had to wash the sheets to prevent the police from knowing about the murder plot.

Facts: Anecdotally, there are several problems with Jack Clemmons's observations. For one, Marilyn's body was discovered (and photographed) lying in a bed with the sheets still on the bed. For this story to be true, Mrs. Murray, along with Drs. Greenson and Engleberg, would have had to remove Marilyn from her bed, clean up her entire body, remove the sheets, put clean sheets on the bed, make those fresh sheets appear as though she had slept in them, place Marilyn back in bed, and hope nothing had soiled the mattress beneath the sheets or that the smell of feces would be apparent to anyone who arrived.

If these three individuals went to the trouble of doing all this, then why would they not think to have the washer finished by the time the police arrived? Wouldn't they wait until the wash cycle was complete so no one could hear it operating and arouse suspicion? And if Jack Clemmons—or any other police officers for that matter—found it suspicious that the washing machine was turned on and running, why not investigate? Police officers were there precisely to investigate the death scene. They would have had every right to not only ask about why a washing machine was running at such an odd time of the morning and after a death, but they also could have simply walked over to it, opened the appliance door, and looked inside.

More than just the anecdotal evidence, though, there is substantial evidence indicating Marilyn didn't own a washer and dryer at all. When Marilyn put an offer in on the house in January 1962, she submitted a list of credits she wanted to be included in the price of the house—the documents do not list any appliances, which means none came with the house.

Marilyn purchased all the appliances for her home on a single day—April 11, 1962—from Kafton Sales Company, located at 1518 North Highland Avenue in Hollywood. Among Marilyn's purchases include an ACME kitchenette for the guesthouse ($280), a Hotpoint refrigerator ($624), Hotpoint range ($227), and two KitchenAid dishwashers ($26.25 and $26.40), presumably one for the main house and one for the guesthouse. There was no mention of a washer and dryer.

The natural question would be how Marilyn washed her clothing. By going through her receipts, it becomes apparent Marilyn had a long history of sending her laundry out to cleaning services. Receipts in New York dating back to when she first moved to the East Coast in 1955 indicate she was using Mme. Apter's Sutton Cleaners, located at 217 East 57th Street in Manhattan. This makes sense because Marilyn was initially living in hotels. Even after settling in her apartment, which she rented, it appears Marilyn continued to have her laundry sent out. After Marilyn died, a list of Marilyn's debts was organized by the estate. Among the creditors listed in New York was B. J.

Denihan for the sum of $1,241.60. In the notes section "for cleaning services" was listed. The cleaner was located at 215 East 64th Street in Manhattan.

In addition to the outstanding cleaning bill in New York, there is also a claim against the estate of Malone Studio Services Inc. in Los Angeles for $111.50. The note states "cleaning of clothes" on the document.

It appears Marilyn had her laundry sent out on both coasts.

After Marilyn Monroe passed away, Dr. Gilbert Nunez bought Marilyn's Los Angeles house for his family. Because so many of the appliances and furnishings were brand new, the Nunezes decided to keep several of Marilyn's items and included them in the price of the sale. Not included in the itemized list of things the Nunez family bought from Marilyn's estate were a washer and dryer.

In addition to the Nunez family purchasing items from Marilyn's home, among the documents associated with her estate included sales of her items to other individuals—none of these purchases indicate a washer and dryer were sold.

Finally, there is an argument that a washer and dryer may have been located in Marilyn's garage. However, there are photos and news footage of Eunice Murray on the driveway getting into her car on the morning of August 5, 1962. The garage door is open and it is clear there are no appliances of any kind located inside.

When combining receipts, real estate documentation, estate information, and photographic evidence, it appears Marilyn used cleaning services to launder her clothes and did not own a washer or dryer.

In the official police report, there is no mention of Sgt. Clemmons raising any concerns about a washer and dryer. Furthermore, although he was the first officer on the scene, he was not the lead investigator. Sgt. Clemmons would have left shortly after Sgt. Robert Byron, a trained detective, arrived on the scene. If Clemmons had concerns, he would have had to have noticed them fairly quickly, but nothing indicates he notified anyone of suspicious activity or behavior by those at the scene.

· 42 ·

Police Reports

Sgt. Robert Byron arrived at Marilyn's house in the early morning hours of August 5. He was a trained detective, and therefore served as lead investigator on the scene. Byron relieved Sgt. Jack Clemmons, who had been the first officer to arrive. Sgt. Byron filed two police reports, the first on August 5 and the second on August 6. A third police report was written by Byron and filed by Officer J. R. Brukles on his behalf. (Notice there is no mention of Clemmons raising concerns about a washer and dryer, or anything else for that matter.)

ORIGINAL POLICE DEATH REPORT
filed by Sergeant Robert Byron on 8-5-1962

Deceased retired on 8-4-62, at about 8PM. At approximately 12AM, P/R [person reporting] observed light on in bedroom of deceased. She (P/R) went to the door, but was unable to arouse deceased. At about 3:30 a.m., she noticed the light was still on and after trying the door found it locked. P/R went to the bedroom window and observed deceased lying in bed on her stomach and seemed unnatural. She (P/R) telephoned Wit #1, who is deceased psychiatrist. Upon arrival, he broke the bedroom window and upon entering found deceased possibly dead. He then called Wit #2, who came and pronounced deceased dead at 3:35AM. Dr. Greenson had seen deceased on 8-4-62, 5:15PM, at her request, because she was unable to sleep. He had been treating her for about one year. When he found deceased, she was nude, lying on her stomach, with phone receiver in her hand. The Police Dept was notified and found deceased in above described condition with the exception of telephone which had been removed by Wit #1. On the night stand were about 15 bottles of medication, some of which were prescription. One bottle with Prescription Number 20853, marked 1½ grain Nembutal, prescribed by Dr. Engelberg. Dr. Engelberg stated that he had prescribed a refill about two days ago and that there probably should have been about 50 capsules at time of refill.

[Information at the bottom of the report indicates Westwood Village Mortuary removed Marilyn's body.]

FOLLOW-UP DEATH REPORT
filed by Sergeant Robert Byron on 8-6-1962

Upon re-interviewing both Dr. Ralph Greenson (Wit #1) and Dr. Hyman Engelberg (Wit #2) they both agree to the following time sequence of their actions.

Dr. Greenson received a phone call from Mrs. Murray (reporting person) at 3:30A, 8-5-62 stating that she was unable to get into Miss Monroe's bedroom and the light was on. He told her to pound on the door and look in the window and call him back. At 3:35A, Mrs. Murray called back and stated Miss Monroe was lying on the bed with the phone in her hand and looked strange. Dr. Greenson was dressed by this time, left for deceased resident which is about one mile away. He also told Mrs. Murray to call Dr. Engelberg.

Dr. Greenson arrived at deceased house at about 3:40A. He broke the window pane and entered through the window and removed the phone from her hand.

Rigor Mortis had set in. At 3:50A, Dr. Engelberg arrived and pronounced Miss Monroe dead. The two doctors talked for a few moments. They both believe that it was about 4A when Dr. Engelberg called the Police Department.

A check with the complaint Board and WLA Desk, indicates that the call was received at 4:25A. Miss Monroe's phone, GM 61890 has been checked and no toll calls were made during the hours of this occurrence. Phone number 472-4830 is being checked at the present time.

Re Death Report of Marilyn Monroe—L.A. Police Dpt.

Death was pronounced on 8/5/62 at 3:45 A.M., Possible Accidental, having taken place between the times of 8/4 and 8/5/62, 3:35 A.M. at residence located at 12305 Fifth Helena Drive, Brentwood, in Rptg. Dist. 814, Report #62-509 463.

Marilyn Monroe on August 4, 1962 retired to her bedroom at about eight o'clock in the evening; Mrs. Eunice Murray of 933 Ocean Ave., Santa Monica, Calif., 395-7752, CR 61890, noted a light in Miss Monroe's bedroom. Mrs. Murray was not able to arouse Miss Monroe when she went to the door, and when she tried the door again at 3:30 A.M. when she noted the light still on, she found it to be locked. Thereupon

Mrs. Murray observed Miss Monroe through the bedroom window and found her lying on her stomach in the bed and the appearance seemed unnatural. Mrs. Murray then called Miss Monroe's psychiatrist, Dr. Ralph Greenson of 436 North Roxbury Drive, Beverly Hills, Calif., CR 14050. Upon entering after breaking that bedroom window he found Miss Monroe possibly dead. Then he telephoned Dr. Hyman Engelberg of 9730 Wilshire Boulevard, also of Beverley Hills, CR 54366, who came over and then pronounced Miss Monroe dead at 3:35 A.M. Miss Monroe was seen by Dr. Greenson on August 4, 1962 at 5:15 P.M., at her request, because she was not able to sleep. She was being treated by him for about a year. She was nude when Dr. Greenson found her dead with the telephone receiver in one hand and lying on her stomach. The Police Department was called and when they arrived they found Miss Monroe in the condition described above, except for the telephone which was removed by Dr. Greenson. There were found to be 15 bottles of medication on the night table and some were prescription. A bottle marked 1½ grains Nembutal, prescription #20853 and prescribed by Dr. Engelberg, and referring to this particular bottle, Dr. Engelberg made the statement that he prescribed a refill for this about two days ago and he further stated there probably should have been about 50 capsules at the time this was refilled by the pharmacist.

Description of Deceased: Female Caucasian, age 36, height 5.4, weight 115 pounds, blonde hair, blue eyes, and slender, medium build.

Occupation: Actress, Probable cause of death: overdose of Nembutal, body discovered 8/5/62 at 3:25 A.M. Taken to County Morgue—from there to Westwood Mortuary. Report made by Sgt. R.E. Byron, #2730, W.L.A. Detective Division. Next of kin: Gladys Baker (Mother).

(8/5/62 11 AM WLA hf—J.R. Brukles 5829)

· 43 ·

Final Days

August 4
5:15 p.m. Marilyn calls Dr. Greenson, who later reports she was "despondent" and having trouble sleeping.
8:00 p.m. Marilyn goes to bed.
August 5
Midnight Eunice Murray observes a phone cord and light on under Marilyn's door and knocks. She gets no response but does not alert anyone.
3:30 a.m. Eunice Murray sees the phone cord still under Marilyn's door and becomes concerned. The door is locked and Marilyn does not respond to a knock on the door. Mrs. Murray goes outside to the bedroom window and sees Marilyn lying on the bed with the phone in her hand. She goes back inside and calls Dr. Greenson. He arrives a few minutes later and breaks the bedroom window to gain entry. Dr. Engelberg also arrives.
3:35 a.m. Dr. Engelberg pronounces Marilyn dead. (The LAPD report indicates the time of death is 3:50 a.m. The coroner's office receives the time as 3:40 and this is the time printed on her death certificate.)
4:00 a.m. The doctors recall this as the time they notify the police to report Marilyn's death. (The LAPD records indicate the call came in at 4:25 a.m.) The first officer on the scene arrives within minutes.
5:25 a.m. Sgt. Clemmons reports the death to the coroner and Marilyn's remains are released to Westwood Village Mortuary for removal. In 1962, the coroner typically only came out to a death site in cases of homicide. Because this case was a probable overdose, the coroner was not called to the scene. At this time, bodies were released to mortuaries for removal on a rotating basis. Westwood happened to be the next mortuary in the rotation; that Marilyn was later interred at this cemetery is a coincidence. No personal property or clothing is brought in with Marilyn.

Marilyn's house on the morning of August 5, 1962. Channel 5 Broadcasting / Photofest ©
Channel 5 Broadcasting

7:45 a.m. The Los Angeles Coroner's Office is dispatched to Westwood to retrieve Marilyn's remains after it is determined Marilyn should be autopsied.
9:00 a.m. Marilyn's remains arrive at the coroner's office and are processed into the facility. No clothing or property is processed.
10:30 a.m. Dr. Noguchi begins Marilyn's postmortem exam.
August 6
8:00 a.m. The toxicological specimens taken from Marilyn arrive at the laboratory.
August 18
Los Angeles County Coroner Dr. Theodore Curphey announces the official ruling of Marilyn Monroe's death: Probable suicide.
August 28
The death certificate for Marilyn Monroe, case #81128, is issued.

· 44 ·

Birth of a Conspiracy

The Pen Is Mightier Than the Sword

> The true things rarely get into circulation. It's usually the false things.
>
> —Marilyn Monroe

$\mathcal{I}$n the years following Marilyn's death, rumors began to swirl of a conspiracy surrounding the events that happened in August 1962. Was Marilyn Monroe murdered? If so, who did it? She was lovers with both John Kennedy and Robert Kennedy. Did they kill her? Did the CIA kill her? What about the Mob?

In reality, there was kind of a conspiracy and it does involve political intrigue—it's just not what most people think it is. The story of Marilyn having affairs with the Kennedy brothers has a definite flashpoint and it was started in 1964 by a political radical with a history of slander and extortion.

Frank Capell was caught up in the anti-Communist movement that swept through the United States beginning in the 1930s. He worked as an investigator for the Subversive Activities Department for the Sheriff of Westchester County in New York. By 1943, he was working for the War Production Board when he and another agent, Richard Atherton, were arrested for soliciting bribes. The September 22, 1943, edition of the *New York Times* ran the headline "Extortion Is Laid to 2 WBG Agents." The opening sentence reads, "Two investigators for the War Production Board's compliance division were held in bail of $7,500 each yesterday, according to United States Attorney James B. M. McNally, while accepting a bribe of $1,000." Capell was fined $2,000 but his career was over.

After his arrest, Capell started a political newspaper, *Herald of Freedom*, in New Jersey. With his publication, Capell was free to be a militant anti-Communist and right-wing extremist. He also fed information to the FBI about alleged Communist activities.

Six weeks after Marilyn Monroe died in 1962, Capell flew to Los Angeles to meet with Maurice Reis, head of the Motion Picture Alliance for the preservation of American Ideals, and Jack Clemmons, the first police officer on the scene at her house on the morning of August 5. Like a lot of people in that era, Clemmons was deeply involved in the anti-Communist movement.

They were discussing Communism in Hollywood, a subject that had once been a hot topic a few years before. Reis kept files on celebrities suspected of Communist ties, Marilyn Monroe included. By the early 1960s, the fervor of Senator Joseph McCarthy's campaign had petered out and the influence of HUAC was dying. Maurice Reis gossiped about an alleged affair between Marilyn and Attorney General Robert Kennedy. Marilyn and Kennedy had met a few times through Peter Lawford, an actor married to his sister, Pat Kennedy, but there was no actual evidence to support rumors of an affair.

Capell, concerned with the increasing popularity of President John F. Kennedy, was eager to create stories that could potentially hurt the Kennedy family's political aspirations. The story of an affair involving Marilyn Monroe and Robert Kennedy, unsubstantiated though it was, proved to be a good starting point. Together, Capell, Reis, and Clemmons concocted a story that Marilyn hadn't committed suicide at all. Instead, she was murdered to protect Robert Kennedy's political ambitions.

Upon Capell's return to the East Coast, he contacted acquaintance Walter Winchell, the popular newspaper columnist, radio personality, and anti-Communist crusader. Capell began feeding Winchell gossip about the "affair" and possible murder. Tidbits were teased in Winchell's column here and there but he never came out and printed the accusations.

Winchell had once been fond of Marilyn—she attended his birthday party at Ciro's on the Sunset Strip in 1953—and a friend to Joe DiMaggio. Or at least, in retrospect maybe the term "frenemy" to Joe is more accurate. It was Winchell who persuaded Joe into attending the publicity stunt on a New York street when Marilyn's skirt billowed up around her legs for *The Seven Year Itch*. It's not an overstatement to say that moment led to the Monroe-DiMaggio divorce. Winchell's opinion of Marilyn soured when she began dating Arthur Miller, who was associated with left-wing causes and accused of Communist affiliations.

In 1964, Robert Kennedy launched a senatorial campaign in the state of New York. With John Kennedy now dead, many political commentators believed this was a step for Robert Kennedy to position himself for the 1968 presidential election. As a response, Capell published *The Strange Death of Marilyn Monroe*, an eighty-page pamphlet that explicitly states Robert

Kennedy had Marilyn killed to protect his career. His primary source in the booklet was Walter Winchell, but because Capell had fed that information to Winchell, he was citing himself.

Meanwhile, an anonymous source from California sent a memo to the Governor's Office of California detailing the Monroe-Kennedy affair. The text was remarkably similar to what had been written in *The Strange Death of Marilyn Monroe*. Although not proven, Maurice Reis is generally believed to be the informant who sent the memo. The letter noted that Robert Kennedy "was deeply involved emotionally with Marilyn" and "repeatedly promised to divorce his wife." Finally, "Marilyn realized that Bobby had no intention" of leaving his wife. It was also noted that Robert Kennedy was in Los Angeles on August 4, the final day of Marilyn's life, and registered at the Beverly Hills Hotel.

The governor's office forwarded the information to the FBI as a precaution but noted the source could not be verified. The cover letter reads "[name redacted] advised that he does not know the source or cannot evaluate the authenticity of this information." Not much became of the letter, but the FBI did learn of the existence of Capell's pamphlet and warned Robert Kennedy in a letter dated July 8, 1964. The FBI noted Capell's information was "very questionable" and did not recommend any action.

The year 1964 was a busy one. That same year Capell and Clemmons collaborated on another pamphlet, this time attacking Sen. Thomas Kuchel, who was running against Barry Goldwater at the time. The California senator was a Republican but not conservative enough for their standards because he had supported the Civil Rights Acts of 1957, 1960, and 1964 and the Voting Rights Act of 1965, which prohibited racial discrimination in voting. In this pamphlet, they claimed Sen. Kuchel had been arrested in 1950 for performing a drunken homosexual act in a car. At the time the accusation was made, in the state of California homosexuality was still illegal and considered a "moral perversion."

This pamphlet failed and saw Capell, Clemmons, and bar owner Norman H. Krause arrested for conspiracy to commit libel; shortly thereafter, a fourth defendant was added, Jack Fergus.

On February 25, 1965, the *Chicago Tribune* reported: "Los Angeles, Feb. 24—Francis A. Capell, 57, one of four men indicted by the Los Angeles county grand jury for conspiracy to criminally libel Sen. Thomas H. Kuchel (R., Cal.) surrendered today for arraignment. Judge David Williams of the superior court ordered Capell to return on March 19 with the three other defendants and freed him on $1,000 bail.

"The four are accused of plotting to commit libel in the distribution of an affidavit depicting Kuchel as having been guilty of a morals offense with another man Feb. 11, 1950. Kuchel was then California state controller. District Atty. Evelle J. Younger has described the allegations in the affidavit as 'false, reckless, malicious and vicious.'

"Capell, publisher of the Herald of Freedom, an anti-communist newspaper, came here voluntarily from Zarephath, N. J. for arraignment. The other three indicted are Norman L. Krause, 44, and Jack D. Clemmons, 41, former Los Angeles policeman, and John F. Fergus, 47, a public relations man."

Charges against Jack Clemmons were dropped in exchange for resigning from the Los Angeles Police Department. The other three pleaded no contest.

On July 7, 1965, a United Features Syndicate Inc. article reported the outcome: "WASHINGTON.—One of the nastiest attempts at character assassination in a long time has been disposed of as expeditiously and as painlessly as possible. Three of the defendants indicted for criminal conspiracy to libel Sen. Thomas H. Kuchel (R., Calif.) in effect pleaded guilty to the charge and submitted letters of abject confessing they had made use of an affidavit wholly false in its allegation of drunkenness and homosexuality."

The article goes on to note Capell's other falsehoods, including a rumor about J. Edgar Hoover, still the head of the FBI at the time.

> One of the defendants in the Kuchel case, Frank A. Capell, has just brought out a book that combines every known variety of smear. Called "Treason is the Reason," it is so full of demonstrable falsehoods as to be ludicrous if it were not such a sad commentary on the gullibility of the audience expects to reach.
>
> As an example the author cites a report that J. Edgar Hoover had approved of the appointment of Adam Yarmolinsky as his successor as head of the FBI. Yarmolinsky was a special assistant to Secretary of Defense Robert S. McNamara who later was at odds with Democratic leaders in the House of a job in the poverty program. Capell reproduces the facsimile of a letter from the FBI head in which Hoover says:
>
> "You may be sure there is no truth to the rumor concerning my choice of a successor and it is my desire to remain in my present capacity as long as I can be of service to my country. It is my earnest hope that my future endeavors will continue to merit your support and approval."
>
> In addition to raking up all the old charges out of the past Capell gives a list of twenty-eight names of high-ranking American diplomats, many of whom have served under Republican and Democratic administrations over the years, whom he alleges are Soviet intelligence agents. The legal counsel for the State Department found that the book contained one libelous statement after another. But to take legal action would only give the book publicity and the outcome would be in doubt.

To laugh off such wild exaggerations is easy enough. But if repeated often enough and particularly in times of tension and national peril they can gain credence. That was one of the most sinister aspects of the rise of Nazism. Hitler understood the technique of the big lie, as he openly boasted. Again and again, as the tragedy of the Weimar Republic drew to a close, decent and well-meaning men were destroyed by deliberate smears against which they found themselves defenseless.

Capell and the other two defendants will be sentenced later this month. Under California law criminal libel is only a misdemeanor subject to a fine of $500 or a year's jail sentence. But on their plea of "no contest," in effect guilty, they can be put on probation for up to three years. This is a demonstration that character assassination does not always pay.

It wasn't long before the libelous stories concocted by Capell and others were largely forgotten, including those in *The Strange Death of Marilyn Monroe*. Things likely would have stayed forgotten had it not been for the release of Norman Mailer's *Marilyn: A Biography* in 1973. It's at this point the conspiracy theories begin to build on one another and with a much broader range.

In Mailer's book, he builds on Capell's theory and adds speculation that the CIA and FBI possibly also played a part in the conspiracy—this time, the organizations would have helped frame the Kennedys for right-wing political gain. The FBI took notice, and created a file titled "Norman Mailer: Information Concerning." The file noted the book provided no actual evidence to back up his claims printed in the book. Ultimately, the FBI did not pursue any action.

While Capell could be fairly easily dismissed as a political zealot with a confirmed history of extortion and libel, Mailer was an accomplished essayist, novelist, and magazine journalist who had cofounded the *Village Voice*. He had won a National Book Award and Pulitzer Prize. Capell's theory had been presented in a fold-and-staple pamphlet, but Mailer's book featured previously rare color photos of Marilyn and became a national bestseller. His standing as an author and the new salacious details ensured the book's success and lent validity to the stories. Mailer even created a new word to describe his claims: "factoid," which he defined as "an event which has no other existence other than it has appeared in print."

Almost immediately, critics began questioning the accuracy of Mailer's book. Under pressure, he was forced to admit his theory was speculation and opinion. At a press conference, Mailer said, "I am not saying once ever that I think she was murdered. I think that there was large motive for her to be murdered. . . . It's opinion entirely. It's my opinion. It is based on no evidence whatsoever that I have. It is my opinion. . . . It is my belief they [Bobby and Marilyn] were not having an affair."

It was too little too late. After years of Vietnam, rumors swirling about President Kennedy's assassination, and Watergate, it was a time of very little trust in the government and authority figures. Most people didn't see Mailer's press conference, but millions of people who bought a copy of the book saw the theory in print.

With Mailer's book continuing to sell well and make money, it was only a matter of time before other writers found a way to capitalize. In January 1975, Robert Slatzer published *The Curious Death of Marilyn Monroe*, or sometimes *The Life and Curious Death of Marilyn Monroe*. What was curious about it was the title's similarity to Capell's *The Strange Death of Marilyn Monroe*.

Slatzer's book used what had already been printed and added his twist by claiming Marilyn kept a red diary in which she wrote down the classified secrets the Kennedys had told her. It was the beginning of a cottage industry for Slatzer, who made a career for himself claiming to have been Marilyn's friend and secret husband.

In recent years, a contract has surfaced between Robert Slatzer and Frank Capell permitting Slatzer to use the information from Capell's original 1964 pamphlet. In exchange, Slatzer got writing credit for the book and Capell's name "will remain secret." It also explains the similarities in the title.

Capell's trouble with the law hadn't stopped his anti-Communism and anti-Democratic crusades. In 1972, he planted a story about Senator McGovern's military service. In a newspaper article from July 25, 1972, "A man named Frank Capell has been identified by the columnist as the source responsible for a vicious slander against Sen. George McGovern, front running Democratic presidential candidate had to be sent home from Europe during World War II because he was a coward." And, "According to Columnist [Jack] Anderson, Capell is the same fellow who linked Robert Kennedy to Marilyn Monroe's suicide and tied ex-Sen. Thomas Kuchel to a homosexual incident. For that latter slander, Capell was indicted for criminal libel and pleaded 'no contest.'"

As the Monroe-Kennedy rumors began to gain momentum and with Capell and Slatzer working together, disgraced former police officer Jack Clemmons resurfaced. He capitalized on being the first officer on the scene at Marilyn's house on the morning of August 5. In interviews, he claimed Marilyn's death scene looked "staged" and he believed that she had been murdered. He also claimed Marilyn couldn't have swallowed enough pills to kill her because there was no drinking glass in her room. (A police photo clearly shows a drinking glass pictured between the nightstand and bed in Marilyn's bedroom.) Furthermore, he said, when he arrived Eunice Murray was washing sheets, implying that something suspicious was going on. He neglects to say that if he believed something was wrong, as a police officer he had the authority to investigate—which he did not. He also couldn't have known at the time that eventually documents detailing Marilyn's estate would come to light and reveal she did not own a washer and dryer.

Jack Clemmons gave many interviews over the years and not once did he divulge that he wasn't at the residence very long. He was the first responding officer, but he did not have the training to conduct an investigation. Clemmons was relieved of his post at Marilyn's house when Sgt. Robert Byron soon showed up and took over.

A Los Angeles police officer points to the pills at Marilyn's bedside. Although conspiracy theorists frequently say Marilyn had no access to water and therefore couldn't swallow enough pills to cause her death, a drinking glass is visible right next to her bed. Channel 5 Broadcasting / Photofest © Channel 5 Broadcasting

Over the years, not one reporter who interviewed Jack Clemmons appears to have checked his record with the LAPD to find his termination, the cause of his termination, or looked through old newspapers to find his name associated with Frank Capell and the indictment for slandering Senator Kuchel. At the very least, no one questioned him about his past.

Meanwhile, publications continued to cash in on the Monroe-Kennedy "affair." The soft-pornographic magazine *Oui* published an article called "Who Killed Marilyn?" in the October 1975 issue. It was written by Anthony Scaduto under the pen name Anthony Sciacca. The article was adapted into a full-length book and released in 1976. The article and book used Capell and Slatzer as a foundation and then introduced a new element—the mafia was involved.

During his career, Robert Kennedy made it a mission to crack down on organized crime. As part of his campaign, he cross-examined mob boss Sam Giancana in front of a congressional committee, an event that was filmed. Giancana repeatedly chuckled at the questions asked of him as Robert Kennedy tried to humiliate him by saying, "I thought only little girls giggled, Mr. Giancana." Kennedy's remark was met with a giggle.

In Scaduto's version, the mafia bugged Marilyn's house, which caught her on tape with one or both of the Kennedys.

In 1982, Milo Speriglio worked with Slatzer and Scaduto to publish *Marilyn Monroe Murder Cover-Up*. The new book was built on the reputations of its predecessors. The mob was still involved, but now they were working *with* the CIA to protect Robert Kennedy. Sam Giancana, the book alleged, personally ordered the hit on Marilyn. Speriglio further claimed a lethal injection because there was no pill residue in Marilyn's stomach. Speriglio's theory makes no sense for a couple of reasons. First, medical evidence proves Marilyn was not killed by injection. Second, the mob, Giancana especially, hated the Kennedys and had no reason to help them. Even if Marilyn had been having an affair with Robert Kennedy, the mob would want her alive because she could confirm the affair, and therefore ruin the Kennedys.

That wasn't the end. In 1985, British journalist Anthony Summers published *Goddess: The Secret Lives of Marilyn Monroe*. Summers was no stranger to the subject of conspiracies, as he had already published *Conspiracy* (1980) about John Kennedy's assassination. *Conspiracy* has since been updated as *Not in Your Lifetime* (1998 and 2013).

Summers claimed to have interviewed more than six hundred sources for *Goddess*, but he relied heavily on Robert Slatzer as a source and repeated the stories already print, which now had a long legacy—the Kennedys, the mob, the CIA, the FBI, and the red diary. Following in the tradition of adding theories, characters, and stories, Marilyn's "best friend" Jeanne Carmen was now part of the narrative. Summers also introduced the unseemly enema story and printed a photo of Marilyn post-autopsy that was never meant for publication—a gross violation of her privacy. In his version, Summers surmises it's possible Robert Kennedy didn't kill Marilyn but helped in the coverup. Another account included an ambulance story about Marilyn being found comatose, loaded into the ambulance only for her to die on the way, and then they turned around and returned Marilyn to bed. This claim came from Walter Schaefer, owner of Schaefer's Ambulance, but he never provided documentation that his company had received a call.

Summers made the talk show circuit with his theories and produced a BBC documentary that interviewed several secondhand and thirdhand sources. Claims ranged from the ambulance theory to hearing the tapes made from within Marilyn's house to the contents of a suicide note to seeing Robert Kennedy at Marilyn's house—and on and on. No one provided evidence to prove their claims.

In 2022, Summers released another documentary, this time for Netflix. Similar to his first documentary in the 1980s, *The Mystery of Marilyn Monroe: The Unheard Tapes* is basically *Goddess* in video format. Much of what Summers claimed in 1985 is simply repackaged for a new generation of viewers.

Remarkably, none of the books that claimed to have insider information or exclusive interviews bothered to look in plain sight and find memoirs of those who had direct access to the Kennedy brothers. If they had, they would have learned Robert was the least likely Kennedy to cheat on his wife or get into trouble.

William Sullivan, deputy director of the FBI, wrote a memoir detailing his thirty-year career with the Bureau, which was released posthumously in 1979. In his book, *The Bureau: My Thirty Years in Hoover's FBI*, he writes, "Although [J. Edgar] Hoover was desperately trying to catch Bobby Kennedy red-handed at anything, he never did. Kennedy was almost a Puritan. We used to watch him at parties, where he would order one glass of scotch and still be sipping from the same glass two hours later. The stories about Bobby Kennedy and Marilyn Monroe were just stories. The original story was invented by a so-called journalist, a right-wing zealot who had a history of spinning wild yarns. It spread like wildfire, of course, and J. Edgar Hoover was right there, gleefully fanning the flames."

Former Agent Clint Hill, who jumped on the trunk of the presidential limousine after John Kennedy was shot, has written four books about his time with the Secret Service, including with the Kennedys. In 2017, the celebrity gossip website TMZ caught up with Hill at the Georgetown campus and a reporter asked him point blank about Marilyn Monroe. Hill waved his hand dismissively, "That's a fallacy."

The reporter asked, "Did you see her sometimes?"

"Never," he replied. "Never saw her and I was there a lot. Never saw her."

With both Kennedys long dead, it would have been easy for either Sullivan or Hill or both to admit if they had seen anything suspicious when it came to Marilyn Monroe.

The "factoids" about "affairs" between Marilyn and the Kennedys have now been repeated so many times over the decades the stories are rarely questioned anymore. Such stories have even made their way into mainstream movies, television, and books. The 2022 movie *Blonde*, directed by Andrew Dominik and based on a "fictional biography" by Joyce Carol Oates, contains a scene depicting Marilyn Monroe (Ana de Armas) performing fellatio on President Kennedy (Caspar Phillipson) in a scene that is so graphic it is nearly pornographic.

Lending credibility to *Blonde* both as a book and a movie is the credibility of Oates, a former Princeton University professor with a long list of prestigious book awards and nominations. *Blonde* was a National Book Award finalist in 2000 and a Pulitzer Prize finalist in 2001. Even Oates falls prey to the murder conspiracy theories and slut-shaming of a woman known for her

The unedited photo of Marilyn with Robert and John Kennedy shows there were many people around them and it was hardly an "intimate" conversation. Cecil W. Stoughton, official White House photographer

positive feminine sexuality. At the end of her novel, Marilyn is assassinated by the "Sharpshooter" sent by the government, or the Agency as she calls it. The Sharpshooter injects Marilyn with a syringe filled with liquid Nembutal. "The President's whore was a junkie & alcoholic & such a death would not be unexpected in Hollywood & vicinity."

The Monroe-Kennedy conspiracies began as a way to derail Robert Kennedy's political ambitions, but it was Marilyn's reputation that was ultimately most damaged. The double standard of promiscuous men looking like studs or heroes while women are slut-shamed is a common, long-standing scenario. Even Joyce Carol Oates, an esteemed writer and professor who has called herself a feminist, belittled Marilyn as a "president's whore."

When tracing the Monroe-Kennedy story back to the real conspiracy—the 1962 meeting with Frank Capell, Maurice Reis, and Jack Clemmons—it seems almost impossible to believe their crackpot scheme worked.

Index

Crawford, J., on, 363; dental work, 230; fashion and jewelry, 51–52, 95–96; fingernails, 94–95; fitness routine and, 52; hairstyle and color in, 38, 86–87, 89, 96–100; hourglass figure and body size, 117–20; individuals responsible for creating, 96–106; makeup and, 92–93, 100–102, 326; memorial service and, 101, 326; modeling career and, 84, 86–87; perfume and, 65, 95, *95*; plastic surgery after fall in shower, 335; public compared with private, 43, 93, 96; "sixth-toe" myth about, 362; skin and skincare, 89–92, *91*; statistics about, 5–7, 118–19; underwear and, 39
Pickford, Mary, 54, 297, 305
Pig & Whistle, 208, 304, 305
places, Marilyn lived or frequented. *See* homes; restaurants, bars, and nightclubs; theatres
plastic surgery, 335
"platinum blonde," 38–39, 41
Platts, Jeff, 99
Playboy, 130, 353
Players Ring Theatre, Los Angeles, 210
plays, Marilyn performance in, 205, 209, 210
poem, 358
police. *See* Los Angeles Police Department
Porterfield, Pearl, 99, 267, 297, 329
Portland, Oregon, 54; mother living in, 228, 289
Powell, William, 42
pregnancies: abortions, rumors about, 332, 334, 345, 363; ectopic, 336; miscarriages, 115, 125, 159, 165, 337, 347, 363; during *Some Like It Hot*, 159, 334, 337
Preminger, Otto, 149–50
prescription drugs. *See* drug use
The Prince, the Showgirl and Me (Clark), 365–67

The Prince and the Showgirl, *156*, 162, 275, 313, 358; Clark book about time with Marilyn during shooting of, 365–66; hairdresser for, 97; home in England while filming, 70; Olivier conflicts during, 155–57, 200, 218, 219, 263, 366; plot and casting, 155, 156; premiere, 213; behind the scenes, 155–57; Strasberg, L., coaching on, 191; therapy during filming of, 338
private life: makeup in, 93; physical appearance in, 43, 93, 96; public image and reputation contrast with, 43–44, 93, 96, 190–91, 259, 358
promiscuousness, 221, 223, 403
psychotherapy: for childhood traumas, 193, 338; under Greenson, R., 72, 168, 173, 341–43, 351, 357; with Hohenberg, 338; with Kris, 335–36, 346–47; the Method use of, 199; from mid-1950s onward, 333; re-traumatization after, 193, 342–43. *See also* mental health/illness
public image and reputation: acting skills and, 213; anxiety and, 101, 140; DiMaggio, J., divorce and, 62–63; Dougherty, J., on, 227; empathy and, 99; evenings out and, 296; inner circle friends and, 348; JFK public schedule/locations relative to, 368–71; private contrasted with, 43–44, 93, 96, 190–91, 259, 358; promiscuous, 221; on set, 138–40; sex symbol and, 40, 122, 123, 191, 221, 372; team of individuals creating, 96–106; while with Hyde, 57, 58, *58*, 185. *See also* clothing design; physical appearance
Pursel, Bill, 221, 303, 312

Quinn, Charles H., 56

Rabwin, Marcus, 334
Racquet Club, Palm Springs, 235, 290